of our own lives. Shannon encourages me to live differently, and I am grateful for her. — Deborah, Columbus, OH, USA

I adore Shannon's podcasts and listen to them repeatedly. She inspires me, and I love her zest for life, enthusiasm, and all things French. Thank you, Shannon. — Kim, Blenheim, New Zealand

I stumbled across *Choosing the Simply Luxurious Life* a few years ago, and I was instantly smitten with everything Shannon creates. She really delivers an intelligent (yet simple) approach to navigating life as a modern woman with her signature *je ne sais quoi* charm! — Kristine, Toronto, ON, Canada

Shannon and her two boys, Oscar and Norman, are not only a necessary but an intricate part of my morning ritual since the early days of *The Simply Luxurious Life* blog. I look forward to my morning coffee with Shannon because she inspires me to LIVE my life to the fullest and with luxury. I am a *femme d'un certain age*, but *TSLL* blog and her book *Choosing the Simply Luxurious Life* are inspirational and motivational for all ages because life isn't about age. Thank you, Shannon, for staying true to your vision and your mission statement. — Michelle, TX, USA

Shannon and I have coffee every morning as I make my lunch and prepare for my day. I swear that our "coffee dates" ground me in the moment and inspire me to set my intention for that day. She has given names to some of my daily rituals and introduced me to so many more. — RJ, Fort Langley, BC, Canada

Shannon is the wise friend we all need in our lives, and I wish I had had her when I was graduating from college and heading out into the world. I treasure all of her posts and use them as an invitation to examine aspects of my life. I firmly believe we all have the potential to live each day well, and Shannon has done the work to give us the action steps to make a beautiful life a reality. — Marina, Kansas City, MO, USA

Shannon and *TSLL* blog have been a guiding light on how to navigate life: combining focused efforts for long-term goals, the notion of self-fulfillment, and the charm of sophistication. All that with the addition of excellent taste and inspiration from the French culture. I cannot wait to read the second book! — Charis, Athens, Greece

I am a long-time follower of Shannon Ables, aspiring to live my own simply luxurious life. Her topics are always interesting. Her ideas and suggestions, many of which I've incorporated into my daily routine, are easy to implement. Even the smallest changes can make such a big difference. I can't wait for the next book. Shannon, you are really so inspiring! Thank you! — Ann, Paso Robles, CA, USA

I stumbled upon Shannon's blog years ago and am a long-time fan of her work. As a "seeker," I love to explore ways to bring more pleasure, passion, and purpose to my life, and Shannon's approach has always resonated with me. Her message is simple yet powerful: through our accumulated, daily choices, we have the power to design the life of our dreams. She encourages women to know themselves, to value themselves, and to celebrate themselves. Her wisdom, guidance, and inspiration have certainly contributed to my own simply luxurious life! — Karen, Port Washington, NY, USA

I am a latecomer but already a huge fan of your blog. It stands out from others for its authenticity and inspiration. You impart a positive energy which is infectious for simple, luxurious living. I can honestly say that it is now one of my *petits plaisirs*. — Kameela, Eastbourne, East Sussex, UK

Thanks to Shannon's many gentle reminders throughout her blog posts, podcasts, and especially her first book, I have been able to cultivate the life I always dreamed of! My days went from hectic and stressed to calm and enjoyable. I think fondly of Shannon's lovely influence each time I enjoy a simple pleasure or soak in a peaceful moment. — Karin, Alabama, USA

Shannon, from the moment I started to read your book, my journey began! Added to the mix were relatable, relevant, and inspiring podcasts and blog posts that became my Monday morning routine. Your tips for cultivating daily rituals have added a touch of magic to my life. Quality versus quantity in all areas . . . from chocolates to finances! — Sarah, Thomasville, GA, USA

Shannon's wonderful book lives permanently on my coffee table. It's a constant reminder that the simple things in life are often the most luxurious . . . a simple bunch of flowers, sitting by a crackling fire with a hot chocolate, or treating yourself to a beautifully scented candle. Fewer possessions and remembering quality over quantity. Can't wait for the new book, Shannon! — Liz Power, Plymouth, Devon, UK

If one is seeking a guide to living their best life, look no further than Shannon Ables. She offers her followers a daily dose of inspiration and encouragement, while embracing the notion that change is always possible. — Carol Belleville, ON, Canada

ALSO BY SHANNON ABLES

Choosing The Simply Luxurious Life: A Modern Woman's Guide

Living

The Simply Luxurious

Life

MAKING YOUR EVERYDAYS EXTRAORDINARY AND
DISCOVERING YOUR BEST SELF

SHANNON ABLES

Simply Luxurious Publishing
BEND, OREGON

Simply Luxurious Publishing

www.thesimplyluxuriouslife.com

Book layout ©2018 BookDesignTemplates.com

Illustrations by Inslee by Design

Cover layout by Dash Creative

Ordering Information:

Quantity sales. Special discounts are available on quantity purchases by corporations, associations, and others. For details, contact the "Special Sales Department" at info@thesimplyluxuriouslife.com.

Living The Simply Luxurious Life/ Shannon Ables. —1st ed.

ISBN: 978-0692085219

Contents

*To my companions during the journey thus far in my new hometown,
my sweet boys, Oscar and Norman*

We all have a better guide in ourselves, if we would attend to it, than any other person can be.

— Jane Austen

Introduction

Each of us is on our own journey, and if you have picked up this book, you are determined to unearth your true potential and discover how your talents, passions, and curiosities can best dance with the world while bringing you true contentment.

Speaking of dancing, if you have chosen to gaze into the unknown of your future and to follow a path that will take you where you want to go, you will feel at times as though you have two left feet. Not because you cannot dance, but because you are learning new steps, new movements that have the potential to showcase your unique gifts. That potential can be revealed only if you hone your intuition and listen to what sparks your curiosity.

Listening to my curiosity was initially an unconscious habit of mine. I remember first visiting Bend, Oregon, as a young girl with my family on a summer vacation. In the mid-eighties, one of the now fastest-growing towns in the country was far smaller and not on the map of travelers from around the globe. Drake Park and Mirror Pond were picturesque, as they still are today, and the nearby neighborhoods were, as recalled in my mind's eye, perfect. I remember the fresh air and the soft silence of simple everyday life unfolding in Bend that summer. That memory remained, and although now the town is twice the size, there was a curiosity in me that lingered as I considered relocating my life there, even though I would be leaving what on the outside looked like a life that was well put together (I owned a house, had a secure job with benefits, etc.) in the small eastern Oregon town I had called home for nine years.

So when I was given the opportunity to step closer toward my dream of living in a town where I could have Mother Nature at my back doorstep for hiking, paddleboarding, and cross-country skiing, and where I could fully experience the four seasons, enjoy delicious dining and cooking options, and be inspired by internationally recognized musical and literary talent (for example, Diana Krall and David Sedaris) who choose to spend a day or two in a small, yet engaged town in central Oregon — I said yes. I wanted to be within a couple of miles of an airport so I could make excursions abroad, to

France or England, quickly and without extra expense, and teach a subject I love deeply. I said yes, even though I knew I would have to sacrifice the likelihood of owning a home immediately and would pay rent that was nearly twice my previous mortgage payment. If it had been any place other than Bend, at that point in my life, I would have said no. But it was Bend. And I had been offered a job in which I could teach what I love. Without any hesitation, I took what was for me a very big step and invested in my dreams in an attempt to reach my full potential.

Now, your "Bend, Oregon" discovery, may be New York City or Luberon, Provence, or Victoria, British Columbia, or Melbourne, Australia, or Devon, England. Wherever you are meant to explore or call home for a couple of years or the rest of your life, the clues are waiting for you to find them.

While I do not know how long Bend will be my hometown, I do know it was meant to be a part of my journey, and over the past three years, I have come to an appreciation for trusting myself and following my curiosities.

I also discovered and unconsciously followed another clue early in my journey. When I was a young teenager, my curiosity was captured by a quote from Henry David Thoreau in his memoir *Walden*, which describes his experience of living in a compact cabin in the wilderness near Walden Pond in Massachusetts.

> *I learned this, at least, by my experiment: that if one advances confidently in the direction of [their] dreams, and endeavors to live the life which [they have] imagined, [they] will meet with a success unexpected in common hours. [They] will put some things behind, will pass an invisible boundary; new, universal, and more liberal laws will begin to establish themselves around and within [them]; or the old laws be expanded, and interpreted in [their] favor in a more liberal sense, and [they] will live with the license of a higher order of beings. In proportion as [they simplify their lives], the laws of the universe will appear less complex, and solitude will not be solitude, nor poverty poverty, nor weakness weakness. If you have built castles in the air, your work need not be lost; that is where they should be. Now put the foundations under them.*

I have adjusted the pronouns for my own purposes so that each time I read this quote (it is posted in my office) I feel as though it is speaking directly to me, encouraging me to stay the course, trust my intuition, and have confidence in what refuses to be ignored. So many of Thoreau's observations — simplifying to reduce complexity and increase clarity, embracing the power of solitude, finding strength in what once was perceived as weakness, continuing to dream extensively, and, most importantly, advancing confidently without promises or assurances — spoke to me as a young girl and now, two decades on, have proven to be true. In many ways, it was when I read this quote that the concept of the simply luxurious life was born.

The unconscious trust I gave to my curiosity in my youth has now become acutely conscious. In many ways, curiosity is my compass, along with my intuition, which continues to be sharpened with each life experience my curiosity leads to and through. These two intangible, priceless entities have opened a world of awareness, understanding, and appreciation that I regularly share with readers on *TSLL* blog, podcast, and vodcast — and now, in even more depth, in this second book, which builds upon my first.

Many readers of the first book, *Choosing The Simply Luxurious Life: A Modern Woman's Guide*, have said they wish they had had it to advise them when they were young women just starting out on the journey of cultivating their lives. Unpacking the fundamentals, the pillars of a life of quality over quantity in each arena of one's life, the first book provides the structure for living a refined life on an everyday income. Once we have paid the attention necessary to create a strong foundation, there is a deeper journey, a more singular journey, one in which the traveler strives toward their full potential. This deeper journey is why I have written *Living The Simply Luxurious Life: Making Your Everyday Extraordinary and Discovering Your Best Self.*

The world is full of clues about which direction to take, which new experience to try, which new skill to attain, which person to introduce yourself to, which person to walk away from, which destination on a map to visit, or perhaps even which food to try at the farmers market. Each of us then needs to own the responsibility to look for these clues, engaging intimately with our everyday lives, discovering how to elevate each seemingly ordinary day to the extraordinary, and enriching our lives and the lives of those around us. And when we enrich our lives, we see hints of what we are innately capable of. We find reasons to shed the layers placed upon us by society and even ourselves that hide the exquisiteness we embody naturally.

Living simply luxuriously is a choice, a decision to find what fascinates and delights you, as well as what the world needs you to share as we progress toward a better future. Your journey will be unique, and in these pages, you will read about tools and skills that will enable you to dance in a way you never thought you could. Read the chapters in order, read them out of order, reread one chapter again and again until you have mastered its lesson — this book is your resource, and each reader will find themselves at a different point along their journey when they begin to read.

The book you hold in your hands is the book I have wanted to write for you, *TSLL* readers, long-time and newly introduced. The first book laid the basic foundation for what it means to live a simply luxurious life; this one deepens and strengthens the roots you have wisely planted. Let this book be a resource with the ultimate goal of enabling you to step toward and reach your full potential. May you savor the journey, be delighted by what you discover, and amazed by all that you are capable of.

CHAPTER ONE

Living a Simply Luxurious Everyday Life

Life is not graded on how fast you can move through it but rather how much you can enjoy it.
— Mary Carlomagno

In the sixteen months following my move to Bend, Oregon, in the summer of 2015, I left my new hometown on only one weekend. In the three years leading up to my move, I had flown more miles, seen more places and more countries than in my entire previous life. All that travel was intoxicating, and while it still is (as this book is being published I have just returned from Provence), in Bend I settled into a life that I loved more completely, sincerely, and serenely than anything I had experienced before.

Choosing Bend and then having the good fortune to land a job there played a significant role in my settling in. But as I gathered my thoughts in preparation for this second book and its founding premise, I realized that settling in had more to do with the person I had become and less about a geographical location on a map.

The last paragraph in the last chapter of my first book, *Choosing the Simply Luxurious Life: A Modern Woman's Guide*, encourages the reader to continue to grow. So long as we choose to continually learn, we move forward toward a life that is more in tune with our values and thus one that gives rise to even more appreciation and satisfaction.

Since the debut of my lifestyle blog *The Simply Luxurious Life*, I have pursued one overarching goal: discovering how to reach one's full potential and helping readers from around the globe — no matter their age, ethnicity, gender, values, relationship status, or money in the bank — to understand what they are capable of, if only they had the tools.

The tools are plenty, and they are the strengths we are born with and the skills we can learn; in chapters eight and nine, I will explain in detail what they are and how to cultivate them. I myself am on a journey of self-growth and discovery, and the learning continues with each day's passing, which is why I feel at peace in my life at this moment. I am savoring the everydays, each and every one.

When a friend of my mother asked her how I was doing after living in Bend for several months, she said, "It would take a stick of dynamite to get her to leave." She was exaggerating, but not by much. I admit that living in Bend has made me very happy, but the deeper truth is that I have fallen in love with my everyday routine and am still enamored. Does it change? Do I tweak it from time to time? Absolutely, but the more I do, the more I realize that so long as I know what makes the everyday sing, I can do so wherever I call home. It all begins with getting back to simple.

The Definition of True Luxury

The most common mistake people make is believing the term "luxury." It's become an excuse for a lack of common sense and invariably stands for over-priced, poorly considered products, whether it's a hotel, an apartment block, a handbag, or a holiday.
— Jasper Morrison

The beautiful quality of focusing on simple luxury is that we pay careful attention to the ease and comfort that luxury is intended to provide. *Luxury* is defined as a state of great comfort or something that is difficult to obtain, but as British designer Jasper Morrison points out, too often the first half of the definition is forgotten, and often people seek luxury as a way of defining themselves to the world, meanwhile paying no real attention to the ease that luxury is supposed to bring. For example, haute couture would certainly be seen as a luxury, but if, when you purchase a tailor-made dress for $4,000, you are not at ease because the purchase puts you in debt up to your ears, that is not comfortable and therefore is not luxury.

On the other hand, if you choose to live in a smaller home rather than a large one — and in so doing create a lifestyle that instills a sense of ease and tranquility and allows you to live well — then you are choosing true luxury even though to the outside world your choices may seem modest.

The definition of true luxury will vary from person to person, based on circumstances and personal preferences, but the key is to remember what true luxury is: great comfort paired with the acquisition of something that took time and conscious effort. And since we are defining luxury, we should also define the concept of being difficult to obtain; it means "needing much effort or skill to accomplish, deal with, or understand."

When we choose to live a simply luxurious life and focus on attaining true luxury, our decisions are carefully and thoughtfully reached. So while the Lanvin flats we purchased may seem excessive to outsiders, we know we have a carefully curated wardrobe, with relatively few items in our closets; we save up to invest in quality over quantity, and we understand the concept of cost per wear (there is a brief definition in chapter eleven).

In other words, in our pursuit of true luxury, we respect our budget, increase our self-confidence, and allow ourselves the comfort provided by the design of the shoe.

True luxury is not . . .

Owning or Renting a Home That Eats Up Too Much of Your Budget so that you cannot enjoy the everyday. I am always amazed at the amount of space or choice of neighborhood many people require to feel that they are living well, even when they can barely afford it. While it may be nice to live in a large place or in a ritzy locale, if doing so exhausts your budget so that you are working just to pay the mortgage or rent and can enjoy little else, you need to reassess. True luxury is a life of comfort and ease, not stress and exhaustion.

Keeping Up with Others' Definition of "the Good Life." When we follow others, we let go of trying to discover ourselves and thus lose track of the best way to attain a truly fulfilling life. If you pattern your life after what others have done, you ignore the unique person you are and the talents you can offer. Choose to live a life that sits well with you at night, a life that makes you want to pinch yourself not because others are applauding but because you are content with yourself and your choices.

More Food, Clothes, Friends, Money, Cars. It is easy to think that having "more" will bring us greater joy, comfort, fulfillment, and pleasure, but ultimately, having more breeds more stress, clutter, and drama, and often a thicker waistline. Anything we bring into our lives or help foster should be done with the intention to create a life of quality — worthwhile friendships, a body that can meet life's demands, enough money to provide comfort as we live within our means, efficient and affordable transportation, and clothes that make us feel our best and last for many seasons.

A Handbag from the Design House of the Moment. If your choice of a handbag is based on a need to show the outside world that you have the latest creation by [insert designer name here] on your arm, then reassess. While many top designers offer quality, long-lasting designs, some do not. Choose a bag because it will last and work well with your life and because you love it.

Visiting Paris or New York City, if such destinations do not interest you. Not everyone finds pleasure and exhilaration in large metropolitan areas. It is important to seek out destinations that capture your attention and curiosity each time you read about them. Again, it is about understanding yourself, being honest with yourself, and then moving forward on your authentic path.

More Responsibilities and Power Positions. With responsibilities come power and potential respect; however, in order to do a quality job, we must carefully choose the responsibilities we welcome into our lives. In order to think clearly, make sound decisions, and respond and lead with poise and assuredness, we must have time to take care of ourselves and rejuvenate regularly.

Welcoming true luxury into our lives involves knowing what to say no to as well. By getting to the core of what each decision will bring into our lives, we can assess what will and what will not bring more ease and comfort into our everyday living.

The Necessary Ingredient for Luxury: Comfort

Luxury must be comfortable, otherwise it is not luxury.
— Coco Chanel

One hundred and thirty-five years ago, Gabrielle "Coco" Chanel was born, and her quote about luxury has always lingered in the back of my mind. After all, owning multiple homes and having endless amounts of money may indeed be someone's definition of luxury, but it is how one spends their money and their time that determines whether it is a luxurious life.

The National Endowment for Financial Education reports that 70 percent of people who come into a financial windfall go broke within a few years. Whether it is poor money management or not having healthy relationships with friends and family, the pressures and lack of knowledge about how to handle the wealth ultimately destroy any opportunity for luxury the money originally presented.

However, that does leave 30 percent who have successfully managed their new good fortune. Needless to say, more money does not make you happier or more comfortable; it is how one goes about living life — big and everyday decisions, self-discipline, etc. — that determine whether a life is full of luxury and contentment.

Stylist Kate Schelter has an insightful approach to this issue: "Luxury is what comes naturally but needs working at through practice, determination, and fine-tuning. Luxury is feeling you do not need anything else to feel whole." Below are a few additional mislabeled "luxurious" ways of living followed by a listing of actual sources of luxury.

Ten Things, Disguised as Luxury, That Cause Stress and Discontent

Working endlessly at an unfulfilling job to earn the big paycheck to pay for "luxurious" purchases and a "luxurious" lifestyle . . . Shoes you cannot walk in . . . A home whose upkeep prevents you from enjoying its supposed riches . . . Hershey's Kisses (or other processed food) that is seemingly delicious but never satisfying, which leads to overeating, which leads to a bad mood and more . . . Purchasing anything that puts you in debt unnecessarily and gives you sleepless nights . . . Purchasing cheap travel tickets only to endure many stops and middle seat assignments . . . Living a life that only looks good on the outside . . . Saying yes to something you do not want, believe in, value, or have time to do, in order to please someone else . . . Living a busy life that leads to short, restless nights as you try to accommodate your demanding schedule . . . More food, larger portions.

Ten Things That Include Comfort and Thus Epitomize Luxury

Real luxury is the pleasure of a real life lived to the fullest and full of imperfections.
— The character Kate, in the film *A Five Star Life*

Time to do with as you please . . . Living in a clean, safe, welcoming home that has just enough space . . . Quality designer clothing that feels as good as it looks and will last for many seasons . . . Traveling on non-stop flights and paying for your ideal preferred seat . . . An uninterrupted night's sleep (after a happy, productive day experienced through a well-balanced schedule) . . . Enjoying one dark chocolate truffle or piece of chocolate from a local chocolatier or homemade in your kitchen . . . Adhering to an eating regimen of moderation, not limitation . . . The voice and freedom to say no . . . Being able to purchase quality clothing, shoes, and accessories without going into debt, and feeling physically and mentally fabulous when you are wearing them . . . Living a life that is fulfilling and authentic despite criticism from those who do not understand.

Living a luxurious life does not require large amounts of money. What it does require is good decision making, a never-ending quest for knowledge, and the ability to live authentically and not be led around by the nose.

Comfort Begets Confidence

Comfort is the root of confidence and not the other way around.
— Haley Mlotek, in the *New York Times Style Magazine*

Confidence is attractive and can be deceiving. It is, however, hard to fake. The truth about confidence is that it is rooted in feeling comfortable. When a woman projects an air of confidence, she feels a sense of security, self-worth, and peace of mind, knowing she is able to think and live independently. Confidence is a dynamic condition that depends on understanding the fluid reality of life, the world, other people, etc. It requires us to always pursue knowledge, ask questions, and remain a participant in the world.

The quote above is from a 2016 article about the trend to no longer wear makeup. The article gave me pause because it is difficult to put down the masks we present to the world, as they are in many ways our armor, and it is far easier to just do what is expected, to project an image or idea that is easy for all to see and hear. Where do we find the comfort that is needed for the confidence we seek?

- We take the time to get to know ourselves and continue this ongoing process.
- We build healthy social networks.
- We stretch ourselves. We try things we have never done before but want to do and someday do well.
- We read and learn voraciously and endlessly.

I can think of more than a few instances when I did not have confidence. For example, I became frustrated as I attempted to converse in French at a local conversation group or with friends and instructors who speak the language. I felt as though I was presenting an entirely different person, one that was not the real Shannon. I gave this some thought and realized why I was not enjoying myself: I was not comfortable and therefore could not relax and be confident. It is a vicious cycle. For quite a long while, I stopped going to the weekly conversations, choosing instead to study on my own. But I realized that in order to increase my comfort, I needed to stretch myself. It is a perplexing paradox. Yes, we need comfort to feel and reflect confidence, but it can be gained only if we choose to grow, learn, and step outside our comfort zone.

Below are a few arenas that require us to experiment, stretch ourselves, and try new things in order to gain the confidence we seek:

- Our preferences in food
- Our way of life
- Our signature style for our wardrobe and our homes
- People with whom we are most compatible: friends, partners, workplace environments
- Interests and hobbies

However, finding comfort requires seeking balance. Do not put yourself in uncomfortable scenarios all of the time. Stretch yourself just enough so that you are able to grow rather than regress. In the French conversation group, I was trying to develop new friendships at the same time I was learning a new language, and I found that I needed to separate the two so that I could be my confident, authentic self with those who were just beginning to know me. So I struck a balance, communicating with them that I wanted dearly to build friendships but felt learning a language simultaneously was not going to work for me.

When we can come home to a place that allows us to feel comfort, we can then be recharged to go back out and try something new, but we must have a sanctuary of comfort to which we can retreat to attain that fix. The sanctuary of comfort may be your house or apartment, or it may be a person, an activity, or a particular place. The solution begins with knowing yourself: knowing not only what you like and dislike, what makes you feel comfortable and uncomfortable, but why your feelings and preferences are what they are. Knowledge is truly power, not only as an approach to life, but also when it comes to understanding ourselves and living our best lives.

Some Examples of True Luxury

To live a luxurious life is to live in a state of great comfort. To an outsider, living luxuriously may appear extravagant or unnecessary, but defining what comfort or extravagant is changes depending upon one's time in history, one's circumstance, one's personal economic situation, and the world's economic situation.

In his *Wall Street Journal* article "Art for Life's Sake," Alain de Botton analyzes Adriaen van Utrecht's painting *Banquet Still Life*. Botton points out that to bring such bounty to the table, it is necessary to appreciate its journey and not ignorantly dismiss the background to the gourmet feast that is presented. What a wonderful lesson for life and the riches we too often take for granted.

Below is a list of thirty true luxuries — some are tangible, and some can only be experienced. What they have in common is that in order to appreciate the riches life presents, we must be mindful of the journey that brought them to us. This simple lesson is one primary key to living a simply luxurious life.

True luxury is . . .

- A restful, deep, uninterrupted night of sleep.
- A Burberry trench coat.
- Having the ability to think for oneself and the strength to do so.
- Access to endless information.
- Saving up for a weeklong cooking class in Provence.
- Having days off each week and vacation time throughout the year to do with as you please.

- Being willing to pay the full price for a product made by a company that pays workers well and respects the environment.
- Having financial security and being a mindful money manager during the good days as well as the rainy ones.
- A healthy body and mind that have been tended to and respected for the gifts that they are.
- Curiosity that leads to a better understanding of how the world works.
- Being able to purchase local food harvested near where you live.
- Being able to purchase imported quality food products to enjoy with a meal or to complete a scrumptious recipe.
- Having the freedom to live as you desire — as Andre Leon Talley shared in *Vogue Living*, "to be able to take control of one's life, health, and the pursuit of happiness in a way that is joyful."
- Cooking with quality utensils, pots, pans, cutlery, and ovens to prepare homemade meals.
- Snuggling up near a crackling fire with a cup of *chocolat chaud*.
- Buying quality clothing made with precise and expert care.
- A handbag that will gain value as the years pass by.
- Clothes that are tailored for your body.
- Turning off the tech.
- Experiencing a theatrical production and having access to art.
- Being the master of your thoughts.
- Having fewer but better items in your life.
- Understanding the difference between need and want, and having the discipline to act on that understanding.
- Having control over your emotions and not allowing others to push your buttons.
- Finding your passion and figuring out how to integrate it into your daily life.
- Clean air.
- Seeing life as a beautiful gift and adventure, and refusing to live someone else's life.
- Having the opportunity to read something new every day.
- Feeling comfortable in your own skin.

- Not having the latest and raved about "thing" on the market, but bringing into your life only what allows you to make it better and more fulfilling.

True luxury does not happen by accident, and it takes time to come to fruition. It does not need pomp and circumstance to attract attention. Its top quality, when experienced, will speak for itself. You enjoy it without a need for approval, but merely for the pleasures of self-satisfaction and achievement.

If we mistakenly purchase excess stuff, we are not making our lives more comfortable but rather bringing more stress into our lives. It is imperative that we live consciously, making decisions based on sound judgment and what is best for the life we want to live and not the life that others want us to live. Because if we choose to listen to what our lives are trying to tell us — about what works, what does not, and why — we will find ourselves living simply luxuriously each and every day in small and large ways.

Live Fully Each Day

According to the Centers for Disease Control and Prevention, the average life expectancy for a woman in the United States was 81.2 years in 2012. Having the opportunity to live to 81+ is wonderful, and exceeding it can be an even greater blessing if one is in good health. However, simply because the average is 81+ does not mean it is guaranteed. After all, this is an average; there are more than 320 million people living in the United States, many of whom are older, and some people will not make it to 81. But rather than focus on statistics like these, let's instead become invigorated to live more fully each and every day.

Why? No matter what your hopes for your life may be, you are not guaranteed anything for certain. Yes, our decisions and proper planning and preparation play a significant effect on our life's trajectory, but the factors we cannot control or predict — the people who cross our paths, world events, the economy, inventions that open an unexpected career path — can only be dealt with as we are introduced to them.

Often if we have had to struggle to achieve a worthwhile goal or suffered an unimaginable loss, there is a silver lining — a greater appreciation for life. And with that appreciation, when simple things and grand opportunities occur, we are more apt to seize them rather than dismiss them because we do not assume there will be another available when we are ready.

A few years ago, a quote from Oprah Winfrey in *O, The Oprah Magazine* caught my attention: "You can either waltz boldly onto the stage of life and live the way you know your spirit is nudging you, or you can sit quietly by the wall, receding into the shadows of your fears and self-doubt."

Some days will be stellar, gold-star, don't-want-them-to-end days, and then there will be some you will want to forget. And if you do have a bad day, learn, apologize if necessary, and then move forward, letting your actions speak for themselves. After all, we are not perfect. But the goal is to always give our best. When we know we have done so, we sleep much better each night. Here are some ways to make sure you give your best:

Stop Postponing Your Life. If you have found someone you click with, do not assume that this will happen with everyone. By no means am I suggesting that you elope. You do not have to dive in headfirst, but recognize the possibilities when you see potential in a relationship or opportunity, and throw your weight in that direction.

Do Not Dismiss Happy Accidents. Whether it is a chance career opportunity or running into a dear friend, appreciate events that take you by surprise. You may not feel ready to act upon them, but make the most of such occurrences, and do not assume they will happen again. All we can be certain of is how we will respond when they occur. Seize these happy accidents.

Spread Kindness. Whether it is helping out without being asked, picking up a loved one's favorite comfort food after a tough day, or some other act of kindness — each day, we should try to wake up determined to act with more care toward our fellow humans. Even being honest, especially if it is not what someone wants to hear, can be an act of kindness so long as we do it tactfully and lovingly. Being sincere when we say yes and refusing to play games, but rather simply saying no to something we do not want to do, are other forms of kindness to incorporate into our everyday lives.

Do What You Love. Do not be afraid to show your passions to others. When asked what you want to do, state your preference, or when given the chance to incorporate a taste of who you are, do it. When we muster up the courage to reveal a glimpse of our authentic selves, we open ourselves to amazing opportunities and connections.

Be Courageous. Choosing to live fully in the present does not mean we can select the emotions we will feel. In fact, such a choice will require us to feel the good and the bad — and feel them deeply at times. Why? Because we are opening ourselves; we are putting down our shields and letting ourselves be fully present. When we decide to be courageous, we are not removing fear; we are mastering it.

Master Your Mind. Your mind is the only thing keeping you from living in the present. Mastering your mind does not mean turning it off, but rather observing your thoughts and recognizing the power they could have if you acted upon them. At the end of chapter eight, I describe nine steps for making your mind your best asset.

The way we proceed through our days, in alignment with the purpose we wish to pursue, will determine what we bring into our lives and what we will let go. And just because life does not look the way we expected, happen when we are ready, or follow a foreseen path does not mean we should not seize it with all of our might.

In 2014, the *New York Times* ran a story under the headline "Does Everything Happen for a Reason?" The two authors, psychologists from Yale, first pointed out that regardless of whether one is religiously inclined, where one lives, and even one's age, humans are inclined to accept that certain things happen for a reason, if only for reassurance that life can be fair. The writers concluded: "Even those who are devout should agree that, at least here on Earth, things just do not naturally work out so that people get what they deserve. . . . Instead, the events of human life unfold in a fair and just manner only when individuals and society work hard to make it happen." In other words, we have to be consciously present so that if indeed a happy accident occurs, we can put into motion the events that must then coincide to lead to the outcome we hope for. And that can only happen if we are living fully each and every day.

Designing Everydays That Flourish

The highs in life that we experience — landing a coveted job, celebrating a hard-earned diploma, signing the papers on a first house, reveling in the magic of a wedding day, visiting a dreamed-about destination, holding a first published book, savoring the arrival of retirement — are momentous occasions that are all the sweeter when you have made persistent efforts and investment to attain that dream.

Having had the opportunity to experience a few of these highs, I can say that the final result would not have been as sweet if I had not sincerely wanted what I sought nor enjoyed the innumerable everydays that paved the way to the end result.

Everyday Habits for a Life of Contentment

While setting, having, and pursing goals is a worthwhile way to achieve a life of contentment, we are mistaken if we think success is measured by the big moments in our lives, the times when we reach the pinnacle and experience such "highs." Rather, success is how we live each day. Success is determined by our everyday approaches to living because we will have far more everydays than celebrations. And if we live the former well, we are cultivating a rich and rewarding life.

Below are daily habits to practice in your everyday life that will ensure a life full of contentment:

Facing Your Doubts. Psychologists say that self-doubt, a cousin of fear, is a natural, healthy human emotion. To not have doubt is to not care, to not be invested. Doubt can be used like a compass, pointing you toward your desires and passions.

Pursuing a Passion That Gives You Purpose. Upon discovering your deeper nature, you discover your strengths, and those strengths will help to lead you to your purpose. It is the marriage of pleasure and purpose that enables you to get lost in your everyday work. Being in love with what you are doing heightens the everyday and helps you reach your goals.

Tending to Your Health. First, know what having good health requires. In other words, understand how your body works, what it needs, and how you can fuel it and care for it properly. You might read *How Not to Die*, a plentiful resource that catalogs every illness and ailment, and answers your questions about reducing the chance of being afflicted with cancer, eliminating the risk of heart disease, and much more; the book provides great advice on what to eat, how much to exercise, and how it all comes together to improve your overall health. In chapter twelve, we will dive deeper into easy and enjoyable ways to tend to your health.

Nurturing Cherished Relationships. The importance of a healthy social network is crucial for enjoying our everydays and weathering unexpected bumps along the way. Such a network begins with the relationship we have with ourselves (see the next paragraph), but nurturing our friendships and romantic partnerships with little, thoughtful gestures, the way we speak, what we say, and how we prioritize and celebrate throughout the year can add up to a strong web of love and support.

Taking Care of You. As with the advice flight attendants give about oxygen masks, we must take care of ourselves — listen to what we need, and heed the requests of our mind and body — before we can give of our time and selves to others. As much as routines are helpful, sometimes we need a break, even a full day, to rejuvenate at a time when we could not have predicted or planned for it. We need to listen to these callings and grant ourselves the time to step back without wandering into the dark byways of guilt.

Thinking Quality Thoughts. We must condense the unnecessary that is not beneficial and curate a home that feeds us well, restores us, and returns us to our best selves. The same is true for our mind. We must toss the trash; we must not gobble up more and more worries and thoughts that will hold us back. Instead, we must be selective and particular about what we choose to think about and engage in. (Again, chapter eight discusses ways to master your mind.)

Giving What You Can and When You Can. Altruism and generosity without the expectation of something in return are magnificent acts. The key is to know your boundaries and limitations. Whether dealing with money, time, or energy, give what you can, when you can to the point where you are still able to live your life well.

Sleeping Well. Experiencing a deep, full sleep each night is key to healthy living and crucial to overall everyday contentment. Creating an evening ritual that tells your mind you are unwinding is a wonderful way to look forward to going to sleep.

Understanding That New Things Will Be Hard Initially but Will Get Easier with Time. Choose to try new things, and be firm with yourself to stick with your resolve, as it may be hard initially. So long as you truly want something or to learn something — a new language, a new skill, an improved social life, a better job, increased savings in your retirement account — do not let the first stage of struggle deter you. The struggling will pass, so long as you do not stop trying.

Leaning into Your Feelings. One greatly beneficial habit is leaning in and examining your emotions, especially those that make you uncomfortable. What do I mean by examining? For me, it is simply taking out my journal and, in the moment, labeling the emotion and why I am feeling it. I do not have to provide a solution and do not have to give the problem value; the objective is simply to understand myself better. Sometimes we really do not know why we are feeling a certain way because we are afraid to look at it squarely. When we do so, we can then move through the emotion, and it does not slow us down or hold the power it did previously.

Competing Only with the Person You Were Yesterday. Competition is best when you are your only opponent. I had the opportunity in 2014 to give a speech to the local high school's National Honor Society inductees, and I chose this topic, as high school is a challenging, stressful time. While refraining from competing with others is a worthwhile lesson for teenagers, it is a valuable reminder in our everyday lives no matter what our age. We will find peace for our everydays when we know we did or were a little bit better than we were yesterday. And who will be the judge of that? Only you.

Remaining Curious. The curiosity you have within you is in many ways a mentor trying to lead you along a path that will excite not only your mind but your inner being. It will lead you to discover your deeper nature, if you have not already tapped into it. Do not let your curiosity be squelched because it may not make sense to those around you or the community you live in. Who cares? Have fun. Be a kid again and lose all track of time. I love these quotes from Elizabeth Gilbert: "If you consistently pursue curiosity, you will live a life of itself that is a work of art," and "Creative living is a life where you routinely make your decisions out of curiosity instead of fear."

Investing in a Way of Life Rather than Things. Yes, we need a roof over our heads. Yes, we need dishes to put food on, and yes, we need clothes and shoes. The key is to know why you are buying what you are buying. Is there a function? Is there a purpose? Purchases that are thoughtfully considered leave you not with regret but instead with a happy everyday life because your budget stays on track, your life is more enjoyable, and the things you buy enhance the overall quality of your life.

Annie Dillard pens in her book *The Writing Life*, "How we spend our days is, of course, how we spend our lives." Living a simply luxurious life is all about the everyday approach to life, and while we can work our tails off for the goals we seek, if we are not enjoying the journey, we need to adjust something. I adore the everydays that life offers me each morning when I rise. I also know that each day will not be glorious and memorable, as we sometimes expect them to be because that idea is what the media uses to keep us intrigued. But what if it could be? What if it is all about how we choose to live the everydays and what our expectations are?

If my experience so far has taught me anything, it is that my assumptions of "what should be" have lead me astray. We must have a mastery of all of the emotions that arise to master life itself. And the funny thing about labeling emotions is that sometimes we misunderstand what life is trying to reveal to us. Follow your doubts, dive deep, and perhaps discover that your doubts are telling you what is worth pursuing. If that is the case, you are traveling down the right road. Keep rolling on.

How to Jump-Start the Day

An essential prelude to a good next day is to get a restful night's sleep. Keep the technology out of your boudoir, sleep in luxuriously soft French or Belgium linen sheets, and make sure the thermostat is dialed down. Then, whether it is Monday morning or Saturday morning, jump-start your day in a way that establishes a positive tone — one that is as simple as being mindful of your basic physiology and the power of your mind — and sets the stage for success. The simple decisions you make before walking out the door can have a powerful effect on the mood you are in when you walk back across the threshold at the end of the day.

Give Your Body a Stretch. Nudging your body to wake up with some simple stretches is a morning routine that takes only five or ten minutes. Run through a few yoga poses or Pilates movements, and take five minutes for quiet meditation.

Read Something Inspiring. You may want to get caught up with the news in the morning, or perhaps you prefer to avoid the morning updates and instead listen to some eye-opening tunes or a soothing classical symphony. Whether you stop by your favorite blogs or read a daily passage in a motivational book, choose to purposefully read something that puts your mind in a positive state and sends you out the door with hope in your step.

Drink a Glass of Water. After eight hours of sleeping, the body is dehydrated. Placing a bottle or glass of water (at least eight ounces) next to your bed each night is a simple habit to get into. When you wake up, drink the water, and not only will your body be hydrated, it will also be jolted awake.

Preview the Day's Agenda. The best way to ensure success in the day that awaits is to know what you wish to accomplish. Take a look at your planner and the day's events. Get clear on where you have to be when, and whether anything needs to be moved to another day. Once you know what you have to do, you can focus and eliminate the stress of the unknown.

Eat to Thrive. A well-fed body is a body that performs at its best — and that includes your brain. Fuel your day with a touch of protein (eggs, for example), fiber, and a few carbs. The protein and fiber will keep your energy levels up far longer than that sugary Danish, and your brain will be fueled to make clear decisions as you move through your day.

Have a Moment with Nature. Whether you live in a cement jungle or next to an open field, take a moment to step outside, feel the air, and remind yourself of your priorities. Even if just for a moment, find some time before the day begins to feel the breeze of the outdoors. In chapter two, see the section "The Power of Nature."

Focus and Then Zone Out. When asked what they were thinking about during a successful play, pitch, putt, or pass, many athletes answered, "Nothing." In other words, their entire focus was on that particular moment and nothing else. No distractions, no overanalysis of previous attempts, and no worries about what might be. As your day begins, become clear about what you want to accomplish, then focus and let go of the unnecessary. The date that did not go so well last night? Do not let it ruin your day. Worried about getting that job interview you want? Relax, knowing you did your best while applying for the job, and focus on the work that is expected of you today so that, at the end of it, you will feel productive.

Strive for Sincere Engagement with Others. Grab a few more moments of cuddling with your significant other, say a few encouraging words to your children, give your dog or cat a much-deserved belly rub. When we connect sincerely with those we love, we not only improve our own mood; we boost theirs as well.

Choose a Confidence-boosting Outfit. Choose an outfit that makes you feel beautiful, strong, confident, professional — whatever you need to feel. After all, first impressions matter, and that begins with what you see in the mirror.

With simple, morning routines, we have the power to set the tone for the remainder of the day. While we may not have control of what we will encounter, we can at least walk out the door with a positive, determined mind-set that helps to make way for even more positive encounters.

Designing a Great Week

This is as true in everyday life as it is in battle: we are given one life, and the decision is ours whether to wait for circumstances to make up our mind, or whether to act, and in acting, to live.
— General Omar N. Bradley

When the week begins, I regularly sign off on my e-mails with "Have a great week!" but what does this actually mean, and how can we indeed insure we will have a great week? Many of us, including myself sometimes, passively move through our weeks, hoping they go well — hoping we do not receive too much to do from our boss, hoping we do not receive a phone call we do not want, hoping an unexpected bill does not arrive in the mail.

Instead, why not encourage a greater possibility that a great week will occur? Why not plan a week that is full of activities, approaches, rituals, and routines that enliven us, make us smile, and foster more of what we love? Sometimes a week is going to throw something our way that we do not want to deal with or did not expect to have to deal with, but these unwanted events do not have to define the entire week. Maybe they will affect that moment or that one particular afternoon, but if we have designed our week to be great, the negative will not outweigh the positive.

Here are a few ideas for designing a great week each week:

Sit Down and Take a Look. Before your week begins, sit down and take a look at your planner. What appointments have you scheduled, what to-dos must get done? Then look at each day and plan it out. Observe closely how much time you actually have in your days. Have you overbooked yourself? Do you have unscheduled time on Wednesday afternoon and evening that you want to protect? Make a change now or vow to protect windows of seemingly "free" time so that you have time to do what you want without something filling that space. When we know what lies ahead, we can prepare and not be surprised or forget things that we have to do.

Plan a Weekly Capsule Menu. We have to eat, so why not eat well? After looking over your schedule, take a moment to plan your menu for the week. You can use the weekly capsule menu concept (see chapter twelve) or simply sketch out notes in your planner. Knowing you have planned healthy, but delicious meals will give you something to look forward to, as well as keep you healthy and well-fed.

Grocery Shop. Make this a weekly ritual that is enjoyable. Pick an ideal time of day, visit your favorite markets, and savor the luxury of all of the options we have.

Take a Day Off. Plan one day a week, or at least an afternoon or morning, to be absolutely yours to do with as you like. Not only does this give you something to look forward to; it also allows you to become comfortable with your own company, figure out what you truly love to do, and listen to what piques your curiosity.

Incorporate Physical Exercise. Even if we love the form of exercise we have chosen, sometimes we fail to make it a priority. Each week, sit down and plan when you will fit your class, walk, swim, or other exercise session into your schedule. Lock it in. Then welcome a feeling of calm, knowing you are taking care of your health, as well as helping your mind and your body sleep better at night.

Schedule Something to Look Forward To. No matter what you do or how you define "something to look forward to," make sure you include at least one experience a week. It will put a skip in your step and enliven your being, and it may just speed up the week.

Make Sleep a Priority and a Luxurious Experience. Block out at least seven or eight hours for sleep each night, and guard them fiercely. To make going to bed even more enticing, adorn your bed with luxurious sheets and your favorite pillows, and have a candle, the proper lighting, and reading material beside the bed.

Set a Work Goal. Consider each week what you would like to complete by the time the week wraps up. Write it down in your planner. And set it in your mind that you will complete this task no matter what happens. Even if you simply make significant progress, when the end of the week arrives, you will feel as though you have accomplished what you had set out to do, and that is a wonderful way to bring tranquility into your weekend.

Nurture Your Cherished Relationships. Whether it is with your friends, partner, children, etc., consider how you can nurture the relationships that mean the most to you this week. Think small. It does not have to be anything grand: a thoughtful text, a rendezvous at a fun new restaurant, helping someone out with a project.

Plan Something to Mark the End of Your Workweek. Perhaps it is a comfort meal or heading out to the theater, but whatever you choose, plan a regular ritual that occurs when the workweek ends and the weekend begins. It will be something to look forward to, and it will be a signal to your mind to transition into a different mode: relaxing.

Get Outside. Mother Nature is a powerful force, and whether you can get outside each day or maybe just once a week, figure out a way or a day to do it.

Make One Day a Week Tech Free. I love what I do as a blogger, but when we set technology down for a moment, we may see that we might have become too attached and not present enough in our real, everyday lives. Perhaps start with an afternoon or evening; try to make one full day a week completely tech free and see what a difference it makes in the quality of your life. If that is impossible, set a time in the evening when the phone goes onto the charger and is out of sight until morning.

Check Your Closet. Are all of the clothes you want to wear cleaned, picked up from the dry cleaner, ironed? When the clothes we want to wear are available in our closets and do not need to be tended, we save time and unnecessary hassle.

Beauty Routine. Whether it is your weekly manicure or time for your bi-weekly pedicure, even if you do them yourself, make sure you have them on your schedule. And what about an at-home spa morning to give yourself whichever weekly masque your skin needs? Make sure your daily beauty necessities are stocked: lotions, makeup, etc. When we feel we are at our best, we relax. And when we relax, there is an improved likelihood that things will go well.

Check In with Yourself Regularly. So far you have planned a great week, one full of things to look forward to. But what if other events occur? What if meetings run long and time becomes tight? At various moments throughout the week, assess how you are feeling. Are you tense? Do you need to talk it out? Do you need to exercise? Do you need to journal and work out your feelings? Checking in with yourself is the quickest and easiest remedy you can give yourself to help get your week back on track. Often we just need to remind ourselves to be present, to slow down and relax, before we make decisions that may spoil the quality of our week.

One of my favorite things to do each Sunday is sit down, take a look at my week, and see what I get to look forward to. I want a life that I am excited to live every day. And even if every day does not offer excitement, I want to give myself opportunities to grow, be challenged, and appreciate the life I live. An ordinary life can truly be extraordinary if we choose to be present and live consciously.

The Joy of Weekend Rituals

No matter how wonderful, productive, or enjoyable the workweek may have been, our weekends (traditional or not) are a wonderful time to savor doing precisely what brings us pleasure. Yes, a getaway weekend every once in a while is certainly a treat, but the everyday, regular Saturday and Sunday can be magnificent if we consciously choose to bring into our lives rituals that we love.

Rituals I regularly look forward to and eagerly await nearly each week include stopping by the local bakery to pick up a croissant; catching up on leisurely reading material; stopping by a friendly local bookstore, finding a comfortable chair, ordering a hot cup of tea, and forgetting about the time; cooking a favorite recipe; and taking a long walk with the pups.

Finding Pleasure in the Essentials

A nice warm shower, a cup of tea, and a caring ear may be all you need to warm your heart.
— Charles F. Glassman

Perhaps there is a nugget of gold in living a busy life: recognizing what it feels like to be so overwhelmed that you can barely find a breath — and then finding a more balanced approach, becoming more appreciative of the essentials, the everyday moments that can be overlooked and camouflaged by the mistaken assumption that you should be pursuing something grander.

One of the gifts I was given as a child was an appreciation for the simple, the everyday, the essentials of life. I became fond of fresh air, cold, crisp water from the well, a sturdy roof over my head, a deep night's sleep without interruption, and homemade food on the table each night served with love and creativity. Daily experiences like these do not produce excitement or make headlines, but they are a simple foundation that, for me, has more beauty than any extravagance.

Each Sunday morning, my ritual is to dive into the newspapers. There is always at least one article worth sharing with followers on my Twitter or Instagram feed.

In the spring, I enjoy waking up with the birds chirping, no alarm clock necessary, and thankful for nature's rhythms and comforts. I love stepping into the kitchen and composing nutritious meals and, especially, spending time outdoors gazing at the sky and basking in the fresh air. Such essentials promote a life of heightened beauty and are a reminder of the importance of finding pleasure in the essentials.

Today, contemplate what the essentials for living your life may be. Are some essentials actually just "wants"? Or perhaps there are a few things you have placed on the "want" side that actually are fundamental for living well and being at peace. Be honest with yourself. Refuse to feel guilty for, as in my case, creating a nightly routine in which I turn in rather early, by eight or eight-thirty, put my thoughts in my journal, and read a few or many pages in a book that has piqued my curiosity until my eyelids become heavy. Whatever it may be, if you are honest with yourself, you will know. Give yourself some time, and begin savoring the essentials so that when those extraordinary "wants" dance into your life, the high will be magnificent and beyond memorable. Even when that moment passes, you will not miss it but will be thankful for it as you step back into the everyday life you love living.

The Essential Ingredient to Elevate the Everyday

We have what we seek. It is there all the time. And if we slow down and be still, it will make itself known to us.
— Thomas Merton

Each of us will design our days a bit differently, which is why the journey of cultivating a simply luxurious life must begin by looking inward. All along, you have had within yourself the essential ingredient for living a life of true contentment, so all that is required is to listen closely to yourself.

When Bob Schieffer hosted the CBS Sunday morning news program *Face the Nation*, he would reserve the final five minutes to elaborate on a variety of his thoughts inspired by the week gone by. I found this to be the best part of the show. A couple of years ago, I was intrigued enough to pick up the book *Bob Schieffer's America*, a catalog of these five-minute commentaries.

I liked one in particular, from April 8, 2007, and I copied it and stuck it to my idea board. The general concept is a beautiful thought to keep in mind during those times when we are perplexed or feel as if no one "gets" us, or when we are unsure about where we are supposed to shine.

Have a look for yourself. The reference is to a man Schieffer interviewed at the Aspen Ideas Festival named T. D. Jakes.

He said something that day that I shall never forget.

He reminded us that no one is perfect, that we are all broken somewhere.

But he said that is not all bad. A key is broken in all the right places to fit a certain lock. When that key is placed in that lock, there is a quiet click. When we meet a person who is broken in the right places to accommodate our brokenness, there is a click.

It can happen in other ways: an introverted person hears that click when [s]he finds a job that can only be done by a person who works well alone.

Whether it is a job, or a relationship . . . something clicks when we find the place that accommodates our uniqueness, or brokenness.

. . . some call it meditation — but there is within each of us some mysterious, inner thing that tells us when something clicks — we don't know how or why, we just know.

We are all broken. But listening for that click can help us to unlock many doors. The voice is always there — we have only to listen.

Are you listening? And if so, what have you heard?

While I would substitute the words "uniquely designed" for "broken," the point Jakes makes is worth contemplating. In order to understand how we can tap into our innate talents, in order to understand what they are and what we are sincerely drawn to without prompting or persuasion from the outside world, we must listen to closely until we hear the "click."

The beginning of the simply luxurious journey requires you to pay attention inwardly. Then the possibilities of what you can achieve in addressing your curiosities and passions become vividly clear, and it becomes easier to let go of the excess and to focus on living well — in a manner that

CHAPTER TWO

Mastering the Complexity of Simplicity

Any intelligent fool can make things bigger, more complex, and more violent. It takes a touch of genius — and a lot of courage — to move in the opposite direction.
— E. F. Schumacher

Even as a young girl, I desired simplicity. I wanted less stuff. I wanted to be free from clutter and able to move at will and use my imagination. It seemed to me that if we had less to take care of, less to worry about, fewer unnecessary problems to deal with, we would have more time to do as we wished. Now that I am in my late thirties, this approach to living has become even more central for me as I go about my everyday life. And it motivated the "simply" in the name of my blog and my first book, *Choosing the Simply Luxurious Life*.

So how is it that the world and daily living in our modern lives have become so complicated? Could it be that as Douglas Horton states, "The art of simplicity is a puzzle of complexity"? In short, yes.

Choosing to live a life of simplicity takes conscious effort.

Here are some of the elements we can include in our day-to-day living to ensure that we can live a life of simplicity — and one of true contentment.

Discipline. Find the courage within yourself to trust that the life you want is more important than a need to acquire or consume. As Peace Pilgrim (Mildred Lisette Norman) has said, "It is those who have enough but not too much who are the happiest." The ability to say no when something does not fit into your life plan or your value system is the key to getting rid of the unnecessary and freeing up your schedule for exactly what you want to focus on.

Patience. Raising mature, independent children, writing a book worth reading, making a mark in your chosen profession, saving enough to buy a house — these and many other worthwhile goals take time, and we must not rush them or give up before they have had a chance to mature. Too many times, we become impatient and create unnecessary problems and drama. Instead of saying too much, buying too much, or trying to do too much, we would do well to take a step back and take a breath. The results will appear in due time, which does not always coincide with the schedule we have devised.

A Clear Direction and Purpose. As Yogi Berra said, "If you don't know where you are going, you'll end up someplace else." The only way to know when to say no in order to not complicate your life is to know where you want to go. Once you understand the life you are attempting to create for yourself, self-discipline becomes much easier to practice. Uncertainty complicates life and prevents us from living simply.

Understanding the Difference between an Advertiser's Desires and Your Own. People bring a lot of unnecessary stress into their lives by trusting that what companies want for them is what they should want for themselves. Upon being offered a product or service, your first questions should be, "Do I need this, and does it contribute to my life goals and priorities?" If you answer honestly, you will end up with fewer unnecessary items, more money in your bank account, and less stress.

Maturity. To live a life of simplicity is to live life consciously: to be aware of your direction and respectful of others, yet strong enough to go in your own direction. Such maturity requires self-knowledge and the courage to step out on your own to understand who you are capable of becoming. When things do not work out as planned, it is the mature person who takes the lesson and moves forward, rather than pouting. Simplicity requires you to not cause extra harm by blaming or whining; doing so would complicate your life unnecessarily. Being an adult in age does not mean we are mature; being mature is a choice. Behaving in a mature manner requires self-discipline, self-examination, and a desire to understand the world — yet more evidence that living simply is indeed complex.

A life of simplicity is not easy to cultivate, but once you become accustomed to tending such a life, it can provide time and energy for the growth of your wildest dreams.

Making Decisions with Tailored Simplicity

People are remarkably bad at remembering long lists of goals. I learned this at a professional level when trying to get my high-performance coaching clients to stay on track; the longer their lists of to-dos and goals, the more overwhelmed and off-track they got. Clarity comes with simplicity.
— Brendon Burchard

The endless choices we have in our modern world — which clothes to wear, what food to eat, which job to pursue, where to travel, what to read, where to live — is a fairly new phenomenon. While having a long list of options for nearly everything can seem wonderful, all those choices can paralyze us if we do not fully understand what we truly want, as psychologist Barry Schwartz reminds readers in his book *The Paradox of Choice: Why More Is Less*.

Have you ever pursued a goal and, upon reaching it, been disappointed by what you had worked so hard to achieve? I have made that mistake more than a few times. What I have realized is that I was not applying "tailored simplicity" guidelines.

Tailored simplicity is the subtle interplay of four aspects of your life: your future, what you wish to achieve; your past, where you have been and how it has gone; your inner life and your values, the priorities that you live by every day and that guide your decisions; and the outer world and your options, understanding what is out of your control and thus what is available.

Tailored simplicity comes into play in our lives any time we make a decision that will change the direction or routine of our lives. Especially when it comes to significant life decisions — career options, relationships, where to live, health habits, where to travel, etc. — understanding how to act with tailored simplicity will reduce your indecisiveness and help you come to a decision that sits well with your conscience. Let me walk you through the process using as an example one of my recent life choices — my move to Bend.

First, I closely examined my past experiences to determine what I liked and did not like about where I lived, what felt comfortable and on target and what did not. When I visited Paris and London, I felt liberated by being able to live without a car and the availability of endless museums, plays, and other events. In Paris and Walla Walla, Washington, I loved the local artisans and their foods, produce, and crafts, and I saw an opportunity to support local businesses and build a sense of community. In Portland, Oregon, so much fresh food was available and the attention to health was refreshing. Bend, Walla Walla, Portland, Paris, and London all provided an abundance of opportunities for mindful stimulation — classes, discussion groups, activities, etc. — so that adults have options to continually grow and be curious. Pendleton, Oregon, Bend, and Walla Walla all offered a sense of community, fantastic neighbors, and quiet neighborhoods. In the negative column, Portland was too big, and I felt boxed in. In London or Paris, the cost of living was too high, and I could not own a home. Walla Walla and Pendleton did not offer the nuanced cultural and community connections and experiences I longed for.

I considered my future. What did I want to change? What was I seeking that I currently lacked? Those aspirations were easy for me to enumerate: opportunities for regular cultural/art events, proximity to college classes for extended learning, fresh produce and other healthy food options, a community with similar values, the ability to walk and paddleboard regularly and to enjoy the four seasons.

Then I turned to my inner world and values, and outlined what I could and could not live without. I wanted a small home to call my own, an affordable cost of living, and a dog-friendly community. I love teaching, and wherever I live, I need to be able to teach. I wanted opportunities to continually grow and explore. I wanted a safe and friendly neighborhood.

When it came to considering the outer world and my options, it was time to get real. As with house-hunting, we can create a dream list of what our house has to have before we buy, but the reality is, we are going to have to give a little, because we cannot create or dictate how it should exist. It is our job to weed through all the options and find the best ones. Where am I willing to move? How far? I searched in state and out, and even considered international destinations. I really had no limits. Upon deciding on two or three locations, I lived or spent significant time in each in order to feel as authentically as I could what it would be like to live there.

By the end of such a process, you have a very concise list of what an option has to have in order for you to even consider it. The guidelines provided an easy way for me to toss aside the alternatives that were not going to ultimately be the best and reduce any energy that would be wasted pursuing dead-end routes. With each step, I began to focus more precisely on the available options.

The principles of tailored simplicity — made specific with five years of searching, exploring, examining, and putting myself in the shoes of someone who lived in each of these towns as much as my budget would allow — made the decision to move to Bend overwhelmingly clear.

When you get to an end point in your decision making, having real conviction about your decision will instill in you a sense of confidence that will pull you through the difficult times along the journey. If you are willing to do the prep work and be very honest with yourself, the answers will be that much easier to find. And those answers will allow more contentment than you ever thought possible.

Getting Back to Simple Every Day

During the summer, when I want to step away from the computer, I take advantage of the sunshine and blue skies to step out onto my back deck with my two dogs. Making such a simple choice several times a day enlivens me, keeps me present, and brings a smile to my face, as well as a happy pup smile from Norman, who is my sunbather. In such moments, the contentment I feel is indescribable.

The reason we work so hard is so that we can have moments like the ones described above. The beauty of such moments is that there is not anything extravagant or excessive about them. Such moments are not hard to attain until we make them so. But we do have to put forth a great amount of effort and work — through weekends at times — to achieve this level of comfort. When each day of the week and sometimes every weekend are overwhelmed with demands, we can become so acclimated to the speed of our lives that we accept it as normal.

Sadly, such living is not simple, and it is not luxurious. Here are a few signs that you have been living at a breakneck speed:

- Your daily to-do list is daunting on a regular basis, leaving you no free time.

- You forget basic information and obligations (recalling people's names, turning off the curling iron, returning calls and e-mails, etc.).
- You have no time for your favorite pastimes (reading, time with friends/family, gardening, etc.)
- Your eating and fitness habits have gone by the wayside.
- Home is merely a place to sleep and eat before you run back out into the world.
- Why you are so busy becomes unclear, and simply making it through the day or week is your goal.

For some, a busy life can exclude time with those we love. Or perhaps the incessant demands of others, even those we love, become constricting because we do not have time to just be on our own, to catch our breath. I am a self-identified introvert, and I find that if I do not have time to step away from others regularly, I am not at my best. Each of us must know what fuels us and include that in our schedule, for when we lose this fuel, we can become disoriented and make decisions that keep us from achieving the dreams we are seeking or the life we wish to live. The good news is that by becoming conscious and mindful, we can get back to simple. Here are some ways to do it:

Start at the Foundation, with Financial Security. Make a bi-weekly or monthly date to balance your budget. Know where your money goes, and manage your assets wisely. When you know how much you can spend, you begin to live more purposefully, and decisions become easier. When you acknowledge that an item of proposed spending would keep you from reaching your goals, saying no becomes easy, and when you are not saying yes to everything — like that fabulous designer skirt that just went on sale — more money stays in your account as you save for your dreams. When you get your finances in order, your life begins to follow. (Read about masterminding your financial security in chapter six; for in-depth information, see chapter three of *Choosing the Simply Luxurious Life*.)

Create a Filing System for Incoming Documents. Because the bills, receipts, tax forms, and other pieces of mail keep arriving, you need to create a filing system that keeps items in their place for easy access. To truly simplify your life, find ways of going entirely paperless. TurboScan and Expensify, for example, are both great apps for electronically filing receipts and other documents. Simply take some quick pics, save, and file in your Dropbox, external hard drive, or the cloud.

Become Comfortable with Saying No. When you become clear about your priorities, you allow yourself to say no to invitations and tasks that do not align with what you need your energy for. Saying no is a way of marking your boundaries and respecting your time and your ability to complete what you say yes to. Saying no when you need to is liberating and rewarding.

Jump-start Your Maintenance Routines. In chapter fifteen, I share a list of routines to help maintain the simply luxurious life you have worked so hard to create. Sometimes these routines get bulldozed by other demands, but later we realize the absence of such routines erodes the quality of our lives. You will be amazed how quickly and easily simply putting these routines back to work can change the tone and increase the ease of your life.

Take Time to Take Care of Your Health. Eating well, working out regularly, getting enough sleep. Often these three vital components get cheated when our lives speed up. Just remember that without the proper fuel, tune-ups, and checkups, our lives can run out of gas and begin to crumble. If setting things right means saying no to a day trip to save on gas so you can buy healthy organic produce for your sack lunches, remember the investment you are making in your health.

Turn Off the Technology Regularly. Master technology before it masters you. When I step away from my technology, even if for just an afternoon or evening, I feel as though I have caught my breath.

Remember Your Purpose. As I revel in my moments in the sunshine with my pups, I am reminded of the life I have been working so hard to create for myself — a life of true simple luxuriousness, a life that allows for moments of leisure and pleasure and time to dabble in hobbies and lose track of time. When we are reminded of the reasons we work so hard, letting go of the unnecessary and embracing self-discipline become that much easier.

You are living your life. You are the only one who is responsible for the path you take. You can say no, or you can be shamed or sufficiently riddled with guilt provoked by societal expectations to say yes to things that will impede the life you are working so hard to create. Only you can find the strength to organize and structure a life that is rich, rewarding, and fulfilling. Take a moment to check your speed. Are you within a reasonable speed limit or are you rushing excessively?

The Benefits of Banishing Busy

No person lives their life more fully, more intensely and more consciously than the one who is calm.
— William George Jordan, *The Majesty of Calmness*

As my yoga instructor began the class one morning, with students in a meditative pose, focusing on the breath, she stated, "Being still is not displaying a lack of energy, but rather demonstrating one's ability to be free from chaos." What an amazing and profound idea. The United States is a nation of hustlers who strive to work more hours, earn one more commission, and achieve more on the job, and often the notion of a life of quality over quantity gets lost in the shuffle. But when we are too involved in the hustle, we miss out on cultivating deep, rich, rewarding days, relationships, and dreams. What values does "banishing busy" bring to our lives?

We Make Better Decisions. When we are calm, no matter what is going on around us, we can take a deep breath and think clearly about what is being asked of us. We can increase our impulse control, eliminate rash decision making, take time before responding to a request. Simply because an e-mail arrives in our inbox does not mean we have to respond immediately. In fact, it is often best to not respond immediately. When we take a breath and contemplate the contents of the e-mail with a clear mind, we can respond in a way that reduces or eliminates regret. Being calm helps us make decisions we are proud of and supports the life we are cultivating.

We Reflect a Life Lived Well. To be content is to have clarity about our priorities and to know we have done our best. Sometimes we think that keeping busy is a way to make up for something we did not do well. Calm people accept that they did their best with what they had and knew at the time, and they move on without the hurry.

We Can Feel Confident in Moments of Uncertainty. Letting go of hurry also means we are confident that we can do our best in the present, that we can think clearly, that we will put our best foot forward. A busy, harried, and rushed state of affairs cannot ruffle us if we are truly calm. So long as we are certain of our direction and our priorities, we will be at ease because we have done our best.

Strong Self-Control Is the Muscle That Will Keep Busy at Bay. We strengthen our self-control when we let go of busy. We keep our impulses in check, giving ourselves time to contemplate, and each time we flex our self-control muscle, it becomes easier to walk away from the temptation to always be busy. Why? Because we know being busy often does not feel good; it can be miserable, exhausting, and unfulfilling. When our lives are full of what we truly value, what we truly love and are passionate about, we do not want to clutter them with excess busyness. Rather, we want to give ourselves more time to savor the life we have created.

We Are Trusting Ourselves and Not Seeking the World's Approval. Often when we are busy, we are on someone else's time schedule. We are trying to meet someone else's demands. When we go at our own pace, when we give ourselves the proper time to do something, we are trusting in ourselves that it will be done, and so long as we have done our best, that is enough. Even if the outside world does not approve, we are not shattered or demoralized because we know we did everything we could in that moment.

We Save Money. Often we waste money when we rush decisions. And remember: "Get rich quick" schemes are always a fool's opportunity. Question anything that offers a quick return. Take the time to do your homework; investigate and inquire for recommendations. Knowing the money you worked hard to earn is invested securely brings a sound night's sleep and peace of mind.

We Develop Strong, Lasting Foundations in Relationships, Work, and Life. Instead of hurrying, if we allow the events in our lives to go at their natural pace, we enhance the quality of our lives. Instead of forcing a relationship to blossom (or even occur), so that we can be married by a certain age or have children by a certain age or "catch up" with our friends who seem to be ahead of us according to society's standards, we can see the true potential that is present. Our journeys through our careers, the strength of our friendships, acquiring the life skills we need to be the success we are each capable of being — each of these takes time, and everyone's time schedule will be different based on what they need and what needs to be learned along the way. Do not rush Mother Nature; do not rush the Universe's plans; do not presume to know how it should all work out and when. Instead, just keep striving down the path that aligns with your priorities and passions.

Not being in a hurry is a necessary component to living a life of quality. According to 19th-century essayist William George Jordan, "Hurry is the deathblow to calmness, to dignity, to poise. Hurry means the breakdown of the nerves. It is the royal road to perpetual worry. Everything that is great in life is the product of slow growth; the newer, and greater, and higher, and nobler the work, the slower is its growth, the surer is its lasting success."

A quality life takes time to develop. It requires us to learn the skills and acquire the tools to live a life that ignores or eradicates the unnecessary and focuses on the areas that are worth our time, attention, and investment.

Sometimes we busy ourselves to keep a protective wall around truths we do not want to acknowledge or confront. But often what we fear is not as awful as we expect. If we will only take the time, we will find keys to unearthing a life that is far more enriching and enjoyable to live because it is a life free from angst, a life lived in truth, and a life lived in the present. I encourage you to let go of the busy to welcome the sublime life that can be yours if only you would set it free.

The Transition from Busy to Balanced

Happiness is not a matter of intensity but of balance and order and rhythm and harmony.
— Thomas Merton

It is a wonderful paradox that in order to live a full life we must not allow our daily schedules to become full. Some responsibilities, some opportunities to be productive, some time to rest, and some time to play — a balance between these key components will enable a full life to bloom. Being busy does not ensure efficiency; in fact, it usually undercuts it. We need to cure our fascination with busyness because it is impeding our ability "to live a fully human life." And the gift we all have been given is the ability to be fully human.

What does being fully human mean? Philosopher and humanitarian Jean Vanier won the 2015 Templeton Prize, awarded to a person who has made an exceptional contribution to affirming life's spiritual dimension. His journey to answering this question began for him in 1960 when he went to Paris "to think, and write, about the meaning of life." In May 2015, he wrote a beautiful article in *The Atlantic* entitled "What It Means to Be Fully Human." I have made a brief list of the points he highlighted:

- To discover who we truly are
- To understand our fragility
- To understand the unity between our head and heart
- To understand the beauty we all possess
- To be willing to open our heart to others, letting go of fear
- To let down the barriers and open up
- To resist the ego and refrain from competition and comparison

To be fully human is to understand that we all, each one of us, is human, and to let this understanding nourish the calm, reassurance, and reflection we need to appreciate this life we have been given. We need to slow down, prioritize, and savor.

There are times in our lives when our schedules are busier than at other times. During the early years of my blog and the two years before the release of my first book, I knew very well what my priorities were, and that made it all the easier to let go of other tasks and responsibilities. Looking back, I know that my clarity of purpose enabled me to eventually recognize when I could slow down and find a better balance in my life.

For each of us, the definition of balance will be different, and it will ebb and flow throughout the course of our lives. Some years, your definition of relaxing will appear to someone else to be drudgery. Other years, your idea of being productive may appear to others as laziness. But it does not matter how others define your approach, so long as you are balanced.

Sometimes it is hard to make the transition from a busy life to a balanced life. You might find yourself sitting on your sofa on a Sunday afternoon, your schedule free and open, scrambling your brain to figure out what you should be doing, unable to relax and just appreciate the balance you have created. You may allow your internal voice to berate you for not taking action, as your goals are not yet accomplished and your life is not where you think it should be. I know this voice. I have heard it in my head, but now I can recognize it and dismiss it — sometimes with just a deep breath or sometimes with an afternoon of reflection and a moment of meditation.

What I also know about the false motivation to remain busy is that a quality life is a thoughtful life. A quality life is a life that involves time to let go. A quality life involves knowing how to de-stress in a healthy manner in order to prevent your mind from turning a snowflake of doubt or worry into a snowball of self-sabotage.

As you make the transition from busy to balanced living, find a practice of de-stressing that works for you. Here are a few options to consider:

- Turn off the TV and read a book.
- Leave your phone at home and go walking.
- Fill your home with music that invites you to escape from the world.
- Take a hot bath.
- Meditate.
- Practice yoga.
- Enjoy a massage.
- Take a nap.
- Attend your favorite exercise class.
- Hang out with Mother Nature (even if it is in your backyard, lounging on a hammock).
- Sip hot tea and journal it out.
- Eat well.
- Talk or spend time with a friend who can bring you closer to calm.
- Partake in your favorite craft or artistic endeavor.

There are many benefits to be experienced when we choose to let go of the habit of busy. One of the most profound and affirming is the opportunity to live an examined life. When we enable ourselves to live an examined life, we discover the path we want to be on; we understand what is actually okay to let go of. We begin to find the permission within ourselves to live fully — to be fully human.

Returning to Calm

Calmness of mind is one of the beautiful jewels of wisdom.
— James Allen

As I have settled into my life in Bend, I am more able to reflect, assess, and determine which manners of living serve me well and which do not.

Following my first summer in Bend, I was asked how my summer went, and my answer was something that I perhaps had never vocalized even to myself before, but it was a powerful truth to discover: For the first time, I enjoyed staying in my hometown during the summer months, as I truly feel Bend is my home, and I enjoy being home. This is the first time I have ever felt this about any place in my adult life.

Such a simple, but profound realization has brought me much tranquility. And I quickly realized that this is the state I needed more of in my life on a regular basis. When we face a busy schedule, it is imperative that we are clear about how we are going to continue to welcome tranquility and calm into our lives. Because the truth is, we need it. Striking a balance between acute stress and restful respite is necessary each day. The key is knowing how. Here are some suggestions:

Spend Time with Positive People who are calm and rational. On the flip side, stop reaching out to people who cannot give you what you need — people you wish could bring you happiness, if only they would change a little. When we reach out to these people, we only bring stress and agony into our lives. A study conducted by the Proceedings of the National Academy of Sciences revealed that while healthy social connections have a strong influence on our happiness, they are "outweighed by the adverse effects of strained relationships." Choose the people you spend time with and are intimate with wisely; they have a significant influence over the quality of your life.

Meditate or Practice Mindfulness Every Day, no matter how much or how little. During the summer months, my days begin with sunrise. Before I sit down for my regular breakfast of steel-cut oats, I step out onto my back porch and meditate for a minimum of ten minutes. When my teaching schedule begins in the fall, I still incorporate meditation into my morning routine, but sometimes I will only be able to do so for three to five minutes. However, meditating daily makes a significant difference in my mood and focus as I begin the day.

Do Not React Immediately if you find yourself in a stressful, chaotic, or unexpected situation. Pause for an hour, a day, a weekend, until your emotions have subsided and you are thinking clearly. Do not let others rush you to speak, act, or get involved.

Set and Maintain Clear Boundaries. The hardest boundaries to maintain will be with people who do not want you to respect them, who will attempt to make you feel guilty or shame you for saying no or not involving yourself. Respect your self-worth, your feelings, and your life's journey, and thereby protect the tranquility you need in your everyday life.

Be Authentically You. Be yourself, tactfully and with decorum. The strain of presenting a false self to the world will eventually build up so that you are not able to relax with others. And even when you are alone, you may stew over who you are trying to be. They can like it or not, they can take it or leave it, but by being authentic, you are investing in a life of tranquility.

Be Silent. Epidemiologists have shown that there is a correlation between high blood pressure and chronic noise. The effect of regular or consistent noise on our beings is not good. It is impossible to be calm when everything around us is cacophonous. As an Arabian proverb says, "The fruit of silence is tranquility."

Savor Your Hobbies. Maybe you can easily list them right now, or maybe you are still exploring. Either way, keep diving into the journey of hobby exploration and enjoyment — whatever makes time disappear and grabs your full attention. Enjoy immersing yourself in your hobbies regularly.

Feel Productive Each Day. In 2017, I shared the "100-Year-Old To-Do List Hack That Still Works Like a Charm." The idea is to list six things you want to accomplish tomorrow. Put them in order of importance. Then, when you wake up the next day, focus solely on the top item until it is complete. Then move on to the next. Any uncompleted items for the day will move to the top of the list tomorrow, but the key is to have only six (or fewer) and to always put them in order of importance.

Give Yourself a Day without a "Have to Do" List. This does not mean you lie on the couch or stay in bed the entire day. What it means is that you give yourself the freedom to do whatever you want. No have-tos, no feeling bad if you do not get something done. Just relax, lose track of time, wander, nap, tinker, play, follow where your curiosity leads.

Incorporate a One-Week-a-Month "No Spending" Practice. Knowing you cannot spend for an entire week relieves the stress of making purchases, perhaps ones that involve more debt or stress or responsibilities, and gives you permission to slow down. If you have your spending well under control, this most likely will not make much of a difference, but sometimes a spending fast is liberating. It slows us down, nudging us to do what truly is fulfilling and not just a quick fix.

Find Something to Be Grateful for Every Day. To alleviate any residual stress at the end of the day, to help make sense of questions I may still have, or simply as a calming end to the day and signal to my mind that it is time to start thinking about falling asleep, I take out my journal and, at a bare minimum, list what I am grateful for from that particular day. If I have more energy, I write about my day and work through my thoughts, but at the least, I share what I am grateful for. It never ceases to amaze me how powerful this small activity is in righting my mind and squelching unnecessary worries before I go to sleep.

An Everyday Necessity: Deliberate Rest

When we take the right to rest, when we make rest fulfilling, and when we practice rest through our days and years, we also make our lives richer and more fulfilling.
— Alex Soojung-Kim Pang, *Rest: Why You Get More Done When You Work Less*

Charles Darwin took regular ten-mile walks. Alice Munro walked three miles each day. Winston Churchill engaged in painting. Lin-Manual Miranda takes his dog each Sunday for strolls through New York City's parks. J.R.R. Tolkien and Ray Bradbury took daily afternoon naps. Workers at Bletchley Park during World War II chose chess as a favorite pastime, and associate justice of the United States Supreme Court Elena Kagan boxes regularly with her personal trainer.

Initially, when the word *rest* is mentioned, we may think of sitting on the sofa, flipping through channels, but the difference between mindless rest and deliberate rest is that the latter "enables productivity." When we truly rest, our minds are not actually stagnant. We are enabling them to do what they need to do — reach understandings and make connections that, when we are actively at work, we cannot manage.

The difference between mindless and deliberate rest is what you are feeding your brain. Sitting down and watching a thoughtful, engaging film can absolutely be deliberate rest. It may offer ideas and insights that eventually help you make connections you did not see prior to viewing the film; the key is to feed your mind well. Give it quality fuel and you will get quality results, even while you sleep.

Rest cultivates calm in your life, and a rested person is in better shape for managing their life. Rest increases your confidence and strengthens your willpower and self-control. It expands your emotional intelligence and your ability to engage. Rested people have more time as they are more able to make their boundaries firm and clear. Being rested increases your success and accomplishment and helps you reach your full potential. Rest allows you to live a long, healthy, invigorating life — a simply luxurious life.

Follow these suggestions for welcoming deliberate rest into your life:

- Make rest a priority.
- Spend only four or five hours each day doing strenuous work.
- Establish a consistent morning routine.
- Set clear boundaries between work and rest.
- Take walks often.
- Nap regularly and nap well.
- Enjoy a deep sleep every night.
- Detach and take that vacation.
- Exercise routinely.
- Cultivate a hobby that you love and that challenges you.

Perhaps when you read the second item on the list above, you said to yourself, Nope, that will never happen, not in my world, not in the job I have to do every day to earn my paycheck. And on the surface, you are absolutely correct. But what if you could look at the job you go to each day and redesign your day? What if you could schedule it so that you address the most strenuous demands at the beginning of the day and then schedule less demanding meetings, projects, and activities toward the end of the day so that you do not tax your mind and resources as heavily?

We do not have to look busy to gain approval. The gift of living well is that our lives often will look paradoxical: How can others live such a life and not be exhausted/stressed and instead have time to enjoy, play, and partake in the pleasures as well? The reality is that it is indeed possible when we choose to live consciously and thoughtfully.

Deliberate rest paired with deliberate work is a partnership: One provides the means to live, while the other gives meaning to life. As Alex Pang writes, "When we treat rest as work's equal and partner, recognize it as a playground for the creative mind and springboard for new ideas, and see it as an activity that we can practice and improve, we elevate rest into something that can help calm our days, organize our lives, give us more time, and help us achieve more while working less."

How to Avoid Unnecessary Stress

Stress. The word often carries a negative connotation, but what the body is doing in a state of stress is releasing adrenaline to allow us to push through a period of time and be successful. When we perpetually place our body in this state, stress takes a negative toll — breaking down our immune system and leaving our bodies more susceptible to aches, pains, and sickness prematurely or unnecessarily.

Why do we stress ourselves? It could be a variety of things, but at the heart of much of our unnecessary stress is a hopeless effort to gain control of everything. Even when we realize that some things will always be out of our control, we can push too hard for too long and ultimately create more problems than solutions.

Striving to do our best leaves us more satisfied, but putting too much on our plate jeopardizes everything. We can end up tying ourselves in knots and tripping over our best-laid plans. Rather than inviting unnecessary stress, let's look at things each of us can let go of that will leave our lives better balanced and more enjoyable.

Being Perfect. The idea that perfection is possible can have a devastating effect on your self-esteem and overall contentment. When I was trying to sell my house, I found myself thinking that every pillow, crevice, and counter needed to be perfectly adorned, styled, and polished. The reality was that I did my best and made my home as neat and attractive as possible, and when the right buyer came along, the sale happened. It is possible to work yourself into a frenzy, examining all of the reasons something may not happen when you so badly want it to, but at some point, you have to let go and live your life.

Creating an Ideal Social Life. Whatever your preferences for enjoying the company of others, nobody can know that but you. So stop trying to create a social circle based on the expectations of other people, and just live the life that brings you the most joy, regardless of outside approval.

Your Past. Each of us has the opportunity to learn from the lessons of our past. Rather than beating yourself up over past blunders and poor judgment calls, be thankful for the opportunities you had and begin striving toward more appropriate journeys that will leave you more fulfilled. Now you know better, and thus you can confidently do better.

Making Enough Money. So long as you have money to live, eat, and sleep comfortably, you should count yourself fortunate, and if you are able to enjoy the means by which you make your money, you can count yourself rich. When we enjoy the work we do, we can live the life we enjoy — which is what actually defines our wealth. Practice sound basic money management and saving practices, and you will soon discover there is no need to compare your income with anyone else's.

Being a Success in the Opinion of Others. Maybe your friends and family do not consider the work you do to be relevant. However, in your heart, you know you are giving your best and loving what you do. True success is being able to live according to your values and at the same time feel a sense of contributing positively to society.

Replace the false ideals discussed above with these practical steps to combat the effects of stress:

Insist on Quality Sleep and a Healthy Diet. Caring for our bodies properly can do amazing things.

Get Regular Exercise, which increases energy and longevity. Exercise is a prime example of how placing temporary stress on our bodies can be a positive practice.

Find a Means to Feel Truly Productive. The feeling of being productive is satisfying at the end of the day and goes a long way toward offsetting the stresses involved in getting there. Weekends and occasional vacation getaways are great, but knowing you are able to produce something of value each day is very rewarding.

Time to Do Nothing. When I have a goal at the forefront of my mind, it can be hard to sit still for a couple of hours. However, if I do not find regular downtime, I am irritable and have a greater tendency to make bad decisions. Taking it easy from time to time is healthy and necessary, especially if we want quality results.

The Value of Solitude

The amount of solitude each of us needs is different. But solitude in some form is a vital ingredient to make sense of our "deeper nature," as Frédéric Lenoir writes in *Happiness: A Philosopher's Guide*: "Happiness consists in living in accordance with our deeper nature. . . . People can never be happy if they go against their deeper natures." And what is the key to discovering our deeper nature? Solitude.

It is in moments of solitude that we have time to discern what we need to be happy or to consider whether we are conforming to others' expectations. Solitude gives us time to reflect without judgment, without impediment. We must build solitude into our schedules, especially when we realize that something feels off or overwhelming or that we are not thinking clearly.

Sometimes things work well for a while, and then they need to shift to another gear to keep the momentum going. The same is true with our lives overall. Not everything needs to be changed. Some things will remain constant, but you will realize that you no longer need the training wheels, which are just slowing you down or depleting you of energy you need.

When we have the time to be with our thoughts, we can discover our deeper nature, our true selves. Do not succumb to societal fear-mongering that says alone time is equivalent to being lonely. Paul Tillich wrote a beautiful retort to such a fallacy: "Language has created the word 'loneliness' to express the pain of being alone. And it has created the word 'solitude' to express the glory of being alone." Anyone who has experienced the rewards of taking time for herself will discover the power of solitude. Solitude opens the door to what will make us happy. But we must become comfortable with our own company so we can find the happiness we seek.

The Power of Nature

Those who contemplate the beauty of the earth find reserves of strength that will endure as long as life lasts. . . . There is something infinitely healing in the repeated refrains of nature — the assurance that dawn comes after night, and spring after winter.
— Rachel Carson, *Silent Spring*

Most of us are indoors a lot. We live in urban environments where nature is not immediately outside our back door. Being cut off from nature can gradually take a toll. Here are specific benefits you gain when you step outside.

You Boost Your Mental Health. A dose of nature can successfully combat stress. According to a 2014 study, those who stepped outside for a constitutional in nature showed a reduction in anxiety and depression. Another study found that being physically active outside thwarts the chances of ever having poor mental health.

You Improve Your Thinking Skills. Students who have regular access to being out in nature perform better on assessments and are more apt to exercise successful critical-thinking skills. One study showed that short-term memory increased as well.

You Revitalize Your Creativity. Separating yourself from a man-made everyday routine frees your mind and unclutters it from the strains that weigh you down when you do not give it a rest. Being present and resisting distraction will refresh your mind and allow you to focus.

You Enhance Your Perspective. When we step out into nature, we are reminded of the simplicity and patience that beauty needs in order to reveal itself, as well as of the ebb and flow of life. As our appreciation is awakened, we are often better able to put our own lives and choices in perspective.

You Age More Gracefully. Strong bones and fewer aches and pains are more common in those who spend regular time outside, and being active while outdoors improves overall physical health. In one study, inflammation within the body decreased in students and elderly people who spent time outdoors, thus helping to prevent some cancers, autoimmune disorders, and other illnesses.

Elevate the Quality of What You Consume

In an article in *Porter* magazine, cookbook author and philanthropist Jessica Seinfeld shared her golden rules for life, and one especially caught my attention: Elevate the quality of your consumption. Let's look further into the areas in which we consume or absorb the products of the outside world, and how we can elevate their quality and thereby the overall quality of our everyday lives.

Food. In his TED Talk "What's Wrong with What We Eat," cookbook author and food journalist Mark Bittman considers the effect of eating mindlessly what is cheap and too often easily accessible. Our food has an effect on our overall health, and on the environment's health as well.

Media. False and restrictive definitions of what it means to be male and what it means to be female inflict injury on innocent children and inhibit the potential of every individual. Lack of awareness of how we individually buy into and even support such images, traditions, and ways of living hurts our own dreams and the dreams of those we love. Television, film, video games, and television news play a significant role in our lives; we must work diligently to understand how they can limit our cultural expectations and keep the culture from shifting for the better.

Reading Material. The way to continue to develop your wealth of knowledge is to continually feed it the proper fuel. Ask yourself, What do you want to bring into your life? What do you value? Based on your answers, seek out publications that support your ideals and deepen your understanding of issues you care about.

Films. Whether it is small independent films or mega summer blockbusters, support movies based on plotlines with substance, and support characters, protagonists, and methods of conflict resolution that align with your values.

Ideas. Are you a TED Talk aficionado? Do you take free online college classes at Coursera or edX? What about book talks at a local bookshop or opinion pieces from credible news organizations? Exposing yourself to a variety of ideas from people with wide-ranging expertise elevates the quality of information you consume.

Energy. Avoid people who bring you down with their mood, their words, or their perspective. Positive energy is just as infectious as negative energy, so find people who enliven you and make you excited about the day and the world you live in.

Clothing, Shoes, and Accessories. Buy less, invest well. We truly do not need much. It is about knowing ourselves and shopping wisely, and therefore less often, but well.

Ultimately, we elevate the quality of our lives when we become educated, conscious, and conscientious consumers. Choose to become informed about what surrounds you and what you are supporting with the money you exchange for the goods you put into your body and fill your mind with.

Letting Go to Gain an Abundance

We must be willing to let go of the life we've planned, so as to have the life that is waiting for us.
—Joseph Campbell

The undeniable life truth remains that change is inevitable. Yet even when we fervently pursue change, letting go of certain aspects of the life we have been living can feel as though we are leaving behind our "Linus blanket." Whether it is the comfort of being accepted in the community we currently live in, the comfort of the walls we have built to protect our heart, or the comfort of a social calendar that may not be to our taste, but at least we have one — letting go of what we have known for what is completely uncertain can cause angst in even the most courageous of people.

As Einstein said, "Everything should be made as simple as possible, but not simpler." And part of striking the right balance is letting go of the unnecessary, which may require change in our lives — change that is on our own terms and for the purpose of improving the overall quality of our lives. And knowing what to hang on to will give our lives the sound structure and direction that will bring fulfillment.

Let go of:

Others' Opinions. It has been my experience that when I am unsure of myself, my abilities, and my path, I seek approval from others more readily and more often. The lesson? Take the time to get to know yourself; hone your strengths, and in doing so, you will begin to approve of yourself, and that is all that matters.

The Number of Likes. Social media offers wonderful ways to stay in touch and share information, but if your value or confidence depends on outside approval, you need to begin doing work on the inside: on your mental strength, self-acceptance, and self-knowledge.

The Size of Your Home. Many people believe they need a large house because they need to take care of many people or they have an immense amount of stuff. The fact is, however, that Americans have lived in far smaller homes in the past with just as many people, and often more.

Societal Expectations That Shrink Who You Are and Could Be. Choose to find the courage to walk to the beat of your own drum; doing otherwise diminishes who you are and what you have to offer. Be brave. We all are capable of discovering the courage within us; it is there, just waiting to be exercised. This is how Raymond Lindquist put it: "Courage is the power to let go of the familiar."

A Busy Schedule. Inevitably there will be times when your life becomes harried, but allowing this to be an everyday occurrence suggests that you are avoiding confronting what you lack in life.

Brand-Name Clothing. The reason I buy Diane von Furstenberg clothing is because it aligns with my signature style: quality, chic, casual attire — and it has to be on sale. However, buying a pair of heels for the red soles or a handbag for the entwining Cs so everyone can see you wearing them reveals your dependence on the approval of others.

Fake Food. It is not only your waistline that will thank you, but also your long-term physical health and especially your mind.

Where Someone Received Their Education. Where someone chose to be trained for their career should not matter in the least. What is important is one's willingness to learn and the ability to grow and apply their knowledge; along with their passion and work ethic, that should catch our attention. Do not focus on where the degree came from, but rather on someone's expertise and passionate pursuit.

Mode of Transportation. Perhaps this is a bigger issue out here on the West Coast, but the only reason one should pay attention to their choice of transportation is to ensure functionality and safety. Beyond that, save your money, and do not forget to change your oil regularly.

Past Mistakes: Leave Them Behind

Steve Maraboli says, "The truth is, unless you let go, unless you forgive yourself, unless you forgive the situation, unless you realize that the situation is over, you cannot move forward." We each leave behind us a textbook full of lessons we can learn from as we move forward, but learning from them and dwelling on them are two different things. When we do the latter, we are longing for a chance to rewrite history — a chance, we undoubtedly know, that will never materialize. When instead we chose to learn from history, we accept our past, remembering that we are human and moving forward with more knowledge.

Just as there are clear things to let go of, there are specific items to hold on to with absolute resolution:

Curiosity. To remain curious, as Diane Sawyer reminds, is to never grow old. The fact that there is always something new to learn is a fire you never want to extinguish.

Books, Information, etc. Whether you choose a book checked out from the library or a news article in *Feedly*, be well read and in the know.

Authenticity. You have something to offer the world that no one else has. Take the time to discover it, have the courage to cultivate it, and pursue it without apology. Your life and legacy will be more fulfilling as a result.

Your Unique Path. People often scoff, question, or try to thwart ideas they do not understand or, due to their experience, could not imagine for themselves. As humans, we consciously view the world from our limited perspective. Knowing this should lift the burden as you pursue and cultivate the life you have imagined.

Gratitude. Being thankful for what is going well keeps the positive energy flowing, motivates us to be more positive by default, and is a magnet for experiences and people. Often, too, when we are thankful for what we have, we do not pursue what we do not need.

Hope. Never lose the fuel that will carry you right up to the moment you were not sure would ever happen.

If lived consciously, life will not always easy, but there are many ways we make it harder than it needs to be. As Henry Havelock Ellis put it, "All the art of living lies in a fine mingling of letting go and holding on." We must strip the unnecessary and revel in the beautiful. While this may sound simple, it requires conscious effort. The key is to recognize what supports you as you courageously choose to be authentically who you are and have the capability to become, and what aligns with your life priorities. Everything else is just filler. In choosing what to hold on to and what to let go of, notice which list is longer. Quality over quantity prevails again.

CHAPTER THREE

Society, Women, and the Woman You Want to Be

Always choose yourself first. Women are very socialized to choose other people. If you put yourself first, it's this incredible path you can forge for yourself.
— Amina Sow, in *All the Single Ladies*, by Rebecca Traister

The first time I watched the documentary *Miss Representation*, directed by Jennifer Siebel Newsom, I gave a sigh of relief. If you have seen this 2011 film, my response at first may sound odd, as the purpose of the film is to reveal how women in America are misrepresented in society and objectified, minimized, and silenced. Since I was a teenager, I had felt that society imposed an indescribable pressure for me to be something that did not sit well with my soul, to be something less than what I was, to be a "thing," a prop, a puzzle piece, a one-dimensional something to complete someone else's idea of how women should live in our society.

When media and government are dominated by one gender, we can get a distorted idea of how all genders can reach their full potential. Eventually, via high school and college and my entry into the world of work, I was able to observe women who spoke the truth about what was going on and why it was not working. *Miss Representation* forwards a point of view that values women as individuals with talents and gifts that should be fostered and celebrated. Thus my sigh of relief.

So many of our assumptions regarding male and female roles in society are the result of nurture — what we learn — not nature. Our brains are plastic, malleable, and not hardwired until we unthinkingly accept what we have been taught. If something works for you and enables you to be your most authentic self, keep traveling down that road, but if it does not — as it did not for me in a variety of areas of my life — you should begin to question any message that gives you pause.

Understanding is a first step toward changing what is not working — understanding the expectations of the people we live and work with, the assumptions and pressures and obstacles we deal with as we strive to reach our fullest potential. Whether or not society acknowledges the equality of women, only women live the experience; therefore, having women in positions to make decisions about how we are represented in society is crucial. And that can begin with you.

The Definition of a Strong Woman

As you read on in this chapter, you will see that a woman can reap great benefits from being strong. But what are the characteristics of a strong woman?

She Values Continual Growth and Knowledge. Endlessly curious about how the world works and how to improve her role in it, a strong woman is consistently seeking knowledge and a better understanding of how to become her best self.

She Has Deeply Rooted Values and a Clear Goal Tied to a Purpose. Because of her incessant quest for knowledge, a strong woman comes to understand more about the world she lives in and develops a value system that is a driving force in her life. And she often lives her life with a goal in mind, one tied to a larger purpose. She understands that hard work is necessary, and the importance of planning and setting goals, and she is not deterred simply because others may not have her vision. She picks her battles, but because she understands the issues revolving around what she values, she is willing to speak up and not cower.

She Is Willing to Take Risks. "Great reward involves great risk" is a mantra that a strong woman understands. She does her homework but knows that not everything comes with a safety hatch. She accepts and understands that growth and progress come from a willingness to step forward, even if the path has not been laid out for her.

She Is Self-sufficient. A strong woman is independent. She is resourceful, capable, and competent, and learns by doing. While she enjoys working with others and excelling together, she is comfortable with her own company, relishing the time alone that will help her achieve balance, unclutter her mind, and care for herself.

She Seeks Out Other Strong Women. She gravitates toward women who are also independent, curious about the world, and helping each other navigate the journey as each strives to live her best life.

She Develops a Thick Skin, as She Will Often Be Misunderstood or Challenged. She may face misunderstanding about the path she has chosen, but in the 21st century, more and more women are pursuing goals, careers, and dreams rather than a partner; once they have come to understand themselves and are able to stand on their own two feet, they open themselves up to someone they can share their lives with. A woman's strength can be stereotyped and labeled negatively by those who do not understand or are fearful of what she might do. A strong woman, knowing herself and her purpose, allows such criticism to flow past her.

She Exhibits Perseverance. Not expecting a handout and certainly not expecting life to be fair, she weathers the storms, the obstacles, and finds the courage from within to keep striving forward. Yet she knows when to let go and move on. She is able to leave a relationship, let a friendship lapse, put herself back in the job market, or even move to a new zip code.

She Values Deep, Thoughtful Conversation. A strong woman does not see value in gossip; rather, she seeks out conversations about ideas and searches for new information. She is a wizard with questions as she works to learn from those who know more than she does.

She Understands the Key to Fulfillment. True success in life resides solely in each of us, and a strong woman is well aware of this reality. Each person must find the courage within herself to live the life of her dreams.

The key to knowing where you want to go lies in listening to what piques your interest, finding the courage to stray from the herd, and having an insatiable desire to forever learn and grow.

Ten Differences Between Women and Girls

One is not born, but rather becomes, a woman.
— Simone de Beauvoir

For some, it occurs when they begin living on their own for the first time, completely free of parental support. For others, it is when they have their first stream of hard-earned money and open their first checking account. For still others, it is a pivotal life event — a relocation, a death, an introduction to a luminary — that opens a new way of looking at the world. We were all, at one point, young, carefree, solely and necessarily dependent on our parents; however, there is a time to evolve, progress, and shed this skin, which has an expiration date.

To be a girl is an experience to cherish, one a child should be allowed to have without coping with adult expectations and responsibilities. For our purposes here, I am referring to someone who is navigating the world of grown-ups, building a life of her own, as a woman — someone capable of being independent and free from parental protections and safety nets. After a certain point, being a girl simply does not serve us well as we pursue our true potential. Here are some differences between women and girls.

Relationships

A **woman** may or may not desire a romantic pairing; if she does, she chooses to do so because it amplifies her life. She will not step into a relationship, and especially will not go as far as to say "I do," simply to not feel left out. A woman would rather be alone pursuing her passions, strengthening her friendships, and building her legacy than be involved with the wrong person. A **girl** is scared of being alone, a fear that is cultivated by those around her and the media she pays attention to. It is also an indicator that she is either not comfortable with who she is or has not taken the time to find out who she is. A girl jumps from one relationship to the next with little regard for the quality of the individual she is involved with.

Dating

A **woman** is strong and confident enough to let another person know she is interested. And while the crucial foundation for building any healthy relationship is one's self-respect and integrity, playing a cat and mouse game is not what a woman does. She may not want to initiate, but even if she does, the goal is to express interest and then let go. Both parties must be interested, and if they are not, both adults move on. No harm, no foul. A **girl** feeds off the drama, finding entertainment in the unknown and the uncertainty about whether the person she is interested in will call or not. A girl has not found something of greater interest in her life, her passion, to focus on.

Finances

A **woman**, regardless of her relationship status, stands on her own feet financially. She understands that successful money management is a skill she can acquire if she chooses to. A woman is disciplined when it comes to spending and saving. A **girl** either assumes she will marry someone who will take care of her financially or fails to educate herself on the power of financial planning because it seems daunting.

Confidence

A **woman** recognizes that true confidence comes from within. While she knows there will be mood shifts, she understands the power of mastering her mind and refuses to be sucked into the debilitating powers of certain emotions. A woman takes the time to get to know herself, to understand her strengths and weaknesses, and realizes she is a work in progress. However, she knows her self-worth and will not be subjected to disrespect from a partner or place of work. A woman recognizes that the only way to gain self-confidence is through experiences, pushing through discomfort from time to time and taking educated risks. A woman has a mind of her own and speaks up for herself and others. A **girl** seeks confidence from external sources — the number of her social media followers, a busy date book, approval from peers of her behavior, clothing, or life choices. A girl without self-confidence can easily be manipulated into believing what others want her to believe about herself.

Appearance

A **woman** knows her body and dresses to flatter it. She may reveal her silhouette, but not too much skin. She knows that while beauty may open the door, intelligence is necessary to cross the threshold. However, she respects the power of dressing well, and while she would not walk out the door without makeup or at least brushing her hair, she does so out of self-respect, not insecurity. A **girl** has only her looks to rely on to close the deal. She shows too much skin or uses too much makeup because she has not invested in her interests, passions, and talents.

Dating Expectations

A **woman** will not expect a date to pay for dinner, tickets, or other expenses when they are together. She will be able to pay for anything she suggests and, if the other person does pay, will not feel obligated to do anything besides say thank you. A **girl** — insecure in her sense of self and aiming only to please — will allow a date to play out on the other person's terms.

Conversation

A **woman** can hold a conversation with just about anyone, and the talk goes deeper than the surface. A woman is well read and aware of the world around her. She is comfortable in existential conversations as well as conversations about local politics. A **girl** is more comfortable gossiping and complaining, focusing on superficial information that does not deepen a conversation.

Social Media

A **woman** reserves her social media accounts for business and curiosities (news, hobby ideas, inspiration) and sees the value in face-to-face conversations, one-on-one texting, or letter writing for thank-yous, invitations, etc. A woman reserves an air of mystery and does not share everything. A **girl** cannot wait to update her social status on Facebook, share gossip on Snapchat, or share a group selfie to demonstrate how popular she is. A girl seeks validation.

Sense of Direction

A **woman** has goals, aspirations, and intentions for her life. She stands on her own but recognizes the value in relationships (working and personal) and helping those she loves work toward their dreams as well. A woman is insatiable in her quest for learning and exploring and does not wait for life to entertain her. A **girl** does not really know what she wants and may default to the dreams and even the journey of someone else.

Standards vs. Expectations

A **woman** has standards. In other words, a woman holds herself in check when it comes to what she needs in her life in order to be her best self and is self-actualized enough that she knows what will be detrimental to her potential and overall mental and physical health. A **girl** has expectations. She projects onto others superficial demands for qualities they must possess before she gets involved and uses them as a way to not look beyond what someone may have to offer.

Becoming a woman, reveling in all that being a woman can entail, is a choice that will empower you to become your best self and surround yourself with a support system of people who offer respect, love, and comfort, just as you afford them the same. It begins with a recognition of your self-worth.

Where True Success Resides

If you consistently pursue curiosity, you will live a life that is a work of art.
— Elizabeth Gilbert, *Big Magic*

On the stage in a sold-out auditorium stood author Elizabeth Gilbert. As I listened to her speak, it was clear that she was "igniting," modeling what her book *Big Magic: Creative Living Beyond Fear* is all about. During the Q&A session, a primary educator asked how to teach her students to be creative, and Gilbert's answer was concise and pointed: "The only way to inspire people is if they see you igniting." In other words, show, don't tell. Do what brings you to life. Model creative living for them. Come alive in your own life.

You may not want to be a writer or a painter, but that does not mean living a creative life is not for you. Living a creative life simply requires each of us to be perpetually curious. To do that, Gilbert says, you must acknowledge that fear exists, yet refuse to let it dictate the decisions in your life. Gilbert says, "Creative living is a life where you routinely make your decisions based on curiosity instead of fear." Living a creative life allows you to live a successful life.

Each of us has within us hidden treasures that are waiting to be brought to the surface. Here's the catch: Unearthing your unique treasures requires, according to Gilbert, "work, faith, focus, courage and hours of devotion." And do you know why many people do not find their treasures? They do not indulge their natural curiosities because they cannot predict what the outcome will be. In other words, they give way to fear rather than recognize it and set it aside. Knowing that the investment you are making may not work out can be daunting. So people bail on the treasure hunt; they surrender to fear of the unknown and put their curiosity on the bench.

While I was reading *Big Magic*, I was also engrossed in *Success Built to Last: Creating a Life That Matters*, by Jerry Porras, Stewart Emery, and Mark Thompson, and the two premises could not have dovetailed more beautifully. Builders, as defined in *Success Built to Last*, are those individuals who love what they do and would secretly do it for free. Builders are people who have found meaning in the work they pursue and "organize their thinking around creating real value." Allowing themselves to ignite will inspire others to continually follow wherever their curiosity leads them.

While we all need a place to live and food to eat, and thus have to figure out how we will pay for those things, we must continue to pursue our curiosities with unabashed devotion. Being curious allows you to cultivate a truly successful life — not as defined by the outside world, but a successful life that you live and enjoy each and every day. When you lose all track of time pursuing what provokes your curiosities, you are in the present; you are engaged and enthralled. You are igniting.

To put it succinctly, true success resides within you. You have had it all along. You just need to face your fear, indulge your curiosity, and revel in your creativity.

Having It All: A New Definition

When I was in my twenties, I was reassured that as women we indeed can have it all; we just cannot have it all at once. "Having it all" meant getting married, working a full-time job, and having children. For some reason, the presumption of this idea never sat well with me. And for nearly ten years, I could not pinpoint why.

One woman's dream come true may indeed be that definition, but it may be a nightmare for another woman, who would rather focus on her career and a strong circle of loving and loyal friends. The good news is that this world can support the many diverse paths women choose to pursue to "have it all."

I love this quote from Gloria Steinem: "I'm completely happy not having children. I mean, everybody does not have to live in the same way. And as somebody said, 'Everybody with a womb doesn't have to have a child any more than everybody with vocal cords has to be an opera singer.'"

There are myriad paths to "having it all" for each of us. Did you get married young to the love of your life — fantastic! Have you put off a long-term relationship as you pursue a once-in-a-lifetime career — amazing! You have adopted two children — bravo! Do you prefer to have a house that is child-free — brilliant! Are you divorced and discovering a long-lost passion — courageous! Whatever your choice, whatever your desired life, it is yours. Just make sure that the life you pursue is not preconditioned by society's expectations but rather adheres to your own principles, values, and goals. You will not make everyone happy, so stop trying, and instead find what makes you blissfully happy, what you have a longing to do.

No matter which path you travel, making the choices you have come to realize are best for your life offers amazing benefits. An inner strength begins to build. You will run up against obstacles and learn how to navigate around them. You will boost your confidence. Do not be limited. Shine brightly. And work very hard. The key is to be the designer of your one and only life. You will thank yourself, as the life events that will unfold will be your reward.

Live Deliberately

Living deliberately means making more conscious and constructive life choices. When you're living deliberately, you're living from a position of responsibility; you're making choices with greater awareness. You've taken yourself off autopilot, so you're better prepared to align your actions with the results you want to achieve.
— Lauren Mackler, *Solemate: Master the Art of Aloneness and Transform Your Life*

While Lauren Mackler's focus is primarily on those who choose to live alone or are currently living alone, the act of living deliberately enhances the quality of your life regardless of your relationship status. Because when we seek out the people and circumstances that speak to our passions, satisfy our purpose, and inspire us to wake up each morning with excitement rather than dread, the relationships we build, professional or personal, are richer because we have chosen to engage in them.

When you decide to put yourself in the driver's seat of your own life — choosing who and what you welcome into your life and how you respond to everyday events — you will see progress toward the goals you have set for your life, whether they are to excel in a certain career, learn a new skill, build stronger relationships, or fall in love with your life again.

So turn off the autopilot; examine your habits and your daily routines, and assess whether they are helping or hindering the development of the life you may only be dreaming about. Spending money unnecessarily rather than saving up for that down payment? Put yourself on a spending diet. Catching yourself engaged in negative self-talk and wondering why your self-esteem is low? Learn to master your mind. After all, we are the curators of our own destiny, and each day is another opportunity to set sail in the right direction.

Refuse to Be Stereotyped

Humans like to know things. We are comforted by certainties, and when we do not know about a group of people, a new concept, or a different way of doing something, it can be unsettling. A simpleton defense is to fear the unknown and seek no further, place a label on it, build barriers to keep it out. A sensible approach is to question, investigate, and gather knowledge. When we have firsthand information from credible sources, we can eliminate irrational fears and reject stereotypes.

Both positive and negative stereotypes exist; both are inaccurate and degrading because they simplify the story, for each of us is indeed quite complex. From *Blondes are dumb* to *Men do not know how to clean* to *Italians are good cooks* and even *French women do not get fat*, stereotypes are abundant and plentiful. Sometimes we do not fight them because they work for us, but we do ourselves and society no favors by not addressing the destruction they can cause, doing our due diligence to defy them, and eventually eliminating them.

Do the Homework. At the heart of prejudice and discrimination is a belief in a stereotype. Most stereotypes are rooted in a partial truth, and often in an individual's experience. But it is up to each of us to find out the truth about, say, race or gender rather than rely on tired, untested ideas.

Determine Why You Do or Do Not Select Certain Options. Getting to know ourselves is at the heart of dismantling stereotypes. Why are we wearing our hair a certain way or falling into certain roles even when they do not feel comfortable? When it comes to our likes and dislikes, it can be hard to determine what is culture and what is chromosome. When we choose to react not in order to gain approval but rather to create authentic satisfaction, we help break down stereotypes.

Keep Your Frustrations in Check. If someone makes an assumption about you that shortchanges your opportunities and negates your possibilities, you might become frustrated, even enraged. In order to slow the tide of stereotyping, we must master our emotions, speak calmly (or wait until we can), and outwit the naysayers — or perhaps outperform them, as actions often speak louder than any words.

Do Not Laugh with the Crowd. The next time someone makes an unfair assumption or laughs at someone for doing the unexpected for their gender, age, sex, position, etc., do not participate. You do not have to correct; instead, simply refrain from feeding the fire, which may allow such discussion to die out quickly.

When we rely on stereotypes, our true gifts are stifled, and our opportunities are limited. None of us wants to be put in such a situation, so why would we do this to others? Power comes from within, not from holding other people down.

Life Beyond Labels

For those of you who are tired of trying to squeeze into constrained categories, who long for integration and wholeness in everything you do, without limits on who you are or who you will become . . . it's time to move beyond labels.
— Maureen Chiquet, *Beyond the Label*

A label that shows the year the grapes in a wine bottle were harvested or where a piece of clothing was made can be helpful, but labels on women, men, ethnicities, races, and generations are limiting, stifling the talent each of us has to offer. Whether it is the assumption that the teaching profession is best suited for women because they are born nurturers or the idea that tall men with deep voices are better at just about everything, we reduce the potential for each person to flourish and find the best fit when we place labels based on outward appearance.

Maureen Chiquet makes clear that she "hates labels and boxes." Her curiosity led her to recognize that many labels are inaccurate and soul-depleting. And it was her curiosity that led her to achieve the success she has enjoyed. She listened to the voice within, was fortunate to have parents who encouraged her curiosity and did not limit her dreams, and was courageous enough to do so even when she did not know what the outcome would be. Below are some key pieces of advice from her book.

Refrain from Following Prescribed Expectations. Find your tribe. Search out people who sing the same song or at least applaud you for staying true to yourself. Along the way, you may have to let go of those who want you to stay in the lane they have become accustomed to traveling; instead, model by example, and support everyone's mode of travel and the paths they have chosen.

If You Feel Something Is Missing, Trust Yourself. Look beyond what Chiquet calls "the world's obstacles, rigid structure, and set definitions." To be able to look beyond, we must first look within. We must become so in tune with ourselves that we know when something is not present and needs to be, even if we cannot put our finger on it at the moment.

Follow Coco Chanel's Approach to Life: Learn the rules, then step outside of them. Chiquet says this about the iconic fashion designer: "Chanel seemed to break every rule by combining seemingly opposite elements and by elegantly subverting convention to create something breathtakingly timeless and fresh . . . a woman who refused to blindly accept the aesthetics of her time in order to invent her own." In the rhetorical writing class I teach, an early lesson is that while there are many rhetorical tools a writer (or artist, speaker, musician, architect, or business leader) can use, they must first know the rules they are breaking, why they are breaking them, and what effect they hope to create.

Savor Life's Beauty. We follow our curiosity in order to live a life we want to dance with each and every day. And when we have cultivated this life, we do not want to rush; we do not want tomorrow to come today. We want to savor each and every moment. In other words, "slow it down, relish it, take it in fully."

Become Comfortable with a Little Discomfort. Often we stay in circumstances or remain under labels that do not fit us because it is what we know, and knowing is, for most people, far more comfortable than uncertainty. Embrace challenging circumstances as you discover the pearl of a life you wish to cultivate.

Be Calm, Confident, Self-Aware, and Clear about Where You Want to Go. Having a map with a clear destination in mind (your goals) and understanding why you refuse to be labeled, and thereby limited, creates a solid foundation that lets you stand strong when others initially may not understand why you persevere amid the temporary headaches when you push back.

All of us can play a role in moving beyond labels. As Maureen Chiquet says, "By moving beyond the label, we can all make our workplaces and our lives more effective and more equitable."

The Woman You Have Always Wanted to Be

I was fortunate to become the woman I always wanted to be.
— Diane von Furstenberg

Diane von Furstenberg revels in her femininity, while reminding us that it is about equality and being free to live the life each of us wants without limitation based on gender. So how exactly does a woman go about becoming the person she has always wanted to be?

Accept That Nothing Is Impossible, and Then Work Hard. If you can dream it, you can create it. What kind of woman do you want to become? Let your answer be your guide as you begin making decisions and moving forward in your life. While we may be clear about what we do not want — to be treated as property, to be disrespected, trapped, etc. — it is even more important for us to be clear about what we do want — an equal partner, a mentor, financial independence, good health, a role as a leader, etc. Be clear about what you want and be able to explain why; then get busy moving forward. How? Be willing to work hard. The woman you wish to become is already within you, waiting for you to reveal her to the world.

Learn to Say No. When you know what you can do and what will enhance your life, it becomes much easier to say no to things that will not be beneficial. While no one wants to hear "no," using this power is a way of respecting yourself.

Become Your Own Best Friend. It is impossible to be genuinely respected and loved if you yourself are not respectful and loving toward yourself. Coming to understand yourself, liking who you discover, accepting the imperfections and celebrating and capitalizing on the strengths is what a best friend who loves you unconditionally would do. Why not be that person for yourself? Refuse to be treated disrespectfully, walk away from those who laugh or poke fun at what you do, and most importantly, be kind to yourself. Find your voice, practice it, exercise it.

Rely on Yourself. Once you come to trust that — no matter what life throws at you, no matter how the future will unfold — you can stand on your own two feet, your insecurities recede. Give yourself the gift of freedom by creating a life in which you respect yourself, and know you can take care of yourself.

Address Insecurities. If you find yourself becoming defensive, upset, or cynical, take some time to get to the root of the feeling. Why do you feel this way? What happened that prompted you to begin behaving in this manner? Upon getting to the bottom of the fear, you can discover how to move beyond it. Become more comfortable with taking risks. Elizabeth Cady Stanton said, "The best protection any woman can have . . . is courage."

Are You Comfortable in Your Own Skin?

As a child I grew up believing that the relationships I had with other people (number of friends, the right partner, etc.) would determine my happiness in life. But I have since discovered that my relationship with myself is at the core of how content I will be as I move through life. I hold the keys to my own happiness.

The French phrase *bien dans sa peau* (literally, "comfortable in one's skin") is simple in theory, but difficult to achieve. As a rule, children are free from outside pressures and expectations; they tend to speak the truth and adhere to their own authentic callings, curiosities, and talents. Now that we are adults who understand the world and its realities, we can either become what the world wants us to be or we can understand the world and then go about creating our own reality. We can be our authentic selves and thrive no matter where we live. We become our best selves, our most assured and successful selves, when we become comfortable in our own skin. Here are a few ways to do it:

Treat Your Body with Respect. Once you understand what your body needs in order to perform its best, feed it, exercise it, and care for it.

Understand What Makes You Come Alive. Then respect and protect it. It is easier to say no when you are clear about what you love and wish to protect.

Hone Your Intuition. Listen to your observations. If you take the time to assess what your intuition is telling you, you will eventually embrace it as an invaluable tool.

Find a Career, a Life, and a Passion That You Fall Madly in Love With. What hobby, pastime, or after-work activity do you ache to indulge in? What makes you lose track of time? Keep following what speaks to you, and so long as you keep listening, you will discover what you have been waiting for.

Become an Insatiable Sponge for Knowledge. Become comfortable with not knowing, and then investigate. We will never have all the answers (when we think we do, it is time to become nervous and double-check our sources), but whatever it is that you wonder about, why not travel there, pick up a book, visit the library, peruse the Internet, or talk to someone who is an expert? Feed your curiosities, and your world will expand in ways you never could have imagined.

Stop Trying to Impress Others. If you are busy trying to impress others, you will never find the time to tickle your own curiosities.

Stop Apologizing. And never speak negatively about yourself to others.

Stop Being Your Own Worst Critic. While pushing yourself to do your best is a noble and rewarding quality, berating yourself when you do not like the outcome can be detrimental to your confidence and sense of yourself.

Become Comfortable with Silence. A woman who is comfortable with silence is a woman who knows when conversation is and is not necessary.

Do Not Use Technology as a Crutch. Be present. Put your phone away, take your earbuds out, and listen to the sounds of nature, the breath of loved ones, the calm in your life, and simply revel in all that you may take for granted. When you become more aware of all that is good in each and every day, you will be amazed at how magnificent it truly is, even if it is not marked by extraordinary occurrences. The everyday has the potential to be extraordinary if only we will take the time to notice.

Give of Your Talents and Time in a Way That Is Comfortable. Do not participate to gain recognition or praise, but because you have something to contribute.

Accept Imperfection, but Strive for Excellence. The most beautiful, confident women are those who own their unique looks, talents, age, and lifestyle — and refuse to apologize. Capitalize on your skills and the opportunities that present themselves, and wisely use your time to pave the way for more opportunities. Do your best, and you will make progress toward excellence.

Realize That Relationship Status Does Not Determine Contentment. A woman who is comfortable in her skin determines her own contentment.

Create a Balanced Schedule. That means including time for hard work and productivity as well as regular pampering and self-rejuvenation.

Six Life Ideals to Let Go

Often, with our good intentions to set goals for our life, we get in our own way instead of allowing happiness or true contentment to unfold naturally. While setting goals is a habit I encourage and support, when we become too rigid, we strangle the magic of life. Below are six life ideals you might consider letting go of.

A Fixed Career Path. Setting a career goal is a wise fundamental component for success, but it would be a mistake to assume you can predict the path your work will take. So long as you are clear about your priorities, have a good work ethic, and are always doing your best, your résumé will continue to grow and shine. However, the world offers many career opportunities we cannot foresee when we set out, so remaining open can help our lives blossom in unexpected ways.

The Checklist Partner. Expecting your life partner to embody a laundry list of ideals is setting yourself up for disappointment. Granted, we need to set certain standards, such as being treated with respect, compassion, and kindness and having physical chemistry, but we need to stop putting up unnecessary barriers that will close us off to opportunities that may exceed our expectations.

The One-Size-Fits-All Traditional Family. A family is not what it looks like to the outside world. Its true meaning and worth lie in the way it cultivates unconditional love, support, and respect for its members. The family we surround ourselves with may not be blood-related, but so long as we have people to turn to and whom we support in kind, we have one. Marry when you are ready, have children of the four-legged variety, no children at all or ten, but whatever you do, do it not because you feel you "should" based on others' values. Be clear about what you value and what your priorities are, and you will cultivate the family you were meant to be with.

Age Stereotypes. We sometimes think that certain abilities, possibilities, and ways of living life must happen at certain milestone ages. But these are more examples of the stereotypes society clings to. Thankfully, they are generally wrong. What fifty-year-olds are able to do directly relates to how well they care for their bodies, the thoughts and attitudes that drive them, and the experiences they have had. When we let go of assumptions based on age, we not only free ourselves to live an amazing life; we also free those we meet to be exactly as they are, regardless of age.

Gender Stereotypes. Like age stereotypes, gender stereotypes limit the possibilities of what each of us is capable of doing. By ignoring expectations about the type of career or relationship a man or a woman should pursue, we allow people to tap into their best and most creative selves.

Perfection and Waiting Until Tomorrow. Studies have shown that women, more often than men, wait until they believe everything is perfect before asking for a promotion. Most men stride into their supervisor's office confident that, while they not be perfect for a new job, they will be able to handle what it requires and do it well. Women often miss opportunities simply because we assume we are not ready for them. The truth is that we will never be perfect for any situation. Yet since perfect does not exist, we are wasting precious time by delaying. Having confidence that you will be able to handle whatever comes your way will open up your world.

When we let go of these fixed life ideas, we open ourselves and free ourselves from the constraints of shortsighted living. While we can never know what the future holds, we will be able to receive whatever may come our way. And often that is when our expectations are exceeded.

How to Live Alone Well

> *Living alone . . . affords an unparalleled opportunity to know yourself, to be yourself, and to develop yourself as a unique and interesting individual.*
> — Phyllis Hobe

Some of us are more apt to prefer living alone than others, but each of us can benefit from the experience at some point in our lives. A crucial component to living a simply luxurious life is discovering who we are, what makes us tick, what makes us shine, what nurtures us to be our best selves.

It was by living alone that I discovered my introversion, my passion for writing, and so many other interests that my younger, less secure self would have never dared to pursue as I tried to please a roommate or significant other. Can I and do I want to live with another? I am confident that I am well equipped to live with another individual, as I am now capable of knowing what I need and realizing what I can compromise on. I am also able to advocate for myself so that I can balance relationships with my passions and not allow them to be pushed aside to please someone else. As for the second part of the question, it depends on the person.

If you are not used to coming home to an empty house or being left to your own devices to entertain yourself, living alone may be difficult . . . at first. Anything of value takes time to reveal its true greatness. Living alone is no exception. Here are some ways to make it part of your simply luxurious lifestyle.

Appreciate, Relax, Enjoy. When you return home, the house will be as you left it. You do not have to compromise. Want risotto for dinner? Done! You can sleep through the night without interruption, always find a quiet space to read, and entertain when you want.

Established Beloved Rituals. Give yourself something to look forward to and savor each and every day.

Cultivate a Healthy Social Circle. Studies have revealed that those who live alone are more socially involved and have a stronger social circle than those who cohabitate. When you get together with friends or family, one of the most blissful moments is returning home to a space that is your own.

Create a Sanctuary. Our homes should be the place that restores us, comforts us, and allows us to rest so that we can be our best when we return to the world the next day. Consider your interior decor as an investment in your well-being.

Master Your Mind. At the end of chapter eight, I share ten ways to master your mind. While having that skill is not necessary in order to live alone, it is vital to the ability to live *well* on your own. When someone lives on her own for the first time, her mind can wander into irrational places. But if you master your mind, perhaps even discover the power of meditation, you will discover a whole new level of living well.

Dive into Your Passion without Apology. Pablo Picasso said, "Without great solitude no serious work is possible." When we live alone, we have the time and space to throw ourselves into our passions without worrying about hurting someone's feelings or balancing with other priorities. If I had not been living alone, I would not have started *The Simply Luxurious Life* blog.

Get to Know Yourself. Often we surround ourselves with nonstop social events and the chatter of others so we do not have to be alone to discover what we fear. But when we explore our fear, we find our purpose and what makes us truly content.

Get to Know Your Neighbors. Whether you live in a house or an apartment, befriend a few of your neighbors. When you step outside your door, seeing a friendly face is a simple luxury. You will not want to get to know every neighbor, but it is good to have at least one person who knows your name.

Watch Television with Purpose. DVR your favorite shows so you do not waste time with commercials. Set up a Netflix account to watch what you want, when you want. Balance your television watching with reading or filling your home with music.

Curate a Positive, Inspired Life. When we live alone, we become the sole artist of our own lives, every single detail. We can choose what to eliminate, what to add, and what to foster into beautiful fruition.

Whether you choose to live alone for a short period or a lifetime, contemplate this quote from actress Ellen Burstyn: "What a lovely surprise to finally discover how unlonely being alone can be."

Make Your Own Life Rules

> *The older you get, the easier it becomes to follow your own rules.*
> — Linda Rodin

At age sixty-nine, beauty mogul Linda Rodin is a force of vitality, independence, and femininity, all according to her own "rules" for how to live her best life. She has always been determined to love the life she has chosen, following no one else's rules.

Choosing to live your own life, to follow your own "rules," is to set yourself free — to respect what works for you, what energizes you, what respects the voice that speaks from within you that may or may not synchronize with the rest of the world. The liberating life truth is that when we listen to that voice, we catapult the quality of our everyday lives into an entirely different dimension of contentment.

I am now in my late thirties, and it has been refreshing and a relief to know that living becomes more enjoyable with each year, so long as we are listening to our lives. As we allow ourselves to become more comfortable following our own rules, the ease will intensify, much like compound interest, as we live each year. How can we become more comfortable living by our own rules?

- Get to know yourself: Begin listening to yourself and thinking for yourself.
- Accept and embrace your uniqueness.
- Step away from the world regularly.
- Strengthen the powerful tool of self-acceptance.
- Stop looking for outside approval of your decisions.

Calling the guidelines by which we live rules is inaccurate, as the word suggests limitation. But I think we all understand what Linda Rodin was implying. We know what works for us; we also know what does not. Below are questions for you to ponder regarding fundamental areas where understanding your rules can lead to more fulfillment. Contemplate what has worked for you, what would benefit you and what you want to achieve. Every person's responses will be unique.

A Schedule That Works for You

- How much sleep do you need? What helps you have a deep, restful sleep?
- At what time do you need to go to bed in order to wake up refreshed and have a productive day?
- What helps you begin the day well?
- When do you need breaks?
- When are you the most productive?

A Style That Speaks to Who You Are

- What are you wearing when you feel your best?
- What works with your lifestyle and regular routine?
- What will you wear regularly and love?

Relationships to Foster or Let Go

- With whom can you relax and be yourself?
- Whom can you trust?
- Who has similar interests and passions?
- Who is kind and thoughtful?

Risks Worth Taking

- What risks have you confronted?
- Whom do you look to for life advice? Have they taken risks and been successful?
- What are you comfortable letting go of in order to gain what you seek?
- Who is telling you something is too risky? Who is telling you to jump? Consider their experience: Do you want to live their life?
- How would you feel if you never took a particular risk?

Your Food and Drink

- Which foods make you feel most energized and productive?
- Which make you feel sluggish, uncomfortable, less mobile or confident?
- How much water do you drink throughout the day?
- Which drinks calm you down or rev up your energy levels?
- How does your skin look? Is it dry, red, glowing, clear?
- After how much time without food do you become irritable, unclear in your thinking, and less calm?

How You Spend Your Money

- What are your financial goals?
- Have you consulted with a financial adviser you trust?
- What risks are you comfortable with? What is worth the investment — a home, a business venture, etc.?
- How much and how long do you want to work?
- Do you have debt? Do you have a plan to eradicate it?
- When do you feel the most in control of your financial life?

Think about the rules you live by. Are they your own? Are you consciously aware of the rules you follow? Why do you follow them? If you see a need for tweaking and improvement, consider helping yourself build a life that cultivates habits that make you excited to wake up each and every day, no matter your age.

How to Age Brilliantly

I was recently inspired by an article in *O Magazine* entitled "Aging Brilliantly." Women between the ages of forty and ninety-two shared bits of wisdom, and the common theme was that they saw each new year as an opportunity to live an even more fulfilling life. The suggestions below mix their advice with some of my own.

Learn, Learn, Learn. I recently read that continually challenging your mind and learning something new — a language, tai chi, how to fly a plane — is like drinking from the fountain of youth. The power of the mind is impressive, and we should all want to keep it quick and agile. Reading is one of the easiest ways to incorporate learning into your daily routine, but learning can also be physical — for instance, exploring tennis, yoga, or dance.

Live Your Passion. Take the time to find your passion and live it. If you have not discovered what makes your heart sing, challenge yourself to do so. It is out there. More often than not, when I talk to people about discovering their passion and purpose, they say it does not happen gradually; it usually smacks you in the face.

Be Resilient. Things can be tough at times, but you can make it. Anyone with years of experience will attest to this statement. You are stronger than you realize. You simply need to get out of your own way.

Find Uplifting People. Once you have chosen a life of hope instead of cynicism, a life of love instead of hate, one in which you seek wisdom instead of remaining ignorant, find people who support this mission.

Take Care of Yourself. You have been given the most magnificent machine you will ever have — your body. Take care of it with the best food, water, and vitamins. Pamper it with sunscreen, lotion, and kindness. My father is a perfect example of someone who is nearing seventy, has always been active, and has vitality and well-being to show for it. His philosophy is that we must take care of ourselves so that when we are free of the office beckoning, we can enjoy life to its fullest. I can honestly say, I have never seen him happier as I have these last nineteen years since he has retired. If he is not out golfing, he is flying, rafting down the river, or simply enjoying time outdoors.

The Wonderful Truth about Health, Happiness, and Getting Older

The effects of becoming older are a result of how we have lived our lives — how well we have taken care of our bodies, how well we have handled stress. The key is knowledge and then putting into practice what you learn. *New York Times* best-selling author Dr. Frank Lipman's book *10 Reasons You Feel Old and Get Fat . . . and How You Can Stay Young, Slim, and Happy!* is a gem of well-organized information that dispels what many people believe and teaches readers how to take charge of their physical health. While there is a correlation between increased age and negative outcomes, old age is not the cause. The cause is how we live our lives.

Eat the Right Foods. Understand the addictive properties of sugar and what eating simple carbohydrates — cookies, white rice, white potatoes — does to your blood sugar levels. A sugar high in full swing feels good, but the inevitable crash does not and leaves you feeling hungry. So you eat more, and if you reach for more sugar and carbs, the nasty cycle continues, with your moods in the throes of sugar highs and lows. Do not beat yourself up about not having willpower. It really is not about that. It is about understanding what makes you feel good. If you have been eating lots of sugar and carbs for a while, you may have a hard time weaning yourself off them. However, once you make it through an initial two- to five-day period, your body will no longer crave them, and you will feel much better.

Eat Fat. Any fat found in nature is usually good for you, unlike fats that have been created in laboratories. For your brain to function properly, you need to eat fats regularly — olive oil, nut butters, organic pasteurized eggs, grass-fed butter, goat and sheep's milk cheese . . . the list goes on. And not only is fat crucial for your brain's health; it is essential for staying fit and feeling your best overall.

Tired and Fatigued No More. Our bodies are made to handle acute stress, as Dr. Lipman points out — but not chronic stress. The body can handle it in the short term, but the long-term result is that you become exhausted and prone to physical ailments and gaining weight. To strike the right balance, you must assess your life. Where is the continual stress coming from? Can you eradicate it? If not, how can you change how you are handling it? When we worry incessantly, when we build a daily schedule that does not allow for regular rejuvenation, we are ratcheting up the stress and decreasing our health and well-being.

Move Your Body Regularly. Dr. Lipman cites Dan Buettner's book on longevity and happiness, *The Blue Zones: 9 Lessons for Living Longer from the People Who've Lived the Longest*. Buettner's Blue Zones are unique communities where common elements of lifestyle, diet, and outlook have led to long lives and excellent quality of life. The author focuses on the one thing all these lifestyles have in common: The individuals were regularly physically active. This can mean going to the gym, but it can also mean getting outside and walking around the neighborhood, working in the garden, swimming, tai chi, anything that moves your body for twenty or thirty minutes a day.

Every Day, Strike a Balance. We must balance acute stress with rest, calm, and tranquility every day. You have an exhausting day at work; nothing bad happens, but a lot is demanded of you, and you are always "on." Make sure, when you come home, that you give yourself time to unwind. Your body and mind need it. Your quality of life needs it.

Adhere to a Healthy Sleep Pattern. A good night's sleep is the best tool you have to turn a good day into a great day. Be aware of what you eat and drink before turning in, and try to settle into a regular pattern.

Understand the Power of Passion, Meaning, and Community. When we discover what makes us come alive, we enrich the quality of our lives, just as we do when we find meaning in what we do and when we find our tribe and feel a part of a community. Taking the time and energy to find your passion is not being selfish. It is necessary. If you want to thrive, if you want to feel youthful and alive, you must have a very close relationship with yourself.

You have an amazing opportunity to live an extraordinary life. Refuse to let the myths that never served you well in the first place get in the way of living a life that is completely within your control. Remember, knowledge is power, and so long as you forever remain curious, your age will be indicated only by the date on your birth certificate, not the life you are living.

Embrace your Unique Journey

When we are traveling toward a desired destination — whether a physical journey or a professional or spiritual one — the best method is to slow down, enjoy the journey, and take in the sights along the way, for it is the journey, not the destination, that is the true prize. Too often, life offers us a bountiful gift, but we are too busy grousing about the one we want that has not arrived yet to recognize the gift sitting before us.

We may not land the job in the city we desire to live in on our first or even second attempt. We may not be accepted into the MBA program we think we need in order to be an entrepreneurial success, and maybe the relationship we thought would go the distance lasted only a short while. But what if life is giving us exactly what we need for the life we are trying to create for ourselves?

CHAPTER FOUR

Be Your Own Brand: Thriving in Your Career

Now that I had started writing, I found cookbookery such fulfilling work that I intended to keep at it for years and years.
— Julia Child

I was introduced to Julia Child in the 1990s, near the end of her career, and immediately became intrigued by the mighty, authentic, and engaging woman who knew how to cook like nobody's business. I fully engaged with Nora Ephron's 2009 film *Julie & Julia*, starring Meryl Streep. I have since dived deeply into Julia's journey in France and Europe, how she came upon her passion of cookbookery, as she called it, and how she knew it was to be her path.

My Life in France, the last book Julia Child wrote before her death, includes the quote above, and the moment I read it, I highlighted, reread, dog-eared, and double-dog-eared it — in other words, I acutely understood the feeling she describes. In her book *The Martha Rules*, Martha Stewart said it another way, and I am sure Julia Child would agree, as she is the best model for this idea one can imagine: "Build your business success around something that you love — something that is inherently and endlessly interesting to you."

Sometimes we simply stumble into our happy place. I share in my first book, *Choosing the Simply Luxurious Life*, how my blog came to life in 2009; by no means was it planned, calculated, or expected. Now, nearly ten years later, like Julia Child, I cannot imagine not writing, blogging, exploring the world, and sharing my discoveries with the readers who stop by the blog, listen to my podcast, or view my cooking vodcast. But, full disclosure: If you had asked me a year before *TSLL* began what I was interested in, I would not have said blogging. I did not know anything about blogging, let alone html coding, linking, etc. But my curiosities led me onward and to where I am now.

The most frequent question I receive from readers is *How do you balance a blog and a writing career while teaching full-time?* The truth is that the fuel comes from my sincere interest in what I do. The second most common question is *How do you always have something to write about?* My answer is that I remain incessantly curious about the life I am living and the world I live in. In the process, I unearth a lot of unknowns, and therein can lie fear, but also the spark of creativity. How so? Elizabeth Gilbert shared the secret in her book *Big Magic*, "Creativity and fear will always be linked. When you try to create a life without fear, you murder your creativity."

A few cases in point from my own life: As I prepared my first book, I elected — without hesitation but without any guarantee of how it would work out — to engage an editor who is an expert in the field (an investment, but a risk that ended up being worth taking). The redesign of *TSLL* blog in 2016 was a significant investment, but one I believed (but was not guaranteed) would enhance the direction of the blog I had in mind. And in many ways my choice to move to Bend (one of the most expensive small towns in the Pacific Northwest) was a complete gamble, and some might have said a foolish decision, but to remain where I was would have been to give in to living with fear, and I knew I was capable of growing even further.

Gilbert says that as long as we do not give fear the wheel to drive our lives, and instead keep it in the back seat, we can use it as motivation for unearthing the truth and not running scared, building a life of structure and rigidity to protect us.

A desire to spark endless creativity and accept that I cannot make my life free of all unknowns informs the simply luxurious life brand (the blog, podcast, vodcast, books, etc.) as I continue to be fueled by the life I live. And as proof that fear of the unknown is a spark for creativity, my move to Bend, Oregon, involved great curiosity. Of course, I had fears, and I still do, which is one reason the brand has evolved into an even more authentic online destination.

Once we set ourselves free, we come upon another truth that can be hard to swallow. Lauren Woolstencroft writes: "There's no magic formula for success. Ultimately, it's about believing in yourself, making realistic goals, believing you can achieve them, and going for them without hesitation." Woolstencroft knows what she is talking about. When she was born, she was missing her left arm below the elbow and both legs below the knees, yet she became a competitive skier as a teenager and was a medalist at the Paralympic Games. She defied the odds, and it began with her belief in herself.

Ultimately, each of us needs to find what interests us tremendously and "keep tremendously interested in it," to borrow Julia Child's sage comment. We do actually have all the answers to realizing the passion we are seeking within ourselves. We just need to find the courage to explore ourselves.

How? Gloria Steinem suggests becoming a scientist in your own experiment and using fear as a significant motivator. Perhaps she is right. Often what we fear is a map/compass pointing us toward what we innately desire, a map that contains unknowns (thus the fear); but beneath the fear is curiosity and, more important, our hopes. If you are willing to try new tasks, learn new skills, travel to unknown places, and step beyond what you know — slowly and gradually, at a pace you can maintain even if you are a bit wobbly — you too, like Julia Child, will find what is "such fulfilling work" that you "intend to keep at it for years and years."

The starting point is igniting from within, which will be your source for infinite propulsion, then effectively managing your journey, building your brand, and enabling it to thrive.

Becoming Your Own CEO

Everything around you that you call life was made up by people that were no smarter than you. And you can change it, you can influence it. Once you learn that, you'll never be the same again.
— Steve Jobs

This statement appears on the back cover of my first book, *Choosing the Simply Luxurious Life: A Modern Woman's Guide:* "Women have never had so many options. Yet we often experience a kind of paralysis, an unconscious willingness to follow societal dictates rather than become the CEOs of our own lives. When we mindlessly follow the dots, we smother our innate gifts and miss opportunities to fulfill our true potential."

Being the head of any company, no matter how successful, can be exhausting, demanding, and emotionally taxing. The primary direction of a company rests squarely on the CEO's shoulders. Think about Apple, OWN, or Berkshire Hathaway. Each has been successful, and one person manned the rudder for all or most of the company's existence. All three CEOs — Steve Jobs, Oprah Winfrey, and Warren Buffett — started from nothing; all had tumultuous times, but all three companies, due to their tenacity, clear vision, and dogged work ethic, still are very successful.

How we go about our lives is not that different from the way a company is run. Each life has the potential for success or catastrophe, depending upon how it is managed. Choosing to be the person in charge can be daunting, intimidating, and frightening because if you are not successful, all the responsibility is yours; however, if success materializes, it is you who will accept all those pats on the back.

Like the stock market, life is unpredictable, but if you choose to incorporate the following approaches into your life's mission statement, you will become your own CEO and will more likely soar with the eagles than remain on the ground.

Look Beyond Others' Approval

Psychologist Lawrence Kohlberg's Ideas of Moral Reasoning is a six-tiered chart of the motivation for making life decisions. He proposes that each of us makes decisions depending upon one of six levels that reflect how morally developed we have become. Placement on the levels is fluid, as we can swiftly change based on maturity and experience, but the primary reason we should let go of what others think is that their opinions may have little do with our aspirations, and if we heed them, they may very well hinder our overall fulfillment in life.

Seeking self-approval is Kohlberg's third level of moral reasoning. On the highest level, one follows a set of self-formulated principles that aspires to go beyond popular or legal dictates in order to determine what is best for society worldwide. It indeed takes a strong person to establish and then follow through on such an elevated way of approaching life. Attaining the sixth level takes time, self-reflection, and inner courage.

Let's take the idea of choosing to have children. Society in many ways still expects, either consciously or unconsciously, that women will desire to have children, and if a woman does not want to reproduce, people can jump to conclusions. In *Selfish, Shallow, and Self-Absorbed: Sixteen Writers on the Decision Not to Have Kids*, edited by Meghan Daum, we learn that the adjectives in the title are far from the truth when it comes to describing such individuals, who have the inner courage to follow their own self-formulated set of principles.

To have children or not, to marry or not, to pursue a particular career or not — these decisions should not be made because we are following the crowd; instead, they should be in alignment with our intended path, our talents, and our passions. If your path is not the one society is accustomed to seeing, you may have to muster your gumption, as the going will at times be difficult. But rest assured, if you know it to be the best path for you, approval from others will be the furthest thing from your mind. A truly fulfilling life can materialize only if we choose the life we are living for ourselves. Rather than seek others' approval, seek first your own, and have the courage to follow through.

Pursue Your Path with Determination

If you're frustrated because you're not getting what you want, stop for a second: Have you actually flat-out asked for it? If you haven't, stop complaining. You can't expect the world to read your mind. You have to put it out there.
— Sophia Amoruso, *#GIRLBOSS*

Very few things worth having, experiencing, or being involved with happen with the snap of the fingers. Rather, life often wants to assess how badly we desire something, be it a job, a new life, or a relationship. And while it may seem that life is shutting the door on our dreams, I have never found the door to be locked if it is indeed something that is possible. Life merely wants to know if we indeed want it as much as we say we do. In other words, continue to knock.

Ultimately, we each have to know what we want in order to pursue it and attain it. And once we know what we want, we need to pursue it without relenting. Such determination will eventually be rewarded.

Care for Your Physical and Mental Health

In order to do our best, be productive, and evolve into the person we know we can become, we must care for our bodies — internally, externally, and mentally — on a regular basis. Adhering to a regular workout routine, practicing regular mind mastery techniques, and tending to our beauty regimen are not vanity; rather, they are an approach that allows us to perform at our best.

A *Huffington Post* writer compared tending to our health to sharpening a saw. If we come to the forest with a sharp utensil, we will slice through a tree trunk in mere minutes, while a dull blade may start out the quickest but will take hours to complete the task. Taking the time, regularly, to take care of your body will help make your dreams a reality.

Mastering your mind involves shifts in default responses that have not been working to your advantage: becoming comfortable with being patient; delaying gratification; refusing to suppress your emotions, instead acknowledging and accurately identifying them; meditating daily, even if only for three minutes; practicing more gratitude; thinking rationally and realistically about distractions that take our minds off course; becoming more comfortable with discomfort, which is often less of a problem than you imagine; and examining your core beliefs, rethinking the limitations you have placed upon yourself. (Chapter eight has a longer section on mastering your mind.) The reality we create in our minds is often what will materialize in the world we live in. Have the strength and the tenacity to boot out the bad, and usher in the good.

Respect the Power of Money

Most of us start off with little, but it is how we care for the money we are given and earn as we start to build our financial foundation that will determine if we will be successful in the long run. Those who turn up their noses at earning money either do not know how to do it or do not understand the power it yields. And so long as the power is used for good, the life you will create will be amazing. For detailed advice, read chapter six, "Money Matters: Masterminding Your Financial Security."

Know How to Market Yourself

Most of us will be on the hunt for a job at some point, and the key is to know how to sell ourselves successfully. While a cover letter is an introduction to who you are, its primary focus should be what you can bring to the organization you are applying to; the best way to do this is to do read up on the organization and draw parallels to your past, your present, and where you want to go in your career. On your résumé, do not hesitate to brag because your strengths will make the enterprise stronger. Be specific, concrete, and straightforward, and keep it simple. There is no need to get too fancy with the design; it is the content that will enable you to shine.

Become an Effective Communicator

Two of the most important factors in becoming an effective communicator are being strong enough to be authentic and knowing your audience. While you will make mistakes along the way, so long as you are doing your best — and being honest and not manipulative or unreliable — you will earn respect. People may not always like what you have to say, but they will trust that you what say is dependable.

Whether in our personal or professional lives, being an active participant when it comes to communication will reap far more success than being passive and assuming others know what we want. Part of the reason there are so few effective communicators is because communicating is not easy. It takes strength, knowledge of the subject matter, and control of one's emotions to effectively convey what we want. But so long as you are willing to practice, learn from your previous missteps, and try again, you will improve.

Design Routines and Stick to Them

Creativity doesn't drive the work; the work drives the creativity. A routine creates a landing place for the muse.
— Alex Soojung-Kim Pang, *Rest*

The power of routines in our lives is that they give us the ability to be free. At first, such a statement may sound contrary or impossible, but when we become accustomed to routines that work for us — getting up at a particular time each day, making ourselves and our partner a cup of tea or coffee, cooking a nourishing breakfast, walking the dogs — we are engaging in activities that fuel us and our good health. That frees our minds to recognize and dance with new ideas when they present themselves.

Redefine Failure

The only way to be successful is to risk what many define as failure. But here's the catch: When something goes wrong, it is never really failure so long as there is a lesson to be learned from the experience. And the good news is that there will always be something to learn.

Keep applying the lessons, refuse to allow others' definition of what success is to stand in for what success is for you. After all, we are each on our own journey. Reaching a peak may take years for one person, while the next climber may require only a few days. Never allow others' evaluations of what you have done to be your barometer for success. So long as you know you have done your best, so long as you refuse to not be or stay defeated, you will be successful.

At the heart of living a simply luxurious life is finding the courage within yourself to live life on your own terms. While we all must learn how to interact effectively with others — communicating and working while thinking of the community and society as a whole — when it comes to the decisions we make, we must spend our entire lives with ourselves. *TSLL* blog, *The Simple Sophisticate* podcast, and the book *Choosing the Simply Luxurious Life* lay out the framework for a sound foundation and clear direction for achieving a life of contentment, but you are the artist, the designer. Your house will look like nobody else's, and that is the beauty. Enjoy the journey and be brave.

Find Your Personal Power

Dance your way to presence. Seize the large, beautiful, powerful parts of yourself — the ones you love and believe. They are, indeed, yours for the taking.
— Amy Cuddy, *Presence*

As with self-worth, we all have personal power within us, and we each must determine whether to access it. For many, especially women in other countries and in centuries past, that personal power has been silenced; women are told it either does not exist or should not exist.

In order for the everyday we seek to become our daily experience, we have to feel in control of our lives. We must have a sense that we are the director of our story, the captain of our ship, the curator of our lives. When we feel we have control of our lives, we take back our personal power. And that is all about three things, as Harvard professor Amy Cuddy points out:

- Confidence
- Being at ease and comfortable with ourselves
- Having a passionate enthusiasm for what we are doing and how we are living

When we exhibit these three qualities at any given moment, we are exhibiting the characteristic Cuddy explores in her book *Presence: Bringing Your Boldest Self to Your Biggest Challenges*. "Presence emerges when we feel personally powerful," when "we are no longer fighting ourselves" but rather "being ourselves." One of the crucial aspects of presence is that it is "about the everyday." If we are present every day, the quality of our lives improves, and that is what living simply luxuriously is all about — refining and enhancing the quality of our everyday lives. You may be asking, "Okay, how do I find my personal power? How to I achieve presence?"

Be Big. As Amy Cuddy shared in her wildly successful 2012 TED Talk "Your Body Language May Shape Who You Are," finding your Superman pose (hands on hips, chest up, eyes looking upward, strong stance) or Starfish pose (arms and hands stretched up and angled straight to the corners of the sky, legs in a wide stance to create a five-pointed star) can have tremendous power over your mind. In her book, Cuddy writes, "Your body shapes your mind. Your mind shapes your behavior. And your behavior shapes your future." In other words, "how you carry your body shapes how you carry your life." Stand up straight, take up some space — head up, eyes up — and walk assuredly. Power is demonstrated first by your behavior, and in order for people to consider that you have power, they must trust that you do. If you believe it, exhibit it. If you don't, practice it until you become it.

Speak Slow and Low. People who exhibit confidence do not feel they have to rush their speech as though they are worried about being interrupted or wasting time. They do not end their sentences on a high note, implying a question or uncertainty with what they have just said.

Listen. When you listen, you gain information; you get to know people and the situation. When you listen, you convey interest and compassion. When you listen, you gain trust because you reveal that you care, and when and if you respond, you want to speak as an informed, thoughtful participant.

Initiate Speech. As much as listening is important, speaking up when it is necessary demonstrates your confidence and personal power. The key is knowing when to speak and knowing you do not need approval. While many people fail to find a balance between speaking and listening, when you do find it, your trustworthiness will be enhanced, as people will see that you are not a pushover, but also not an indifferent, heavy-handed bulldozer.

Make Eye Contact. While there is a fine line with eye contact (staring down someone into submission is generally not a good idea), looking directly at the person you are conversing with has powerful effects. Again, the goal is trust. When people try to discern if someone is lying, they may see shifting eyes and avoiding eye contact as signs that a person is not to be trusted, even if they are telling the truth. What an observer is picking up on in such a situation is a person's sense of powerlessness. Cuddy offers an alternative for situations in which looking too long into someone's eyes may make the other person unnecessarily uncomfortable: Look upward. Looking skyward offers the perception of thoughtfulness, imagination, and creativity instead of domination.

Have Self-Control. When we have self-control, we demonstrate self-awareness. We always want to be aware of our feelings, why we are feeling what we feel, and why we are responding the way we are. At the same time, we can remain calm and not be a slave to rash thinking.

Be Calm. Studies reveal that those who are seen and defined as being powerful have two things in common biologically: higher levels of basal testosterone and lower levels of cortisol. As Amy Cuddy points out, we may not be surprised at the power of testosterone; what many people do not realize is that in order to be effective as a powerful person, they must also be physically calm, and that is where the lower levels of cortisol come in. Cortisol is the hormone released when we are under stress. Feelings of anxiety, stress, self-doubt, and uncertainty cause our levels of cortisol to rise, and when that happens, we must have a way of combating these feelings. Writing in my journal, engaging in my favorite hobbies, walking my dogs, paddleboarding, cooking, slipping away to see a good movie or reminding myself of all that I should be grateful for on any given day — these are just a few of the many ways I welcome more tranquility into my daily life.

Know Yourself. The only way to exhibit passionate enthusiasm for anything in your life, the only way to be truly comfortable at nearly any moment, is to know who you are, what you value, what tickles your fancy, and how you perform at your best. When you know yourself, when you know your mind, you can head in a direction that will mesh with your curiosities. Become informed and know how things work so you are not locked in a state of fear when unknowns arise.

Control Your Breathing. Studies of patients suffering with PTSD were shown to have decreased anxiety after attending regular yoga sessions. In yoga, the focus on the breath correlates to reduced anxiety and better control over the thoughts we allow to be present. To relax, slow down your breaths — in through your nose and out through your mouth. Begin by counting to four as you inhale and four again as you exhale. Extend it to six, and then breathe normally again. The beauty of learning how to breathe well is that it can be practiced anywhere and whenever you need to gain composure, calm, or clarity: at home in a quiet space, in your office, even on your commute. Placing your attention on your breathing lets you step outside the moment that is causing your angst.

Flip Your Negative Emotions. Feeling anxious before a big speech, interview, or first attempt at a new skill? Flip the feeling on its head and see it as an opportunity.

Again, the power of our mind is a wonderful thing to harness. Exhibiting personal power each day will take time and daily practice. Each of the ten ways mentioned above will ensure that if you regularly demonstrate such a presence, you will have positive results. Some of the ideas may be uncomfortable to step into, especially in scenarios such as work or relationships where our change in actions may be a noticeable shift. So why integrate them into your everyday life? Because the benefits are absolutely worth it.

What Your Personal Power Can Do for You

Liberates Your Thinking. Amy Cuddy says, "Presence stems from believing and trusting your story." When you have presence, you set yourself free. And when you set yourself free, you do not feel the need to fit in or think like the group if the group does not align with what is true for you. When you are able to be present each day, you think independently and are not swayed by the outside world. You become less self-conscious because you are not trying to fit in; you are not self-absorbed, trying to be an imposter. Instead, your ideas spark, your creativity blossoms, and you can think more abstractly.

Buffers Negative Emotions. When we are full of anxiety, we become more self-absorbed. We are worried about being accepted, concerned about what other people think of what we are doing. We may try to overcome the negative feelings by becoming an imposter: being outgoing when we really prefer to work alone; saying yes when our schedule is already too full; not sharing what we truly enjoy for fear it will be laughed at. We will never achieve our best life or meet the people who will bring out our best selves if we are not genuine. When we have presence, we are better able to allow stress, worry, rejection, even physical pain to slip away. When we are confident in the direction we are heading, in the life we are living in alignment with who we are, the only approval we are seeking is our own, and we have already given that to ourselves.

Increases Your Proactivity. Powerful people, those with a firmly anchored sense of personal power, procrastinate less and therefore complete tasks and reach goals more of the time and get more accomplished. And when we do something, as with our posture (be big!), we see results. Confidence comes from knowing we can or have done something, and that can only occur when we actually do something.

Helps You Achieve Goals. Because we are able to be more proactive and because our confidence is increased, we are better able to reach our goals. And so the upward cycle continues.

Frees You to Be Your Best Self. Ultimately, the best and most profound gift we give ourselves by having presence is that we are able to become our best selves.

Having presence takes time and many small steps and attempts. As Amy Cuddy points out, "Being inauthentic takes hard work." But being yourself does not take effort. What takes effort is trying to squeeze into boxes you think you need to fit into when you are in particular situations or around certain people. This can be exhausting. It depletes your energy, which leaves you with few resources for mustering the strength to reach your full potential. Part of the journey is finding out the how: how to be ourselves, how to exhibit the personal power we have within us.

How to Be Your Own Brand

The only person you are destined to become is the person you decide to be.
— Ralph Waldo Emerson

Brands — think Chanel, Nike, Apple, Vogue, Le Creuset, Manolo Blahnik — create an image in our minds: luxurious, efficient, feminine, masculine, powerful, trustworthy, daring — any number of descriptors come to mind. Each brand has made decisions in order to establish itself, and the way it responds to its market and the world in general is solely in its control.

One of our most important tasks in life is to recognize that each of us is our own brand. The way we present ourselves to the world can result in not only stronger professional relationships, but stronger personal ones as well.

Because every day is an opportunity to build the brand we wish to present and leave as a legacy, it is vitally important to maintain a protected private life. We must have a sanctuary to come home to at night, people we can trust, and a space where we do not need to worry about perception. If we do not have a strong personal sanctuary, we will not be at our best when we go out into the world.

George Washington, Jane Austen, Susan B. Anthony, Mark Twain, Rosa Parks, Ralph Waldo Emerson — each had a similar amount of time as each of us to leave their stamp on the world. Because of their actions, choices, and ways of living, we still mention them in conversation, look to them for inspiration, and hold them in high regard. Each was human, with no special powers that any of us could not acquire, yet their legacies inspire awe. Whether you leave a legacy the entire world will know about or your effect is simply on the community you live in, leaving a legacy you are proud of and a brand you have purposefully created will bring you much contentment and joy.

There are many components to consider when establishing the brand you desire. Let's begin with actions because, as the timeless maxim states, they speak louder than words.

Actions

The universe doesn't give you what you ask for with your thoughts — it gives you what you demand with your actions.
— Steve Maraboli

Proactive or Reactive. Do you set goals, plan, and remain focused until they are met, or are you a victim of life's events that occur around you?

Constructive or Destructive. Look at the habits you have adopted, the behaviors you exhibit, and the predilections you embrace. Are they building the life of quality you want or slowly destroying it? Are you moderate when it comes to eating well, or do you indulge randomly and then starve yourself in an attempt to compensate? Do you speak up and enforce your boundaries, or let them slide as a way to avoid confrontation? Do you choose to be generous when considering the intentions of others or immediately assume the worst?

Helpful or Hurtful. Do you step in with compassion or pounce on the downtrodden?

Work Ethic. Do you give your absolute best even when it is not expected or needed, or do you give just enough to get by?

Sponge or Stone. Do you have an insatiable curiosity for life and continue to be a student beyond the classroom, or are you satisfied with the status quo?

And while actions are indeed powerful, some of the most powerful means to cheer someone up or pull someone down are the words we choose.

Words

Think twice before you speak, because your words and influence will plant the seed of either success or failure in the mind of another.
— Napoleon Hill

Diction. Your word choice matters. Do you reveal yourself to be knowledgeable or close-minded? Honest or deceitful? Observant or ignorant?

Tone. Regardless of what you say, what feeling is created in those who hear you? Are you sincere or sarcastic, lighthearted or hurtful, comforting or cold?

Projection and Pitch. When you speak, do you command attention? Do you show yourself to be strong or meek, certain or doubtful?

Appearance

You can have whatever you want if you dress for it.
— Edith Head

Physical Health. Your projection of good health conveys to others your good sense and respect for yourself. There is no certain weight, height, or age that a brand cannot have. An appearance of respecting one's body and caring for it accordingly conveys knowledge and the potential for success in other endeavors as well.

Cleanliness and Grooming. When you project an image of cleanliness, again you project self-confident and self-respect. If you are willing to take care of yourself, you build a subtle level of trust.

Wardrobe. Humans are visual, and what they see, they respond to, so choose your "wrapping" carefully. Your clothing choices will depend on the circumstance and the brand you want to build. For example, a person pursuing success in the fashion industry will have to dress differently than a teacher in a schoolroom. Dressing appropriately for a job conveys one's preparedness and awareness of expectations.

Thoughts

The mind is everything. What you think you become.
— Buddha

Attitude. Positive or negative, possible or impossible, hopeful or cynical. Do you approach life with a determination that your best days are in front of you or behind you? The attitude you convey will draw to you similar-minded people, so be sure you attract those you want to associate with.

Internal Dialogue. What does the conversation in your mind sound like? Your thoughts predict your words and your actions, so be mindful to encourage a supportive, positive flow of thought in your mind day in and day out.

Every day, we project an image, an attitude, an idea of who we are out into the world that either draws toward us the connections we want or keeps them at bay. While establishing your brand will take time and discipline, when you have created a habit of living that you are proud of, your entire life will be elevated — your mood, the quality of your days, your relationships with others and with yourself — and you will cultivate a most amazing brand and a simply luxurious life.

Women in the Workplace

Did you know . . .

- According to the National Association of Women Business Owners, more than 9.4 million business firms are owned by women, and those firms employed nearly 7.9 million people and generated $1.5 trillion in sales in 2015.
- A report from the Institute for Women's Policy Research says that about 29 percent of America's business owners are women, up from 26 percent in 1997. The number of women-owned firms has grown 68 percent since 2007, compared with 47 percent for all businesses.
- The progress for minority women has been particularly swift, with business ownership skyrocketing by 265 percent since 1997, the same report says. And minorities now make up one in three female-owned businesses, up from only one in six less than two decades ago.

Work and life. The two are not mutually exclusive because our lives include the work we do, and doing a job we love and pursuing a career we are passionate about requires much of our time and is often our life's pursuit. After all, it is the combination of a pleasurable life with a productive life that results in true contentment at the end of each day.

With more than 51 percent of the workforce in the United States predicted to be women at the end of 2018, women have the opportunity to create and model for others how to cultivate a productive, engaging, and enjoyable work environment. Four arenas are key to not just productivity, but our engagement in and enjoyment of the work we do.

Office Space and Energy

For many of us, much of the workweek is spent in the office, and it is important to do what you can to create an environment you want to walk into each day. Below is a list of details that can ensure that the workday — from beginning to end, each day of the week — runs as smoothly as possible. When we control what is in our control, we can better handle what is not.

Organize the Space. Arrange furniture, desk, files, tables, etc., in a way that is inviting not only to anyone who comes in to see you, but also to yourself when you arrive each morning. I was quite drawn to Dr. Paula Agard's office in the fifth season of *Suits*, with its neutral color palette, comfortable furniture, and organized workspace. Of course, having such a lavish budget is not typical, but keeping in mind the details of comfort, calm, and thoughtful touches makes a difference, especially over time.

Organize Your Desk to create a zen, yet inspiring place to work.

Understand How You Work Best, and adjust what you can to create a space in which you thrive.

Create Clear Expectations and Rules for clients, colleagues, and superiors that enable you to do your job well and thus provide support for others to do their job well also. For example, set a clear understanding about when you will respond to e-mails, messages, and other communications; once people know they will be hearing from you in a timely manner but perhaps not immediately, you are less likely to be bombarded by unnecessary e-mails checking to see if you received their last one.

Keep the Conversation Elevated. Squash the gossip, and instead talk, first and foremost, about work or the job at hand; insert a bit of personal sharing based on what each person is comfortable with, and have a good sense of humor that is playful but not hurtful. Establishing necessary boundaries protects your energy throughout the day and improves the quality of your support for others throughout the organization. Once it is clear you are not someone who gossips, coworkers will stop coming to you with the latest dirt.

Celebrate Special as Well as Random Occasions. The monotony of a work environment benefits from celebratory events — whether it is the holidays, first Fridays (time for making an office croissant run), or coworkers' birthdays. Such celebrations create an enjoyable culture of support and congeniality.

Working with Colleagues

- Communicate clearly and promptly via e-mail or in person.
- When in charge of a meeting or small group conversation, welcome everyone to share.
- Do the job you are expected to do well and on time. Be the team player everyone wants to work with.
- Keep e-mails concise, polite, and brief. Adhere to respectful e-mail etiquette, and send out group e-mails only when absolutely necessary.
- Keep it positive and lighthearted, and assume the best when communicating via e-mail. Be aware of the tone you create; the words we choose can draw us closer together or further apart.
- If you are a manager or a head of a small group, set rules and expectations, such as speaking directly to the person you are having a difficult time with and not talking behind their back to another colleague. You might begin each meeting with "thirty seconds of positive" (our English department head established this opening for our department meetings, and it enables us to get to know each other on a more personal level — our hobbies, passions, etc.).
- Respect the time that will be allotted for each meeting and adhere to the expectations for each occasion.
- Respect your coworkers' personal privacy. Instead of asking too many personal questions and invading someone's space, let them open up to you. Let their willingness to share be the barometer for what you can ask them.
- A simple "Good morning" and "Have a nice weekend" go a long way to establish rapport with colleagues you may not see outside of your workday.
- Engage in chitchat to say hello and see how the weekend or a particular event went. Just remember to not linger too long.
- When you have a choice, work with "growth mind-set" individuals.

Reporting to a Supervisor

Unless you are your own boss, you report in some capacity to a supervisor, administrator, or other type of manager. Specific expectations and norms will be unique to your profession, but in general, the list below offers ideas for cultivating a relationship of respect and professionalism as well as opportunities to rise:

- Do what is expected of you in the role you were hired to perform.
- Do your work to the best of your ability.
- If you can exceed expectations, do so.
- Keep track of successes, advancements, ideas for growth, expansion, etc., and share them when the time is appropriate or your supervisor asks you for ideas or suggestions.
- Keep your conversations professional.
- Be trustworthy and dependable; do the job well and on time. Do not make more work for those you report to.

Doing what we love and enjoying the way we do it is the path to success. Doing it in a way that respects each individual but also provides clear expectations is a certain route to not only productivity, but more contentment on the job.

How to Succeed as an Entrepreneur

You don't "succeed" because you have no weaknesses; you succeed because you find your unique strengths and focus on developing habits around them.
— Timothy Ferriss

There is no need to wistfully look back upon your college years and wonder why you could not have come up with the next new start-up idea and risen to financial success during your early twenties. The truth behind successful entrepreneurships is that being older is better. In fact, according to the U.S. Bureau of Labor Statistics, entrepreneurs who were 35 or older were 50 percent more likely to start their own business, and the study also showed —this is the most important detail — that "midcareer entrepreneurs were nearly five times more likely" to be passionate about their pursuit five years into their venture than those who began a business right after graduating from college.

As Carl Schramm wrote in the *Wall Street Journal* in February 2018, mid-career entrepreneurs bring two components that are hard to find when one is young: more varied and extensive experiences, whether in professional or personal endeavors, and the financial means to fund a start-up, whether in liquid assets or through having a day job, to pay the expenses while they hone their small business on the weekends and at night.

More women than ever before are starting their own businesses, but only three percent of female-owned businesses have revenue of a million dollars or more. My challenge to those who are considering or who are already running their own business: While the goal should never be to earn a certain amount of money, it should be to thrive and not just get by. In order to choose and then run a business that can thrive, you need to look to those who have been successful doing what you want to do, learn the necessary tools and skills, and apply them effectively. In other words, you need to do your homework.

From my own experience, I concur completely with Schramm as to why I have been able to slowly, but steadily become an entrepreneur: I have a sincere passion for the message I share with the world in my writing, and my teaching career's skills overlap with what I do, but teaching also give me windows of time each year when I can dedicate myself entirely to exploring more fully my business ideas, such as writing a book during the summer months and traveling during seasonal week- or month-long breaks. As well, I do my best to continually learn what is new in the blogging industry, as it seems to constantly change. For example, at the beginning of my journey, I was slow to start my business Facebook page and was gently, but adamantly encouraged to get mine up and running (in 2011 — yes, much later than I should have done it).

I do not want to find myself behind the curve again, and so I regularly read various industry blogs and columns to stay abreast as much as possible, and I follow other bloggers I trust and who are experts at what they do. On the flip side, the reason my blog continues to grow is because of *TSLL* readers who share what they discover with those they love. The takeaway for me from this fact about my readership was that I needed to listen to my readers. Case in point: I wrote this section of the book in response to requests from many of you.

The bottom line is that it is never too late to consider becoming an entrepreneur. While the uncertainties in doing so are vast as you begin to lay the groundwork, here are some tips and advice that can put the odds for lasting success in your favor.

What to Pursue

The Intersection. Find where what the world needs meets your talents and passion.

Knowledge. Never stop learning and discovering new information about the world, its past, its people, and its potential. Especially stay cognizant of your particular industry.

What to Establish

A Routine That Works for You. W. H. Auden wrote, "Routine, in an intelligent man, is a sign of ambition." Thoughtfully be aware of what works best for your personality and productivity, and stick to it. Each of our routines will be different.

Strong Relationships. Customers or clients, contractors in a field of expertise vital to the success of your business, the community — invest in building relationships in these arenas as they are a foundation from which you can rise as well as help those you connect with.

Sincerity. Choose a business that you would do for free, but because you know your value and intend to be taken seriously, put a price on the services or products you offer. In other words, pursue a business concept you believe in and want to see in the world, so much so that you would be its first customer should someone offer such an idea to the public.

Credibility. Success stories take time, and we build our credibility by continuing to learn from those who know more, even though we will apply the knowledge using our unique touch.

Self-Motivation. You are solely responsible for completing tasks, meeting deadlines, and being the composed and enthusiastic face of your organization, so make sure you have the desire to fill all of these roles. Being an entrepreneur can be very rewarding, but you must be able to wear many different hats. Make sure you are comfortable doing this or have the ability to hire people to fill roles that are not your strengths.

How to Thrive

Master Marketing. Not all marketing needs to be expensive, and you do not need a MBA to be a successful entrepreneur, but choosing to be a student of how to market well, however and wherever you gather the information, is crucial for introducing your brand to the world. For example, using social media effectively rather than placing any paid advertisements at all can be a frugal marketing strategy. Build relationships with potential customers first, and establish trust by offering a quality product and being willing to continually improve. Do your research to see what type of marketing is worth investing in when you have the available capital.

Work Smart. The concept of quality effort over quantity comes into play once again, this time with the business you wish to build. You may have to work long hours at certain points throughout your business's life span or during certain seasons of the year, but if you are working long hours all the time, rethink your approach. Optimize your creativity by either investing in an employee to do tasks you no longer need to do or devise systems that cut down on the time you need to put in while maintaining or increasing production quality. Never assume there is only one way to accomplish what others have done before you.

Master the Money Flow. In other words, get your budget in order. Understand very clearly how much and where you are spending money and if you are pricing your services or products properly for the time and money you have invested and will continue to invest.

Making the Leap

Be Logical, Not Emotional. Leap into your entrepreneurial business as your sole endeavor when you make enough annually to pay not only your mandatory and discretionary expenses, but also your health insurance premiums and meaningful contributions to your retirement. Conversely, do not leave your current employer simply because you want to be free from time constraints, do not like where you work, or do not want to work for a boss; most likely you will be putting in longer hours than in your current job as your new business finds its footing. Success in one career contributes to success in another, so leave on good terms.

Consult Solid Resources

The section above is merely a starting-off point to remind you that if an idea has been dancing around in your mind for years and it just will not disappear, perhaps you should consider the reality that you do indeed have the passion to fuel a step into a new world of opportunity.

Now all you need are the tools, and below I have listed books I highly recommend on a handful of different areas of entrepreneurship.

- To find and trust your creative inspiration: *Big Magic: Creative Living Beyond Fear*, by Elizabeth Gilbert
- To cultivate rituals and routines that work well for you: *Daily Rituals: How Artists Work*, by Mason Currey
- To fund your dream: No, you don't need an angel investor: *The $100 Startup: Reinvent the Way You Make a Living, Do What You Love, and Create a New Future*, by Chris Guillebeau
- To learn the necessary skills to acquire and build for success, consult this "toolkit for changing your life": *Tools of Titans*, by Timothy Ferriss
- To learn from seven highly successful female entrepreneurs about how they took their idea to the next level: *Million Dollar Women: The Essential Guide for Female Entrepreneurs Who Want to Go Big*, by Julia Pimsleur
- To help determine your ideal side gig and how to turn it into your career: *The Economy of You: Discover your Inner Entrepreneur and Recession-Proof Your Life*, by Kimberly Palmer
- To understand how to move forward successfully with smart decision making: *Pivot: The Only Move That Matters Is the Next One*, by Jenny Blake
- To ignore your critics and hold on to your passion: *Be Obsessed or Be Average*, by Grant Cardone
- To engage potential customers: *Influence: The Psychology of Persuasion*, by Robert B. Cialdini
- To gain knowledge of the past and how it came to be, and to understand the present, why it works, and where the tech industry is predicted to be heading next: *The Third Wave: An Entrepreneur's Vision of the Future*, by Steve Case
- To understand the importance of interpersonal skills and realize that formal education is not the only way to success: *The 4 Essentials of Entrepreneurial Thinking: What Successful People Didn't Learn in School*, by Cliff Michaels

Running a Small Business

While I have been running my blog for nearly nine years, I am still a neophyte when it comes to running my own business (although I am thoroughly loving the opportunity to learn as I go forward). In my few short years as an entrepreneur, I have learned a few principles from my accountant, lawyer, and financial adviser that have helped me along my journey thus far:

- Hire a good accountant.
- Have a lawyer you trust answer any questions or help you create your business corporation, LLC, etc.
- Make sure to have the proper insurance.
- Save for retirement with a SEP (Simplified Employee Pension).
- When you are the only person on staff or when you work from home, set business hours that keep you focused, accountable, and thus productive.
- Choose contractors and other talented collaborators who understand your vision and have a growth mind-set, just as you do.

Again, the most frequent questions I receive are *How do you do it all? How do you find the energy and ideas day after day?* As much as I want to share a logical, specific schedule and tell you why it works, the truth is that it all depends on my absolute passion and dedication to what I do. I sleep and breathe living a life of quality and quantity and figuring out how to do it well as the world around us continues to shift and change.

I grappled and sorted through this question unconsciously beginning when I was a young girl and continued to do so until I was nearing thirty and finally decided to just write about it, having no idea what might unfold.

And here we are, nine years later, and my curiosity is only more excited and bursting with questions and writing ideas. Look to your energy source: your passion. If it is an authentic source, trust that you have what it takes to strive forward successfully.

Eight Ways to Remain Interested in Your Passion

Julia Child did not taste her first French meal until she was thirty-six, yet following that meal, eating and cooking French food became a lifelong passion for her. Ian Fleming, the creator of James Bond, did not write his first novel, *Casino Royale*, until he was forty-three; then he churned out thirteen more works of fiction over the next fourteen years. And Edith Wharton, author of *The House of Mirth* and *Ethan Frome*, after being discouraged by her parents from writing as a young girl, finally dove back in when she was thirty-five and created her own financial wealth from her talents.

Discovering what one is passionate about is not an easy task, but it will eventually be revealed if one keeps looking. Once we find our passion, there may be times when our interest wanes or we begin to question whether we should keep investing time and energy in what we have discovered. If what you are pursuing is what you are passionate about, these moments of doubt do not mean you should stop doing what you are doing; instead, they are a sign that you need some time to re-energize yourself. And this re-energizing must happen on a regular basis. Much like your body and its need to be fed, hydrated, and rested each day, your passions must be nourished if you wish them to flourish.

How can we reboot our interest in something we fell head over heels in love with years ago? Here are eight tips.

Step Away from the Financial Aspects. Try this for a day or two. If your passion is what you do for a living — and if that is the case, what an amazing career to have — the pressures of making sure it is making enough money to pay the bills can be a wet blanket. Make sure your finances are in order so that you can step away for a few days in order to focus primarily on what made you get involved with your work in the first place. Submersing yourself in the passion of what you do helps lift the burdens of financial stress, and often that is just what you need to strengthen your creative mind. Upon returning to your financial needs after taking a break, try to find a way to streamline your finances. Whether that is creating a simple budget system or purchasing a program such as QuickBooks or Xero, consider this an investment in yourself and your future happiness.

Investigate Others' Lives. Read biographies of those who have traveled the path you are just beginning. If you are an into sports, read a biography about a successful athlete you look up to. If you are pursuing political science, read a biography about Winston Churchill or

Condoleezza Rice or Abraham Lincoln. In other words, place yourself in the world of someone who inspired you to jump into what you are doing currently. Observe their struggles, discover how they overcame them, be inspired by their story, and most likely you will be refueled to jump back in with fervor.

Delegate the Necessary Have-tos. Often, with my busy schedule, what stresses me out the most is not being able to complete all of the have-tos (cleaning the house, mowing the lawn, etc.), and while these chores need to be done, when I figure out how to delegate or simplify them, I free myself up to spend time doing what I love — writing, reading, traveling, cooking, endlessly looking for inspiration. The details of your life may mean you are not able to enjoy doing what you are doing. If that is the case, rearrange your life, edit, delegate. Prioritize the elements in your life so that you are in the driver's seat.

Schedule Breaks to Recharge. Regular vacations or weekends in which you are free from responsibility or can be away from the office without the phone attached to your ear are necessary to remind yourself that you love what you are doing. Even if you are only able to take one vacation a year, take it. Taking the time to be reassured that your passion is worth your continued involvement will set your mind at ease when you have to dive headfirst back into the fray.

Be Willing to Take a Risk. Often the best way to reboot your interest in your passion is to do something with it you have never done. Do you love cooking but have never attempted a soufflé? Give it a try until you have mastered it. The success you eventually arrive at will boost your confidence and add a lilt in your step as you get back in the kitchen and take it up a notch.

Find the Drains on Your Energy. Then find a solution. If you are feeling less than inspired about your passion, plug the leaks. Somewhere you are being drained unnecessarily, and it is time to flush out the energy leeches. It could be people who are draining you, or it could be obligations you have signed up for without acknowledging there are not thirty hours in the day. Find them, plug them, move on.

Change Your Environment. Travel, move, rearrange the furniture. Open a new book, step off a plane into a new city, state, or country. Create a new perspective for yourself. A change of environment will allow you to be nudged out of your rut and begin to see things differently. There is always a lesson to learn, a new sight to analyze, and something new to discover about your life and yourself.

Record Your Thoughts. Never underestimate the power of keeping a journal. I journal regularly, so I make sure I have my Moleskine either by my bed, in my office, or in my tote, even when I travel. Begin by writing down what happened during your day, and if you want, note how you felt or what you are hoping for; let your thoughts direct your pen. The journal is a sacred space, a you-only space, and the more often you write in it, the more honest you will become, breathing new life into your hidden hopes, fears, and ideas. Whether you experience *aha* moments while you are writing or looking back over older entries, insights will leap off the page if you are honest and pay attention to what you have written.

Imagine your life without the ability to pursue your passion. If the eight ideas above fail to keep you interested, imagine your life without being able to write, to swim, to travel, to parent, to teach, to protect, to build, to lead, etc. Would you want that life? I didn't think so.

Often our passions are strangled by the things we either have to do to keep our lives running smoothly or believe we have to do. Be protective about what you bring into your life and into your schedule. Your passion is a life source for contentment, joy, becoming your best self for those around you, and enjoying your own company. Do not let that flame die.

How to Find Infinite Motivation

A few years ago, I watched a film I had been meaning to see since it was released in 2010. Afterward, I was inspired and reinvigorated, and reminded that anything is possible so long as you possess one important attribute . . . internal motivation. The story of the last horse to win the Triple Crown, *Secretariat* (1973), offers a plethora of lessons, but two very important characteristics came into play in the horse also known as Big Red (1970–1989). Upon his death, as is standard practice for a racing champion, an autopsy was performed, and it was discovered that Secretariat's heart weighed an estimated 22 pounds, compared to 8.5 pounds for a normal horse.

Such a phenomenal anomaly has still not been matched. But it was what his trainer, owner, jockey, groom, and other observers noticed about him that made for an unbeatable competitor: He loved to run. In fact, in preparation for the Belmont Stakes, the final race to earn the Triple Crown, the trainer ran him rather than resting him in the days leading up to the main event.

Obviously, we cannot get inside a horse's head, but those who have spent their lives around animals, paying close attention to their behavior, discern particular predilections and motivations in horses. And Secretariat's was to run simply because he enjoyed it. Blessed with a powerful heart that enabled unbeatable endurance, he outran a worthy opponent in Sham (whose heart weighed 18 pounds), winning the Belmont Stakes by 31 lengths.

The lesson? Regardless of how talented we are in any arena — speaking, math, music, sports — if our heart is not sincerely enamored with the task at hand, our fullest potential is less likely to be reached.

Yale professor of psychology and organizational behavior Barry Schwartz led a study involving more than 11,000 West Point cadets regarding what type of motivation — internal (seek understanding, grow as an individual, improve the world) or instrumental (external reward such as money, prestige, attention) — provided the better or desired outcomes.

As you might expect, cadets with a strong internal motivation (coupled with a weak instrumental motivation) were more likely to graduate and be successful in their military career. What was unexpected was that the cadets who felt both internal and instrumental motives performed worse on every evaluative measure compared to those who had a strong internal motivation along with a weak instrumental motivation.

The study revealed that in order to attain a favorable outcome, activities and instruction should be structured in such a way that instrumental outcomes do not become the motive, even if such outcomes occur as a by-product. For example, eating well and working out should not be done to fit into a particular dress to impress your former classmates at the upcoming reunion. Rather, living healthily should be done to improve your longevity and increase your physical capabilities and thus the quality of your life. The idea is not to pursue paths that have no instrumental value, but to make sure that instrumental value is not the primary motivator.

Take some time to be with yourself and take part in a bit of self-reflection. Secretariat did not do what he did to gain accolades, a movie deal, or higher stud fees; he was born with a gift and happened to love doing something that a large heart helped him to excel at. I have no doubt that even if his heart had been the standard 8.5 pounds, Secretariat would still have loved to run and would have been absolutely content. The Triple Crown was just the cherry on top.

Be the Captain of Your Ship

Whatever circumstances you were born into, whatever family life and education you had or didn't have, you came here to make your dreams come true, and no matter where you are now, you are fully equipped with everything you need to do it.
— Rhonda Byrne, *Hero*

Benjamin Franklin was twenty years old in 1726 when he laid out his thirteen virtues, which he offered as a way to cultivate strong character. His resolute determination to adhere to his core principles undoubtedly aided him as he chartered the path he carved for himself and are in part why American history holds him in such high regard. Here is Franklin's list of virtues.

Temperance. Eat not to dullness. Drink not to elevation.
Silence. Speak not but what may benefit others or yourself. Avoid trifling conversation.
Order. Let all your things have their places. Let each part of your business have its time.
Resolution. Resolve to perform what you ought. Perform without fail what you resolve.
Frugality. Make no expense but to do good to others or yourself: i.e., waste nothing.
Industry. Lose no time. Be always employed in something useful. Cut off all unnecessary actions.
Sincerity. Use no hurtful deceit. Think innocently and justly; and, if you speak, speak accordingly.
Justice. Wrong none by doing injuries or omitting the benefits that are your duty.
Moderation. Avoid extremes. Forbear resenting injuries so much as you think they deserve.
Cleanliness. Tolerate no uncleanliness in body, clothes, or habitation.
Tranquility. Be not disturbed at trifles, or at accidents common or unavoidable.

Chastity. Rarely use venery but for health or offspring, never to dullness, weakness, or the injury of your own or another's peace or reputation.

Humility. Imitate Jesus and Socrates.

We too, with determination and clarity, can chart the path we wish to create for ourselves. We too can navigate the wind and the currents of life to propel us toward our desired destination. A horrific storm that may seem to throw us off course can take us to better waters if we learn the proper lessons along the way. Whether we are given an inflatable dinghy or a grand yacht to make our journey, we can turn our dreams into reality.

Those who feel they have been dealt an unfair hand may need to rely on more creative means to acquire a safer vessel, but imagine the skills they will have gained along the way. Those skills will forever exist for those who have had to scratch and claw to get where they wish to go; it is those skills that can strengthen your foundation and allow you to potentially exceed your initial dreams.

So long as you have a sound mind to absorb knowledge, a voice to ask questions, and ears to gather information, you can weather Mother Nature's turbulent moments and come to appreciate the pearls gathered up along the way.

As Steve Jobs reminded Stanford graduates in 2005, "You can't connect the dots looking forward; you can only connect them looking backward." In the meantime, never waste an opportunity to learn something new, gain new knowledge, or feed your curiosity. Life has a funny way of answering our questions, but we first must be willing to step forward and ask them.

CHAPTER FIVE

Building Your Community

The good we secure for ourselves is precarious and uncertain until it is secured for all of us and incorporated into our common life.
— Jane Addams

Imagine for a moment a community you enjoy being a part of — whether it is a place you once called home, your workplace, a city you have resided in or perhaps a different city, state, or country you have visited but felt a strong connection to. What was it about the environment that drew you to that community?

As I examined this question for myself — including my love affair with my new hometown, Bend, but also my appreciation for my time on NW 23rd in Portland, my study-abroad experience in Angers, and my adoration for the limestone neighborhood of Maida Vale, in London — I began to see, first, that there was one quality each place provided that I highly valued: trustworthiness, the sense that I could be authentically myself and could exercise my strengths and curiosities without fear of being ostracized. Second, I identified the opportunity to explore, grow, and be challenged, balanced by opportunities to relax, unwind, reconnect with the natural world, and become restored. Third, I saw potential to grow, if I invested myself, and to assist those around me to grow as well.

As the quote from Jane Adams suggests, if we only look out for ourselves, we ironically are not looking out for ourselves at all. We each exist within a community, whether it is the neighborhood we live in, the people we work with, the town we call home, or our state/province and country.

In a democracy, the majority rules, and minority rights are protected as well, but we must educate ourselves, speak up, and be involved, whether we are in the majority or the minority on any given issue, in order to be ensured that the world we enjoy living in each day remains and progresses successfully into the future.

How can we do that? On a small scale, be a neighbor you would want to live next to, attend city council meetings, stay informed, refrain from running to your "tribe" on every issue. Remember, communities involve a diverse congregation of individuals, experiences, dreams, beliefs, and generations. Understanding is needed, along with a recognition of the humanity in each individual we meet. When we think of others and consider our own needs, it is more likely we can strike a balance, but being someone who refuses to understand the other side or who is entirely too flexible and easily swayed will not be helpful either.

An enjoyable way to become involved in your community is to attend local events and gatherings — strolling local farmers markets, attending annual festivals, volunteering. Become acquainted with local businesses and support them with your patronage. Get outside on a regular basis and acknowledge your neighbors, if only in passing or with a short conversation.

A Sense of Community: Be Part of Something Larger

We can begin by doing small things at the local level, like planting community gardens or looking out for our neighbors. That is how change takes place in living systems, not from above but from within, from many local actions occurring simultaneously.
— Grace Lee Boggs

If we cling to a single relationship, assuming it will cure all of our ills and provide all of the solutions, we are deceiving ourselves. In order for any relationship to thrive, we must build a community founded on trust, growth, acceptance, support, and possibility, and that community begins with healthy individuals who understand themselves and can provide, for themselves, this knowledge and self-love. It begins with each of us being an active part of the beauty in our community.

I still remember vividly how difficult it was to leave my old neighborhood in eastern Oregon and my house of nine years, which I had remodeled extensively. Bend was calling, but it was hard to say good-bye to two things. The house was the most difficult to walk away from, as I had poured my heart and soul, as well as hard-earned money, into my sanctuary. And on my street, I had built relationships with my neighbors; we experienced the seasons together — the hard winters, the hot summers, the beautiful springs and falls — as we worked in our yards. We created a community of trust and protection, and I will be forever thankful to have been a part of that.

Aside from the relationships you build in your neighborhood, becoming involved in your town's planning and development is a way to invest in your community. As Supreme Court Justice Felix Frankfurter stated, "In a democracy, the highest office is the office of citizen."

If you use the local parks regularly, take part in volunteering for the annual clean-up or spring plantings of flower beds. When new city council seats become available, get to know the potential candidates and cast your vote for someone who has the vision you desire (or perhaps run yourself).

But the component of community that will always be with us — one that can heighten the quality of all the other parts of our community — is ourselves.

To Cultivate Social Well-Being: First Become Comfortable with Yourself

Striking a balance between time on your own and building a healthy community is an ever-shifting task, one that requires you to be present and live consciously so that you welcome healthy people and activities and edit out those that squelch or restrict your growth and keep you from more fulfilling experiences.

The value of solitude is that it lets us investigate and discover our deepest nature in order to live a life that brings us fulfillment and satisfaction. It is also during the moments of regular solitude that we discover how much social interaction we need and what type of interaction best suits our temperament.

However, it is important to understand what being "social" means. As I will share later in the book in more detail, the realization that I am an introvert was life-changing and liberating. And as Michaela Chung points out in her book *The Irresistible Introvert*, "[introverts] are lonelier when we spend too much time focusing outward. Turning in is both a joy and a necessity for introverts." In other words, some of us are simply happiest in our own company.

Whether our nature gravitates toward gregarious encounters or thrives on limited, but substantive intimate time together, we do need connection. It is a matter of determining what kind we need.

What does a healthy social fabric consist of? What must we invest in? What must we not forget as we navigate the conscious development of a healthy social life? Everyone's social quilt will be unique. Your "tribe" may be made up entirely of friends you consider family, while for someone else, it may include some relatives and family members as well as friends who feel like birth siblings. Others still will have friends of varying ages, backgrounds, experiences, and perspectives. And not everyone in your community will be a friend; many people include acquaintances from different circles: work, hobbies, the past, the neighborhood, etc.

The quilt that becomes your social network will be dynamic in many ways, evolving and changing as you move through your own life and as the people you connect with move through theirs. The one constant is that your quilt will be unique to you.

Be Your Own Best Friend. Diane von Furstenberg has said, "When a woman becomes her own best friend, life is easier." At the heart of living well is knowing who you are. Without such knowledge, we cannot understand how to create a life that will bring us contentment. And then we must like who we are and who we are becoming. If we enjoy our own company, we put that self-respect out into the world in every interaction we have with others, for the way we treat ourselves teaches others how to treat us. Start with yourself. Become your own best friend, and learn whom to allow into your life and whom to let go.

Invest in a Social Network. One of the best examples of the importance of building a social network is the life of an expat. Tamara Micner shared in the *Wall Street Journal* in 2016 the strategies she used for subverting the loneliness that inevitably pops up after the honeymoon stage of living in a new country; at the top of the list is building a social network. Begin to seek out entities, organizations, and interests that maintain your well-being and peace of mind. From building rapport at work with a few like-minded colleagues to seeking out a church, temple, mosque, or other spiritual venue, start with small steps, but continue to put yourself out there in arenas that are congruent with your values, interests, and lifestyle. Before long, you will have a few friends and more than a handful of acquaintances.

Take Your Time Finding Your Partner. A partner can play a tremendous role in our lives. However, maintaining a relationship can be tremendously amazing or tremendously exhausting and draining. And while relationships take continued investment and attention, they also should not be something to rush into. Often we are not ready to be in the relationship we seek; we need to evolve and explore as an individual so we can be a partner worthy of the relationship we dream about. In any case, trust your timing. By no means refrain from an opportunity to meet new people and go on dates, but certainly do not throw yourself into just any relationship simply to avoid being alone. The best strategy is to live our lives, do our thing, and be our best selves. Binge on life, and that will draw to you a bevy of people — potential friends, acquaintances, and perhaps even a partner.

If we wish to have a rich social network, we need to be clear about what will and what will not allow it to flourish.

How to Cultivate a Healthy Social Circle

That which we elect to surround ourselves with becomes the museum of our soul and the archive of our experience.
— Thomas Jefferson

The people we choose, the events we attend, the road we take, the media we listen to, the places we visit, how we spend our time — all of these things gradually mold us, shaping us into the person we consciously want to become. The people we welcome into or release from our lives, and the ways we interact with those we want in our lives, play a significant role in the contentment we feel and the overall quality of our professional and personal lives. So whom should we welcome and whom should we usher to the door?

People to Avoid

People think being alone makes you lonely, but I don't think that's true. Being surrounded by the wrong people is the loneliest thing in the world.
— Kim Culbertson

Politely show these types of people the door:

Disrespectful Individuals. When you first meet someone, you may not be able to discern whether they will be respectful, but this will become clear fairly soon. For example, they may show their attitude in what they don't do rather than what they actually do, so pay attention, and do not make excuses for them. If someone continually lacks appreciation for your situation or the time and energy you have expended on them, let them go. If they are disrespectful with their actions or words, let them go.

Stressors. With some people, you will experience stressful situations — a boss who tightens purse strings, unexpected family situations, a travel itinerary that is not going as planned. Simply because you feel stress while you are with some people does not mean they are "stressors" and should be let go from your life. If, on the other hand, someone routinely causes stress with contentious arguments, inappropriate behavior, and being heedless of their effect on others, let them go.

Two-Faced Talkers. Such individuals are lethal to your ability to trust. They will tell you what is pleasing to hear to your face or in your presence, but when you are beyond audible reach, their commentary takes an about-face. Let these people go. Their behavior is a reflection of their need to please and their inability to speak the truth even when it is uncomfortable.

Pain Instigators. While there will be times when our friends, spouses, or colleagues hurt our feelings or overstep their bounds, this is not necessarily a reason to boot them from our lives. So long as we have the courage to speak up and clarify our boundaries, such relationships can be repaired and grow stronger. However, it sometimes happens that someone hurts us, we explain why we were hurt, and they do it again; if this pattern continues, we must release these people from our lives.

Takers. When it comes to relationships, giving and taking is a balance that both parties need to understand. When people constantly take from you — asking favors, borrowing money and not repaying, enjoying your connection without being appreciative — they need to be removed from your life. They either are ignorant about what they are doing and not aware that they need to be more appreciative, or they expect you to accommodate them and will never change. Either way, you must speak up and protect yourself.

Negative Nellies/Wet Blankets. At the core of both of these types is the weight of negativity that weighs down the receiver (you). Each morning we wake up with a finite amount of energy. When we spend time with someone who comments only on the negative (complains, whines, etc.) or cannot seem to find the good in the day, our positive energy quotient is slowly drained because we have to expend more of it to stay positive. A wet blanket can douse a spark of hope or excitement by saying nothing at all, responding with a cynical comment, or simply not relating to the reason you are cheerful. This may happen unexpectedly when a true friend or family member has pressing matters on their mind, but if this is the modus operandi of someone close to you, its effects on you can be negative.

Constant Competitors. Constant competitors feel the need to perpetually "one up" anything that someone else offers. Due to their insecurities and need for validation, they have to demonstrate that they also are successful and happy, or have had it much worse than you. This does not mean a friend cannot share a similar experience, but rather than recognizing a moment in which you want to be heard and celebrated, or heard and supported, some people flip the tables and instead bring everything back to themselves.

Passive-Aggressives. Someone who is unable to speak directly to the issue at hand and instead mopes or withholds affection or attention is trying to maintain power or intimidate. These folks can be difficult to recognize, but they can gradually and harmfully affect your everyday life if you spend time with them regularly. Such people are cowardly and weak by nature, and this is the only way they know to maintain whatever power they think they have. Instead of confronting an issue, they bury it and stew, which negatively affects not only them but all their relationships. The key, if you must interact with them, is to confront them tactfully but directly, and then move on.

The Expired Relationship. It can be a romantic relationship that was meant to help you grow or learn something, a colleague or boss who taught you and helped you excel in your career, or a friend who was your confidante, but now you are traveling separate paths. Each individual we have a relationship with has the opportunity to enhance our lives, but not all relationships are meant to remain a part of our lives forever. Maintaining any healthy relationship takes energy, and we have only so much emotional energy on any given day. To expect more than a relationship can give is to ruin what its original purpose was. Honor it, and move on.

Now that we have talked about those who should not be in our lives, we have made room for whom we should welcome into our personal and professional social circles.

People to Cherish

As with nearly every arena of our lives, it is not the number of people we interact with and build relationships with that is important; it is the quality, the type of people with whom we spend our precious hours every day. Sometimes one person can fulfill more than one role in your life, and that is perfectly fine. Each of our social circles is different. The people we cherish will also evolve over time, and your community will constantly be in a state of flux based on where you are, where you wish to go, and what life tosses your way. But without a doubt, the following types of people will improve the contentment and fulfillment in your life.

The Cheerleader. Cheerleaders are people who keep you going, remind you of your strengths, and help you plow forward when the world seems to hand you too much. They are also there to celebrate with you when success comes your way. Cheerleaders are not Pollyannas who sugarcoat or ignore reality, but they help you find your grit and provide boosts of energy when you feel you have nothing left to give. A cheerleader sends you a text just before you step up to the plate for that important interview and reminds you how amazing you are before you go out on a date. A cheerleader is also the person you talk to after these events occur and is just as excited as you are when all goes well.

The Mentor. We all need mentors, whether we speak directly to them or simply observe them from afar. A person who embodies qualities we aspire to, has been successful, and lives their life in a way we wish could be our own — that is a mentor. Preferably, the mentor in your life will be someone you can check in with from time to time, discuss life and career issues, and receive feedback.

The Realist. Not to be confused with a cynic, the realist in many ways is your conscience and your gut, but also someone who has all the facts. This person is often someone older, with more experience and wisdom, who has learned lessons in the business of life and has succeeded. A realist points out the options, the pros and the cons, the bottom line, and breaks down everything without sugar-coating anything. Realists do not try to squash your dreams; they do give you the necessary facts, so that, should you go forward, you will be well-informed.

The Connector. This is someone who opens doors for you that you cannot open for yourself, no matter how amazing your résumé. The saying I remember hearing as a young adult was, "It's not what you know; it's who you know." The connector is sometimes also a mentor in that they see something in you and wish to help. Having been where you are or knowing they can help you get where you wish to go, they gladly do so.

The Giver. To give without expectation is a characteristic of a secure individual. Such a person does not grease the wheels in order to see what she can receive in return. Rather, the giver gives simply because she sees a need and feels a desire to help, motivate, or express her love. The receiver should express appreciation and should not take advantage. These are not people you can seek out. They typically will find you.

The Motivator. Reminding you of all the possibilities life has to offer — that is what a motivator brings into your everyday life. Motivators may take on the role of cheerleader from time to time, but their main ability is to bring the world and its beauty to your front step, remind you of all the possibilities, and show you that you can and should be participating regularly. The motivator's energy enlivens you and helps you stay excited about living each day.

Do not feel guilt-ridden for removing certain people from your life and working hard to include positive influences. Learning how to navigate our lives as we interact with others is a constant dance. But with conscious attention and a willingness to remember that we must be positive contributors in others' lives, just as we need positive influences in our own, the overall quality of our lives will improve, and all that we have to be grateful for will grow exponentially.

Fourteen Ways to Be a Friend Worth Having

Good friends help you find important things when you have lost them . . . your smile, your hope, and your courage.
— Doe Zantamata

The word *friend* has been diluted in our world of social media. We can be friends with more than 800 people and only have met a handful of them in person. By definition, a friend is someone with whom we share a mutual affection, someone who is not hostile toward us, someone we enjoy spending time with, and someone who helps or supports us. There are healthy friendships, and then there are friendships that give the appearance of wholesome beneficence but actually are eroding and destructive, preventing us from reaching our true potential.

Below are fourteen attributes of a true friend who is worth having. Keep in mind that, in order to have such devoted, worthwhile friends, we must also be a true friend, so the list is not only what to seek in a friend, but what to aspire to.

Is Present. A friend is not someone to use and abuse and call at all hours, expecting them to be there when you want them, regardless of their schedule. A true friend becomes an active member of your life — someone who is aware of what is going on, calls to see how an interview or presentation went, and makes time to see you. In other words, a true friend makes the friendship a priority and strengthens it over time.

Shows Up. Being supportive of each other's big events sends a significant message — that you are there to support what matters to them. While life can get in the way at times, so long as you show up more often than not, the friendship will be strengthened.

Remembers the Two-Way-Street Rule. It can be easy to unload on good friends and share all of our good and bad news, but find the balance. Remember that a friendship involves two people, so begin by asking how they are doing, then sit back and listen. We should not be afraid to talk about what we are passionate, excited, or upset about, so long as we encourage our friends to do the same.

Gives Thoughtful Advice. A secure and supportive friend not only gives thoughtful advice but also is not offended when their advice is not taken. Being a good friend may involve saying, "I don't know what you should do, but I know someone who you might want to talk to or a book you might want to read." By giving an honest response, you help build a bond of trust, so that when you do end up giving advice, your friend has faith that it is coming from a place of love.

Encourages Authenticity. A true friend does not expect their friends to conform to what they understand, but rather revels in their uniqueness, celebrates their strengths, and supports them as they strive to reach their full potential. In so doing, a true friend does not compete or tear down her friends to bolster her own self-confidence. Often this issue is why it is easier for strong friendships to form when two friends are thriving in different arenas. However, it is possible for two friends to work in the same field or compete in the same arena; it simply requires strong, secure individuals.

Listens and Remembers. Listening — letting your friend recognize that you are attentive to them and your conversation above anything else — is a supreme form of respect for the relationship. It is easy to be distracted by our phones or other people, but when we give our undivided attention, we communicate without saying a word. Remembering what was said solidifies the trust. Whether it is remembering a dear friend's birthday, sending a brief "best of luck" card before an exciting new venture, or sending a quick text when a friend is about to meet someone they are anxious to meet — such simple gestures can mean the world.

Is Loyal. A true friend refrains from speaking ill of a friend even if others talk negatively about her. In fact, a true friend, should it be necessary, will speak up for their friend and attempt to stop the vitriol.

Is Flexible. Not all friendships will stand the test of time. Short-term friendships can help us navigate particular periods in our lives; however, a handful of friendships persevere throughout the chapters of our childhood and adult lives. Any healthy friendship that has successfully navigated this process has been flexible enough to let the two people grow, experiment, and step away from each other for extended periods of time and celebrate new pathways in each other's lives.

Speaks the Truth. Whether it is good or bad feedback, a true friend has the courage to tactfully and lovingly tell the other person the truth. If a friend has had a great success, even if they do not understand how it came to be, they are excited and celebratory in all sincerity; however, if a close friend is becoming increasingly negative and difficult to be around, it takes a strong and well-meaning friend to point out the change in behavior — not to nag, but to help them find greater contentment.

Is Supportive. It can be easy to be supportive of a friend when we approve of what they are doing, but a true test of friendship is to support a loved one when they pursue a path we do not understand. By no means am I advocating for supporting a friend when they are choosing a self-destructing, downward spiral; but if a friend is choosing a career or relationship that we ourselves would not pursue but that could be ideal for someone else, then we need to take a moment, let go of our judgment, and be honest with our reservations, but then move on and be supportive.

Tries to Improve Each Other's Lives. A good friend looks out not only for herself as she navigates life, but also her dear friends — whether by simply being a positive person or by providing information, ideas, and inspiration.

Communicates Kindly. While there may be moments of passion and heated disagreement, after things calm down, a true friend recognizes that such heated tones only exacerbate the situation. A true friend can apologize and not hold a grudge, recognizing that we all make mistakes; we are all human and have bad days.

Respects Boundaries. Each friendship is different, and thus each friendship will have different boundaries for what can be discussed, how we should behave, and what issues are sensitive and not to be shared. Having a romantic partner does not mean a friendship has to end; however, the friendship may shift or change, and a true friend respects this reality. Knowing when we need to give our friends space to be on their own and when we need to pry, even if they say they do not want us to, presents a tricky tightrope to walk; with time, knowing how to respond becomes easier.

Is Observant of Moods. With any friendship, this understanding will take time, but it is possible to discern when it is acceptable to be silly and tongue-in-cheek and when our friend needs us to be serious and listen or support. On a similar note, taking note of a dear friend's mood and asking them if they are okay, even if they say they do not want to talk about it, at least conveys that you are concerned.

Building a friendship is not something that happens magically over coffee one day. It takes time to slowly discover who each person is and build trust. However, no matter who you are, the key to any healthy relationship is to gradually allow yourself to be vulnerable and observe how the friend you choose to be vulnerable with handles such a trusting gesture. Throwing everything on the table in the first meeting probably is not the best idea, but gradually, as you share bits and pieces of yourself, you will eventually be able to see how much you can trust someone. Creating a lasting bond is a dynamic commitment, because as we grow and progress toward our best selves, so do our friends, and in order for the friendship to continue to "fit," we must always be an active participant.

Master the Art of Conversation

Cheerfulness, unaffected cheerfulness, a sincere desire to please and be pleased, unchecked by any efforts to shine, are the qualities you must bring with you into society, if you wish to succeed in conversation . . . a light and airy equanimity of temper — that spirit which never rises to boisterousness, and never sinks to immovable dullness; that moves gracefully from "grave to gay, from serious to serene," and by mere manner gives proof of a feeling heart and generous mind.
— Arthur Martine

The good news about knowing how to navigate any conversational situation is that nobody is born an expert. Conversation is a learned skill that is honed with practice and observation. Often young adults seem to have an innate ability to talk and converse with anyone, but if you were to delve into their childhood, you would no doubt find an adult, parent, or sibling they learned from, consciously or unconsciously. Some become more comfortable with this ability than others, but we can all master the art of conversation.

After all, whether for work, building personal relationships, or navigating the world at large — traveling, doing our errands, hiring people to work on our homes, negotiating a deal — knowing how to politely, yet effectively converse with people, whether or not we know them or like them, can greatly affect our mood, stress levels, success, and ease as we go about our everyday business.

Below are some tips on how to skillfully navigate any conversation. I am not perfect at all of these as each situation brings its own nuances, but I try diligently to improve or recognize when I could have done better. Like anyone else, I have good days and bad days, but I try to remember each of these pointers when I can, and that has shown me what can be accomplished with a skilled conversation.

Know Your Audience. Knowing your audience — what their backgrounds, beliefs, and ages are — is crucial for deciding what would be the appropriate and most engaging conversation. Everything is not open for discussion all of the time, and a tactful conversationalist recognizes this.

Pose a Question. Ask questions you think the other person would be comfortable answering or ones that would allow them to use their knowledge to provide better insight. A few years ago, I was introduced to a federal attorney at a summer gathering, and as a civics teacher, I was eager to ask him about a recent Supreme Court ruling. Not only did I learn something, but I was able to gain a bit of perspective beyond the classroom.

Acknowledge Other Points of View. In any conversation with one or more people, the quickest way to show genuine interest is to demonstrate that you are listening. Acknowledge their story, emotion, etc., either by remembering it later in the conversation ("As Lori informed us earlier . . .") or by saying you agree ("I never thought about it from that perspective").

Create Moments of Inspiration. Sometimes, asking a question can be tricky if you do not know the people you are talking with very well. In such a case, often it is the topics we discuss or the stories we tell that prompt someone else to want to share something, and that is quite a compliment in itself. Whether it is sharing something that grabs their attention or opens their eyes to the unexpected, or is a bit of news that perks up the conversation, come with a few fail-safe, inspiring stories.

Prefer Selfless to Selfish Conversation. The easiest topic for anyone to talk about is themselves; keep this in mind when you do not know where to take a conversation. Begin by asking another guest how they know the host, and perhaps another topic will present itself. As Dale Carnegie said, "It's much easier to become interested in others than it is to convince them to be interested in you." If both parties follow this advice, the conversation will be pleasantly balanced.

Brevity Provokes Curiosity. Long-windedness kills the flow. Have you ever listened to someone tell a story and go back months to provide context? Then the story finishes up, and you realize there was no need for the extra details. Do not be that person. It is better to share just enough or a sliver shy of enough than to drone on, leaving your listeners wondering what the point of the story is.

Know When Silence Is Best. "Eloquent silence," a term coined by Arthur Martine in his 1866 book *Martine's Hand-Book of Etiquette and Guide to True Politeness*, is knowing when to simply listen, which is just as polite as knowing the appropriate thing to say or how to speak politely. Martine says that silence, if practiced or timed correctly, is a way of encouraging others to speak. Speak less. Listen more. And as a practice, paraphrase what you heard the other person say, to show respect and that you are paying attention, and to make sure you understood them correctly.

Do Not Over-Share. While sharing all of your "war stories," relationship gaffs, or children's accolades may be something you are comfortable with, do not assume those you are conversing with will be interested. Proceed slowly when it comes to offering personal information; test the waters to see how comfortable others are with certain issues before diving right in. And when in doubt, don't.

Be Humble. Always accept compliments with gratitude, making sure to point out others' contributions; this is a way to display humility and build respect. Droning on about how successful you have been is not a useful conversation starter. When such successes come up naturally, you should own them, but then revert back to the first sentence of the paragraph.

Try to Understand Rather Than Be Right. We have all encountered people who are adamant that their point of view is the only way to see the world. They would rather be right than consider other perspectives. These people drive listeners away. A skillful conversationalist invites other viewpoints, sincerely considers them, and sees the colloquy as an opportunity to finesse their point of view or broaden their understanding.

Omit When Necessary, But Always Speak the Truth. If you know that certain information will hurt somebody or would be inappropriate in a particular setting, refrain from bringing the information to the table. If you are asked directly, be honest, or simply say, "I don't feel comfortable talking about it here." Either way, respect the scenario you are in at the moment.

Respect Comfort Levels. A sense of mystery is always a valuable quality to have, and that means also respecting others' privacy. Ask only questions you know they are comfortable with, and do not assume that simply because you are comfortable, they must be too. A skilled conversationalist remembers past conversations with individuals and recalls the topics people enjoyed discussing and those that have never been broached.

Navigate Disagreements Respectfully. If you disagree with a stated opinion, begin by finding common ground — what you agree with, what you see eye to eye on. For example, if you are talking about the inability of Congress to compromise, but you disagree with what the other person feels the problem is, begin by stating, "I could not agree more. Congress certainly needs to change the way they function because it isn't helpful to the country." When you recognize common ground, you acknowledge that you have listened and have validated the premise that inspired their opinion. Then transition with "and" rather than "but." When you use "and," you are adding to, not deflating, the conversation. For example, ". . . and while [their opinion] is one idea, another solution may be [your opinion]."

Know When a Conversation Is Over. End any conversation, formal or not, on a positive note, even if you are interrupted, and be sure to smile and convey that you enjoyed it — with a lighthearted quip, for example — before moving on.

Part of the reason diving into a conversation is so daunting is because so much is out of our hands. While that can be intimidating, it is also what makes conversations exciting. You never know where they will go, who you will meet, what you will learn, etc. And if you break a few rules along the way, if you are paying attention to the people involved, you will get a feeling for what people are comfortable with. Simply pay attention. Part of conversation, like life, is simply being aware, in the moment, of yourself, those around you, and your overall environment.

How to Deal with Toxic People

Until you let go of all the toxic people in your life, you will never grow into your fullest potential. Let them go so you can grow.
— Anonymous

Toxic weeds, toxic chemicals, toxins in our bodies — each of these entities negatively affects the environment. The same can be said for toxic people. We all have encountered a toxic person — perhaps even a stranger on the street, someone we will never see again — but the interaction leaves our minds reeling and our confidence depleted. Or it can be someone we are related to or someone we once thought was a friend. Work can bring toxic people into our lives, and we may have less control regarding those interactions; however, with the proper tools, each of us can effectively maneuver and handle toxic people.

Do Not Rely on Responses from Others to Dictate Your Happiness. Even if we master all the tools discussed here, we will still run into toxic people from time to time, but if we are mentally strong, such events will not ruin our day. It is when we happen upon a toxic person and the interaction invades our thoughts and poisons our potential happiness that the toxic person has won. We need instead to not be dependent upon what others say or think about us; if we do, we hand over our happiness to them as well. If you truly believe you are doing what is best for you and no one is being harmed, then revel in your strength to follow your path, and do not be deterred by those who always see obstacles.

Limit Interaction. Once you have determined that a person is not someone you wish to continue a relationship with (though you may see them from time to time or even regularly, such as at the workplace), make the conscious decision to limit spending time with them. Politely decline their invitations, and eventually they will no longer continue to ask; elect to work with people who add value to any collaboration, and use the most powerful one-word sentence when it comes to setting boundaries: "No." Do not waiver. Refrain from being nice and putting yourself in a position that leaves you drained or disrespected.

Set Boundaries Preemptively. It has been said that we teach people how to treat us. In other words, when we initially meet someone, our self-respect is either clear, absent, or somewhere in between. A respectful person would not take advantage of another's lack of self-respect, but a toxic person will determine rather quickly whether someone can be messed with. When we set clear boundaries for ourselves, determining what we need in our lives to thrive and what we cannot tolerate, we are showing ourselves self-respect. When someone crosses a boundary, perhaps our first response is simply to speak up; if we do not, it may be assumed that the behavior was okay. If the boundary is crossed again, we must be strong and stand up firmly, perhaps even walking away entirely. Setting boundaries teaches others how to treat us.

Shift Your Thoughts about Them. Marianne Williamson shared with Oprah Winfrey a few years ago an intriguing idea about how to deal with people who have betrayed you. And without question, someone who betrays you, promises their loyalty until it is inconvenient for them, and destroys your trust is a toxic person, as is someone who hurts you. Williamson suggests that you stop spending time and energy being angry and instead pray for them and their happiness. Initially, that sounds absurd, and Oprah was shocked as well until Williamson explained. The purpose in praying (or meditating, whichever works best for you) is to shift your mind and actually has nothing to do with the other person. She states that one of two things will happen: Either the person will change or the person praying eventually will not care anymore. Either way, you win.

Master Your Emotions. One of the destructive aspects of a toxic person is that they seem to masterfully know how to push our emotional buttons. They know our Achilles' heel, our sacred cows, and will attack them to gain control. How? We lose control when we allow our emotions to dominate our actions. Rather than allowing our emotions to drive our actions, we can feel angry, hurt, and betrayed, then go on to recognize how and why we are feeling. And sooner rather than later, we need to take the reins and think rationally: What is the best way to act in the situation to reach the best outcome? When you can master your emotions, no one can have control over you. Chapter eight provides detailed guidance on this key strength.

Do Not Get into the Arena with Them. Perhaps the first time you engage with someone you now define as toxic, you have no idea. In fact, you approach them as you approach anyone, politely, with a friendly smile and a curiosity to get to know them. However, you may soon realize the person does not behave logically (for reasons you should not try to deduce, as it will waste your energy) and any commonsense reasoning is falling on deaf ears. Walk away. Do not try to reason with them. Do not try to win the battle, because it is a war you will never win. This is hard to do because you do not want to assume or jump to conclusions, but with time and experience, you will be able to ascertain that, every once in a while, there will be people you must not engage with. Keep Mark Twain's words of advice in mind, and you will be just fine, "Never argue with stupid people. They will drag you down to their level and then beat you with experience."

Learn and Do Not Repeat. Often toxic people enter our lives to expose something within us that needs to improve or be repaired. Rather than dwell on the situation or the person, take a moment and ask, What can I learn? How could I have handled the situation better or avoided it altogether? Often there is a lesson waiting to be discovered. The simple saying "Forgive, but don't forget" applies to toxic people. Forgiving is good for your mental health, but forgetting can expose you to more hurt down the road.

Gain Perspective. While whining about a situation or person that is causing you angst is not productive, it is a good idea to share your experience with someone in order to see it from a different perspective. Perhaps you were wrong and they are not toxic at all. Or perhaps, while yes, they are toxic, you could have handled the situation better. By gaining a wider perspective, you are attempting to learn a larger lesson so that the lesson will not keep repeating itself.

Solve and Move Forward. In order to successfully handle toxic people, focus on the solution, not the problem. Remember, most likely you are not going to change them or even reason with them, but you can decide how you will change or improve to better handle future interactions. Once you have a plan in place, put it into practice, and devote your energies to more fruitful projects, people, and experiences. In other words, dwelling on a tainted relationship is wasted energy.

Toxicity robs us of our joy, reduces our creative energies, and depletes our ability to reach our full potential. We cannot control everything in our lives, but we can control much more than we realize. When you use these tools, you will begin to find more energy, feel less stress, and live a more fulfilling life. Such a practice is a conscious effort. It is by living consciously that we know how to navigate situations and people, and how to make the most of those we enjoy having in our lives.

The Gifts of a Healthy Neighborhood

It was July 2012, and I was visiting London for the first time. I had the opportunity, for a week, to call a multi-million-dollar flat in the Maida

Vale neighborhood home; a friend of a friend had offered a spare bedroom during the Olympics. Complete with tall windows that overlooked a tranquil communal garden, it tempered the urban hustle and bustle with an escape to the garden each day, a balance that heightened my level of appreciation for a city that is now near the top of my list of favorite places to visit.

Initially we may not know why we are drawn to a particular community, but it is important to understand the components that enable it to thrive. It is also important to look behind the curtain and explore how the machinery works, so to speak, to see if you indeed are part of something you can be proud of.

Ultimately, as with Mr. Rogers on PBS, a healthy neighborhood involves a sincere kindness. You find yourself taking deep breaths of contentment, laughing and playing, while tending to what you care about. There are times to rise up and organize, there are times to have conversations that may be uncomfortable, but when we feel a connection and have a common thread with our neighbors and with the people we have welcomed into our most intimate lives, those conversations, when handled well, can lead to tremendous growth.

Neighbors: Dos & Don'ts

Keep the golden rule in mind: Be the neighbor you would want to live next to.

Do:

- Introduce yourself when you or someone else is new in the neighborhood.
- Be observant and respectful of your neighbors' lifestyles.
- Be cognizant of shared walls and reducing noise by placing rugs or moving entertainment systems.
- Pick up after your dog, and control your pets' behavior.
- Engage in good parking etiquette.
- If neighbors are traveling, return their trash and recycling bins to their property and off the street. Tuck their newspapers out of sight so it is not obvious they are gone.
- Keep an overall eye out without being too nosy. If a stranger is nosing around while your neighbors are gone, speak to the individual or call local authorities.
- Keep your noise levels low.

- If you are planning a soirée, yard sale, or anything involving traffic and noise, inform your neighbors and invite them to join, if that makes sense.
- Acknowledge the holiday season by either dropping a holiday card in their mailbox or homemade goodies on their doorstep.
- Keep your yard, driveway, and front door welcoming and clean. The value of your home increases if the entire neighborhood is cared for.

Don't:

- Get too close too fast.
- Be too nosy.
- Ask for too many favors or ask a neighbor to do something you would not want to be asked to do.
- Date your neighbor.
- Ignore neighbors entirely, even if you do want your privacy. Acknowledge them, at a minimum, with a nod of the head or a wave.

The Strength of Any Community Begins with Each of Us

Most of us meet many individuals throughout a given day or week — people we live next to, are introduced to and shake hands with, work with, have coffee with — and our connection with each person is unique. With each encounter, we should work to understand how our role, our mannerisms, our open-mindedness, and our decorum can play a role in strengthening or weakening relationships with those we work with, live in a neighborhood with, make a home with. When we are thoughtful and purposeful, we can be part of the foundation of the community we wish to be a part of.

Spread what you wish to see more of, model what you seek, and be cognizant of the journey each individual is doing their best to navigate. In so doing, we all grow rather than constrict, and growth is what is necessary to not only survive but thrive individually and as a community.

CHAPTER SIX

Money Matters: Masterminding Your Financial Security

The reason I have been able to be so financially successful is my focus has never, ever for one minute been about money.
— Oprah Winfrey

oney. Some of us love it, some of us loathe it, and all of us need it in some capacity to live our lives. I begin with Oprah Winfrey's quote because sustained financial success comes from keeping your eye on a bigger prize — pursuing a passion, giving the world what only you can uniquely bring to it, wholeheartedly believing in what you are doing. However, if you ignore money and the value of it in your life, you harm yourself, those you love, and the society you live in. Which leads me to the importance of knowing your value.

Talk show host Mika Brzezinski puts it this way: "It doesn't matter if they like you. They need to respect you. They need to show that respect for you in your paycheck. And that needs to be okay." Just as money has value — it provides us with shelter, food, comfort, education, protection — so too must we understand our value.

Living to make ever-increasing amounts of money can become a destructive cycle, but so too can undervaluing what you bring to the world. Again, knowing yourself is crucial — your skills and abilities, the time you have invested, your achievements and experience — but you may not be comfortable communicating that to those who write your paycheck. You must learn to communicate and clearly assert your value, particularly if you are being undervalued.

Whenever we recognize that there is a disparity in what we are paid and speak up, we gradually reduce the likelihood that it will happen to someone after us. Communicating unapologetically but with tact and clarity will aid in our efforts. There is only so much we can control, and the only entity we have full control over is ourselves, which is why we must value ourselves — even if it means putting our foot down and saying no, I will leave if you do not rectify this situation. Refuse to be undervalued and you will help not only yourself but others to be paid fairly.

Nine Ways Money Can Buy Happiness

Money, while it can't always buy happiness, is an important means to achieving higher living standards.
— Fortune magazine (May 1, 2013)

As a high school student, I can remember doodling the phrase "Be Happy" on my worn-out homework folders whenever I had free time and was lost in thought. Whether that was due to the success of Bobby McFerrin's song "Don't Worry, Be Happy" or my innate desire to seek a life of bliss, I will never know. Regardless, as humans, when we make decisions, at the core of our motivation is usually a desire to attain happiness.

In other words, we seek a sense of living that is not overrun by fear, pain, and loss, but rather adoration, appreciation, and affection.

The notion that more income does not increase one's happiness (stated in 1974 as the Easterlin paradox) was accepted and perpetuated in the clichéd maxim "Money can't buy you happiness." However, it is a maxim without teeth — in other words, actual data. In an effort to see if it did indeed have substance, a 2013 study from the Brookings Institution proved the opposite: More money does, in fact, increase one's level of happiness.

But before you see this as an excuse to work harder and longer hours to bring in more money, the evidence must be qualified. Simply having more money does not necessarily make you happier; it is how you spend it that equates to more happiness. Upon completing Elizabeth Dunn and Michael Norton's 2012 book *Happy Money: The Science of Smarter Spending*, I was reassured that if managed wisely, the money I have worked so hard for can indeed enhance the quality of my life. The ideas below are a combination of research-based findings from the book as well as a few discoveries of my own.

Money Can Buy Time. Time is definite and stubborn. There is only so much of it, and no matter how long we complain about not having enough, the universe will never give us a twenty-five-hour day. How does one buy time? After seven years, I finally installed an automatic sprinkler system in my yard in eastern Oregon. I cannot fully express how elated I was to have time on the weekends and during vacations to spend as I pleased, without my plans revolving around how I would get my yard watered. You might hire a house cleaner so you can spend more time with your family or purchase plane tickets in order to not have to drive and to enjoy more time at your destination. When you use your money to get more time to enjoy what you love to do, your happiness is increased.

Money Can Buy Experiences. Whenever the holidays or birthdays roll around, I advocate for family and friends to spend their money, if they wish to give gifts, on time together, doing things that create memories, rather than on another "thing" that brings immediate pleasure that quickly dissipates. Consider this approach even when you are planning how you will spend money on yourself. Choosing to spend it on a class, a tour, or an event rather than on another item of clothing, gadget, or souvenir creates an opportunity for connection, growth, and fulfillment.

Money Can Buy Quality. A large part of the mission of *TSLL* blog is the idea that quality surpasses quantity on the path to creating a life of contentment and fulfillment. Whether it reduces clutter, saves money in the long run, or allows for dependable performance, you have confidence that the car, tool, or item of clothing will do what it is supposed to do. In other words, it will perform at the expected level for a reasonable period of time, reduce your frustration, and keep the money that would have been spent on replacements in your pocket.

Money Can Buy Knowledge. Similar to buying experiences, buying knowledge — whether you find it in a book, in a classroom, or on a vacation to a travel destination — greatly enhances the quality of your life. When you have knowledge, you make better decisions, which reduce stress and allow you to be healthier and enjoy life more fully.

Money Lets You Invest in Yourself and Others. Having more money allows you to invest it for your retirement or place it in a savings account in case of emergencies. Knowing your financial future is taken care of allows you to enjoy your present life, as well as a better night's sleep, which is needed to maintain good health. Also, whether you donate to a favorite charity, create a scholarship fund for a deserving graduate, or save for your children's future, knowing you are helping someone attain their own happiness is a tremendous happiness booster.

Money Can Bring People Together. Creating healthy and rewarding connections with others is a fantastic way to boost your health and happiness. We all have our preferences for the social scenarios that bring us the most joy, but whenever you spend your money organizing a dinner party, a special date night, or a grand gathering of friends or family, these shared memories and moments allow happiness to increase for the host as well as the guests.

Money Can Help Secure Good Health. When you can purchase quality food (not processed, which is typically cheaper), have access to clean water, the means to buy something as simple as sunscreen or as significant as health care, you improve the quality of your life, which reduces your worries and ultimately increases your happiness and longevity.

Money Lets You Buy Now, Enjoy Later. Buying on credit — purchase now, pay later — can decrease long-term happiness, while the reverse can increase it. Buying now, knowing that what you have purchased is paid for in full and looking forward to its benefits, can increase your happiness. For example, if you make travel plans — airfare and accommodations — in advance and pay for the big-ticket items upfront, the trip is guaranteed, and you can spend the time in the interim dreaming and anticipating all that is to come.

By making wise decisions about how we spend our money, we can directly affect how happy our lives are. I recommend reading *Happy Money* for specific examples and the evidence for the authors' findings.

Money: How to Know If You Have Enough

Enough is the quality of having everything you need and want but nothing in excess, nothing that burdens you.
— Vicki Robin, *Your Money or Your Life*

While there is not a magic number that equates to having enough money, it may seem impossible at first to answer the question of how much is sufficient. However, there are fundamental questions to ask yourself and habits to bring into your daily living that will help you determine a number that is right for you.

Have You Let Go of Comparisons? Now, more than ever, as we live in a world where lives are displayed in great detail on social media, we need to refrain from comparing ourselves to others. A dependable way to stop comparing is to become clear about your life's path — what excites you, what you want to improve upon —and create a vision for your life. Often in my own past, if I found myself making comparisons with others, it was, I realized later, because they were striving toward something — an experience, a way of living — that I was eager to try myself but felt unable to attempt. When I finally found the courage to do what I desired, to place my toes over the edge and sometimes even leap, I found that I was not interested in comparing, and instead applauded others and then went about my journey.

Have You Eliminated Debt? Debt is a broad term. Many of us, if we own a house, will have a mortgage, and business debt may be necessary at times. However, your personal credit card debt should be at zero. If you can look at the balances on your bills and know you can pay them in full each month without denting your monthly living budget, your finances are in great order.

Do You Live within Your Means? A quote from Suze Orman has become part of my approach to money: "The nicest thing you can say about a woman is that she lives well, and she lives below her means." Our means shift, change, and hopefully grow from year to year. Conducting a financial check-in each year is a great way to see if you are spending too much or not enough in order to live the life you want.
Do You Meet or Exceed Your Monthly Savings Goal? Currently I am saving for a down payment, and with this goal in mind, I have designated that a certain part of my monthly income will be put into my

money market account. When I hit my target amount, I will be doing a little dance.

Are You Spending Wisely? Take a moment and compare your current spending habits with your habits from five years ago. Are you spending more? Less? More wisely? Staying within your budget? Reflecting regularly will help you to spend consciously. If you see that your spending has increased, ask yourself why. Then ask yourself, is it necessary? Am I able to spend more? Living well is not a bad thing to do. The key is to make sure you can afford it.

Do You Pay Proper Attention to Retirement Savings? While there is no magic formula for retirement savings, the one thing that will not work is doing nothing. The first thing is to begin now, if you have not already. Then sit down and examine how much you will need to retire so that you can set a goal and create a plan to make it happen. I have shared many financial and retirement savings posts in *TSLL* "Money" archives.

Do You Adhere to a Monthly Budget? A sensible budget supports the life you want to build and live. Massachusetts senator and former Harvard bankruptcy law professor Elizabeth Warren suggests organizing one's monthly budget around these percentages: "Spend 50 percent on needs, 30 percent on wants, and 20 percent on savings." You may have to dip into your wants for your needs from time to time, depending on where you live and during different periods, but saving 15 to 20 percent for retirement, emergencies, dreams, and vacations is a must for peace of mind and the ability to respond to life's unexpected hurdles and adventures. Similarly, keep your housing payment (rent or mortgage) to 33 percent.

It has been suggested that we have a tendency to unconsciously move away from achieving "enough" rather than toward it (Tim Maurer, *Simple Money*). I would argue that being financially comfortable is a choice, based on our appreciation for what it can mean.

Why Not . . . Be Attractive to Wealth?

If we believe we are incapable of achieving financial success, we are quickly steering ourselves down the path of sabotage. If, on the other hand, we educate ourselves about the ways money is transferred, accrues in value, and functions in our lives, we begin to navigate a life that is open to more financial prosperity.

T. Harv Eker's best-selling book *Secrets of the Millionaire Mind* enumerates the many ways we train our minds to either acquire or avoid wealth. As I thought about the book's ideas, I observed many parallels to living a conscious life in order to live the life of our dreams. Both require intention, education, dedication, and a mastering of our minds. Once we realize that we are the masters of our future, it is up to us to figure out what we want so that we can get about the business of attaining our goals. How do we do that?

Master What You Fear. Rather than letting fear stop you — I don't know if I can handle the responsibility that comes with the promotion; investing in the stock market makes me nervous; investing in my education may not pay off; what about paying back the loans? — see fear as an opportunity to gain more knowledge. The power of fear is that it seeks to control you. You need to take back the power and educate yourself, regaining your power because you know how to navigate past fear.

Welcome Hard Work. It will result in many riches. Rather than taking the route that is easy and convenient, choose to understand what you desire, what will make you happy, what will create a better life for you and your family and improve the world at large.

Train, Manage, and Master Your Thoughts. First, come to understand where your mind wanders to when it is left to its own devices. Then understand why it travels to unhelpful destinations. Often the culprit is fear spawned from lack of knowledge. Replace any unhelpful, debilitating thoughts with helpful, supportive positive mantras. Chapter eight devotes a section to this topic.

Let Your Money Work for You. You will have to work very hard to end up in a place where you can afford to let your money work for you, but aim for that goal. That initial front-end loading will be the difference. How can your money work for you? Through investments, freed-up time to focus on important business matters and projects, owning property, licensing your ideas, earning royalties, etc.

Become Savvy with Your Money. Start small and create a budget on an Excel spreadsheet; track where your money goes, refuse to overspend, and never make a purchase without being certain you need it and can afford it. When you have control of your spending, you can pay off debt, and then begin investing and taking risks with your money wisely. Either you control your money, or it will control you.

Choose Your Company Wisely. The people you spend time with have an indirect effect on how you view money, how you spend money, and your overall motivation to achieve the success you wish. Spend time with those who respect themselves and their dreams and who wish to continually gain knowledge about life. Spend time with people who inspire you, motivate you, and are positive influences.

Seek What Makes You Happy. If you are not happy without money, you are far less likely to be happy with it. Ultimately, money provides an opportunity for you to bring amazing experiences into your life, to support charities and institutions that you want to help grow and flourish, but simply earning money to show how worthy you are is the wrong motivator to achieve true financial success and wealth. Money will make you more of what you already are — hopeful or cynical, determined or defeated, etc.

View Obstacles as Opportunities. Every barrier comes with a lesson attached. Did your first credit card become a crutch? Use that as a lesson about how to handle debt properly. Did you become impatient and buy a hot stock only to realize you should have done more research? No mistake is a waste of time if you learn the lesson it is trying to teach.

Adopt an Attitude of Appreciation. Skip the resentment. So what if someone else makes more money than you do and is doing well? Rather than scoff at people who have done well and assume the worst about their character or their means of acquiring success, choose to learn from them. While certainly some excessively rich people came by their money questionably, there are far more people who earned it fair and square. Shift your attitude, and gather as much knowledge as you can; it is yours to gain or cast aside.

Provide Something of Value. Whether it is a particular skill, your compassion, your patience, or your expertise on a particular topic, so long as you can provide something that is helpful to others, you will be successful. Come to understand your strengths, continue to work at them and improve them, and they may just be your path to success and financial wealth.

Accept the Fact That You Create Your Destiny. The moment you realize that you really do hold the reins to your success or defeat is the moment, if you are like me, when you ignore the naysayers, put your nose to the grindstone, and work like you have never worked before.

Money is simply energy, and when you realize that you are either open to this energy or closed off to it, you realize you have tremendous power in creating the life you have imagined. Will it be easy? Heck no! Will it be worth it? If the path you choose leads to a life of fulfillment and remains in tune with your values and priorities, it will be more amazing than you can imagine.

Believe it or not, there is such a thing as magnetic energy when it comes to attracting wealth. Jean Chatzky's book *The Difference: How Anyone Can Prosper in Even the Toughest Times* says that a person's ability to be appreciative and grateful for what they already have is essential to attracting more of what they desire. Simply put, no matter how little or how much you have in the bank, it is vital to realize that you are responsible for discovering your own contentment. In order to achieve that, you must recognize the abundance you already have around you. After all, if you are not satisfied now, you will never be satisfied when you get more because you will not have learned the gift of being grateful. How does one acquire this magnetic chemistry? Here is what Chatzky suggests:

Wear Rosier Glasses. See things more optimistically. Eliminate the cynicism, and elect to see how abundantly rich you truly are — not necessarily always in cash value, but in your relationships, lifestyle, and community. Appreciating what you have instead of focusing on what you lack creates a tremendous positive change.

Stop Comparing Yourself to Others. When you value who you are and the talents and gifts you have to offer, you are again focusing on your self-worth. If you constantly belittle yourself for not being like the Joneses or a beautiful model on the cover of a magazine, you will always feel as though you are lacking. Change what you focus on and your positive energy will multiply.

Use Visual Cues. Put yourself on the offensive by framing your favorite inspiring quote and hanging it above your desk; write it in your planner and put it on your phone's screen saver, and use it to check in with yourself when you are in doubt.

Be There for Someone Else. Choose to pay it forward by helping someone who is not expecting your aid. It may be someone you know, it may not be, but when you do this, you are giving of yourself and your good fortune to someone else who could benefit from your time and energy. It does not have to be a grand, expensive gesture. In fact, it does not need to cost any money; it can be a simple thirty-minute visit with a senior citizen who enjoys your conversation. Whatever you do, remember to do it without wanting anything in return. Truly wealthy people realize how fortunate they are and want to give back when they can simply because they can.

Mastering Your Money

If money be not thy servant, it will be thy master. The covetous man cannot so properly be said to possess wealth, as that may be said to possess him.
— Francis Bacon

Whatever your goals are for creating your simply luxurious life, the good news when it comes to mastering your finances, as Jean Chatzky reminds us in *The Difference*, is that you do not need to be born rich, attend an Ivy League college, receive a windfall of money out of the blue, catch a lucky break, or bring home a six-figure salary. The key to building a strong foundation — one that will provide sturdy roots from which you can stretch, bend, and try new things, resting assured that you will always be safe and secure — is mastering your money.

Some people hear the word *money* and cringe; others hear it and think of opportunity. Simply being flush with money and living a lavish lifestyle does not guarantee you will be happy. Let's put money into the context of our everyday lives. In order to thrive in any environment, we must first come to understand how money functions in our lives and, more importantly, in the world we live in. Money is a source of energy reflecting the value of a thing you want to buy. When you transfer money to another individual, they are gaining more energy (money). You want enough energy not only to survive but to thrive. Refusing to let money master you will allow you to sleep soundly, knowing your financial house is in order, so that you can go about living the life of your dreams.

Below are a dozen steps for mastering your money so that you can enjoy the process and the value that money can bring into your life if you handle it well. Rather than dreading dealing with your money every month, create a process in which you celebrate your life and become more engaged with your money, mastering it, and using that energy to propel you forward to pursue your dreams.

Set Up a Simple Monthly Budget

Create a "money date" with yourself each month. Track your spending, pay bills, and plan for the month ahead. Perhaps you already have a program to track your finances, but if you want a simple budget template, go to *TSLL*'s "Simple Budget Template" in the archived Money posts and print a free copy.

Once you know where your money is going, you can make a plan tailored to what you think your needs and wants actually are. In order to accurately determine what is a need (necessary) and what is a want (discretionary), go through your past month's bank statement and put each expenditure in one of those two categories. The goal is to build your knowledge about where your money is going. If you are sharing a budget with a roommate or significant other, all parties should go through this process. An itemized monthly budget needs to be as simple as necessary for your needs. By keeping it simple, you will be less likely to put off dealing with it and will not dread it.

The last step in creating a budget is making a monthly or bi-monthly date with yourself to sit down and work through the numbers. Block out this time as you would for an appointment with your doctor; it is that important. Once you know where your money is going and how much you have, be honest with yourself about where you can cut some corners: Program your thermostat, bundle utilities, check your phone's data plan, reduce the number of television channels you need (or cut the cord and use Netflix, Amazon, Hulu, Acorn, BritBox, etc.), understand how retailers promote impulse buying, purchase a Smart Strip and reduce the energy vampires in your home, and, at the supermarket, look for the unit price to get the most for your money.

Create a Plan to Pay Off Debt

There are different types of debt — good (education, mortgage, business loan) and bad (credit card, etc.). Either way, create a plan for eliminating it, and then stick to it. Determine the interest rate on each debt, pay off the card with the highest interest rate first (while paying the minimum on the others), transfer balances when you can, and negotiate lower rates if possible. See my first book and *TSLL* blog for more details.

Sleep on It Before You Splurge

Any time you are about to make a large purchase or investment — car, wardrobe item, home, business, etc. — do your stress level a favor and sleep on it. The excitement in the moment when the beautiful new designer coat is before you, begging to be taken back to your closet, is hard to walk away from, but you will feel far better when you know you have decided with a clear mind rather than letting your emotions determine your decision.

Save Regularly

In *Smart Women Finish Rich: 9 Steps to Achieving Financial Security and Funding Your Dreams*, David Bach describes three baskets of savings: retirement, emergency, and dreams. I have found this scheme to be greatly beneficial; it provides peace of mind for the future and a sound night's sleep, as I am prepared for the unknown and excited as I plan for dream vacations and expenditures. Fifteen to 20 percent of our monthly budget should be divided into these three baskets. While retirement should receive the largest chunk (10–15 percent), make sure to contribute to the other two baskets as well. Each month, put a certain amount of money, no matter how small, into each account.

Invest Regularly and Keep It Simple

This is the best thing you can do to create peace of mind. As you begin to save regularly, invest in more than a savings account in order to accrue interest that will compound favorably over time. Whether you choose a 401K, a 403B, a Roth IRA, a SEP, specific stocks, or bonds, keep it simple and do it regularly, as in each month. Tuck away $50 as you get your feet wet, and increase the amount as you feel comfortable. The key to making money is to understand why you are investing, be consistent, and remain knowledgeable about where your money is going.

Monitor Your Money

Track each expense, come to understand where your money goes, and assess whether you are spending it wisely. Monitoring your spending also allows you to catch any nefarious behavior and become aware quickly if someone has hacked your account.

Become Financially Savvy

Continue reading, learning, and rereading books, blogs, and magazines that deal with money and how to handle it. I reread Jean Chatzky's book *The Difference* simply because every couple of years I am in a different financial place and will grab on to other bits of the wisdom she shares. Here are a few other financial books I recommend: *Live, Spend, Save, Repeat*, by Kim Anderson; *Simple Money*, by Tim Maurer; *The Automatic Millionaire*, by David Bach; *The Intelligent Investor*, by Benjamin Graham; and *The Law of Divine Compensation*, by Marianne Williamson.

Be Willing to Take Risks

While being in the black (having no debt) is a wonderful goal, there may be times when you should invest, for example, in a business venture or home remodeling. While we will never know with 100 percent certainty if something will work out, of the 5 percent of Americans who are deemed millionaires or more, 85 percent are self-made. In other words, they invested in themselves. Dare to dream, do your homework, and work your tail off. Life has a funny way of rewarding this winning combination.

Evaluate Past Failures and Successes

Often the most valuable lessons are the ones we learn firsthand, but that does not mean we have to continue to make the same mistakes. The goal is to learn from the ignorance we once had and turn it into gold. By evaluating what worked, what did not, what our weaknesses are, and when our intuition has paid off, we will be better able to make the best financial decisions as we move forward.

Create a Lifestyle That Does Not Drain Your Budget

As you reorganize your budget so that you are living below your means, paying off and staying out of debt, and allowing yourself to sleep soundly at night, you may realize your lifestyle has to change. Downsize: Limit your shopping, purchase quality when you have saved up, but bring fewer items into your life to take care of. Find a job closer to home. Reduce your discretionary spending.

Use Cash

Not only is it a good idea to have cash in your wallet and to use only cash when you are out and about; you should also have cash available for emergencies. Have an emergency fund that is accessible within one to three days so that if you need extra money for an unexpected but necessary expense, you have it. The goal is to refrain from living paycheck to paycheck. Once you get into the habit of saving regularly, you will create a cushion of savings and cash. You can sleep soundly knowing that if an emergency hits, you will be able to deal with it without destroying your budget.

Achieve Credit Card Mastery

A credit card is not inherently bad, but it can easily become a monster. But so long as we understand the power of a credit card, we can master it. It can build your credit score; it allows wiggle room for big-ticket items so long as you can pay it off in full each month; and many cards have a rewards program offering discounts on purchases and travel. I do not suggest getting rid of credit cards altogether unless you absolutely cannot be trusted with them, but limiting the number of cards you have is a wise decision. Be savvy about finding the best rate and understanding the rewards and benefits and determining what works best for your use of the card.

Everyone's financial path is different, and just because someone makes more does not mean they have a better handle on their finances. Whatever your income, master the money you have worked so hard to earn. You will feel richer and more attractive to wealth. Once you become the master of your money, you are dictating the terms on which your life will move forward. The more you take control of what is in your power, the more successful you will be.

Try One Week of No Spending Each Month

In 2011, I posed a challenge of sorts not only to readers, but also to myself. And this monthly ritual that I brought into my life has been worth its weight in gold. What is this challenge? The refusal to spend money for one entire week each month.

You may be thinking, How is that possible? What about emergencies? What about _____? What about _____? Sometimes my attempt at not spending for an entire week can be thwarted by a must-have purchase for dog care or gas or something that is a necessity (steel-cut oats, for example, a breakfast must-have). However, even when that happens, the week is not a loss; it still saves me from spending money. Not spending for an entire week has consistently been a benefit to my budget and overall to my peace of mind and contentment.

The degree of your success will be determined almost entirely by planning. You must be very clear about what you need: food, supplies, appointments, prescriptions, etc. Beyond the immediate savings, your planning helps you to become clear about how you are living and to determine if your money is supporting something that does not fit with the life you want. This simple monthly ritual can save you money not only in the short term, but in the long term as well.

Have a Well-Stocked *Épicerie*. There are essentials that are needed for most meals. While *épicerie* translates literally as "grocery," I use it for the collection of the items in your pantry, cupboards, and refrigerator that should always be stocked (they are listed in chapter twelve). These items are not the fresh food you pick up weekly, so you can stock up ahead of time. Knowing your pantry is properly stocked helps you stick to the no-spending approach, as you are less tempted to pick up takeout when you know you can cook your favorite meals at home.

Pick the Best Week. The week does not need to start on Monday or end on the weekend; it can be any seven days in a row that works best with your schedule. While I mentioned in 2011 that the second and third weeks work best for me, I have since changed my preference. I typically balance my monthly budget (pay my bills, deposit my savings, etc.) on the last day of the month. This allows a fresh start on day one (my day one is the first of the month, but everyone's first of the month will be unique based on when paychecks are distributed). So now I have chosen the first week of the month to be my no-spending week. Motivation is high — my paycheck has just come in, and much of it must be paid out for bills. Wanting to keep as much as I can in my accounts motivates me to not spend. I know I have money for the rest of the month, so I do not feel truly deprived. My spending month is now three weeks rather than four, which makes it feel as though my money is worth more. Sometimes, the first of the week will not work due to appointments, dates, visiting guests, travel plans, etc., but overall this week has worked very well for me.

Buy Prepaid Cards. What about my regular stop at the café? My weekly yoga class? Won't this monthly ritual make me antisocial? Absolutely not. Look into prepaying or buying a card at your favorite coffee shop and placing a set amount on it for each month. You can do the same thing with your weekly fitness classes.

Stick to a Capsule Menu. While keeping your *épicerie* well-stocked is key, so too is having the fresh ingredients on hand to make the dishes and meals you love. As a weekly ritual, I go to the markets once, sometimes twice a week (for fresh produce and seafood) and pick up these ingredients. My capsule menu approach (see chapter twelve) not only helps me buy within my budget, but also allows me to organize my meals so that I use the same ingredients multiple times, but in different ways throughout the week. For example, chicken is often on my capsule menu grocery list, as I can pan-fry and slice it to top my vinaigrette-dressed spinach salad for lunch, and I can make it the main entrée in a dinner of Parmesan chicken with a side of roasted vegetables and black rice.

Get Creative with Entertainment. Pull out Scrabble, clear the table after dinner, pour some wine, and settle in as you display your vocabulary prowess. Or take an evening hike to watch the sunset. Watch your favorite classic film. Or maybe this one week of the month is a time to complete some household chores or dive into projects you have been waiting to find time to do. The key is to find hobbies and take pleasure in things that do not cost a dime.

Visit the Library. Speaking of simple pleasures, dive into reading . . . for free. Visit your local library. If you have an Amazon Prime account, you have access to one free e-book download a month.

Change Your Perspective on Living Well. The beautiful gift you can give yourself by not spending for one week is the gift of being less busy. If you have to watch your gas level, if you are not ordering takeout and are not running to the market every night, you can be more present and less hurried. You can dive into a conversation, pull out a book you have been wanting to read, or simply sit on the back porch with a cup of coffee, put your feet up, and watch the birds twitter away in the yard. Before long, you may look forward to this week each month; it is a respite that gives you even more time to breathe, relax, and appreciate the life you have cultivated.

Place a Carrot on a Stick. As you begin to put this monthly ritual in place, give yourself some extra motivation. Nothing big or extravagant, but something that will motivate you so that you can enjoy a reward the morning of day eight. Recently I was enjoying an afternoon relaxing with my dogs and observing how many birds were in my backyard. At that moment, I could have kicked myself for not having a bird feeder. I promised myself that I could go pick one out if I made it through the no-spending week. Much like a kid waiting for her birthday to arrive, I was now even more okay with my week of no spending. I am happy to report that I have been giddily enjoying the lovely new birds that are visiting my yard.

Choosing to not open your wallet for one week is a small way to increase control of your spending, no matter how much control you already have. It allows you to assess the conscious spending you do and recognize unconscious spending that needs to be curtailed. The funny thing I have also discovered is that when the second week of the month begins, I am more reluctant to pull out my debit card and to hand over my cash. While this reluctance subsides as the month goes on, when the first of the month rolls around again, it is like a tightened rubber band, pulling me back in and reminding me to keep my spending in check. And remember, if you have to run to the store for a basic food item, let yourself do it and know that you are still doing yourself a great service. The goal is to reduce unnecessary spending, not deprive yourself.

Acting Rich vs. Being Rich

More people look richer than they really are, and the really rich often don't look anything like what we think they should look like.
— Thomas J. Stanley

Perception versus reality. The primary goal of someone working in public relations is to present an exterior that will prompt a desired result: sales, confidence, change, movement, acceptance, etc. But as those who have been behind the scenes know, just because there is an image of what "rich" looks like does not mean it is so. The multi-million-dollar contracts signed by athletes and the lavish homes owned by starlets do not reflect what being financially rich actually is.

Thomas J. Stanley, in his 2009 book *Stop Acting Rich: And Start Living Like a Real Millionaire*, enumerates the many ways those who desire to be rich are misled to believe what rich actually is: living in an expensive, well-located, spacious home, owning a Rolex, driving a BMW, enjoying a well-stocked wine cellar, wearing top designer clothing, owning a vacation home, employing hired help. In reality, those who are rich generally do not conform with that list. Stanley says that the image of "rich" presented by the media, advertisers, and celebrities misrepresents the truth.

What is the true definition of rich? The U.S. Census Bureau quantifies "wealthy" as 30 times the median net worth of U.S. households, which Credit Suisse Global Wealth reported in 2014 to be $44,900 per adult; based on this math, with all assets considered, along with annual income, one would have to have a net worth of $1,347,000 to be considered "rich." The Economic Policy Institute reported in 2016 that to be in the 1 percent in America in terms of annual household income, "a family needs an income of $389,436." The true definition of being rich is not what is revealed externally, but rather the assets one has earned. Needing to prove to the world that we are rich is akin to Margaret Thatcher's aphorism about being powerful: "Power is like being a lady . . . if you have to tell people you are, you aren't."

Owning a house is often described as the only way to become financially secure, but as we saw in the Great Recession, many took a financial face-plant because of their real estate choices. This is not to say real estate is a bad financial decision. In fact, it is usually a very good idea in the long run, but the key is to understand that there are many routes to attaining a secure financial life.

Become Well Educated. According to Thomas Stanley, 90 percent of millionaires who were happy in their lives had graduated from college, 62 percent had advanced degrees, and only 19 percent were in the top 5 percent of their class. The key to making sound life decisions — not only in finance, but in general — is to become savvy about what you will be doing for your career, as that will be your foundation. Being at the top is not necessary, but it is clear that education makes a tremendous difference.

Have Patience. It takes time to accrue wealth. Stanley interviewed baby boomers in their mid-fifties who were millionaires. Many of them began investing in their mid-twenties, and it was evident that they did not achieve their wealth overnight; rather, they did it gradually over decades of smart decision making.

Make More Than You Spend. Another commonality was that millionaires lived in a smaller or less expensive house than they could afford and refrained from buying status symbol items such as vehicles, watches, and clothing.

Invest in Real Estate, but Purchase Less Than You Can Afford. Most millionaires bought their first house at age twenty-six; while they did not still live there, they tended to purchase less than what their income allows. Not only does this approach alleviate stress; it also frees up money to be invested elsewhere, such as in experiences that support personal growth.

Don't Live in the Most Expensive Neighborhood. While location is key in real estate, investing in a neighborhood purely to maintain appearances, regardless of how much it will cost, will do you no favors in the long run. In fact, Stanley found that most millionaires were better off than their neighbors.

Be Generous. Sixty percent of happy millionaires gave to charitable causes, while only 38 percent of unsatisfied millionaires did the same. Helping and giving when we can is easier when we make more than we spend; overall they leave us feeling more connected to our community and those we love.

Make Smart Purchases. Is wearing Manolo Blahniks off the table if we want to become rich? It depends. A frugal shopper who appreciates quality over quantity can purchase a pair of Manolos, perhaps in a consignment shop, and wear them for years. It is people who believe they must have designer everything and pay full price each time who are wasting their money. Part of the mission of living simply luxuriously is not to feel deprived, but instead to live intelligently. You know what you need and how much you can afford, and you are a savvy shopper.

Reconsider a Second Home or Extra Discretionary Anything. Stanley shares a long list of experiences and activities that deca-millionaires spend their money on versus buying a second home, a boat, and expensive watches, wines, cars, and the like. Here is just a taste: gardening, vacationing in Paris, visiting museums, attending Broadway plays, jogging, attending lectures, socializing with loved ones, raising money for charities, participating in civic activities, studying art, golfing — and this is just a start. In other words, as Stanley states,

166 | SHANNON ABLES

"You cannot be in two places at one time," so why spend your money unnecessarily on two mortgages or paying down debt you do not need to thrive?

Refuse to Fall Prey to the Newest Model. Whether it is the latest iPhone or the latest model car, new does not necessarily mean better. There is no need to invest every time a new version is introduced. Being financially secure and independent allows me to dictate my future. As much as I wish I could have been über financially secure when I was in my twenties, I have realized that it is a gradual process and the key is to make savvy decisions, take educated risks, and consult those who can educate us.

Why Not . . . Purchase Quality That Is Worth the High Price Tag?

Choosing quality over quantity plays a paramount role in our overall contentment. For instance, there was one item in my daily routine that was not performing, but I had not taken the time to investigate if I should invest in a higher-quality product and pay a significantly higher price. For years, I invested in quality conditioners, deep conditioners, and a well-trained stylist and colorist, but not in my shampoo. The extremely dry climate in Bend made me realize that I had to care for and protect my hair more consciously. So I began using a quality shampoo, and it was worth the higher price tag. That revelation made me ponder more broadly what else was worth the greater cost. Below is a list of items I think are worth the extra pennies.

Shampoo and Conditioner. Quality shampoo and conditioner are worth the purchase price if it is in your budget. I used an $8 shampoo for years, until my stylist informed me that the waxy build-up it causes and the false "silky finish" actually strips hair of its natural oils and dehydrates it. Cheaper options may contain some high-grade ingredients, but only in small amounts.

Bedroom Pillows. Not only should your bedroom beckon you to sleep, it should also enable you to sleep soundly and in deep comfort.

Essential Wardrobe Items. For years, *TSLL* blog has recommended building a capsule wardrobe created with ten to fifteen investment items for each season (fall and spring), as well as a cost-per-wear approach. Learn more in chapter eleven.

Shoes. Quality shoes last. They protect your feet and can look like new for years if properly cared for.

Cutlery. A good knife will save not only your fingers, but time, and your cooking experience will become far more enjoyable. Consider my recommendations in the *TSLL* "Kitchen" shop.

Bed Linens. We spend a third of our lives in bed, so quality sheets (French or Belgium linen or Egyptian cotton, minimum 400 thread count) are a necessity. Spending $50–$100 more will make a noticeable difference in the quality of your sleep, and quality sheets last for years.

Lingerie. A bra that fits well, is made of lace or silk so that it gently lays upon the body, and holds its shape and color is an investment you will be thrilled with.

A Non-Stop Flight. Unless your budget is very tight, a non-stop flight gives you time, ease, and comfort that is irreplaceable.

Fragrance. A quality fragrance from a reputable boutique or department store is worth the money. Discount shops use inferior ingredients that dilute the scent.

Electric Toothbrush. It provides a more thorough cleaning.

Face Creams. Professional-grade creams, oils, serums, etc. are worth the price if you can afford them. With higher-grade ingredients and far less water (check the ingredients), the results you seek for younger, brighter skin require some extra cash. When choosing, look at reviews and how long the product has been available.

Quality Cookware. Quality cookware — copper, Le Creuset, All-Clad, etc. — will entirely change your experience in the kitchen.

A Down Duvet. All I had to do was sleep under a quality down duvet at a top-tier hotel. The fill was higher, the warmth was immediate, and I did not need extra sheets and blankets. I am currently sleeping under one of my own and loving each night.

KitchenAid Mixer. All you will need is one for your entire life.

Concert Tickets. Listening in person to your favorite band or singer is worth the wait in line and the money. Purchasing front-row tickets or sitting in the VIP section is not necessary; just being present is something to splurge on.

The Theater. Each time I see a Broadway show or a play in the London theater district, time stops, and I am completely present.

Travel or Anything on Your Bucket List. Save up and do it. Study after study proves that enjoyable experiences have a huge influence on our overall happiness.

Smart shopping means knowing first what you can afford and then purchasing the best quality you can find.

Facing the Unavoidable: Taxes

Each year in late January or early February, I take a weekend day to organize my taxes. I try to remind myself of the many benefits I receive from investing in education, national parks, safe roads, protection, etc. Regardless of how tax season makes you feel, it is a task that cannot be avoided. Often, it can be a moment to celebrate if you are among the 52 percent of Americans who receive a refund instead of having to pay. Below, I have rounded up some tips that help keep me organized throughout the year so that January and February are a bit less stressful.

Keep a Tax Year File. At the beginning of each year, I create a file labeled "Taxes 2018" or whatever the coming year is. Whenever I have a check stub, business document, or important tax document, such as a 1099, 1098, W-2, or receipt from a charity, I file it. If you prefer to do away with all paper receipts, a free app called Expensify electronically captures the images and files.

Create a Separate Folder for Expenses. Be sure to save this file for seven years, in case you are audited.

Use the Tax Organizer from Your CPA. If you have an accountant, they will probably send you a tax organizer (worksheet) to gather all the necessary details prior to coming into their office.

Teachers and Students, Keep Track of Your Expenses. Most states have a maximum amount you can deduct for education expenses, union dues, etc.

Create a Checklist. Each January, as W-2 forms begin arriving, I make a list of all the items I expect to receive and the information I will need prior to scheduling my appointment with my CPA. Here is a list of things you may need:

- W-2s from your employers
- 1098 form (for mortgage interest)
- 1099-INT (for interest earned)
- 1099-DIV (for dividends you received)
- 1099-B forms (for transactions involving stocks, bonds, etc.)
- 1099-MISC forms (for any income from self-employment or to send to contractors you paid throughout the year)
- K-1 forms (if you have a partnership, small business, or trust)
- 1099-SSA (if you receive social security)

Deductions:

- Medical receipts
- Receipts from charitable donations
- Education receipts
- Moving expenses
- Mortgage interest
- Childcare costs
- Business/work-related receipts

Once everything has arrived, get started or schedule an appointment. The earlier you file, the more quickly your refund will arrive.

Note Important Deadlines. While April 15 is the most important date, January 31 is also one to keep in mind. If you do not receive your expected W-2, 1098, or 1099 forms by this date, contact your employer and banking and investment institutions to inquire about the delay. By law, you must receive them by January 31.

Choose Your Best Filing Option. I prefer to use an accountant, one my family has worked with for years. Whether you use a professional preparer or fill out the forms yourself, make sure you know what you are going to do well in advance of April 15. E-filing, using a tax-filing software program, and filling out the paperwork by hand yourself are all options. Filing late is not, without significant penalties, unless you file for an extension. Keep it simple, and make sure you do it right the first time.

Small Business Owners/Sole Proprietors

Because I try to reduce my stress and responsibilities, I have my taxes prepared by a CPA, one whom I trust and who can answer all of my questions. The fee I end up paying him relieves me of the worry I might experience if I rely on myself to read all of the laws and forms correctly. However, by no means is this to imply you cannot do them on your own.

If You Work at Home, Keep Track of Your Payments for utilities, mortgage/rent, repairs, etc., as you can deduct a portion of your expenses.

Keep a Separate Budget for Your Business Expenses. Ideally, you will have a separate checking/credit account as well (a requirement if you own an S corp). I have begun using QuickBooks online as my business has grown over the years, and each month I keep track of the expenses paid out and earnings coming in so that when January arrives, I can quickly assess my total income, search for the receipts necessary, and, best of all, sync all information with my accountant's system without additional work.

Create a System for Your Receipts. When you receive a receipt, label it with the event it relates to — "trip to Portland for KATU appearance," "meal with potential client," etc.

Make a Plan for Paying/Saving for Taxes Owed. Based on your tax bracket, when tax season arrives, you will need to pay taxes based on your income. Either decide to set aside a certain percentage each time income is deposited or build your savings through the year so you are able to make payments when they are due. Most likely, your accountant will advise setting you up to pay quarterly taxes.

The Money Paradox

The most important investment you can make is in yourself.
— Warren Buffett

In order to invest in ourselves, we must, first, be courageous enough to get to know ourselves, and, second, find the willpower to save more often, as saving and investing will enable us to have the financial security we need not only today but, most significantly, tomorrow.

From the money to purchase a home we desire rather than one we have to settle for, to the money to retire early and dive into our second act rather than continuing to work in a career that has grown stale in order to pay the bills, to the money that allows us to breathe comfortably during hardships rather than living from paycheck to paycheck — when we take the same amount of pleasure in saving and seeing our cushions and retirement accounts grow as we do spending our money, we have become financially savvy. We have mastered our financial security.

CHAPTER SEVEN

Matters of the Heart

Love is as much an art as painting or living; it requires practice, finesse, determination, humility, energy, and delicacy.
— Hannah Rothschild, *The Improbability of Love*

As young children, we were told of Prince Charming and a damsel needing rescue. Perhaps we saw *Cinderella*, *The Little Mermaid*, or *Snow White* too many times. As we got older, we absorbed and unconsciously accepted the idea that we are incomplete, incapable, and reeking of subtle desperation until that one special person finds us; we errantly accepted the myth that this is "how it will all someday work out if I am to be truly happy." (Think *Pretty Woman*, *Dirty Dancing*, *Jerry Maguire*, *The Proposal*, *The Holiday* — the list goes on.) While some films are trying to make a shift — *Frozen*, *Home Again*, *A Five Star Life* — the myth of a soul mate continues to be peddled and accepted as the one thing we need for true contentment.

I am absolutely a romantic, but some things need to be de-romanticized. The soul mate myth is one of them. Even if you think your love life is flourishing, the relationship you treasure can be strengthened by letting go of this cultural marketing myth. Often we presume that our partner will fill our voids, fix our hurts, and protect us from the parts of the world that scare us, but when we seek this solution to our woes, it is just a bandage covering a wound that has not been tended to properly.

In fact, rather than a soul mate, the person we are seeking is, simply put, a partner. The role of a soul mate is actually someone who will break you down, break you open, as Elizabeth Gilbert shares, so that you can see where and how you need to be transformed to reach your full potential — in other words, who you can become in order to be your best self and thus a better partner. A true soul mate offers a relationship that is often too intense to endure, a relationship that offers an opportunity for growth rather than an opportunity for a lifetime partnership. And so, yes, we can and most likely will have more than one soul mate, as we are on a journey of growth and discovery and the journey never ends. As Gilbert shares, a soul mate is an individual who . . .

> . . . *is a mirror, the person who shows you everything that is holding you back, the person who brings you to your own attention so you can change your life. . . . A true soul mate is probably the most important person you'll ever meet, because they tear down your walls and smack you awake. But to live with a soul mate forever? Nah. Too painful. Soul mates, they come into your life just to reveal another layer of yourself to you, and then leave. . . . A soul mate's purpose is to shake you up, tear apart your ego a little bit, show you your obstacles and addictions, break your heart open so new light can get in, make you so desperate and out of control that you have to transform your life.*

When we can differentiate a soul mate from a life partner with whom we can share and enjoy our lives, we recognize the gifts a soul mate can bring into our lives and are thankful for the time spent with them. And then the responsibility is on us to do the work. No one will fix us, no one will show us how, but a soul mate shows us why it is necessary and, most importantly, that it is possible to reach our full potential, something that we may have thought was not possible until they came into our life.

So how can we heal the parts of ourselves that seem impossible to fix, but clearly need to be fixed and can be fixed? By addressing them. By doing the dirty and seemingly difficult work of understanding why certain things are not working as we would like them to. Investing time in winnowing away aspects of your life that are no longer serving you — coming to better understand how to handle your emotions, recognizing barriers you have in your life, and discovering the tools to work around them, as well as learning how to effectively communicate with others — is a gift not only to anyone you are in a relationship with, but to yourself as well.

Once you invest in yourself, you most likely will find you enjoy your own company. You will no longer need to fill your life with appointments, responsibilities that do not support the life you wish you live, anything to busy yourself so that you do not have to sit quietly with yourself from time to time. You will achieve a peace that multiplies your comfort, contentment, and happiness. The person you need in your life is your best self.

It is up to each of us to recognize the perversion of love portrayed in the media and understand what a loving relationship truly is, while dropping the need to label the person we would like to welcome into the most intimate part of our lives as a soul mate. Because the truth is that for a lifetime, rather than a soul mate, what we truly seek is a partner to move with us through life's journey.

The soul mate theory is a fallacy because it presumes we are fixed entities. But "growing apart" is a common reason that marriages fail. Humans are forever changing, learning new information about themselves and the world, and trying various ways to move forward. This does not mean relationships cannot endure, but acknowledging the reality of change is crucial. The story of a new relationship — two individuals meet, connect, and seem to speak the same language — is only the first chapter. The rest is a conscious choice to invest, learn, listen, and communicate, to express kindness and recognize within ourselves the truth behind what we feel. To quote Alain de Botton, "Love is a skill."

So let the term *soul mate* go and liberate yourself, whether you are in a relationship or not, seeking a relationship or not, because when you do, you open the door to more responsibility on your part. And, as they say (albeit in reverse), when you take on such great responsibility, you give yourself power to live a life that will bring you true contentment.

Love and the Independent Woman

Love — whether romantic or platonic or a love for a passion we pursue doggedly and without apology — is an electric force that provides infinite fuel for life. Love is a necessity for living a life of fulfillment, contentment, and reaching our full potential. And it is the goal of reaching her full potential that drives the woman who is independent.

Her Enjoyment of Her Own Company Is Real, though that does not mean she does not enjoy the company of others. Alone time is delicious to her. She revels in it, finds immense pleasure in it, and does not need someone else to entertain her or keep her company. She will spend an evening by herself because she wants to.

When She Expresses Love or Affection, It Is Real. She will not waste time with games or ego-lifting flirtations. She is secure in who she is and does not need to drum up interest from others to confirm her worth. Because an independent woman relies on herself for her income and fulfillment, she is engaged, she is driven, and when she welcomes the possibility of a relationship into her life, she does so thoughtfully.

She Is Self-Aware and Therefore Will Not Hold on to a Relationship That Is Not Working. She knows what she wants to accomplish. For the most part, she knows what it will take and what she can do. She also knows at this point in her life what works and sees very clearly what does not. And if the fit is not right, she will not beat around the bush, hanging on and hoping it will iron itself out.

Her Friends May Be Few, but They Are Mighty. Her planner is full, her goals are clear, and her days are often long, but she sleeps well and is excited when she wakes up in the morning, thankful for the opportunities she has. Because of her full life, the friendships she builds are strong and provide support. She places quality over quantity. Her need for strength is important, her need for trust is vital, and she wants to give fully to those she cares about.

She Is Looking for an Equal Partnership. Any relationship will ebb and flow based on the needs of the individuals, but the partnership an independent woman is looking for is not about fulfilling traditional roles. It is about setting each person in the relationship free to be themselves.

Drama Is for Television and the Theater. The independent woman does not engage in drama. She recognizes the unnecessary burden she puts on others when she involves them in drama. An independent woman seeks to be productive, honest, and clear. While she knows how to negotiate, she also understands that people have feelings and keeps this in mind when dealing with them professionally and personally.

Living Together Is Not Off the Table. It simply must be with the right person. Living together is an opportunity to connect more intimately, but only when the independent woman can trust that the other person will be her true partner, not someone who will add tasks and chores to her list. Living together should be an enhancement, not a burden.

She Is Looking for Real Love. Living alone is a wonderful experience. But to change or tweak the life that works well for you is a significant decision, and the person who provokes such a possibility must be someone who surpasses most others you have met.

Real love enters our lives in a variety of ways: through our careers, children, pets, hobbies, service, families, etc. But it should always begin with having sincere love and appreciation for ourselves. An independent woman understands this. She may struggle with who she is becoming, as it seems to change as she grows and strives. Once she figures out who she is at her core, that truth does not change. And knowing that truth brings a comfort and a sanctuary no one can take away.

Why Not . . . Stop the Pursuit?

A common comment from those who learned I was moving to Bend was "It will be so much easier to find someone in Bend." Now the comment has changed to a question: "Have you found someone yet?" I know they mean well and want me to be happy. But if you are a long-term reader of *TSLL* blog, you know it is not a "You complete me" site. Rather it is an "I complete me" site. My response was and is, No, I moved to Bend because I fell in love with Bend — the lifestyle and the contentment it allowed me to foster in my everyday life — and thus I fell in love even more deeply with my life and the community I feel fortunate to be a part of.

Some people understand this, some people do not, and maybe I am ignorant of the bliss that is awaiting me should I find myself in a romantic relationship that blows my mind. But I would argue that, when you truly fall in love with your life, that is a truly mind-blowing experience, and I hope you all have the opportunity to experience it for yourselves. Should you have a romantic relationship, it will undoubtedly add to the quality of your life if you are in a place to understand how to foster it. In the following section, I invite you think about what we should stop doing and start doing when it comes to love and romantic partnerships.

Stop looking for a fix, and start fixing yourself. None of us will ever be perfect, and no one we enter into a partnership with will be perfect. But what personal qualities in yourself were you not pleased with in the past? Were you too quick to anger or to jump to jealousy? Do you understand why you were drawn to the wrong people? This may be something you can do on your own, or you may look to a counselor to help navigate what you do not understand. Either way, take the time, as it will pay dividends in all arenas of your life.

Stop limiting yourself to one relationship that is worth investing in, and start building a community of love, support, and respect. In an interview with Garance Doré, Esther Perel said, "We have been sold an ideal that your life is incomplete if you do not have a romantic partner . . . the people who are single with a solid group of friends are continuously still hoping and thinking this is the holy grail, that this is the thing that completes a life, and I think that it creates a misguided hunger." The key is to build a social network, a community, that allows your needs to be met without relying on one person to be everything.

Stop having expectations, and start stretching and realizing the vast possibilities you never considered. Let go of the script in your head that lays out how it is supposed to go, how quickly a relationship must move along, and begin to make authentic connections with others. Set boundaries, but be open to new opportunities. Let yourself be curious, see what or whom you are drawn to, take your time, and see where your options lead.

Stop seeking what someone can give you, and start putting love out into the world. In Alain de Botton's book *The Course of Love*, the main takeaway for me was "Love is a skill, not just an enthusiasm." If we wish to be loved, we must know how to love and be willing to love.

Stop seeing being single as something to be fixed, and start seeing life as an opportunity to leave your legacy, improve the world, inspire someone to find their path, or simply make their day brighter, easier, or more enjoyable.

Stop thinking about your biological clock, and start diving deep into your life. Often we are so laser-focused on what we think we need, on what we think must happen, that we shut the door on unexpected opportunity. Loosen your grip on life; come to understand and be more at peace with uncertainty. It may just surprise you and open your eyes to a life of even more wonderful amazement.

Stop trying to be perfect, and start being you, really you. Dig deep for your courage, begin to let go of what others may think, and jump in to show the world who you really are. We all have unique gifts, passions, and talents that the world is hoping we will find the courage to reveal.

Stop looking to fill what you perceive to be the gaps in your life, and start observing and expressing gratitude for all that is already in your life. I am going to let Oprah be the teacher here: "The single greatest thing you can do to change your life today would be to start being grateful for what you have right now. And the more grateful you are, the more you get."

Enjoy the journey rather than trying to control the outcome, and begin creating a life you are passionately in love with, no matter the state of your romantic life at any given moment.

Eight Things to Accomplish Before You Step into a Relationship

As I look back on my past — which contains a handful of relationships, which were unique, and which began and ended for different reasons — I know I am a different person now. I have learned to be a far better partner, but also a far better and more content individual overall, whether I am in a relationship or not. Earlier, I did not know either what I needed or where to find the knowledge I sought. Most importantly, I was still growing and discovering myself, and thankfully, that journey has never ceased. Why am I thankful the journey has continued? Because it has led me to valuable resources for understanding what I was lacking when it came to being in a healthy relationship. Here is some advice based on my personal experience.

Explore What Interests You. First, be sincere in your interest. Second, have more than just a few interests. For if one falls through or wanes, you have others that can fill the gap. To put all of our time and interest into one basket of interest is to put a tremendous amount of pressure on that focus. Often the focus is a relationship, and while tending to and investing in a relationship that brings us much joy is a worthwhile interest, it should not be the only one we have. You also need to pursue things that you are naturally drawn to and that enhance your life without weighing you down.

Investigate Your Barriers to Healthy Relationships. The work you do to understand yourself will reap awesome, lasting benefits that enable you to see and experience lasting growth and recognize the amazing possibilities you are presented with. Investing in yourself by scheduling time with a counselor is an investment in a quality way of life that will equip you to attain true contentment.

Learn How to Communicate Effectively. If we have not seen effective communication modeled in our own lives, it is up to each of us to learn, and fortunately, the information on this topic is abundant. Ultimately, in order to communicate well, we must know what we want to say and why we want to say it. And in order to understand the why, we must get to know ourselves. We need to understand why we are angry at particular moments; we need to understand why we are fearful, why we get defensive, why we get jealous, and look within ourselves to understand our unconscious reactions before we speak and do damage unnecessarily. On the flip side, we must not cower and become passive. We must communicate without attacking, express how we feel, be able to objectively observe our emotions, and listen with the intention to understand more deeply.

Cultivate a Healthy, Strong Social Life. Our social worlds are often tied to our interests as well as our work. Once you devote time to them, you are free to be yourself, and your social life becomes a place of enjoyment, pleasure, and respite — an integral piece in your contented life.

Actively Pursue Your Dreams. Let go of the have-tos and must-dos, and instead dive into your dream. Perhaps it requires you to work on the weekends or each night after work for a few hours. Maybe your dream prevents you from celebrating when Friday evening arrives, but it enables you to come alive when you immerse yourself in the pursuit. Trust your dreams, not the fears the outside world throws at you. People are intrigued by those who have the courage to tap into something and pursue it doggedly. Not everyone will understand, but those who respect and admire your efforts will be people you will be happy to connect with.

Cultivate Self-compassion. When we look within ourselves for compassion, we give ourselves permission to be imperfect. We recognize that we must first be kind to ourselves in order for others to know that is how we deserve to be treated. Often, we are our harshest critics, but the belief that self-criticism is the best path to success is false. In fact, it is quite detrimental. Instead, being self-compassionate reveals a high emotional intelligence; we are able to have a broad perspective on our circumstances and move on rather than get bogged down in self-criticism. Because we can take care of our emotional needs, we look less to the outside world to build us up and are able to build healthier relationships.

Become Comfortable with Validating Yourself. If we do not first validate ourselves, approve of the life and the decisions we make, we will constantly seek approval from others. Dependent upon approval and desperate for acceptance, we will only harm ourselves as we will never find true contentment. As I wrote in a 2011 post, "You can succeed if nobody else believes it, but you will never succeed if you don't believe in yourself." Why do many of us fall into the trap of asking whether we should do something instead of simply trusting what we know will make us happy? It is scary to stop seeking validation from others, especially from our parents, our peers, and those we may have been in relationships with. But when we forget about the power of our self-approval, we limit the quality of the life we could be living.

Build a Life You Love Living on Your Own. Cultivating a simply luxurious life centers around the premise of building a life that is congruent with your authentic and most true self. If you will stop trying for a life you think you should live and instead focus on what truly suits you, the quality way of living you seek will materialize.

When we begin to really listen to what works for us — rather than gravitating toward what we have done, what we have seen, what we know — we curate a life that is in alignment with our values, one that enables us to live and pursue what we love and thus to become enlivened from within. We will undoubtedly be involved in many different types of relationships, and all will teach us something about ourselves and the world. But when it comes to enduring relationships (keeping in mind that nothing is infinite), we multiply the happiness quotient not only for ourselves but also for those we love.

First Date Cheat Sheet

The Internet is full of dos and don'ts when it comes to first dates. The two parties are unknowns to each other, ratcheting uncertainty to a high level. And while each first-date experience will be different, the one variable you control is you. As I look back on the many first dates I have had, the one thing I have learned is to stop worrying about impressing and start seeing the encounter more as a fact-finding mission. I am not suggesting that the first date be Interrogation 101, but the goal is to see if there is compatibility. Sure, you both said yes to the first date, which means there was mutual curiosity, but is there potential for an enduring connection?

Don't Let Physical Attraction Be the Only Selling Point. *Psychology Today* once reported that evaluating a potential partner on physical attraction alone does not ensure a relationship that will deepen or endure. Admittedly, there must be some level of attraction, but the key is to ask yourself, Why am I interested in this person? What non-physical qualities do I respect or find attractive? Are they thoughtful, generous, intelligent, humorous, disciplined, determined, or any number of other reasons to be interested in them?

Express Appreciation. Finding the right balance between nonchalance and adulation is imperative, but when in doubt, say thank you when someone opens a door, pays for a meal, or performs any action that considers your comfort or enjoyment.

If You Want a Second Date, Be Honest. Most likely, you will feel a vibe, perhaps based on comments made during your conversation, on body language, or on how the date went (did it end abruptly or go longer than expected?). Before the date ends, if you want to see the person again, make it known: "I'd like to do this again." State it short and sweet. At this point, the tennis match of reciprocation has begun, and you can gauge how they respond. As I have dated in my thirties versus my twenties, I have observed that more secure people play fewer games and are more direct. Also, there is no need to wait three days (or whatever number of days the "rules" require) to be in touch to set up the next date if both parties are interested. Texting the next day to briefly say you had a nice time shows interest and intention, no matter when the next date may be.

Engage in Equal Inquiry. Each person must let the other talk, but it is crucial that the sharing be evenly distributed. After all, you are looking for a partner who wants to be with you because of who you are, what you bring to the table.

Offer a Trailer, Not the Entire Movie. The gift of a first date is that the slate is clean, no mistakes, no gaffs or faux pas. But that does not mean the person is your trusted confidant. Introduce yourself, but do not expose yourself. Mystery is attractive initially. (Keeping up the walls after time has passed is another story.) But the first date should offer a glimpse of who you are and what excites you about life.

Authenticity Invites Authenticity. The best way to get to know someone as they truly are is to be yourself. Being vulnerable creates a safe place for the other person to open up as well. Not everyone will engage, but on the first date, if you want the compatibility meters to register accurately, you must show the truth of who you are.

Let Go of Assumptions. Since a first date is typically a few hours at most, the conversation may cover a lot of ground without going too deep, or you may just touch on one or two topics and get to know someone on a single dimension. Give the other person a chance to reveal themselves. Your background and experiences have helped you arrive where you are in your life. The person you are on a date with cannot possibly see all those twists and turns on your first meeting. Therefore, have patience in getting to know them as you would hope they would do with you.

As Steve Martin's character in *It's Complicated* states over his croque monsieur with Meryl Streep, "Dating is exhausting." Trying to be aware of how we are coming across, trying to be our best, authentic selves, emotionally putting ourselves out there — each of these alone is taxing and demanding, let alone all of them at once.

Most importantly, be kind to yourself. Whether the first date leads to a second date and beyond, or even if it leads to a second date that confirms your concerns from the first and things end thereafter, at least you gave it a shot and broadened your knowledge of who lives in this big, amazing world.

Eighteen Red Flags

The relationships that did not work out can offer long-lasting gifts as we go about building new lasting, loving, and supportive relationships. The biggest gift may be the chance to step away from a relationship when we realize it is not going to be a good path for us. We can prevent heartbreak, devastation, and unnecessary pain by heeding glaring red flags.

Not all red flags speak negatively of the person we are getting to know. For example, sometimes someone's values are so different from your own that an intimate relationship might not be the wisest path to take. Let yourself move on. And when a red flag highlights qualities that might crush the vibrant person you are, move on as of yesterday. (I do not include below the most obvious red flags — physical abuse, cheating, real mental problems, etc.)

You will not necessarily see red flags on the first date, or even the second or third, but these are warning signs of trouble ahead.

They Have a Hurtful Sense of Humor. Seeing different things as funny does not mean you should bail. However, if their humor is a direct result of seeing other people, animals, or things suffer, then yes, this is a red flag worth respecting. Know the difference between hurtful humor and playful humor.

They Are Amazed You Could Like Them. Sometimes when we are just gaining our self-confidence or are rebounding from a blow to our self-esteem, we can be thrilled when anyone pays attention to us. If by date three or week two, your date tells you they cannot believe you would be with someone like them, nine times out of ten that is a sign that you have not been paying close enough attention. This may sound snobby, but trust me, it is not. While such a comment may sound like flattery, you need to get to know this person better.

They Do Not Respect Your Boundaries. One key component to developing trust is the issue of respect for your boundaries. For example, if you tell someone you need some time alone or are exhausted after a long week and just want to stay home, yet they ignore your wishes and intrude or make plans for you to go out, that is ignoring your boundaries. If this behavior happens repeatedly, they are not respecting what you need.

An Ex Is Still in the Picture. Note how often the person you are dating mentions an ex (or exes). If there is still a relationship there, determine what type it is: friendly, respectful, best buds? What role does the ex have in their life? Continued involvement with an ex is not an immediate red flag, but as you move forward, ensure that whatever the ex's role is, you are truly comfortable with it.

They Impose Guilt. Imposing guilt is a weak person's way of communicating when they do not get what they want. The key to any healthy relationship is clear, honest, thoughtful conversation. Someone who is tossing around guilt is trying to manipulate your behavior. It could be a comment they make in passing, such as "If you really liked me, you'd stop being friends with her," or it may take the form of passive-aggressive behavior — that is, the silent treatment. Either way, your date is not communicating what they want in an adult fashion.

They Lack Direction. Perhaps you have heard of the Peter Pan syndrome. If the person you are dating appears to have not grown up or does not have a desire to be a grown-up who is responsible for their life without reliance on mom and dad, you may have met your very own Peter Pan.

They Need a Relationship, and Anyone Will Do. Relationship hoppers are people who do not know what it is like to be alone. Everyone's time between relationships will be different, for a myriad of reasons, but when you find someone who seems overly ready to jump into a relationship, you need to back up a step and find out why. If it feels like they have a canned speech or first-date routine, if their personality comes across as insincere, or if they really do not want to get to know you, they just want you to like them, put this relationship on permanent pause.

You Are Their Only Means to Happiness. A healthy relationship will find you spending more and more of your time together, but each of you should be independent, secure beings, capable of enjoying some of life's moments without each other. Codependency often provides us with security and stability when the relationship begins because we are uncertain about where it stands, but in the long run, a codependent relationship is not healthy. You must be secure with yourself and enjoy your own company, and the other person must feel the same about themselves if you are to enjoy life together.

They Live according to Different Life Values. Having different values — perhaps in religion or politics or the direction you want your future to take (kids, no kids, etc.) — does not mean either of you are bad people or something is wrong. It just means this person is not a good prospect for a long-term relationship.

They Want to Improve You for Their Benefit. When we encourage our partner to be the best they can be, we may not understand why they want to do what they are doing, but we do need to support and encourage them. However, it is not our partner's job to change us, fix us, and assist us in improving so that they are happier with us. Do not allow someone to see you as a project.

They Share with Others Things You Told Them in Confidence. If we share something that is to be kept between the two people in the room and that promise is violated, trust is destroyed. The first time may be a mistake, a misunderstanding, and communication to clarify needs to take place. But if it happens again, see the behavior as a red flag and move on.

They Have More than One Friend Who Has Troubling Values. Sometimes the people we date have friends who are going through hard times. We all have ups and downs, and being a good friend involves hanging in there. But if their friends' behaviors are troubling to you and your way of life, take a step back and ask yourself why this person is friends with people like this. While we do not expect to love their friends as they do, we do need to see what type of relationships they surround themselves with, which speaks to what they are comfortable with.

They Latch on Too Quickly. They quickly assimilate to your world without hesitation, and after close inspection, it becomes apparent they do not have much going on in their own life: goals, dreams, projects, etc. Choose someone who loves the life they are living, and you will have a happy relationship.

Your Only Attraction Is Physical. These types of relationships are excusable when we are young and do not understand the hormones rushing around our bodies. This is not to say we should not have some chemistry with a person; there at least needs to be a hint — otherwise you are just friends. But basing your interest solely on someone's looks or your physical attraction foretells disaster down the road.

They Are Always Asking Something of You. If your partner sees you as a maid, cook, babysitter — if they see you as someone who will help them out without taking into consideration how it makes you feel — either sit them down and have a conversation or just be done with it tactfully. Relationships are partnerships, not a way to have someone to do your laundry or cook your dinner.

How Do They Treat Strangers? The way someone treats service staff, people on the street, or other people's property can be a helpful indicator of their true character. Sometimes they will put on their best behavior when you are present, so pay attention when their guard is down. Their actions may reveal habits they might not even be aware of.

They Never Ask Questions to Get to Know You. A red flag from the beginning is when someone you are intently interested in allows you to do all of the asking and conversation starting but asks nothing about you.

Your Gut Feels Uncomfortable about Them . . . Still. If we have taken the time to get to know ourselves and learned lessons from the past, often we can sense when something is off, when someone is being disrespectful or does not have the same intentions as we have. Instincts are like muscles: All of us have them, but not all of us use them effectively. If your instincts are not well-honed, you may have to take more time to get to know them. But either way, eventually the red flag, if it is there, will raise its ugly head. Trust it. However, know the difference between your gut speaking to you and fear of the unknown. Our intuition is established based on previous experiences, but when we have not experienced something, it could be fear that is speaking because we do not know how things will unfold. The test that life coach Marie Forleo offers is to ask yourself, "Does it make you feel expansive or retractive." In other words, when you think about the possibilities, do you feel the relationship will reduce the quality of your life or expand it? If the answer is the latter, go forward. If it is the former, walk away now.

If a red flag does pop up, be thankful that you avoided difficulties or heartache and now have the opportunity to look for a person who will be a pleasure to be with.

Adults vs. Grown-Ups: Fifteen Differences

Becoming an adult does not mean we have grown up. Growing up requires that we purposely choose to mature, that we recognize certain realities and how the world works and thus how we must behave and think. This is not to say that we conform and become robots, walking in step to whatever society dictates. But we do need to become aware of how we each contribute to and are part of a bigger picture and take responsibility for our actions. Initially, such awareness and responsibility may not sound like much fun. When we were children, most of us did not have the stresses we have as adults, and being able to handle life's difficulties is a choice, not just something that happens when we turn eighteen.

Here is how I see the differences between being merely an adult and being a grown-up:

Clothing. *Adult:* Wears clothing that expresses personal style regardless of its rightness for the occasion. *Grown-up:* Understands that dressing appropriately shows respect not only for oneself, but also for the occasion and people involved.

Friendships and Relationships. *Adult:* Expects friends and family to be there for them simply because they are related or were friends in the past. *Grown-up:* Consciously chooses to strengthen and build friendships; does not take them for granted but respects and supports them with consistent attention.

Oops, You Were Wrong. *Adult:* Shifts blame to others or circumstances; must always be right and believes admitting mistakes is a sign of weakness. *Grown-up:* Upon realizing they have made a mistake or should apologize, they do so sincerely, doing their best to not repeat it. Then they move forward.

Adult Substances. *Adult:* Drinks and smokes because they can, regardless of consequence to themselves, others, or how it affects their professional or personal lives. *Grown-up:* Respects and understands the effects of drinking and smoking; acts responsibly, understanding the situation and how it affects them individually; refuses to cave to peer pressure.

Conversation. *Adult:* Unaware of their presence in a conversation — monopolizing it, not acknowledging other opinions, being passive-aggressive when they hear something they disagree with. *Grown-up:* Understands the art of conversation.

Emotions. *Adult:* Acts immediately based on an emotional response or exhibits passive-aggressive behavior toward someone they are upset with as a way to punish or gain control rather than resolve the issue. *Grown-up:* Controls their emotions; waits until they are calm and in a favorable setting to discuss contentious matters.

Citizenship. *Adult:* Breaks rules because they can get away with it; does not understand or care what the effects are on others. *Grown-up:* Values their role as a citizen of the community and the world at large; recognizes that civility not only improves the world at large but enhances their own world as well.

Decision Making. *Adult:* Makes rash decisions driven by how good it will feel, disregarding the consequences for themselves or others. *Grown-up:* Makes rational decisions based on conscious, patient thought; considers how it will affect not only their present, but also the future and those around them.

Planning and Goal Setting. *Adult:* Shortsighted; does not plan and lives only in the moment, not thinking about potential consequences. *Grown-up:* Revels in the moment, but has a plan for the future and keeps themselves in check regarding money, behavior, etc.

The Story Line. *Adult:* Plays the victim — "Someone will help me" or "It's not my fault." *Grown-up:* Chooses to be the hero of their own life.

Money. *Adult:* Ignores spending issues that ultimately undo them, followed by asking for help. *Grown-up:* Masters their finances even when it gets hairy.

A Changing World. *Adult:* Becomes cynical about the world, constantly complaining, yet refusing to take action to improve the situation. *Grown-up:* Contributes positively to the world in their own way.

Getting Along with Others. *Adult:* Becomes jealous of others and competitive with them rather than simply trying to be better than the person they were yesterday. *Grown-up:* Applauds the success of others, seeing it as motivation and inspiration.

Doing/Having It All. *Adult:* Endlessly tries to keep up with the latest trend on social media and has a schedule that leaves them no time to appreciate their beautiful life. *Grown-up:* Takes the time to understand themselves, is clear about their values and passions, and lets go of trying to keep up with outside expectations, thus creating a life of true fulfillment.

Perspective. *Adult:* Upon meeting someone whose choices do not sync with their worldview, strews guilt, shame, or negativity about freely in an attempt to make the other party feel inferior. *Grown-up:* Understands that not everyone has to see the world through their lens and celebrates the differences. While they may not choose to spend time with people who have differing approaches to living, they can do so respectfully, as they hope others would do for them.

Refusing to be a grown-up creates unnecessary stress and prevents moments of joy and pleasure to occur without guilt. In other words, growing up is an investment, and it will pay off.

Let's Talk about Sex

Women are thirsty for society to recognize what Peggy Orenstein points out in her book *Girls & Sex*: In order to have a strong well-being, we must have the ability to seek "full, healthy sexual expression." Each of us, upon reaching the zenith of complete, healthy sexual expression, will define it uniquely, but how do we get there? How do we emancipate ourselves from societal or familial harnesses that limit the ability to cultivate an overall strong well-being?

Get to Know Your Body. Just as we need to get to know ourselves in the mental or spiritual sense, we must also get to know our bodies, biologically and sensually. What is where? What does it do? Why does it look like that? What arouses me?

Understand What Real Intimacy Is. If we accept what the media projects and if we do not see healthy, loving relationships modeled by our parents or those closest to us, it is easy to understand why sex may be seen as the only way to intimacy with a partner. In truth, intimacy is sharing a close bond with a loved one. It can be platonic, it can be romantic, but it involves trust, shared experiences, and authentic and honest expression, and it is not always physical.

Understand the Difference between Sensuality and Sexuality.
Sensuality is anything that involves pleasure enjoyed through the
senses. Sensuality requires us to be fully present, to pay attention to
what surrounds us, and to drink in its feel, sense, taste, sound, and
sight. With our partner, this could include a foot massage at the end of
the day, the aroma of the dinner you are making, or taking baths
together. Sexuality is simply about sex. But sex can be far more
enjoyable when sensuality is involved, and one does not need to involve
sex to be sensual. Embracing the sensual details of our everyday lives
heightens our appreciation for all that surrounds us.

Focus on What Is Best for You. Whatever your thoughts about sex,
intimacy, and sensuality, be able to separate what is true for you from
what others may project onto you. Is sex a means of control? Does it
reveal insecurity or lack of knowledge? Is it based on past experiences?
Refrain from judging other's choices, and never push someone where
they are not comfortable going.

Talk about It. Being curious is the beginning of understanding
ourselves sexually so that we can communicate our needs and desires.
The best person to have conversations about sex with is the person you
are sexually involved with, but that does not have to be the only person.
Talking to your gynecologist is one valuable resource. When your body
feels good, think about why. And when it is acting out of character,
inquire as well.

As an adult, you know what is best for you, your body, and the life you
wish to lead. Honor your truth, and find a partner who respects your
wishes.

Six Components of Healthy Relationships

Here are six key components for building a strong, healthy
relationship, primarily with your romantic partner, but each of these
actions will help to build relationships in every arena of your life.

Cultivate a Healthy Self-Esteem. Self-esteem is something no one can
give us, but once we give it to ourselves, no one can take it away;
without self-esteem, a relationship can wander into codependency,
jealousy can erupt, and we may no longer be able to be supportive,
loving, and helping.

Be Selfless. We must strike a conscious balance when we choose to be selfless. Being selfless does not mean disappearing so our partner can shine; it does not mean that our dreams, needs, and desires no longer matter. It does mean that when we give of ourselves, we are not doing it to get something in return.

Accept the Natural Pace. When we allow a relationship to unfold naturally, taking note of opportunities when they arise without being forced or manipulated, we know the speed we are traveling is just right. Part of knowing the proper speed is being observant, listening, and communicating clearly.

Accumulate Moments. Whether moments with your partner are unexpected or planned, ordinary or monumental, simple or grand, revel in them. Be present. Put down your phone, stop checking your e-mail, and lose track of time. Moments that help cultivate a sincere relationship require our full attention. And by giving our full attention, we are letting the other person know they matter.

Be Vulnerable. This one is very tough for me, and most likely for many of you as well. We carry memories of being hurt as a means to protect ourselves in the future. But this can create a wall that keeps us from finding and establishing sincere relationships and connections with others. While we should by no means be open to everyone we meet, what we can do is observe those we are getting to know, slowly testing the waters as we go and seeing how they respond to the true selves we put out there.

Practice Kindness. Being thoughtful, being gentle with your words, not trying to punish — these are examples of everyday kindness. Kindness comes in how we communicate, even when it is tough to do so. Kindness comes in simple gestures throughout the day to help, to acknowledge, or to express love. Kindness is being selfless and paying attention to the lives of those we care about.

Relationships are not always going to be easy, and there is no definite road map. Each one takes its own course, which may be frustrating initially, but when we understand that two unique individuals are coming together, it only makes sense. And that is when a sort of magical adventure can begin.

Making Your Partner Feel Special

Each of us wants to feel special — not necessarily to everyone or to a huge group, but to at least a handful of people who truly care about how we are doing and who would miss us terribly if we were not in their lives.

In a romantic relationship, it is imperative that both parties feel they are special to their partner. In other words, when you feel you are irreplaceable and hold a place of priority in your partner's life, you understand clearly that you are important in that person's present and future. When you feel special to someone, you understand that having an argument does not threaten the existence of the relationship. When you feel special, you know you will have a much more enjoyable time with them than without them, because there is an intimacy, a comfort that no one else can provide.

The way we treat those who are special to us is something we learn as a child, and I am very thankful to my parents, who modeled behavior I try to emulate. My mother has always been thoughtful when it comes to small and big occasions and knowing when someone needs a little special something (not always a tangible gift, but giving of her time, a truly listening ear, and, most precious of all, her presence), and my father is always available with an extra hand. Neither expects anything in return.

As we continue to build either the relationships we hold dear or improve upon past failed relationships, here are a couple dozen small ways to show someone how special they are as you create the most important part of your life. Some of these suggestions can work in a variety of different settings and relationships (work, family, friends, etc.), but primarily my suggestions are for strengthening your relationship with your significant other:

Turn to them when you have had a bad day . . . Be specific in your compliments . . . Always be their teammate, not more competition . . . Tell them you believe in them . . . Laugh with them . . . Smile when you see them . . . Keep their confidence; maintain trust . . . Point out what they do well . . . Be their biggest cheerleader, not a critic . . . Always have their back in group conversations . . . Be willing to wait until they are ready — to talk, to share, to move forward, etc. . . . . Show appreciation for the little and big things they do . . . Listen . . . Set goals together . . . Be kind . . . Never point out their flaws in public, and in private, focus on their positive qualities and build those up . . . Just be together . . . Let them know that they are enough, that your life is full because they are in it . . . Leave unexpected notes just because . . . Offer to help before they ask . . . When you tell them you love them, look into their eyes . . . Respect their passions . . . Celebrate when they reach small or big milestones toward their personal or professional goals . . . Give a hug just because you want to be close to them . . . When you say you will do something, do it . . . Never let them feel like the third wheel, whether with friends, family, or coworkers . . . Experience things together without others' involvement . . . When they are wrong, do not point it out . . . Let them vent without judgment . . . Call just to see how their day is going . . . Be their safe place, their rock, their number-one fan.

What I Have Learned about Love So Far

If you are looking for the love of your life, stop; they will be waiting for you when you start doing things you love.
— Anonymous

The unexpected adventure you embark upon when you step into a relationship with a potential life partner is that you embark on a journey of self-discovery.

Of course, we can and should go on sojourns of self-discovery before we choose to step into a relationship, but because of the nature of a romantic relationship, often our less developed and tender spots do not fully become exposed. After all, when we care for someone and see potential for spending our future with them, we experience emotions at a more intense level than we may have before and perhaps emotions we may have never experienced before.

Whether you are in a relationship that spans decades, are just beginning to get to know one another, or are not in a relationship at all except the one with yourself, understanding what Esther Perel means when she states, "If you want to change your partner, change yourself" is essential to enjoying your love journey.

A simple truth that most people accept is that nobody is perfect, but sometimes we skip over this truth and jump to assumptions and high expectations rather than understanding the person we are involved with and finding the strength to truthfully express who we are, our curiosities, and our boundaries.

Ultimately, the only individual we have control over and should have control over is ourselves. A healthy relationship requires each of the individuals to honor this sacred understanding, but too often we "belong" to someone. And when we think or speak in this manner, we are speaking unconsciously as though we (or they) are an item to possess, a thing to acquire. And while it can be hard to accept the idea that we are truly magnificent all on our own, when we honestly come to understand it, any relationship we enter into will be greater because of our security within ourselves.

Each of us is on a love journey. Our love stories are unfolding page by page, and we cannot skip ahead to read the last chapter. That is not how it works. Love is mysterious and magical — this I have finally realized. Read on for more realizations about love that I have come to understand.

You must become a good partner in order to find and develop a healthy relationship. Come into a relationship as someone who is content in their own company, someone who is self-aware and therefore also aware of who might make a good partner.

High emotional intelligence will help both you and your partner. When you can accurately identify how you feel and why, you can refrain from needlessly acting on emotions that will soon pass. Chapter nine offers tips on strengthening your emotional intelligence.

Courage and bravery are required. We need to be courageous to reveal who we truly are and what we actually need, and honest about where we can let go. And we also have to be brave to open our lives to another individual.

It is easy to react but more difficult to respond. With thoughtful practice and conscious effort, responding can become your default rather than reacting.

Both partners must figure out how to make the relationship work. What do you want? What does your partner want? What do you want as a couple? Have these conversations. Talk calmly and when you are ready. Explain what makes you feel loved and what makes you feel anxious. Communicating about what works for you, where you can compromise, and where you cannot is the best way to make a relationship work for both individuals.

Treat your partner lovingly even during frustrating times. It will take a conscious choice to respond rather than react. Being aware of how we are feeling and why, and not being led around by our emotions is key to maintaining and growing stable, healthy relationships.

Work through new feelings, circumstances, conflicts, etc. Everything that is not working out in this moment does not need to be solved in this moment. When we understand our emotions, we will also be able to be strong and to step away from a conversation that may be highly charged. Respectfully explain that you need a walk or some time to collect your thoughts; then step back to gain some perspective and come back with a calm and clear head.

Understand that your partner is not perfect. The key is to have hope rather than expectations. If we default to expectations, we set traps to fall through and get caught. But if we have hope, we remain optimistic while being open to what may be.

Have perspective on what is truly important. There will be moments when things do not work out as you had hoped and disappointment arises. While it is okay to express disappointment, it is also important to put it into perspective with the entire journey you are on together.

Understand that the value of being single strengthens future relationships. Allowing yourself time to be single — to be alone and have moments of solitude in which to understand yourself — is crucial when it comes to entering into a healthy relationship down the road, should you choose. A healthy relationship begins with two healthy, stable, secure, and content individuals.

Understand the truth about having physical chemistry. Chemistry is not bad, but it should not be the only thing, let alone the determining factor, when choosing a partner.

The most important must-have is emotional responsiveness. A relationship without emotional responsiveness is not a relationship you want to be in. We have to want to be emotionally invested; we have to want to love in a way we may have never loved before. And we need to feel our partner doing the same.

Know how to balance self-love with loving our partner. It is important to know how to be kind and gentle with ourselves, to know how to eradicate the negative voice, to refuse to let others bring us down, and to respect the boundaries we need in our lives. Finding the right partner begins with understanding and then loving ourselves because when we embody love for the life we live, we are then truly able to give it sincerely to others.

We may not know when we will meet the right partner or potential right partner. The good news is there are plenty of opportunities to do so as long as we choose to live in accordance with our unique compass and temperament. Love asks us to look within and examine ourselves. Love also asks each of us to have faith, stop looking around, and instead look within and trust the journey. This can be scary, but often when something is scary, it is life's way of saying, Look a little closer, examine what is really going on. When you do so, you set yourself free to spend your life doing what you love, and a loving intimate relationship can be part of that.

CHAPTER EIGHT

Stock Your Toolbox I: Own Your Strengths

If you are under the impression you have already perfected yourself, you will never rise to the heights you are no doubt capable of.
— Kazuo Ishiguro

Nurture. Nature. Each of us has evolved into the person we are today based on both. We have genetic coding from our parents, and we also have the nurture they surrounded us with. To better distinguish between nature and nurture, look at them through the lens of a child. Newborns do not have a pre-programmed language they will begin speaking; that is nurture. However, all healthy newborns have the ability to learn how to speak (nature). Hate is a learned behavior (nurture). In order to reach our full potential, we have to find the strength to not only let go of limiting assumptions we hear from ourselves and those around us, but to look the unknowns in the face and walk toward them.

We do not have to rely on empty promises or abstract beliefs with no substance, trusting that fate and the unknown will take care of us. Instead, we can learn how to navigate this ever-changing world by educating ourselves. So much of our power resides within us. We just need to find the gumption to understand how we work (our minds, our emotions, etc.) and why certain things may not be working, and then apply this new knowledge.

Nurture What Nature Gave You

After teaching for almost two decades, I have seen so many wonderful, talented, and diamond-in-the-rough students that I never cease to be inspired. The students who are able to be themselves in the morass of insecurity that high school breeds are those who are unique unto themselves. One may be the quiet creative in the class who is humble with her talents but reveals her magic with each essay; the other may be a bully's target who refuses to conform, ultimately negating the bully's power; or perhaps it is the unlikely athlete who after the first three years of high school and hours of dedicated practice finally earns a position on the team their senior year.

I recently heard this truism: "The first half of our lives we spend trying to fit in; the second half we spend trying to stand out." The quicker we can break free from the first half — erroneously believing we must fit someone else's definition in order to be deemed a "success" or accepted — the sooner we will achieve contentment. Below are a few examples of why nurturing what is innately yours is the best decision you can make.

You Can Shine Like a Diamond. The difference between shining a pebble and shining a diamond is that no matter how hard you try, a pebble will still be a pebble. However, when a diamond is cut and polished to look its best, it is a magnificent sight to behold. So too are your innate abilities. Fine-tuning the skills, looks, and behaviors that you feel you should have but can only develop to a modest degree, will never result in a shiny diamond. However, when you tend to what comes naturally to you, the results can be astounding.

An Imitation Does Not Make History. We can choose to follow or we can choose to be ourselves. Learn from trailblazers' journeys, be inspired by them, then be yourself. As Eleanor Roosevelt put it, "One's philosophy is not best expressed in words; it is expressed in the choices one makes. In the long run, we shape our lives, and we shape ourselves. The process never ends until we die. And the choices we make are ultimately our own responsibility."

You Will Use Your Energy Wisely. The most amazing gift of being ourselves is that it replenishes us. When we conform and contort ourselves to fit others' expectations, values, and demands, we deplete ourselves of energy because we are out of alignment with where we truly wish to go. Nature rewards us for being ourselves. When you find time to do what you love, are you watching the clock? Most likely, you have no interest in checking the time because you have lost track of it.

You Gain Control. We humans seek to "know" in order to rid ourselves of "unknowns." Knowing allows us to lose our fear and gain a sense of control. Others, in their attempt to try to understand us, may try to force their perceptions on us. If we let them become our perceptions, we hinder our potential. Even when people are genuinely trying to help, if we have done our homework, we can quickly discern how shortsighted their ideas can be. It is crucial that we trust ourselves, remain in tune with what we know we are capable of, and take on the responsibility of owning our own destiny.

You Will Unearth Your True Beauty. Helped along by magazines, red carpets, advertisements, and the runways, each decade gravitates to a particular set of ideals of beauty. How boring. Women such as Diana Vreeland, Barbra Streisand, Mindy Kaling, and Tina Fey have each said that their "look" fails to fit society's definition of beauty, and that it was their talent that catapulted them to success. I would argue that most people do indeed find them each quite beautiful. As Steve Maraboli said, "There is nothing more rare, nor more beautiful, than a woman being unapologetically herself; comfortable in her perfect imperfection. To me, that is the true essence of beauty."

You Can Stop Complicating Your Life. John Lennon put it simply: "You don't need anybody to tell you who you are or what you are. You are what you are!" I would not venture to say that life is easy, but it is simple: Find your truth and how it can improve the world, and get busy doing the best you can. Stop spending your energy and emotion trying to be someone you are not in an effort to please people who are blindly following the dots.

Ask yourself, what can I do, what do I love doing, what comes naturally to me, and then practice, fine-tune, and put forth the time and energy to excel. In other words, keep it simple, and the opportunities will unfold before you.

Strengths vs. Skills

A candidate for a job is commonly asked "What are your strengths?" But what does that question actually mean? Strength and skill often are taken to be synonymous, when actually they are quite different. Strengths are innate abilities, curiosities, passions you do not need to put on a wish list. They are the talents you possess, abilities that come to you innately. Strengths will be with you for a lifetime and have been with you in some form since you were a child. Skills, on the other hand, can be taught, but they can be forgotten if they are not practiced consistently. Learning to speak French and, with practice, becoming fluent is a skill, as is learning to type or mastering Excel or PowerPoint.

Strengths and skills are interrelated. After sixteen years of teaching, I possess many well-honed skills, classroom management being one. However, my strength of social intelligence — awareness of others' motives and feelings — helped me become proficient as a teacher more quickly. We are often unconscious of our strengths, and it is only when we get to know ourselves and follow our curiosities and the opportunities that our strengths make available to us that we realize what they are.

Once you discover your strengths, what then? Martin E. P. Seligman says in his book *Authentic Happiness* that there are three types of work: job, career, and calling. A job is merely for the paycheck. A career involves a deeper personal investment as you advance up the ladder; however, you can be completely fine retiring from your career. A calling is derived more directly from your strengths. Seligman says a calling is a *passionate commitment to work for its own sake*. For one person, being a teacher can be a calling, while for another it is a career. Being a landscaper can be a job for one individual, but for another a calling. The difference is you. Your strengths will determine what your calling is.

When we practice a skill, we do it for a purpose: money, advancement, to gain something outside of ourselves. When we invest in our strengths, the only return we seek is the pleasure of being immersed in what we are doing. You may be thinking, I need to stay in my job or career because it pays the bills. I understand, and you should. But when you have given yourself permission to start spending more of your free time focusing on your strengths, your willingness to trust yourself could lead to amazing opportunities.

Abilities to Strengthen: Why Not . . . Create a To Be List?

Your ultimate goal in life is to become your best self. Your immediate goal is to get on the path that will lead you there.
— David Viscott, MD

A to-do list is often concrete: actions, tasks, etc. However, I became intrigued after reading an article in *Porter* magazine in which the writer suggested we focus not on a to-do list but rather on a to-be list. When we focus on what we want to be, we are doing the work of being our best selves. And while being our best selves will not guarantee everything we wish to attain or become, it reminds us to focus on depth, connections, and skills that take time to master. Below is an informal list of sixteen things "to be." Each approach to living invites us to deepen our appreciation, our awareness, and thus the quality of our everyday lives.

> Why not be . . . self-accepting . . . authentic . . . calm . . . self-actualized . . . confident . . . the CEO of your own life . . . emotionally intelligent . . . happy . . . productive, yet balanced . . . self-reliant and self-sufficient . . . disciplined, able to employ willpower . . . a grown-up . . . brave . . . trusting . . . truly wealthy . . . charismatic?

We might not be able to cross off all the items on our to-do list each day, but perhaps we can embody each "to be" quality. If so, we will live more consciously and thoughtfully.

Self-Acceptance

The most powerful tool you can use to achieve success is self-acceptance. Ironically, accepting yourself as who you are at this very moment — strengths and weaknesses — is the first step toward changing the things you are accepting (accepting something does not mean you like it). Self-acceptance opens up greater possibilities of succeeding because you are not fighting yourself along the way. For example, if you know you have a killer voice, but you are overweight and so body-conscious that you will not step onstage, you have not accepted yourself or your life for what it is. You are getting in your own way. Accept that you need to work on your weight, but in the meantime, get up on that stage and sing your lungs out.

Self-acceptance is being happy with who you are in the present moment and loving yourself for who you are right now — even those aspects you are not thrilled with. Here are a few benefits of embracing the idea of self-acceptance:

- You become less defensive.
- It becomes easier to maintain close relationships.
- You value and appreciate yourself and others more fully.
- You tune in to your true essence and stop wasting energy on your faults.
- You celebrate your strengths, laugh at your weaknesses, and, if need be, make positive changes in your life.
- You become more effective in setting and reaching your goals and dreams.

To move toward being more accepting, adopt some daily habits that keep you from being hindered by negative self-talk and focused on your imperfections: Monitor your self-talk. Be an optimistic realist and eliminate your worst critic (you) from your head. Do not compare yourself to others. Learn to say no. When you respect yourself enough to put the kibosh on people's negative comments about you, you take your power back. By saying no to things you do not agree with, do not want to be a part of, and do not feel right about, you are saying that your needs and your ideas are worth attending to.

Figure Out How You Are Hard-Wired

Coming to understand how we are hard-wired — our innate abilities and the past experiences that have shaped our mind's navigation and sensitivities — can be akin to learning a new language. And if you have ever tried to learn a new language, you know it requires dutiful attention and time. But you also know that when you finally do become proficient, navigating through any conversation that arises becomes second nature. What does proficient understanding of your unique language look and feel like?

You Make the Right Decisions. When you become aware of your internal wiring, you know where you will and will not feel comfortable: a room filled with strangers, yes; one-on-one time with an acquaintance, not so much — or vice versa. When you are in tune with your internal wiring, you can spare yourself unnecessary anxiety and maybe even uncomfortable conversations and arguments. Saying no becomes something you are comfortable with, and you say it without guilt. We can conserve so much time and energy when we choose the right decision for ourselves the first time around. When we utilize our resources — our creative mind, our finite energy — we open up our world for even more exciting and unimaginable opportunities to occur, and because we have not squandered our energy elsewhere, we can capitalize on them.

You Will Strengthen Your Relationships. If you are involved with someone who enjoys situations that you do not, clearly communicating this is crucial. When you do, while there will be times when you and they will compromise and push past your comfort zones, you can also do things apart and, in so doing, build mutual respect and understanding. When we care for others, we want them to feel comfortable. Instead of pushing their buttons, we can treat them with the same kindness and respect we hope to be treated with.

You Will Live Unapologetically. The hard-wiring that makes us who we are, which is a combination of innate and early-life experiences, will help us discover what we value, what we place at the top of our priority list, and what we will pursue once we find the courage. When we are clear about our passions, decision making becomes easier (if we will marry, who to marry, if we will have children, which traditions to let go of, etc.). When decision making is this simple, we avoid the temptation to care about what others will think.

You Will Discover an Inner Peace. Through these steps — making the right decisions, cultivating healthy relationships, immersing ourselves in a life we love, and letting go of what others think — we find the peace we have been seeking. Whether you want a better salary, a relationship, or a house to call home, you are looking for a way to feel at ease, to find contentment. All it requires is slowing down, taking the time to listen to ourselves and our feelings and investigating their source, and then applying that wisdom to our lives.

Get to Know Yourself: Introvert and HSP

It is vital to figure out how you are hard-wired. When I made the connection about my introversion in 2011 and my high sensitivities a few years later, my world was made new. My revelations came about because of my journey inward to get to know myself. I unconsciously knew what I loved as well as what made me uncomfortable from an early age, but it took the validation of gaining knowledge from others who were experts in the fields of psychology and neurology to enable me to release one of my deepest breaths and attempt to help those who love me better understand me. When my brother read the introduction to my first book, which exemplified my introversion, he told me he now understands me better — not only how we are different but why I sought to live the way I do.

Not everyone who reads this book will identify with these temperaments; however, even if you are an extrovert or an introvert who is not highly sensitive, perhaps you know someone who may be — a partner, parent, child, friend, student, or colleague. If you understand how they function best, your relationship with them will become strengthened as you begin to understand their "language."

Enjoy Being an Introvert

Getting lost in an intriguing book; enjoying time with a good friend or significant other, just the two of us catching up and sipping some wine; going alone to a Saturday matinee; strolling the streets window shopping without anyone else to fill my thoughts with conversation; longing for the time of day when I take my dogs for a walk and get lost in their unabashed enjoyment. These are just a few of the many activities I find exhilarating and uplifting; while engaged in them, I tap into my creativity, can see things from different perspectives, and can contemplate a sticky problem or a new plan without distraction. I am re-energized after I have time alone to explore, relax, plan, or just be, while most extroverts are fueled by multiple interactions in a social setting.

Even if you are not an introvert, you may have introvert tendencies. And that is fine, because being absolutely introverted or extroverted is not the healthiest situation. There are many reasons to embrace your introverted nature, so that you no longer feel guilty about asking for an evening at home or a quiet coffee for two. We are all wired differently, and it is vital, if we wish to reach our full potential, to heed what our bodies and minds need. While yes, being an extrovert has its perks as well, you may find comfort in knowing that there are amazing things waiting for you when you choose to embrace the introvert that you are.

The Gifts of Being an HSP

Abraham Lincoln, Jane Goodall, Princess Diana, Katherine Hepburn, Martin Luther King Jr., Albert Einstein, Glenn Close, Steve Martin, Eleanor Roosevelt, Ralph Waldo Emerson, Robert Frost, Emily Dickinson — all are or were highly sensitive persons. Here are a few more: Frank Lloyd Wright, Ansel Adams, Frida Kahlo, Barbra Streisand, Mozart, Neil Young, Alanis Morissette, Elton John.

What does highly sensitive mean? Elaine Aron, author of *The Highly Sensitive Person: How to Thrive When the World Overwhelms You*, says HSPs have an "increased sensitivity to stimulation" and "are more aware of subtleties and process information in a deeper, more reflective way." Someone who identifies as an HSP knows she was born with a sensitive nervous system. If you are a highly sensitive person, you:

. . . are conscientious; you have keen awareness of details that cultivates a highly accurate intuition. HSPs may become perfectionists or people-pleasers, so it is vital to find a balance.

. . . define "fun" differently. Classes, lectures, concerts, art exhibits, yoga, cooking classes, any event that is intimate and has a thoughtful purpose is more enjoyable for an HSP than a busy happy hour at a bar, a crowded gym, or a lively cocktail party.

. . . are sensitive to subtle qualities in the air, light, or fabrics. Hay fever, pollens, scents, odors, and itchy fabrics are much more perceptible to HSPs.

. . . are good at tasks that involve observing minor differences. Many scientists, detectives, caretakers, parents, teachers, psychologists, etc. are HSPs.

. . . are able to focus and concentrate deeply.

. . . have an active imagination. The creative mind is the engine of the HSP, and ideas can spark at any moment.

. . . have an artistic side.

. . . prefer conversations of substance, philosophy, and feelings, and dislike idle chitchat.

. . . are able to process material at deeper levels. Many HSPs are told, "You over-analyze everything," but so long as the analysis does not veer down a destructive path, it can lead to wonderful creations, inventions, and ideas.

. . . enjoy time at home to decompress. HSPs self-reflect regularly.

. . . find that your greatest social fulfillment tends to come from close relationships; this is where you can shine. HSPs are skilled in close, personal relationships but can put up a wall if they are hurt.

. . . tend not to share openly with just anyone.
. . . find that group brainstorming and team projects are not productive.
. . . find tranquility in nature, especially water.
. . . are observant and can understand and build trust with children and animals.

What an HSP Needs to Thrive

- **Balance.** When it comes to arousal and overstimulation, getting to know yourself is crucial. Know and be able to recognize when you are over-aroused, so you can either avoid such situations or have a plan about how to tactfully remove yourself.
- **Boundaries.** Gathering your courage to say no, and knowing why, not only protects your ability to be at your best; it also makes clear who you should be spending time with.
- **Plenty of downtime**, including daily alone time. Whether it is a much-needed evening alone at the end of the workweek or a half hour each day after arriving home before diving into chores around the house, alone time is a refueling time, a centering and decompressing time to allow yourself to be buoyed and fully present.
- **Rest.** Establish clear evening rituals to alert your mind that you are going to bed soon. Create an environment that is conducive to a restful night's sleep.
- **Clear communication.** While communication with significant others, friends, family, and colleagues is key for everyone, it is crucial for an HSP; most people do not have the HSP makeup and will be thankful for the heads-up.
- **Relationships that strike a balance between giving to others and giving to yourself.** If someone cannot or will not try to understand what you need, you may need to move on, but often it simply takes communication.
- **Time to step away from ordinary thinking.** Meditation, cooking, watching TV — engage in activities that shift your mind away from your thoughts and onto the task at hand.
- **Time in nature.** A deep appreciation of natural beauty refuels the HSP.
- **Independence and a strong sense of self and identity.** HSPs have a strong need for independence; they abhor feeling trapped.

- **Time-outs from heated or emotional interactions.** When you are feeling over-aroused or trapped, step away — postponing, though not ending, the conversation.
- **Care for your body.** Physical pampering — the food we prepare, the amount of sleep we get each night — gives us what we need to forge ahead successfully.
- **Experiencing new things and realizing that most of what you encounter will leave you safe.** Experiencing positive new events builds your self-esteem and self-confidence.
- **Understanding that simple is best.** When there is too much clutter or an extremely busy schedule, HSPs become overwhelmed. Simplicity is their best friend.

At the heart of living a simply luxurious life is getting to know yourself, and if you realize you are an HSP, it will hopefully be an *aha* moment; perhaps a burden will be lifted from your shoulders, as it was from mine. As you move forward, embracing your amazing strengths and learning how to handle your weaker tendencies, know that you have something amazing to offer the world.

Address Your Insecurities

We all have insecurities. Some of us have figured out how to accept the reality of being human and refused to let it stand in our way. The key is to observe and recognize when we are feeling insecure, then ask ourselves why and seek ways to improve and reduce the insecurity. Of course, as soon as you improve one insecurity and begin to stretch yourself, you will experience another, as you may be entering new territory, but that is evidence that you are growing and remaining curious about the world.

To better understand how insecurities arise, we need to understand self-doubt and its antithesis, self-efficacy. As defined by psychologist Albert Bandura, self-efficacy is the belief in your ability to influence events that affect your life and control the way you experience them. When we feel insecure, we feel we lack control over how our lives will unfold or whether we will be able to achieve the outcomes we seek.

It is important to understand where self-doubt comes from and how insecurities arise. Self-doubt begins when we are young as we unconsciously absorb the ideas and beliefs of those who protect and guide us. If we were discouraged from trying or doing something we were curious about, if we acquired a belief system that involved a lack of expansion, growth, or a means to indulge and follow our curiosity, it may be more difficult for us as adults to trust ourselves when we explore outside our comfort zones. If we have never had the experience we are curious to try, and therefore it is completely unknown, we may doubt our abilities. And if we have had bad experiences or disappointment without positive nurturing that helped us navigate successfully, self-doubt will strengthen.

How can we cultivate self-efficacy? The good news is that when we do run up against difficult life events, we can curtail the negative by reaching for the tools (shared in this chapter and chapter nine) that will help us navigate successfully. Let's take a look at eight tools that will help extinguish self-doubt from our lives and strengthen our confidence.

Have a Clear Vision of Your Desired Self. Studies show that individuals with a clear idea of their desired self (realistic goals to be achieved with time and effort) have less self-doubt. Because their idea is so clear, the way such a person operates is detailed, measurable, and can be organized step by step.

Take on Challenging Goals. If we set only simple goals that can be achieved in a short period of time without much effort, on the surface it may seem as though we are building our self-efficacy and reducing self-doubt, but in actuality we are building a false sense of our abilities. When you choose a goal that may take years or an immense amount of focus or discipline to achieve, you are enabling your ability to eradicate self-doubt. You may have moments of self-doubt, but as you see yourself make progress, you will be reminded that the little voice of self-doubt is full of empty worries.

Find the Right Mentor. The right mentor is someone who can truly see you even if you cannot see your strengths yourself. The right mentor encourages and pushes you, but always provides an environment in which it is safe to try and stumble. The right mentor points you to opportunities for growth and encourages you to practice being your desired self.

Nurture Yourself. If you have just been through a whirlwind of emotion and upheaval, step back and care for yourself. Self-doubt can increase when we refuse to acknowledge that we need to recharge. Remember that while unwanted events can happen, they do not always, and when they do, it may be for a good reason — to set us down the path to what we truly desire. It is hard to see such a truth when we are emotionally frazzled, so be kind to yourself until you are ready to get up and step forward again.

Take Small Steps Regularly. Create small, daily habits and routines that gradually take you toward where you want to end up.

Be Selective about the Company You Keep. If there are people in your life whose words and actions degrade your confidence, weigh you down, and take away your energy to strive forward, limit or eliminate your time with them.

Set Clear Boundaries. Boundaries let you step away from what erodes your confidence, energy, and ability to grow. Boundaries also offer a buffer from things that make you feel stressed and overwhelmed. When you reduce the instances when you feel these negative emotions, you have the opportunity to be more successful.

Find a Person Who Offers Objective Advice. While this individual may be your mentor as well, it also may be an entirely different person — perhaps a counselor, a friend who passes no judgment whatsoever, anyone who will allow you to move forward to a solution. It usually will be someone who has been where you wish to go or sees clearly where you wish to go and will help you reach your destination safely and successfully. I often find that when I talk things out with my trusted person, I hear myself more clearly and discover new *aha*s I had not been able to see on my own. When we let go instead of holding in our worries, doubts, and fears, we are saying, I know I can move forward, I just do not know how. Seeking out someone to help us is a sign of strength and resilience.

The elimination of insecurities begins with self-knowledge. It is crucial to recognize when we need a little assistance to nudge us over an obstacle. When we do not, we feed our insecurities, but that no longer has to be our default. When we know the tools to reach for, we can become unstuck and move forward rather than be held captive by self-doubt.

Authenticity

To be true to who you are — you might think this aspiration should be simple to attain. After all, who knows who we are at our core better than ourselves? But in fact, it is hard. In a world of doctored reality television, plastic surgery, and social media where we post our best selves, it can be daring to show ourselves — flaws, strengths, and all. Here are a few reasons many of us find it challenging to be authentic:

- We know we are not perfect, but coming to terms with our weaknesses is not easy.
- When we expose our weaknesses, we fear others may not have our best interests at heart and use our shortcomings against us.
- Tapping into our authentic selves is a never-ending process as we are always learning something new.

Once we accept that it will not be easy, and that we are not alone in feeling a bit unnerved about exposing ourselves, for better or for worse, the benefits are unmatched. Psychologists Michael Kernis and Brian Goldman say that authenticity is "the unimpeded operation of one's true or core self in one's daily enterprise." But how do we get there? What must we do to achieve this? Kernis and Goldman offer four steps to take:

Increase Your Self-awareness. Understand who you are, why you feel certain emotions at certain times, your preferences for things as simple as favorite foods and as complicated as what makes you feel anxiety or stress, what you are passionate about and why.

Develop the Ability to Evaluate Your Strengths and Weaknesses. Once you understand them, you can use your strengths and work through your weaknesses so that they do not become your Achilles' heel, but rather opportunities to move forward. You may discover ways to do this immediately, or you can seek guidance from a family member, therapist, or expert whose advice you respect. Other options are educating yourself — reading books, taking courses, journaling to make sense of what you are feeling. When you make the most of your gifts and work to improve your weaknesses, you take control of your life.

Act in Alignment with Your Values and Needs. When you understand yourself, you can more clearly discern what you can and cannot compromise on. Decision making will become easier. Your willingness to say "no" and "yes" without hesitation or guilt will come more freely.

Build Healthy Relationships. In order to have healthy relationships, you must be willing to be authentic. And in order to present your true self to those you are building relationships with, you must be vulnerable. When you are, you discover who will appreciate your vulnerability, and you respond in kind, which allows the relationship to grow.

When we talk about investing in authenticity, the benefits should far outweigh any initial trepidation. The quality of your life will improve, and that is the basic premise for trying to reform anything in our lives.

You Avoid Second-Guessing. When you know that the decisions you are making are in alignment with your values and needs, you do not have to think twice about them. You will move forward with confidence and free yourself from unnecessary worry, angst, and stress.

You Let Go of What Others Think. Those who judge are often frustrated with the life path they are on. While we do not need to feel sorry for them, we can have compassion because most of us, at some point in our lives, will find ourselves not quite where we want to be.

You Build Trust and Respect in Relationships. In order to connect with others, we must be able to share ourselves. By no means does this require that you reveal all. But, little by little, you give and see if they give. If they respond in kind, you give again and so on. It is a process that takes time, but one that helps build trust and respect.

You Receive a Confidence Boost. Putting ourselves out there and sharing what we are passionate about yields many rewards, and one is a boost to our confidence. Regardless of the response from others, our demonstrated ability to do something we initially thought we could not accomplish is cataloged in our memory to draw upon the next time we doubt ourselves.

You Reach Your Full Potential. Nearly all of us are trying to figure out our gifts, our path, what we can do that makes us happy. Guess what? The only way to discover this is to be authentic. In choosing such a path, we are choosing uncertainty, and understandably, that holds us back at times. Fight through this. Realizing your full potential is your reward.

You Improve Your Mental Health. Once we let go of what others think, as well as the bad habit of second-guessing ourselves, we let go of unnecessary stress and anxiety. Once we refuse to over-analyze, we are not bringing into our daily lives stress that can erode our health. Instead, our peace of mind grows, and our health improves as well, along with our productivity and the quality of our lives.

We each must find the courage to present ourselves to the world. We do not know what life will grant us if we follow such a path, and while that may be frustrating initially, keep in mind something Amy Poehler said: "You attract the right things when you have a sense of who you are." If we want success, contentment, and happiness, we must simply do what comes naturally — be ourselves.

Self-Reliance

Fortune helps them that help themselves.
— English proverb

The circumstances we are born into are determined entirely by luck. Gabrielle Bonheur Chanel was born into quite undesirable conditions; as she became Coco Chanel, it was her determination and self-reliance that put her at the apex of the fashion world.

Nearly a century before Chanel opened her first clothing boutique in Deauville, France, and began selling what has remained a classic, the *marinière* (the sailor blouse), American transcendentalist Ralph Waldo Emerson wrote his 1841 essay "Self-Reliance." What that title describes is reliance on one's own powers and resources rather than those of others, and the rewards for those who find the courage and strength to be self-reliant are magnificent.

You Will Embrace Your Unique Gifts. As children, we do not hesitate to walk toward what piques our interest. We are not yet swayed by what society applauds or disapproves. Sadly, as we grow up, our inner voice becomes harder and harder to hear. But your calling, your passions are exactly what you must trust. No one else will offer the world what you can give it, and should you not tap into this ability, the world will be denied your uniqueness.

You Will Become Fulfilled and Content. You will not feel true contentment until you put forth the effort and the time and persevere to understand who you are and what you can create and share with the world.

You Will Discover an Inner Peace. When you listen to yourself and let your unique talents soar, you are not looking to see if others applaud. You will not care, so long as you are truly pursuing your authentic path. When you let go of what others think, you set yourself free.

Your Struggles Will Result in More Knowledge, Strength, and Contentment. When we pursue a life of self-reliance, we run up against obstacles. These obstacles are not to stop us, but to strengthen us. And ultimately, like an Olympian who trains for years, meets defeat along the way, but keeps improving, we are stronger as we step beyond each obstacle. We are more content because we know how to successfully deal with any difficulty that presents itself. And that brings tremendous peace of mind.

You Will Find That Loving Your Unique Self Is a Magnet for More Love. Choosing to love who we are and who we are discovering we can be is a self-love that lifts us up. It is not arrogance, but an appreciation for what we have been given and a promise not to squander those gifts. This realization, this way of living to rely on ourselves and make the most of our gifts, is intoxicating to the outside world.

More "Luck" Will Occur in Your Life. Choosing to be self-reliant is choosing a courageous path in life. It will be hard work; it will involve many setbacks and frustrations. It will involve sleepless nights as you doubt and question your decision; sometimes it will be lonely. But so long as you continue to learn lessons from the setback and continue to put forth effort, more and more luck will seemingly drop into your lap.

Choosing to be self-reliant in an increasingly "social" world may at first seem impossible. The key is to quiet yourself from time to time. Step away from the noise, the technology that bombards your senses, and the voices of others in an effort to discern what your inner voice is saying. If you do this regularly, little by little, your life will begin to blossom.

Self-Actualization

Happiness and well-being are strictly personal concepts. For some people, the sense of freedom and adventure is an essential part of the experience. Trust your instinct. This is your journey. The route to take is up to you.
— A Five Star Life

Being self-actualized is having knowledge of oneself and the world around you. You are no longer limited by what society purports to define as a "happy life," but rather investigate and discover what happiness is for you, while accepting that others may have a different definition. Abraham Maslow introduced the psychological theory of self-actualization in the mid-20th century when he introduced his Hierarchy of Needs, with self-actualization at the pinnacle. Maslow's definition: "What a man can be, he must be. This need we may call self-actualization. . . . It refers to the desire for self-fulfillment, namely, to the tendency for him to become actualized in what he is potentially . . . to become everything that one is capable of becoming."

Put simply, to reach self-actualization is to reach your full potential. The benefits of attaining self-actualization are plentiful: inner peace, mastery of one's emotions, improved physical health, enhanced creativity, increased ability to learn new concepts, becoming an inspiration for others, and contributing positively to society.

How does one become self-actualized? Actually, there is no end point, as our degree of self-actualization constantly ebbs and flows; it is not a static state. Maslow believed that, in order to attain it, we must first meet four key needs in order to be free to explore our true potential:

- **Physiological Security:** Good nutrition, adequate shelter, and a healthy body.
- **Safety:** A home that provides safety, security, and consistent routines that free your mind to explore, wander, and relax. Financial security is key for these first two needs.
- **A Social Life:** Healthy, comforting, supportive relationships — at work, at home, or with friends — allow us to feel respected and be ourselves.

- **Self-Esteem:** Having honed your expertise in one or two fields, you earn respect for your talents, efforts, and expertise. The validation need not come from outside sources; it can just be your own self-knowledge that you have achieved something of value.

Once you have met the four needs, you are free to pursue what speaks to you. However, you still need to take a leap to arrive at self-actualization. It will be slightly different for each person, but psychologists suggest that any of the following can do the trick:

- Be willing to try something new, travel paths unknown, and face your fears.
- Be willing to trust your inner voice, especially if something does not ring true for you.
- Avoid putting up walls by playing games and being dishonest. Honesty is crucial.
- Have the courage to be unpopular or even ostracized if you are doing something out of the ordinary.
- Regardless of your age, dive into life as you did when you were a child. Lose track of time and indulge yourself in what you love doing.
- Practice regular self-examination. Be in tune with your emotions and why they occur. When your defenses go up, determine why, so you can maneuver past them.
- Take responsibility for your life.
- Understand that a good life takes time and hard work.
- Practice a solid work ethic regardless of who is watching.

Determine the Why

Whether it is the biggest "why" of them all — "Why am I here?" — or a seemingly small and insignificant one, such as "Why do I want to dye my hair red instead of blond?" we must get to the bottom of the motivation for our decisions. As you travel through life, proceed consciously, understanding your reasons for pursuing a certain career, marrying a particular person, taking or not taking a risk, deciding whether to have children, etc. Ask yourself: Is it fear or courage that motivates me? Is it certainty or doubt that comforts me? More importantly, Is it my own internal compass that points the way, or it is society's?

With every life-altering decision you make, ask "why?" This may slow the pace of your journey from time to time, but like racing to the station and hopping on the first train that comes by, only to discover it is going in the wrong direction, being well grounded in your knowledge of what you are doing will save valuable time and reduce stress along the way.

Understand Your Currency

We determine the fuel that will carry us through life. And the only way to discover it is to get to know ourselves, be truthful, be loving, and, most importantly, be honest. If you are not certain what your currency is, ask those you love and trust to point out what they see as your strengths and to remind you of weaknesses that may be holding you back. Sometimes we cannot see ourselves clearly, and often it is not until we see ourselves through others' eyes that we are reminded of how amazing we can be.

Exercise Self-Control

There are two types of pleasures: lower and higher. Lower pleasures, which some philosophers say are not really pleasures at all, are merely a result of avoiding pain — for example, too much comfort food after a bad day, sex with just anybody because you are lonely, or using drugs to avoid realities of your life that are not going as planned.

You pursue higher pleasures not because you have unfulfilled desires, but in order to attain what you want — for example, anything that will increase your overall or general happiness versus a fleeting "high" that afterward leaves you with regret or worse off than you were initially. Enjoying a chocolate truffle at the end of the day is not bad if it is a reward for eating well throughout the rest of the day or if it helps you unwind and relax. The same can be said for intimate moments with a significant other, which are opportunities to build a bond and establish trust. Other higher pleasures stimulate the intellect; while often the "feel good" emotion does not occur instantaneously, when it does blossom, the pleasure and delight exceed any momentary thrill.

Understand the Power of Money

Many assume that more money equates to more happiness. However, it is not money, but what we do with it that determines our happiness — saving for the future, investing in experiences. It is when money is used wisely that good outcomes and feelings follow. Read chapter six for tips on masterminding your financial security.

Determine What Is Truly Just

An aphorism states, "One must first learn the rules before one can break them," and the same can be true for living the examined life. We must first understand the context or reason for the laws and unwritten rules society imposes before we can stand up against them if they are unjust or unsound. Martin Luther King Jr. reminds in his letter from Birmingham Jail, "One has not only a legal, but a moral responsibility to obey just laws. Conversely, one has a moral responsibility to disobey unjust laws."

The key is to examine closely and carefully, and then find the courage to act with discipline and restraint if indeed laws are just, and, if they are not, to disobey in a way that is responsible and allows for improvement or progress. Make it a regular practice to converse with yourself and others and accept that while we will never have all the answers, we do ourselves a tremendous favor when we refuse to live blindly.

Master Your Mind

If you correct your mind, the rest of your life will fall into place.
— Lao Tzu

What we think has an amazing effect on the reality of our lives. If we believe we deserve a particular career path, set our minds to achieving it, and refuse to give up, nothing can stand in our way. Contrarily, if we think we do not deserve a partner who respects us, we will allow ourselves to stay in an underwhelming relationship. The gift, the beauty, is that our mind is under our control, and with purposeful attention, we can allow our minds to be our best asset rather than a vehicle for a wild, hurtful ride. Much like athletes who filter out everything the moment they are on the field, you can filter out negative thoughts, doubts, and worries so you can achieve your desired success and peace of mind.

We can cultivate a habit of refraining from assumptions, communicating clearly, and letting go until the time arrives for us to know the truth. This is not easy to do; it requires patience, blind faith, and the ability to shut down negative thinking, but it is possible. Your mind and your life will be vastly improved when you claim this power.

Examine Your Core Beliefs

We ourselves often are the source behind the debilitating thoughts that creep into our minds. Based on our past experiences, whether successes or heartbreaks, we believe we know how everything will work out in the future. But while the past did indeed happen, the future cannot be predicted entirely. Examine your core beliefs. Do you think you are too old to do something? Let it go. Do you believe no one will accept you because you have made missteps in your past? Let it go. Your thoughts about how things "should" unfold may be getting in the way of the possibilities life wants to unveil to you. Be open to the unexpected.

Do Not Give Up After the First Attempt

As any successful athlete will tell you, you will not become proficient unless you practice regularly. Didn't get the job you were seeking on your first or maybe even second attempt? Ask for feedback, build your résumé, and try again. We learn by our mistakes, and to allow our minds to think otherwise is letting them have control. The only way you will be able to build your confidence, and thus strengthen your mind into believing you can do something, is to refuse to give up.

Exhibit More Gratitude

If you are like me, sometimes you wake up in the middle of the night and your mind takes control. And often these late-night or early-morning mind trips lead nowhere positive, as doubt, worry, and fear dance freely through my thoughts. Part of the problem, I realized, was that my mind was controlling me, not the other way around. Two things have helped me master this dilemma when it occurs: I read a book, or I think about all that I am grateful for.

Let's look at the latter option. When you decide to think about all that is going well in your life, you reclaim control of your mind. You stop the fearful worrying and doubt in its tracks and remind yourself that there is a lot that is going well.

Whether you are waking up in the middle of the night or are plagued with doubts and worries during the middle of the day, turn to gratitude. It should provide a reminder that things are not nearly as bad as your uncontrolled mind might have you believe.

Use Brain Energy Productively

Just like any muscle in our body, our brain can become taxed after extended use. Once we understand this biological fact, we can be more selective about what we ask it to do on any given day. Why bog it down with unnecessary worry and fretting?

I find that when school begins and I am back teaching in the classroom, my creative bursts are less frequent. I have come to understand this fact about myself, so I waste no time in writing something down when it pops into my head because I know such creative bursts are less frequent during the school year. Conversely, during holiday breaks or the summer, my mind is flooded with ideas as it does not have to focus on as many demands.

If we worry about why we did not get the job, why someone did not call, why our lives are not going as planned, we waste valuable resources that could be used to improve the quality of our lives. Monitor your thoughts, toss the garbage, and keep the gems.

Practice Regularly

Part of the power of meditation is that it asks us to still our mind, or at least recognize when it is running free and we are at its mercy. Even if, at first, we are not able to rein in our minds, the ability to recognize when we have lost control is a tremendous step in the right direction. Whether you practice yoga, meditation, or simply pay attention and stop your thoughts when they lead somewhere that is not beneficial, do so regularly, and you will take the beast by the horns and charm it into submission.

Think Rationally and Realistically

When we choose to be Positive Poppy about all that is going on in our lives, even during events of turmoil and frustration, we disrespect our feelings and those of the people around us who need us to be sympathetic. By no means am I suggesting cynicism is the path to mastering your mind — absolutely not. Rather, be aware of what your mind is thinking, recognize when your emotions are getting the better of you, and bring yourself back to reality. When we can think rationally even when it would be easy to get angry (and lash out) or excited (and make a rash decision), we have mastered our minds.

Do Not Suppress Emotions

We need to be rational and realistic, but this is not to suggest we should suppress our emotions. Rather, mastering our minds requires us is to recognize how we are feeling and why, and makes us able to experience our emotions in a healthy manner. For example, during a time of grieving, we should absolutely allow ourselves to feel the loss. To deny this authentic emotion would only lead to frustrations down the road. If we are feeling ecstatic about something that is going well in our lives, we should definitely celebrate, dance, raise a glass, and cheer. In such a situation, we are respecting the emotion and giving it permission to be felt rather than letting the emotion control us.

Be Patient, Delay Gratification, and Become More Comfortable with Discomfort

Someone who has mastered their mind can exercise self-control. While instant gratification can be tempting, keeping our goals and purpose in mind makes it easy to be patient and say no. For the most part, we live in a world with very few threats if we employ common sense (use seat belts, lock our doors, etc.). This means that most likely we can stretch our comfort zone. For example, if you want to be more physically fit, you will have to get out of your comfort zone and take that fitness class or spend time at the gym. You must choose to step out of your comfort zone repeatedly if you are going to master your mind.

Become Self-Compassionate

Olivia Fox Cabane explains in *The Charisma Myth* that self-compassion is "the warmth we have for ourselves especially when we are going through a difficult experience." In other words, we are able to forgive ourselves so that we can move forward; we tame our inner critic so that we can be productive and not self-destructive. All of this begins with our thoughts about ourselves. Cabane highlights studies showing that people who are self-compassionate have greater emotional resilience in the face of daily difficulties and fewer negative reactions to difficult situations.

Part of the frustration of life in our modern age, especially in America, is that we feel that something is wrong if we are not happy every moment. Notice that I use the word *feel*. Feelings bounce around and come and go. The trick is to recognize the good feelings and capture them in your memory.

Neuropsychologist Rick Hanson says, in his book *Hardwiring Happiness*, that it all comes down to our brains: "Change your brain, change your life for the better." Simply put, we need to deeply savor the good that occurs in our lives, the small as well as the large; as we do, we build new synapses, training our brain to expect the good rather than look for the bad. The skill that we all need to develop, practice multiple times a day, and then use habitually is to take in the good. In other words, be present in your life, be engaged, pay attention, and savor the good moments, no matter how small or large. Hanson says, "By taking just a few extra seconds to stay with a positive experience, you'll help turn a passing mental state into lasting neural structure. . . . This practice brings you into the present moment . . . [and] teaches you to have more control over your attention."

This may sound simplistic, but after coming to understand how the brain works, how it creates paths of memory, and why it has evolved the way it has, Hanson shows that our daily routines and the tracks we allow to run through our mind can create a happier way of living, every day, no matter what is going on. Here's Hanson's one-sentence synopsis: "In a positive circle, feeling better helps you act better, which helps the world treat you better, which helps you feel better."

On the flip side, if we let negative events run through our minds and become absorbed by them, we are laying down negative tracks in our mind, strengthening synapses that are on the lookout for the negative. Hanson points out that our ancestral need for survival continues to impede our way of life in the 21st century; our brain is designed in such a way that "negative stimuli are perceived more rapidly and easily than positive stimuli." In other words, "the default setting of the brain is to overestimate threats and underestimate opportunities and underestimate resources both for coping with threats and for fulfilling opportunities." Which is why it takes conscious effort to rewire the brain to be less fearful and more positive-seeking. If we do nothing, the hereditary tendency of the brain to anticipate danger will persist, blocking us from attaining our full potential. There are many habits that help us savor the good moments, among them:

Slowing Down. In order to recognize and absorb a good moment, we need to slow down. Take ten seconds to fully observe and imprint in your memory what is going well.

Becoming Aware of What Surrounds You. Being present helps you to be fully aware of all that is happening. Even if certain things are not going well, you can put them into perspective and ratchet down the not so good so it does not become more important than it needs to be.

Strengthening Your Emotional Intelligence. The key component to rewiring your brain is being able to accurately understand what you are feeling. If it is positive, you can expand the feeling into a mood. As Hanson points out, you can expand a feeling of gladness and gratitude into a mood of contentment. Conversely, if you recognize you are feeling sad, you can stop the feeling from becoming a mood of depression by recognizing what you are feeling, why you are feeling it, and shifting your mind to a positive scenario so that it does not become fixated on something that is not productive or helpful.

Instead of Wanting, Choosing to Appreciate the Moment. Often, we are fully aware that a moment or an experience is good, and because we know it is good, we want more of it. But this wanting, Hanson points out, can keep us from experiencing what is going on right now. We are removing ourselves from the situation and acting in a way that says we feel we lack something. In fact, the "want" is killing the growth of more goodness. Instead, be present, enjoy what is occurring, appreciate it for what it is, and relish your opportunities. When beautiful moments happen, savor the experience, allow your memory to absorb it fully, and then replay it to brighten your day. Again, more is not better; instead, deepen what you are given by following this three-step process: Have a good experience, savor and absorb it, and commit it to memory.

When we shift away from seeking more happiness and trying to avoid pain, we recognize that we have the ability to be content wherever we are at any given moment. We have that power. We do not have to chase happiness, and we do not have to run from what we perceive as bad moments. Because as we begin to live more consciously, as we begin to focus on the good, take it in fully, and commit it to memory, we build a life that snowballs in the best of ways. We attract people, moments, and environments that are full of goodness, and we cultivate moments of goodness in our lives and for those around us.

Every human being has doubts throughout the day — fears that they are not enough and are not where they want to be. There are a million different advertisers, businesses, and people vying for our attention, dollars, and time that want us to think a certain way of living is the best. And when we think we have not measured up, our minds start to beat us up.

Do not let this happen. Master your mind, choose your path, choose your response. It will determine the success and contentment of your life. At the core of this equation is mastering your thoughts rather than allowing your mind to be manipulated and letting it manipulate you. You can do it, but it must be a conscious effort.

The hallmark of capable people — secure in who they are and clear about where they are going, confident that they can arrive at their destination — is resiliency. A resilient person carries a toolbox of acknowledged and liberated strengths and well-honed skills. When we acknowledge and liberate our strengths, we are better able to manage the obstacles we run up against and move beyond them.

Resilient individuals build a toolbox and understand when they need to use one or more of the abilities inside. When we know we can curtail the negative by reaching for a strength that helps us navigate to the other side, we see how improving our skills would be beneficial as well. Developing skills that deepen the quality of our everyday lives is the topic of the next chapter.

CHAPTER NINE

Stock Your Toolbox II: Hone the Skills You Need to Succeed

Our innate nature is fixed; whether we ignore it or embrace it, it is concrete. As we considered in chapter eight, each of us has hard-wired strengths. It is up to each of us to recognize and fully embrace them.

Contrarily, what we nurture is invited into our lives, but we must understand what to invite and why. Nurture means warmth, comfort, and growth, which leads to blossoming. In other words, based on what we set our attention upon, our lives can produce a bountiful, beautiful garden to nourish us with majestic blooms and foliage, as well as sustenance. If we lapse into neglect and ignorance, however, our lives can gradually become a plot of weeds — or, worse still, untilled infertile soil, littered with rocks and begging for attention if only someone would recognize the potential.

Each one of us, no matter what our formal education, where or by whom we were raised, and which generation we are part of, can cultivate a garden of magnificence in which the bounty exceeds expectations each year as the gardener's savvy and skill improve. In this chapter, part II of Stocking Your Toolbox, we will examine the skills each of us can acquire and strengthen so that you too can become a master gardener of your life.

Emotional Intelligence

The uncertainties in life are vast. But to ignore the ability to master the certainties is a mistake. Each of us is capable of cultivating a life that is fulfilling and attains true contentment — no matter what changes life may bring — by honing the tool of emotional intelligence, or EQ.

A term created by researchers Peter Salavoy and John Mayer and brought into the mainstream culture by Dan Goleman in his 1996 book *Emotional Intelligence*, EQ is often overlooked. That is unfortunate, as tending to EQ makes a significant difference in the quality of our lives, no matter what the circumstances may be. And each of us has the ability to improve our EQ.

Emotional intelligence is often broken down into three components and skills:

- Emotional awareness, including the ability to identify your own emotions and those of others
- The ability to harness emotions and apply them to tasks like thinking and problem solving
- The ability to manage emotions, including the ability to regulate your own emotions and the ability to cheer someone up or calm someone down.

At the foundation of developing a strong EQ is awareness of a balance that is often discussed on *TSLL* blog. Exploring and understanding ourselves while respectfully and thoughtfully navigating the world around us, whether we are at work or at play, is what living well should be all about. EQ is ensuring the relationships we build with ourselves and others are in a healthy balance, as well as respectful, thoughtful, loving, and kind.

EQ is simple in theory and eventually becomes simple in practice, but initially, it takes time, attention, and patience to build a muscle that many leave undeveloped. Most of us are proficient in some areas, but consciously or unconsciously weak in others. And with any eventual success, the first step toward improving is knowing where you need to improve. But first, let's look at what can be gained by improving our EQ.

Take Charge of Your Happiness

When you increase your emotional intelligence, you become the curator of your own happiness. You gain the power, regardless of outside forces, events, or people, to shape situations and relationships so that they contribute to your happiness and success. A person with high EQ:

- Can solve a variety of emotionally charged problems accurately and quickly.
- Manages emotions — both one's own and those of others — effectively, especially under pressure.
- Regulates emotions such as anger or jealously and keeps them at a healthy level.
- Calmly find solutions to problems.
- Exudes confidence based on trusting one's intuition and not allowing emotions to get out of control.
- Is self-aware: can look honestly at oneself — observing strengths and weaknesses — and work on areas that need improvement.
- Becomes comfortable with change.
- Has the strength to say no.
- Is able to be disciplined and therefore able to distinguish between immediate and long-term effects, thereby experiencing much success, effectiveness, and productivity.
- Has strong listening skills.
- Is unlikely to judge and stereotype.
- Can identify with and understand the wants, needs, and viewpoints of others.
- Manages disputes effectively, becomes an excellent communicator, and is adept at building and maintaining relationships.

Tools to Enhance EQ

As I continue to hone my emotional intelligence and apply it to my personal and professional relationships, I have begun to see remarkable improvements, which is why I want to share with you some tools I have found to work for me.

Reduce Negative Personalization. If your tendency is to assume the worst when an individual does something that upsets or confuses you, instead take a step back. Refrain from jumping to conclusions and making negative assumptions. Examine the situation from multiple perspectives. Doing this gives you a more objective perspective; it gives you room to breathe, collect your emotions, and, quite often, recognize that others' actions and reactions often have nothing to do with you and everything to do with them and what they are dealing with, experiencing, and feeling.

Avoid an All-or-Nothing Attitude. Whether in relationships or at work, provide yourself with a banquet of options. For example, do not link your socializing entirely with a single relationship with one friend; instead, build a handful of strong, healthy friendships. When you have a romantic partner, be sure to build a life you love living, whether or not that individual is with you; your partner should add to your contentment, not be the sole reason for it. Professionally, give yourself options; if you are considering a career move, apply for a handful of jobs rather than just one.

Learn to Manage Stress Effectively. First, be able to recognize that you are stressed, and identify the triggers. Then find a way to manage the stress. This can be as simple, perhaps, as engaging in some physical exercise or simply going outside, getting some fresh air, and convening with Mother Nature. It may mean sitting down and hashing out a work problem with colleagues. Or it can be done in more solitary fashion, by journaling out your thoughts.

Discuss Difficult Emotions with the Right Person. Knowing your boundaries, priorities, and values will help you determine when this will be beneficial. Not all negative emotions and anger need to be shared with the individual who angered you. But there are times when you must speak up. Knowing the difference is imperative. When we decide that we must discuss how we feel — to help those we either work with or are in relationships with to better understand us — "I feel . . ." statements are often simple but effective conversation starters. When you are seeking clarification during a time of emotional confusion, share what you know for certain: how you feel and why.

Learn to Rebound from Adversity. Running up against unexpected challenges, obstacles, and setbacks is inevitable if we choose to continually evolve, learn, and be curious about the world and seek to improve our position and potential. How can we best respond? By asking the right questions: What can I learn from this experience? What are other perspectives and solutions beyond the limited box I have put myself in? What is important? What can I be thankful for?

Allow Yourself to Be Vulnerable in Intimate Relationships. It is not easy to be vulnerable — by definition, it opens us up to hurt and potential pain — but we cannot experience true intimacy and deep, fulfilling relationships if we do not reveal who we truly are to other people.

Improve Your Emotional Vocabulary. Knowing how you feel and how to accurately pinpoint the emotion through words — spoken and written — is a powerful way to improve connections with others, build understanding, and enhance relationships.

Pause Before You Speak. The primary component of exercising emotional intelligence is acting consciously, and that includes speaking. Pausing to find the words that are the most accurate, as well as supportive and constructive, begins to build and strengthen the bond between two individuals.

Emotional intelligence has been proven to be more vital and a more accurate determinate than IQ when it comes to long-term success in building a rewarding quality of life. And the good news is that, unlike one's IQ, EQ is a learned skill. It is something we can practice and improve upon, no matter our age.

Quality is something that does not just occur; it is cultivated, it is conscious, and it requires consistency. Yes, it might be helpful if the improvements in our lives could occur by simply buying a particular product or a certain type of home or outfit, but the reality is that, no matter what clothes you wear, what size your home is, or what type of degree you have, knowing how to understand your emotions and how to observe them accurately in others — followed by healthy action that respects who you are as well as those around you — is the yeast of life. If you want to rise, if you want what you value to rise, invest in your emotional intelligence.

Be an Optimist

One of the simplest, but not easiest, things each of us can do on a minute-by-minute basis is to be hopeful — in other words, to be an optimist. While there are many things that are out of our control on a daily basis, choosing to be an optimist allows what we do control to live up to its full potential.

Jomny Sun once said, "I think people who ridicule positivity think positivity is easy." I could not agree more that being positive is a conscious choice. To begin with, being realistic about optimism requires that we accept responsibility for the thoughts we allow to run around in our minds and, consequently, our words and actions. This is where the "not easy" part comes into play. Being optimistic requires focus (which, of course, has many other benefits as well). Once we determine that we will live life looking for and striving for the good, amazing results begin to be revealed. Our mind is a muscle, and what we regularly practice becomes easier, but we must consciously focus on what we want our default approach to thinking to be.

It is far less difficult to think optimistically when things are going well, but a true test of whether you are an optimist is when things do not go as planned. This is precisely why it is essential to put yourself on the offensive and to be resolute in your decision to be an optimist. Our thoughts truly have an amazing force behind them.

Eight Reasons Why

There are eight ways your personal life will benefit from the simple decision to see the glass as half full. Or as Shawn Achor, author of *The Happiness Advantage*, suggests, it does not matter, if you realize there is always a pitcher full of water nearby. Let's get started.

It Is Therapeutic. Optimists are people who understand and accept reality, but refuse to give in, refuse to be stopped by barriers, and instead see opportunities for growth. And because they are able to have this vision, they can talk themselves and thus walk themselves through problems that arise. Being able to analyze a situation for what it can provide them with on the other side is healthy self-therapy. After all, instead of getting in our own way, allowing ourselves to be stuck in the mud of cynicism and pessimism, we become our own therapist, and that healthy outlook affects every aspect of our lives.

It Gives You a Blossoming Social Life. Speaking of every aspect, humans are social creatures who thrive on social contact (some more than others), and people want to be around others who bring opportunity and joy into their lives. When we are determined to be optimistic, we gain respect; we attract people who choose to be around others who continually try to create a more fulfilling life, and this is truly possible only when we see opportunity and gems along life's winding journey. We must be a magnet for good in the world if we wish to see good in the world around us.

It Promotes Healthy Relationships. Optimists tend to attract other optimistic people. But we have to be able to see clearly those who want to be a positive force in our lives versus those who want to squash our hopes. If we maintain a constant perspective of optimism, we will be able to weed out those who are, for lack of a better term, "downers." Instead of establishing close relationships with those who sap our energy, why not be with people who fill us up and inspire us to be our best selves?

Your Productivity Increases. As a result of staying true to our resolve to be positive, slowly we see things change; slowly the energy we have put out into the world returns. There are many ways and forms in which our energy can manifest: We may attract hard workers into a venture we are involved in; we may see greater respect from others and thus better treatment from them; people may become friendlier, and those around us may gain confidence. Because we are a magnet that draws back to us what we put out into the world, it is imperative that we choose a positive path if we hope to see a better world unfold around us.

If You Fail, You Fail Fruitfully. Once you commit to being an optimist, you will be tested. This is almost guaranteed, and this is when we must summon our true grit. An optimist facing moments of frustration has an opportunity to grow, to look at a problem differently, to see the good, and to walk away with a lesson learned instead of simply walking away. Failure truly is not failure until we refuse to learn the lesson.

You Will Have a Healthier Life. Studies have proven that having an optimistic outlook while navigating through trying circumstances does have a positive effect. In a twenty-five-year study done through the University of Michigan, researchers demonstrated that a person with a pessimistic outlook on life was more likely to have poor health in middle and late years.

You Feel an Abundance of Gratitude. Whether I write down one or ten things that happened during my day that made it better, I am focusing on the positive. I am reminding myself of all the good in my life that I may otherwise take for granted and lose sight of. When we choose to live life consciously, we become more aware of how good things really are.

Your Dreams Begin to Materialize. When we continue to believe that we will reach our dreams, that we can make them happen and then take steps to get there, our positive attitude is helping propel each step we take.

What you cater to, you create and bring to yourself. So why not cater to optimism? Why not cater to a world you wish to live in? Why not have hope? Why not continue to believe in the goodness and possibility of the world?

How to Be Optimistic

Below are five strategies for combating situations that try or test your ability to maintain an attitude of seeing the best in any situation. When things are going well, it is easy to keep hope in your heart, but the real test comes when it seems you just cannot get a leg up. Let's take a look.

Change Your Language. One of the simplest things each of us can do to change the tone of our days is to change the words we use in our conversations, comments, and descriptions. When we force ourselves to eliminate *cannot* and replace it with *can* or when we point out what is working instead of what is not, it is amazing how quickly the tone shifts to a positive, more hopeful outlook.

Ask Yourself Why. When we do tend to unconsciously gravitate toward negative thoughts about our abilities, the world, our relationships, and so on, we need to stop and ask ourselves why we immediately jump to negative conclusions. More often than not, it is because of fears or a lack of belief in ourselves. Once we confront the problem, we can move past it and refuse to allow it to affect how we go about our days.

Change What Surrounds You. It is hard to remain positive when we are involved on a daily basis with people we do not respect, a job that does not fulfill us, or a relationship that tears us down. However, we have the freedom to change all such scenarios. Some will most certainly be easier than others, and we sometimes put ourselves in unfortunate situations, but we can do the right and grown-up thing and put forth the effort to get ourselves out of them. I am of the opinion that one should not utter a complaint unless they are willing to do something to change what they are complaining about. I truly believe more would get accomplished and less empty flapdoodle would take place if more people followed this philosophy.

Accept Success. Not everything in our lives is going to run smoothly. Nothing is entirely perfect and flawless. No matter what occurs, why not focus on what went well and allow yourself to celebrate your successes and use them as fuel to continue to have hope? The small hurdles we jump make a difference, and we must not mindlessly take them for granted.

Look for the Meaning. When life seems too overwhelming and fraught with questions that seem to have no answers, having a foundation of something greater than ourselves is a reason to live better, give more, and continue to grow and be our best selves. While hopefully you can find the inspiration within yourself, when you cannot and need something more, look for the meaning of life, and do your best to leave this world better than when you found it. Knowing you are doing your best and contributing in a productive way will help you have sleep-filled nights and calm your mind.

The beauty of all of this effort to remain hopeful is that with time it becomes ingrained in our nature, and we begin to see things right side up without having to try. That is the gift of being an optimist.

Nine Tools to Squash Negativity

Despite the fact that we are all dynamic individuals, continually growing and stretching, trying new things and becoming improved versions of ourselves, we will never entirely rid our lives of negative thoughts. The key is in how we handle these moments when they arise.

Here are nine tools to help you squash negativity and continue living a fulfilling life.

When You Need Love, Give Love

This simple formula works. Not only does it shift the focus from momentary feelings of loneliness or lack, but it lets others feel what you know is truly uplifting and heart-warming. The giving can be to anyone, but it should be something that improves their lives, no matter how small, reminds them of how special they are, or merely gives them reassurance. Perhaps it is a phone call to catch up with a friend from a distance or a card to let someone know you are thinking of them. Or you could plan on doing something with someone that they have been wanting to do.

Dive into What You Love

One of the best things I ever made a regular habit of was diving into what I loved. In fact, *TSLL* blog came about because I was not satisfied with the quality of my days, and so I dove into a place where my curiosities resided. I have never looked back. Sure, sometimes I have to remind myself of this self-taught lesson, but when I sit down to write, explore, go on walks with my dogs, capture pictures of scenes that bring a smile to my face, play in the kitchen, putter in the garden, or attempt anything for the first time that tickles my curiosity, I am present. I am in the moment, and I have no time to let negativity grab hold.

Focus on What Went Well

In *Flourish*, Martin E. P. Seligman discusses the psychology behind fixating on what is going wrong versus focusing on what is going well. He reminds us that our ancestors who prepared for disasters were more likely to survive than those who just sat basking in the sunshine. However, in our modern world, we often take the worrying too far. Instead, we can hone a skill that will reduce our habit of jumping on the worry wagon. Simply write in your journal each night three things that went well. Try to stick to this for one whole week, and in time it will become a positive habit that reinforces your perception of what is going well.

Re-examine Your Well-Being

Often our mind slips into the negative when we have not been tending to our well-being as diligently as we should. What is our well-being? It is "the state of being comfortable, healthy, or happy." It involves many different areas of our lives: mental, physical, social, emotional, personal, and professional. It is a combination of many different aspects, including feeling satisfied with your overall life; feeling a sense of accomplishment or of having a satisfying direction in your life; being involved in healthy, happy, supportive relationships; feeling engaged in your life — your community, your neighborhood, and the world; and tending to your health with physical exercise, diet, and mental strength. Sometimes, a slip or dip in one of these areas that has been strong in the past can make us doubt ourselves in other areas. The tricky part can be figuring out what needs attention, and then we must take the time to mend.

Release Your Emotions in Healthy Ways

There are moments in our lives when we have built-up emotions and must get them out. Sometimes we have to release our frustrations. The key is to indulge in an activity that is not relationship-damaging or self-destructive. Each of us will have different releases, so you need to find a few ways that work for you. Maybe you just need to cry it out. Maybe it is an intense cross-fit class or squashing garlic with your knife and fist. For such an exercise to be successful, you must know why you are feeling what you are feeling. And when you are engaged in the healthy practice of releasing these emotions, say the reason out loud (or, if in a class, under your breath). Maybe your mother-in-law stepped on your toes one too many times, and even though you stood up for yourself and things are going in the right direction, you just need to let off some steam. Or maybe a colleague became extremely difficult to work with. While there is nothing you can do about the facts of what happened, you can release your negative energy so that you do not inflict unnecessary damage on yourself or anyone you love.

Exercise Is Good for Your Mind

Regular exercise is a great way to eradicate the "yuck" from your day. It sometimes is not anything of importance or anything to talk about, but sweating it out lets it roll off our shoulders that much more easily. When we are working out, we are too busy and focused on the moment to feel dragged down, and when we are done, we are exhausted and our minds want nothing more than to relax.

Get a Good Night's Sleep

Equally important, get a good night's sleep each and every night. Your mind needs to be recharged and re-energized so that it can think clearly, and when we give it the seven to nine hours of sleep it needs, we are less likely to resort to negativity.

See a Therapist/Counselor

For many years, I wanted to see a therapist or a counselor as a preventive tool. When I finally found someone I was comfortable with and who understood my reason for scheduling sessions, I found it to be immensely beneficial. Some feel that seeing a counselor is a sign of weakness, but whether you are going for assistance to fix an aspect of your life or as preventive means of self-exploration, you should never see an investment in your overall well-being as a flaw. In fact, it takes great strength to say, I want to improve, and I know that, on my own, I cannot do everything or know everything. Perhaps an objective outsider can help me reach my full potential. In fact, in my first session, I was giddy. My counselor smiled, but it truly was me saying, I am here to continue to improve myself and make sense of my goals and better figure out how to make them a reality, while assisting myself and getting out of my own way.

Create and Maintain Rituals

Something we talk about often on *TSLL* blog is including rituals in your everyday routine. Whether they are daily, weekly, monthly, or seasonal, rituals provide regular moments of pleasure with a minimum of effort. In order to have rituals that hold a powerful positive influence over our lives, keep them clear and simple and enact them regularly. Stick to your walk in the morning, sip a cup of hot tea in the evening, and paint your toes on Sunday while watching Oprah's latest segment on *60 Minutes*. Rituals relax you and tend to your well-being all at the same time.

Sometimes we are not aware that our well-being is out of whack. And until we recognize why we are feeling the way we are, we can get down on ourselves and our lives. The good news is that while we are human and negativity will creep in from time to time, we know how to move past it so that it does not unduly affect ourselves or those we love.

Be Brave

I believe that the most important single thing, beyond discipline and creativity is daring to dare.
— Maya Angelou

Often, as we seek new experiences and achievements, we have to let go of our comfortable ways and change our approach as we go about our everyday lives. And that can make us fearful. We need to realize that what we fear is often an indication of the direction we desire to take. And if we are willing to tap into our bravery, the most amazing changes and an enriched life can become our reality. What do you receive by being brave?

You Become the Director of Your Life. The only way to ensure that your life is your own is to have the courage to step forward toward what you are curious about. Choose to seek a career path that speaks to your skills, rather than just your strengths. Decide to follow where your wandering mind leads you; be willing to do things on your own, and often you will discover what makes your soul truly come to life.

You Accept Room for Growth and Choose to Improve. Being brave is also about owning your mistakes, understanding that you are a work in progress, and finding the strength to seek guidance, support, and information when you do not have the answers to make the change or improvements you seek.

You Grab Hold of Opportunities. The true definition of luck is preparedness meeting opportunity; it is in moments of opportunity that we choose to step forward and seize what could be rather than fearing what could be lost. Often we are too concerned about what we know and refuse to discover what we do not know.

You Can Embrace Spontaneity. Yes, being brave can make us feel uncomfortable as we step outside of our comfort zone. Being disciplined and making tough decisions as we prioritize our lives is not always fun. Yet being brave is also about trusting ourselves — knowing that we can be spontaneous from time to time, let our hair down, and simply see where the moment takes us — because we know we have established a strong foundation to return to.

You Accept That Life's Events Are Not Always in Your Hands. Similarly, when we know we have a secure foundation, it becomes easier to recognize what is and what is not within our control. And when we are cognizant of the difference, we can detach from results we have no control over.

You Introduce Others to Your Talents. A scary task to embrace is showing others the heart and soul of who we are and what we can do. Those things that we hold dear, that we are passionate about, can make us vulnerable, and that can be intensely frightening. However, when we do begin to show others our talents and passions, people who we might work with, who might have similar passions and curiosities, begin to gravitate toward us, and relationships and opportunities begin to materialize.

You Avoid Unnecessary Energy Drains. Being brave can mean saying no, letting go, and walking away. Whether it is a relationship, a job, or a way of life, this is not always an easy decision, but energy is power, and when we use our energy defending ourselves or getting trapped in others' pointless dramas, we take away energy for living the life we desire.

You Unearth Your Fullest Potential. If we are not brave, we lose what the world would like to reveal to us. We lose the amazing life that wants to be our life.

You Turn Your Dreams into Reality. Those dreams you have as you are daydreaming at work or while driving are not random. They keep popping up again and again in the hope that you will do something with them, make something of them, bring them to fruition. After all, you will do something with that idea that no one else will because no one else is you.

Why Not . . . Meditate?

As more and more scientific research shows that meditation has direct effects on one's health, many who may have shied away from this simple, yet powerful practice are giving it a second thought. Meditation gives you back your mind, which becomes a muscle you can use to your benefit, rather than letting it run wickedly wild and pull you down with worries and fret.

You Will Have a Better Brain. Regular meditation improves memory and keeps your mind from wandering.

You Will Become More Present. When we are present, we are better able to appreciate and strengthen the conversations we are in, the life we are living, and the world around us. Meditation enhances the ability to be present as it allows us to control our thoughts, focus on our breathing, and relax our minds.

You Will Thwart Depression and Anxiety. When we lose control of our minds, we can drive ourselves batty with worry. As we practice controlling our thoughts through meditation, they become an instrument of success.

You Will Reduce Stress. Regular meditation can lower levels of cortisol (the stress hormone that, if secreted excessively and regularly, can damage blood vessels and weaken the heart) and decrease blood pressure.

You Will Find Emotional Balance. Whenever I find myself flustered or emotionally agitated, I retreat to my office or classroom, shut the door, sit down, and meditate for a few minutes. This practice generally brings me back to my more stable self.

How to Meditate. Do not make it too difficult. It really is simple, and you can craft it to fit your needs and comforts. Here are a few of the things that work for me, just as examples. Incorporate your own ideas as you see fit.

- **Find several minutes of quiet time without distraction.** Sit still and quiet your mind for two minutes. As you become more comfortable and able, increase the time.
- **Find a quiet, soothing spot.** I place my yoga mat on the floor in a room with natural light or outside on my back porch during the summer months. Even though my eyes will be closed, I want Mother Nature to be the first thing they see

when they open. Turn off all extra noise and reduce distractions.

- **Add personal components that will aid you in your practice.** Wear comfortable clothing, and if you do not want absolute silence, play tranquil music without words. I prefer the sounds of water — ocean waves, raindrops, etc.
- **Choose a regular time of day.** Perhaps you want to begin your day with a quiet moment to set the tone. Or maybe you would prefer quiet at the end of the busy workday to calm your mind before bed.
- **Establish a quiet mind.** The key is to not beat yourself up as thoughts begin to swirl. They will. Noticing active thoughts is evidence that you are paying attention to your mind (Andy of Headspace calls this "noting" — is it a thought or a feeling?); with time, you will be able to slow these thoughts and eventually cease them when you wish. The best way I have discovered to quiet my mind is to count my breath. Mix up the counts. For example, breathe in for 4 and out for 2. Breathe in for 4 and out for 4. Strengthen your breath and breathe in for 8 and out for 4. When you focus on breathing, your mind is not focusing on your thoughts.

I am far from a master at meditation, merely an amateur getting my sea legs. I do know that when I meditate, I feel a calmness that I wish to bring more of into my life.

Confidence: How to Build It

A person with confidence has a sense of assuredness, a sense of knowledge and understanding. Being confident does not mean you have to be confident in all aspects of your life. Based on your skill set, your experience, and your natural abilities, you may find certain tasks and expectations easier to perform. However, even though you may not be an expert in everything you attempt, you can still have a certain level of confidence at all times. How? Read on.

Know Your Style. Did you know that 55 percent of someone's first impression of you is your visual presentation? That leaves 38 percent based on how you speak, and 7 percent based on what you say. One's visual presentation also includes how we stand (good posture), our mannerisms (smiling, frowning, etc.), hair, accessories, and overall appearance. And so long as we are comfortable with our authentic style and can share our sincere personality, we are likely to feel comfortable. And when we are comfortable in our own skin, we project confidence.

Face Your Fears. When we attempt something we do not think we can do and eventually conquer this fear, we receive a shot of confidence that is through the roof.

Take Care of Yourself. Guilt should not be even considered as you take a little time each day or a lot each weekend to rejuvenate, rest, and begin anew with fresh legs the next day.

Take Action. Some people would say, "Fake it until you make it," but as Katty Kay and Claire Shipman point out in *The Confidence Code*, confidence is an authentic action, so "faking it" is not needed in order to acquire it. Instead, simply take action. Move forward. You will figure it out as you go, and the mistakes you make along the way will be invaluable. And your confidence will gradually, yet steadily rise.

The Power of the Spoken Word

Understanding the power of one's voice is important. Granted, looks play a significant role as well, but speech often begins the journey of understanding who someone is. How you speak — both the sounds you make and the words you utter — matters. Here is how to make sure your spoken words work to your advantage:

Speak Slowly. Speaking slowly suggests confidence that what we are saying should be listened to, that we will not be interrupted, and that something worthwhile is being shared. Much of this is about perception, but if you have something to say, gather your composure and maintain it as you speak . . . slowly and steadily.

Adjust Your Pitch and Tone. In 2010, researchers at Duke University released a study that showed that both men and women who spoke in low, deep voices were perceived as strong, dominant, and healthy. The catch that many women find to be a double standard is that women are assumed to be more attractive when they do not speak in lower tones, while men can continue to remain attractive doing the same thing. This assumption has much to do with traditional gender roles, in which women are subservient and docile, and men are strong, dominant, and authoritative. A potential employer or romantic partner who wants a weak woman may gravitate toward a high voice, but if someone is looking for a confident, equal woman, a lower pitch is certainly more attractive.

Eliminate the Up Talk. If you end declarative statements with a high pitch of heightened intonation, your statement comes across instead as an interrogative sentence — a question, a wondering, not a fact, not a point of resolution. However, if you end your statement with a lower pitch, the door is not open for questioning, wondering, or doubt. If you are indeed asking a question, a slightly higher pitch is understandable, but keep the end of your sentences low when you are making statements of fact or opinion.

Drop Filler Words. One of the most difficult habits to break is using filler words such as *like*, *uh*, *er*, and *um*. While often this way of speaking is just a habit, it makes the speaker seem unsure or unprepared.

Project. Even if you speak clearly and concisely, if people cannot hear you, what you say is not going to stick. Much has to do with posture; you project best when you breathe deeply from the abdomen, clear your throat, and speak confidently. The primary reason people speak softly is uncertainty about how they will be received. Speak up, do so with confidence, and allow yourself to be heard.

Smile. Even in times of trauma, warmth and comfort are reassuring. Perhaps you have noticed that someone who is a joy to talk to often is smiling, not scowling. When you speak, be aware of the face you are presenting to your listeners.

Eliminate the Apology. In June 2015, the *New York Times* published an article — "Why Women Apologize and Should Stop," by Sloane Crosley — about the excessive amount of apologizing women engage in, both consciously and unconsciously. Why should they stop? To put it succinctly, we should use our words to say what we really mean, to be declarative, tactful, and accurate, and to refrain from being passive. We can still be polite, respectful, and elegant, but we no longer need to reflexively apologize.

Know Your Audience. Whether you are being interviewed for a promotion at work or speaking to an acquaintance who might be someone to build a friendship with, note your diction, the subject matter, and items that should or should not be discussed. This finishing touch will show your awareness of and respect for the person you are talking with, and that is exceedingly powerful.

Because we so often communicate via technology, speaking with others — on the phone, via Skype, or in person — has increased in value. In those moments, we either confirm or erase the impression we created via the keyboard.

How to Increase Your Willpower

Willpower is the missing link in reaching human potential.
— Barry Michels

Much like a tank of gas, when we wake up after a good night's sleep, our minds contain a finite amount of willpower that will gradually be reduced but is never increased until we fuel it up again with rest and/or the proper food. Have you ever wondered why you are more quickly annoyed or less able to hold your tongue at the end of the workday? Most likely, it is because your willpower has been reduced or weakened. How can we preserve as much willpower as possible throughout each of our days?

Be a Planner. Stop procrastinating, and think about what you will do to reach your goals.

Play Offense Instead of Defense. Schedule preventive care and maintenance of your health, your home, your beauty routines, your savings, etc.

Know Your Individual Language. Become in tune with yourself so you can recognize when you are becoming more frustrated than normal or losing control of your impulses (eating, spending, etc.). Understanding how you are hard-wired (as shared in chapter eight) helps you understand the language you speak. Then take steps to get back in control.

Make To-Do Lists. Set goals, and be clear about why you want to pursue them. Refrain from setting too many, and discover the small steps it will take to get there.

Always Get a Full Night's Sleep. Sleep is a key fuel for the engine that is our willpower. Without it, no matter how we try, the quality of our lives will suffer.

Take Care of Your Health. Listen to your body. Maintain a regimen that includes aerobic, strength, and flexibility exercises, as well as a healthy diet and regular visits to your medical practitioner. Tend to what your body needs when something is not functioning properly; take time off when you get a cold, and see a doctor when something is not working as it should.

Monitor Yourself. Let your jeans tell you when to limit bread and desserts. Write down what you have done to progress toward your goals.

Include Rewards. Building up your self-control to better manage your willpower will take time, so reward yourself for the progress you make. Give yourself the motivation to keep going until the habit becomes ingrained.

Form Daily Habits That Are Beneficial. By doing so, you expend less energy in the long run.

What Having Strong Willpower Can Do for You

The benefits of having strong willpower can be summarized as the ability to create positive outcomes in our lives. Here's how:

It Improves Your Social Relationships. When we can successfully monitor our impulses, we are less likely to say or do something without first considering the outcome, particularly how others might feel or what might be gained or lost.

Attraction Builds. One of the most basic human needs is to feel included, recognized, and heard. Those who exhibit willpower are better able to step outside of themselves and consider those around them.

You Can Control Your Emotions. This is not about suppressing emotions; that would absolutely be unhelpful. Instead, become aware of how you are feeling, and exercise willpower to successfully address your emotions or communicate about them with others in a way that is helpful, not hurtful.

And Your Thoughts. Mastering our minds is hard when our willpower is depleted. The key is to recognize helpful or hurtful thoughts and shift gears into more productive and uplifting images and ideas.

Your Performance Improves. Whether at work or at home, when we are able to focus, we are better able to manage our time, manage or ignore distractions, and think clearly about how to successfully do what needs to be done. Most importantly, we are able to finish what we set out to do. Willpower enables us to focus, enables us to complete, and complete well, the task at hand.

Is it any wonder that those with strong willpower live successful and contented lives? While we always can and should try to increase our knowledge, our IQ is basically the same as when we were a child. We cannot radically change our intelligence, but we can radically change our willpower (a learned skill), and if we eliminate all unnecessary stressors, temptations, etc., we reduce the need to use it as often so that we can think freely and well to make the most of each and every day. Whether we are pursuing a goal or strengthening relationships, willpower is the key.

Be Productive

Accomplishing something is one of the most exhilarating and assured routes to contentment. When I do not know what to do with myself, it is usually because I do not feel I have been productive. However, the ability to relax is just as important, so we must find a balance between exerting effort to accomplish necessary tasks and allowing our bodies and minds to be rejuvenated.

Fuel Up. In order to do our best work and project our best selves into the world, we must fuel our body. When we eat a healthy, balanced breakfast (protein, fiber, and carbs), we are taking control of what is in our power. Follow up with a light, yet healthy lunch, an afternoon snack, and a dinner that is filling, but not bloating. And we must also fuel our mind — the attitude we carry with us throughout the day.

Turn It Off. It is easy to become distracted by the many offerings of the Internet — e-mail, favorite websites for news, shopping, and inspiration, as well as social media. Occasionally turn off your connection to the Internet, cell phones, and other devices, and just allow yourself to completely focus on the tasks before you. Whether it is your work or personal e-mail, set a limit on how many times you check it every day.

Get Organized. When you work in an organized space, office or home, you are also freeing your mind of unnecessary distractions and expanding its capacity to be more creative, focused, and productive. Take time to toss what you no longer need, file what you want to save, and create an organizational system that works best for your needs.

Regular Planning. Get into the habit of setting monthly, weekly, and daily goals or tasks you would like to accomplish. I look forward to the end of the month for the simple reason that it is when I plan the next (seriously, it does not take all that much to thrill me). I set three to five goals I want to accomplish by month's end. Sometimes they deal with finances, other times fitness — but no matter what it is, I write concrete goals that are measurable; for example, attend four yoga classes, reach out to two potential guests for the podcast, drink two bottles of water each day. As for weekly planning, create an enjoyable ritual for yourself; on a day that signifies the end of your weekend, take a look at the week ahead. Write down what you want to accomplish by the end of the week; while these goals might not be as easy to measure, when you write down something such as "contribute to a positive atmosphere at work," you are helping yourself to focus on this task the entire week. Daily planning begins by looking at your daily schedule the morning of the day at hand or the night before you go to bed. When I have completed my appointments and required tasks early, I feel okay just relaxing and do not feel I have to fill the empty time with more work. Remember, it is vital to find the balance and allow yourself to unwind regularly.

Keep It Simple. As consumers, we are offered many gadgets, gizmos, and creative new ways to do just about anything; however, more technology often makes things unnecessarily more complicated. I carry around a small notebook to write down ideas that pop into my head at random times. I use just one planning system; there are so many out there that if I were to use them all, I would be completely disorganized.

Be Flexible. No matter what your goal may be or how you hope to accomplish something, be flexible when unexpected events and obstacles get in your way. If you can maneuver successfully around them and not demand that things be completed in a certain way, you will reap far more rewards and earn the respect of others as they recognize your ability to adapt and work with their ideas.

Never Stop Learning. The key to remaining vital, "in the know," and relevant is to be a learner for life. Whether in the classroom or not, there are lessons just waiting to reveal themselves if only you choose to seize the opportunity. Remember, knowledge is key: Knowing what is available and what is possible is putting the odds in your favor.

Regular Creativity Breaks. If you are working in a creative field, you must treat your mind as a muscle that needs to be rested, especially after bouts of exhaustive effort. After a certain number of days of constant creative writing or brainstorming, it becomes difficult to think of one more creative and unique idea, but after a day or two off, I am fresh with ideas from experiences I have had or articles I have read. Breaks are a must if we are to continually be creative and successful.

Eliminate What Is Unnecessary. Examine the activities and expenditures you make every week. Which ones are not tied to any of your top priorities? Can you eliminate them? Will they free up time and resources that can be put to better use? The key is to live consciously and to recognize why you are doing something. If you are simply acting out of habit, think about dropping activities that do not add real value to your life.

Be a Problem Solver. Difficulties will arise — that is a given — but it is the way we compose ourselves and deal with the issue that will determine the effect of the problem at hand. There are many things we are capable of tackling and completing on our own, even when we do not think we can (simple plumbing and electrical fixes around the house, negotiating to lower a bill or a price on an item you need). There are also times when it is wise to call someone who is an expert and can save you time, eliminate unnecessary frustration, and possibly teach you something.

Do Not Be Shy. No matter where you work, it is imperative that you be your own advocate when it comes to earning the respect and credit you deserve. Especially when you are running your own business, you must be comfortable with tooting your own horn. Be bold and tactfully boastful and you are sure to garner more deserved attention.

Self-Assess. One of the most helpful tools that leads to greater productivity is to plan regular times throughout the year to assess how well you are progressing toward your intended targets. By sitting down often (perhaps monthly) and looking at what you want to achieve and what has worked so far, you can eliminate what is not working and make adjustments.

Revel in Down Time. Occasionally take an afternoon or a whole day to just do nothing. Do not try to glean inspiration, cultivate new ideas, or complete home projects. Just be. We need to regularly refuel, to allow ourselves to do as we please. Sometimes it is during your vacations and days off that you come across what intrigues you.

Take Tasks One at a Time. There is a misunderstanding about multitasking. There is an assumption that the more you can do at one time, the more you will accomplish, but this is simply not an effective way to become more productive. As with anything in life, when we devote our entire focus to a task, we are able to do our best because we are not distracted. The same is true for any task you choose to take on: Do it well so that you only have to do it once. Knowing you did a quality job will also provide a peace of mind that is priceless.

Ask for Advice. Often we run up against a question that we do not have an answer for. Instead of becoming frustrated with yourself, seek out someone you trust and respect, and ask for their advice and guidance. They will most likely be flattered, and you will be stretching yourself to continually learn.

Pick Your Battles. In both your personal life and professional life, sometimes voicing your opinion, confronting someone, or getting in the middle just is not worth your time. While you may become agitated by something someone says at work, ask yourself: Is this worth my energy? Does this take something away from me on a deeper level or devalue me as a person? If you answer no, then let it go.

Finding a Balance

Regularly reassess the balance you have that will propel you to work at your optimal best, help you meet your goals and aspirations, and bring harmony into your life as a whole. I love to go back and reread many books that I keep on my shelves; one of them is Mireille Guiliano's *Women, Work and the Art of Savoir Faire: Business Sense and Sensibility.* Guiliano writes that one of the important anchors of each of our lives is the work-life balance. She describes it as a four-legged support system. These points, which I lay out below, are fairly self-explanatory, but she notes that each person will have a different approach to them — especially the fourth element, your personal zen.

One ritual I love to partake in at the end of August and beginning of September, as well with the start of each new calendar year and my personal new year, my birthday, is to go through each of these four points and set goals, make schedules, and determine how I will be sure to find this balance.

Good Health. I create a weekly schedule of how many times I would like to walk and which days and times would work best with my schedule, and when I will carve out time for yoga and strength training. If I have it in my planner and set in my mind that I want to complete two strength training sessions a week, do yoga on Saturday mornings, and walk with my dogs every morning, I have a goal in mind, and I view it as an appointment. Sometimes things do not occur exactly as I have planned and I have to move some days around, but when you have a goal, you can feel accomplished when you know you have completed your fitness regimen. The same approach works for eating as well.

Healthy/Supportive Social Network. Some people need more time with others, some need less. Some find it through friends, some through family, some through both. The key is to have an outlet for sharing and discussing with people you trust. Everyone's groups will be different, and they will change as you go through life, but be sure you have one or more trusted confidants who have your back.

Solid Work Situation. I am a writer and a high school humanities teacher, and I appreciate the time to reboot for my teaching career during the summer. As well, I am cognizant that I need to protect my wells of creative energy for my writing career throughout the year, doubly so when I am engaged in both careers for nine months. At the beginning of each school year, I try to design my day so that I will have less stress and enjoy increased productivity. Whether it is stocking healthy treats ahead of time so that when I need a boost I reach for almonds instead of donuts or examining which days are best for completing particular themed posts throughout the week for the blog, I try to learn from what worked in the past and tweak what needs adjusting. On a larger scale, we all need to take time to assess whether we are in a career with opportunities for growth and whether we are taking advantage of them.

Your Personal Zen. We all need regular time to immerse ourselves in hobbies and leisurely pursuits that lower our stress and bring utter joy. This can be regular pampering at a spa, kayaking in a nearby lake, going out on the town to listen to a favorite musician, having a novel waiting for you on your nightstand, or cooking with your significant other. Whatever it is that brings you pleasure, erase the thought that it is selfish because, in fact, it is necessary.

Skills Worth Practicing No Matter What Your Age

Before Serena Williams won her first grand slam tennis final in 1999 at age eighteen, she had been practicing and finessing her game since she was three years old. That's fifteen years of practice. Success not only in our careers but in our daily lives comes from intentionally choosing to improve, to grow, again and again and again, day after day, even when seemingly no reward has been achieved . . . yet. The glory of Williams winning twenty-three grand slam titles did not just occur. Yes, she has been at the top of the leader board many times over the past fifteen years, but there were many stumbles, setbacks, and significant challenges along the way.

Living well is not something we innately know how to do. We have to be a student of life. We have to be willing to not get it right from time to time. We have to be willing to refuse to settle for what we know if what we know does not work for us, does not sit well, or is not giving us the results, deeper connections, and peace of mind we seek.

The good news about so much of the life we want to create for ourselves, for those we love, and for the world is that with repeated practice, we can retrain our mind, which is not dependent on external conditions but rather on inner strength. Inner strength is something we all are capable of. This section takes a look at invaluable skills we all can practice that can have profoundly positive effects on the overall quality of our everyday lives.

Loving Well. Often the kink in not being able to find contentment is not understanding how the love we seek actually works. Too often we are seeking it rather than cultivating it. When we cultivate it and do it well, we recognize that it is a skill — something we can bring into our lives simply by embodying it in our daily actions and thoughts.

Refining Your Craft. Generally, someone who appears to be an overnight success has worked for years at their craft — exploring, tweaking, learning, making mistakes, and continuing to practice what they love, whether the response is applause or stone-cold silence. Whatever it is that you love to do, simply practice it a little every single day.

Learning Endlessly. There are many different learning styles, but all of us can learn. Discover how to learn. Discover how to ask questions. And ask questions, constantly.

Thinking Critically. Christopher Hitchens said, "The essence of the independent mind lies not in what it thinks, but in how it thinks." With everything that you observe, hear, and experience, think critically. Why? While it is simpler and far less straining to be led around by the nose — whether by society, family, friends, or an institution — that is supremely dangerous.

Being Grateful. Exercising gratitude in your everyday life not only improves your peace of mind; it also can improve your job prospects and income, and thus the quality of your overall life. Daily gratitude has been shown to enhance alertness, enthusiasm, determination, attentiveness, and energy — qualities that employers look for in prospective employees and in those they want to promote.

Being Present. Mindfulness is a skill that requires us to first master our mind; in doing so, we become able to be fully present in the moment. Meditation has been proven to condition us to be more mindful, and there are many other benefits as well (see the section above). The gifts of being mindful are plentiful, but it ultimately reveals to us the life we are truly living — allowing us to see the good, to see the truth — and if we are not content with what we see, to be motivated to do what needs to be done.

Letting Go. We must practice letting go of what we have no control over and finding peace with outcomes that may not be what we desire but nonetheless are a reality. The sooner we practice letting go with grace, the sooner we welcome peace into our lives and recognize that we are much better served when we focus on what we can control.

Being Vulnerable and Setting Boundaries. Knowing how and when to set boundaries takes practice. The process is most definitely a ying and yang situation, but both are needed in order to attain and maintain healthy relationships.

Taking Chances. "Take chances, make mistakes. That's how you grow. Pain nourishes your courage. You have to fail in order to practice being brave." So said Mary Tyler Moore. At first, taking chances is scary. And sadly, some take a chance and do not reap what they had hoped, so they never take a chance again, certain that it will not be worth it. Such a fear, while understandable and natural, is unfounded. As Mary Tyler Moore attests, it is through mistakes and pain that we realize we are tougher and mightier and more amazing than we realized, and that builds our confidence. So take chances now and often. I promise you your life will continue to amaze you.

A Complete Toolbox

Our strengths will be amplified by the skills we take the time to learn and integrate into our everyday lives. Below is a summation of the key strengths and skills we have discussed in chapters eight and nine.

Strengths: self-acceptance . . . understanding your temperament: how you are hard-wired . . . your ability to address insecurities . . . authenticity . . . self-reliance . . . self-actualization.

Skills: your emotional intelligence . . . your ability to be an optimist . . . bravery . . . confidence . . . effective communication . . . willpower . . . productivity.

Much like the patience that is needed as we wait for a contractor to finish a project we have envisioned, we must be patient with ourselves as we complete our toolbox with the strengths and skills that will enhance the quality of our lives.

CHAPTER TEN

How to Make a Successful Fresh Start

A fresh start. A clean slate. A second chance. All are ways to describe the gift of starting over. Perhaps a relationship has ended or you have relocated to a new city. Or maybe you are starting a new job, redecorating a room in your home, reorganizing your files, or simply pressing the reset button on any aspect of your life that has not been working or did not work out as you had hoped.

While beginning from scratch can feel as though you are a novice again, in reality you are more of an expert than you realize, should you choose to use your powers. When you begin again, you bring with you the wisdom of what did and did not work, the insight of knowing how something will turn out in a particular circumstance, and the ability to not waste precious time and energy doing something that will not yield the results you seek.

Take Time to Assess

Before moving forward, take time to assess in detail what went well, what did not work, and why. Write down your insights so that during times of frustration in any new endeavor, you can remind yourself how to overcome the roadblocks that stood in your way the last time. Even with a simple change, such as switching from a PC to a Mac, begin with an assessment to ensure a successful path forward. Write down what went wrong that impeded your ability to work efficiently on your computer. What do you want to make sure your new computer will be capable of doing?

Be Clear

As you begin again, be clear about what your expectations are. Then be willing to be flexible about how you get there. Maybe the computer will not be the size you want because of your budget, but it still offers what you need for productivity. The key is to know what you need versus what you want. Knowing the difference will reduce unnecessary headaches and help you achieve your goals at a faster pace.

Have Patience

You have learned some valuable lessons, but that does not mean your new journey will be free of frustrations. For example, even if the new job is one you have worked toward for years, there will still be a learning curve in understanding the new work environment. Have patience with yourself, and do not throw in the towel too quickly. I have come to define such initial headaches as checkpoints assessing whether or not we are willing to be where we have longed to be.

Keep Your Courage

The moments of doubt are greatest when you make the initial leap of change — when you do something different from what you have done in the past — putting the down payment on your first home, saying "I do," or taking out a loan for your own business. In such moments, you must hang on to the courage it took you to make the initial mistake that provided the lesson. That courage is always there, waiting to be tapped, and each time you learn the lesson and pick yourself up to try it again differently, the strength of your courage increases.

Having the opportunity to do something again is the opportunity to do it better and to tailor it exactly as you would prefer. Not everything in life offers a second chance. After all, we only get to be eighteen years old once, thirty-four once, fifty once, and so on. But regardless of your age, when you get the chance to improve, do not be discouraged by mistakes in past relationships, past employment, money management, or anything that has tripped you up. Choose to turn coal into diamonds, and be amazed at the rewards life will offer you.

Ways to Fix a Bad Day

There are days when, even when you walk out the door with a spring in your step, you still cannot seem to catch a break. Perhaps incessant demands, unexpected delays, last-minute changes, or any number of events beyond your control occur, and you are dumbfounded as to how the day shifted from where you intended it to go.

It would be ideal if we could press a restart button or take a time out to catch our breath, but sometimes these options are not available when we desperately need them and you feel you might be losing all control. Below are a few remedies to help you end such a day in the manner in which you began it — with a spring in your step, a hopeful smile on your face, and a reassured state of mind.

Control What You Can. We always have control over what we say and what we do. During such stressful times, we must exercise self-control so that we do not erupt simply to relieve our frustrations. When you feel out of control, remind yourself that the day will end and aim for the goal of applauding yourself for watching your tongue and your temper. You will sleep far better knowing you did.

Find Time to Power Down. When you get home, shut off your devices, turn off the television, and just breathe. No noise, no demands, just separation from a bad day that is thankfully winding down.

Time with Loved Ones. When I cross the threshold into my home and hear the quick pitter-patter of my dogs' feet, their smiling, wiggly happiness lifts my mood instantly. Whether it is your pets, your children, your spouse, or your closest friend, try to spend some time with them or at least connect on the phone (maybe not with the dogs). Let your hair down, vent if necessary, and just be in the company of those who love you.

Write It Out. Sometimes the safest and best therapy is to pick up your journal or computer and just write. Simply putting your frustrations on paper can act as a release and a way to organize why you became so frazzled and uptight. Sometimes we do not realize in the moment what has set us off, and when we take the time to assess after the events have taken place, we give ourselves an opportunity to learn and handle similar situations differently.

Exercise. When I step into a yoga class and have to hold a pose, there is nothing else on my mind except for my muscles screaming at me for not keeping them in better shape. And when I finish, I feel a sense of accomplishment that may not have been achieved during a bad day.

Do Not Drown or Overindulge Your Stressors. Keep your eating and drinking in check on days when your patience and nerves are frazzled. In fact, do not put yourself in a situation where your willpower will be tested. Instead, prepare a simple, yet comforting meal (or purchase takeout at your favorite eatery); fuel your body with something that will leave you feeling good about at least one thing you had control over during the day — your diet and health.

Take a Bath. Surround yourself with warmth — literally. Soak in a hot bath and close your eyes. Necessary me-time is not a luxury; it is mandatory.

Refrain from Making Significant Decisions. Do yourself a favor and put any big decisions on hold when you run up against a day that just is not working in your favor. Tomorrow you will be glad you heeded this advice, as you will have averted another day of frustration caused by rash decision making. Often, instead of making the right decision, we simply make a decision to get it done, but really the only thing we are doing is making more work for ourselves down the road.

Slow Down and Have a Cup of Tea. Or the hot drink of your choice. Heating up the water to have a cup of my favorite tea slows me down. I have to find time to enjoy it, press pause for a moment, and enjoy the warmth. This can also be a wonderful time to close your eyes and have a mini-meditation session to clear your mind.

Seven Tricks for a Successful Leap

Last summer, while sitting on a swinging bench at my country getaway (my childhood home, aka my parents' house), I was greeted by the sight of a haphazardly flying bird — a young robin — coming directly toward my face. Wings flailing, it hit me square in the cheek and continued to soar to a rocky landing a few yards away in the garden. Needless to say, my attention had been captured.

I recognized the young fledgling, as I had rescued it earlier in the morning from a handful of curious dogs and cats after it fell during an early trip from the nest. Throughout the rest of the day, I kept a curious lookout for the amateur flyer as it found a temporary safe sanctuary in a lilac tree. While the parent kept feeding and nudging the young bird to continue to try to fly, for the remainder of the afternoon the fledgling kept close to its newfound perch.

What became apparent during my daylong observation was that a new journey can be fraught with unsteadiness, anxiety about whether it will all work out, and fear that we may fall flat on our face (or into someone's face, as was the case for this little fledgling). But with each subsequent attempt, the young robin's strength grew, its ability to fly improved, and its direction became more precise. What can we do to turn a frightful journey, yet one we are eager for, into a successful endeavor?

Listen and Heed What Comes Naturally. What do you love to do, what are you passionate about, what keeps calling your name, and what are you drawn to like a moth to a flame? Such passion will be the fuel to help you through initially frustrating or frightening moments.

Create a Strong Support System. Find people who sincerely believe in you. Reach out and discover those who have traveled the path you are about to take, and learn from their journey.

Understand Your Fear and Master It. Fear is natural, as it is our mind recognizing that we do not know what an outcome will be; therefore, it is trying to protect us from suffering. But if we are striving toward an unknown and doing something purposefully, often fear is a sign that we are headed in the right direction, because part of the fear is wondering what our lives will be like if we do not succeed.

Keep Striving Forward. No matter how small the steps may seem, with each one we learn what works, what it feels like to follow this new path, what a successful step looks like, and how to improve. The power of small steps is that they add up, and along the way you have created a strong foundation of knowledge and understanding of what it took to get where you are.

Proceed at a Pace That Is Comfortable for You. We cannot expect everyone to travel at the same speed or to gain their sea legs at the same moment because everyone has had a different set of past experiences.

As you begin to move forward, keep checking in with yourself. Perhaps someone in your support system genuinely believes you can move more quickly; even though they may mean well, if that pace does not sit well with you, respect how you feel. So long as you resolve to never give up, you will get there — in your own time.

Learn from Your Mistakes Along the Way. A perfect life would be a boring life. So rather than cursing when mistakes and setbacks occur, mine them for all the valuable knowledge they can offer. There is always something to discover that will help you along your way.

Pay Attention to People You Can Trust and People to Avoid. Who cheers when you succeed, and who is only there when you are down but disappears when you are soaring? Hold fast to those who genuinely cheer for your happiness, and let go of those who only want your company to bolster their own contentment.

As much as we want our journey to a new life, career path, or destination to be unobstructed, more often than not, we will encounter something we had not planned on. Instead of being defeated, tuck the valuable, unique knowledge into the back of your mind as it may turn out to be a life saver at a later point.

The Difference between Being Scared and Having Doubts

New things are scary. Anything worth having is scary.
— Shonda Rhimes, series finale of *Private Practice*

While reading Hope Alcocer's contributing blog post to *Verily* regarding red flags when it comes to relationships, I was reminded of doubt, and how instinctually, when I have doubts, it is my subconscious pointing out something that I have not fully grasped but need to take time to investigate. In contrast, while reading Barbara Stanny's book *Secrets of Six-Figure Women*, I was reassured that having fears is natural if what we are seeking is something we genuinely want — a life change, a new job, etc.

There is significant evidence to support the claim that having doubts is much different than being scared or feeling fear. Simply stated, doubt is a red flag that exists because of your life's experience, and fear is a natural uncertainty based not on experience but perhaps the voices of others or society in general, but not doubt you have regarding your own abilities.

When you are fearful or scared, it is because you have no evidence that you can or cannot do something, which is all the more reason to try. It is natural to feel apprehension, as you have no proof that you will succeed, but then again, you have no proof that you will not either. If we desire to take that leap of faith and work toward a dream that others may not grasp yet or pursue a life change that breaks the mold, we are fearful partially because we feel we will not be able to make it happen. In this case, so long as you believe more resolutely that you can rather than that you cannot, you will be successful.

On the other hand, having doubts involves previous experience, knowledge of similar behavior, and an ability to know more about a situation than others either want you to know, or perhaps they do not even understand it themselves. For example, in a previous relationship that I eventually ended, I began seeing red flags (or having doubts) five months prior to the relationship ending; however, I did not want to accept what I knew instinctually to be true, so I kept working at the relationship. It was not until I saw evidence of my doubts realized that I recognized my instincts were correct, and I thankfully chose to follow what I had subconsciously been aware of all along. Much later, further evidence reassured me that I had made the correct decision. The good news about doubts is that they are our constant warriors of protection, and it is our job to investigate what they are trying to tell us.

The key to discerning the difference between whether you are feeling doubt or fear is to know yourself fully. Only you can honestly say why you are feeling what you are feeling. Only you can say, I want it so badly that if I do not achieve it, I will ache incessantly. Only you can say, I don't trust what is promised. There is a great difference between these two statements. Know yourself, and you will know how to proceed.

Fifteen Ways to Banish Worry

If you are distressed by anything external, the pain is not due to the thing itself, but to your estimate of it; and this you have the power to revoke at any moment.
— Marcus Aurelius

A handful of years ago, I was speaking with a fellow blogger about resolutions. One that we discovered we had in common for 2013 was the desire to be able to be more present in our daily lives. Sounds simple enough, but in my experience, plans for the future can too often infiltrate the present, thereby squashing potentially memorable moments. For others, the obstacle that impedes the ability to fully enjoy the present may be hanging on to the past, refusing to let go or move forward.

Whether the past or the future is hog-tying your mind, the foundation for many of the reservations that prevent people from being fully present and living a rich and full life involves an element of worry: worry that things will never be the same after something loved is lost or uncertainty about how things will work out in the future.

Did you know that worry, stress, despair, angst, selfishness, anxiousness, and anger can cause a long list of diseases such as ulcers, headaches, insomnia, depression, tumors, and rheumatism, just to name a few? It is what the worry causes the body to do internally that prevents it from doing the job it was meant to do — heal itself. Our bodies are amazing machines, so much so that we do not realize how well they take care of themselves, so long as we allow them to.

Dale Carnegie's book *How to Stop Worrying and Start Living* is based on common sense, science, and many firsthand stories that demonstrate that worry is unnecessary, plus advice for how to conquer it and the benefits of doing so. After pouring over the book, I have come up with my own list, which includes Carnegie's tips that I have found to work for myself.

Respond Rationally to What You Are Worried About. This four-step plan eliminates 99 percent of the worries I have running around in my head: Write down exactly what you are worried about, write down what you can do about it, decide the best course of action, and start immediately to fulfill the course of action you have decided upon.

Realize That Most Things We Worry about Never Materialize. If you look at the law of averages, it is easy to see that we worry far too much. Think of all that could be imagined, created, and enjoyed with the energy saved when we stop worrying unnecessarily.

Master Your Thoughts. If we believe we are living a grand, full life that is brimming with potential, our attitude is projected out into the world, and we draw to ourselves others of like thinking. The opposite is true as well. One of the first pieces of advice Carnegie offers is to "be content to live the only time we can possibly live: from now until bedtime." It is imperative in order to live our best life that we stay in the present, remaining confident that we have assessed and learned the lessons of the past and have adequately put ourselves on the right path for the future to work out in the best possible way. When you know these two things, it is much simpler to live in the present. For a more extended discussion, see "Master Your Mind" in chapter eight.

Never Stop Gaining Knowledge. Whatever it is that is causing your fear, stop fretting and start doing something productive, beginning with gaining credible knowledge so that you can squash unnecessary fear and, if need be, make a plan to deal with what is ahead of you in a constructive manner. "Confusion is the chief cause of worry." Eliminate the confusion and eliminate your worries.

Relax, Before You Need It, and Do So Regularly. It has happened to me a few times — once in college after finals and another time at the end of a seemingly endless build-up of demands at work that I refused to say no to; when I finally stopped to rest, I became quite sick. Had I balanced my workload with intermittent respites to relax and unwind, taken time away from work and simply put my responsibilities down even if they were not entirely done quite yet, I may have saved myself the utter exhaustion that finally forced me to stop. In order to do our best, we must be at our best. And that means resting our minds (as well as our bodies) regularly to allow them both to recharge.

Get Busy. This may sound counter to the advice above, but after a difficult emotional event, often the best way to silence our worries is to throw ourselves into a project — something physically or mentally challenging, so that the brain has to focus on that one task and is not able to wander or worry. While there must come a time to slow down and assess (because we cannot run from what scares us forever if we wish to live a contented life), until we have some distance, sometimes the best thing is to focus on something that is purposeful and distracting.

Sit Down Regularly and Self-assess. Benjamin Franklin was regular in this practice, sitting down every evening to pause, reflect, gain wisdom from his mistakes, and decide what he should do the following day to productively move forward. While you may not want to do it every day (though your evening journal time is a great time to indulge), structure your life to include this valuable routine.

Do Your Best and Let It Go. Perfection is impossible, so we cannot expect things to always go off without a hitch. However, you can control whether you bring your best self to the table. So long as you know you did your best at that given moment, based on the experience and resources you were able to gather, let any criticism roll off your back. Had you known better, you would have done better.

Do Not Waste a Minute on Your Enemies. At some point in your life, someone may have hurt you or you may have been unjustly wronged, but it is a waste of time, energy, and the chances for potential opportunity to give them any of your thoughts. Move forward and let the past worry about itself. Stay in the present.

Be Grateful. Remember that tune from the movie *White Christmas* — "Count your blessings instead of sheep, and you'll fall asleep counting your blessings"? When we realize how fortunate we already are, we bring peace to our mind, calming ourselves down and instilling a state of contentment.

Do Not Imitate Others. Find yourself and be yourself. The most powerful and life-changing discovery we can each make is to take the time to discover who we are. Self-discovery takes time and continues until the day we die. By refusing to be anyone but who we are, we offer our gift to the world; we stop trying to fit in and be accepted; we reveal to the world the gift that we are — and that is when the magic happens (and a lot of unnecessary pressure falls away).

Let Go of the Little Things. It can take a significant lesson to remind us what we should and should not be filling our minds with. Once you have survived a plane crash or a car wreck, worrying about matching socks is not that big of a deal. Learn this lesson now before a grand lesson has to take place, and free your mind of worry so that you can enjoy all that is going well.

Accept the Inevitable and Focus on Making Your New Life Richer. There will be things that happen that we do not want, that cause great pain and destroy the vision we may have had for our lives; however, the most productive and helpful thing is to accept the facts and vow to make your life going forward as rich as humanly possible.

"Don't saw sawdust." Stop worrying about the past. This is such simple advice, yet based on how much we have emotionally invested ourselves in something, it can be hard to do. However, so long as we know we did our best and take time to learn a lesson that ensures it does not happen again, we help ourselves to move forward.

Never Give More Energy to a Thing than It Is Worth. While it is healthy to grieve, cry, and mourn for something that is lost, set a limit, and then once that limit is met, dry your eyes and move forward. You may need someone to help you do this initially; the goal is to ensure you do not spend more energy on something that does not deserve more than what you have already given it.

Trust the Timing of Your Life

Pasta must be cooked for a particular length of time to reach the perfect al dente state, and it is best for the health of a newborn to remain in the womb for the full gestation period. Timing is important. It makes a difference. If you allow a steak to remain on the grill for two minutes more, it can go from medium-rare to medium; add two minutes and you are at medium-well. But you must cook it for at least four minutes on each side for it to be worth eating at all. Everything has a timing that works best for the desired results.

Trusting the timing of our lives is hard. While we may look up to other individuals and try to pattern our lives after them, we each come from unique circumstances and need to learn specific lessons to reach our final destination. So how do we successfully trust the timing of our lives and not fight it?

Let Go of Impatience. Having goals is a brilliant idea, and striving for them each day with small steps is the best plan, but you may need to be flexible about when you are expecting to arrive at the goal. You do not know what you do not know, so you will not know the lessons you need to learn until they are presented. And how long it will take to learn these lessons will depend upon you.

Accept the Lessons. Do not try to avoid them. The first time you make a mistake is forgivable. How could you have known, right? But when you continue to make the same mistake again and again, perhaps life is trying to teach you a lesson that you are refusing to absorb. Do you keep dating the same type of person and it never works out? Do you continue to communicate in a manner that is riddled with emotion rather than calm, rational thoughts and never seem to feel that you are being heard or respected? Perhaps a change of approach is needed. Learn the lesson.

Learn to Trust Yourself. The most important element of building trust with others is to learn how to trust yourself. How do you begin to trust yourself? It may sound simple and commonsensical, but I am always amazed by how many people do not do this: Get to know yourself. When you come to understand who you are — what makes you tick, what can get under your skin and why, what you need, and where you can be flexible in life — decisions become much easier to make. This job or that job. That house or this apartment. Continue dating this person or move on. You get the idea. When we do not know ourselves, we cannot trust ourselves, and therefore, we cannot be sure about the lessons we need to learn. This affects the timing of our lives.

Enjoy Your Own Company. When you are comfortable with time on your own, you do not make decisions just to avoid being alone. Often you truly want to do what you say yes to, but if you are uncomfortable being alone from time to time, you will say yes when you really do not want to and potentially keep making mistakes that disrupt the timing of your life. Again, it comes back to getting to know yourself so that the decisions, when they need to be made, are easier.

Be Willing to Persevere. Simply because you were denied something you were aching for — traveling abroad, having children, owning a house, getting a particular job, finding the love of your life, etc. — does not mean life is denying you that path. The question is, What is it you truly desire? Is the desire coming from you or from society? If the desire is coming from within you — if you cannot squash it and it remains at the forefront of your mind — listen to it. Perhaps the universe or God, whatever you call divine intervention in your life, is saying, You are not ready. But "You are not ready" does not mean denial. What it means is you have not learned the necessary lessons to either appreciate or make the most of the opportunity that will come when you are actually ready.

Be Honest with Yourself. Sometimes it can be uncomfortable to admit where we need to improve. Perhaps we have trust issues. Perhaps we do not know how to communicate effectively or lovingly. Perhaps we do not know how to balance our budget. In each of these instances, simply getting to this realization is a huge step. When we are honest about what we do not know how to do in order to successfully pursue our goals, we can then find assistance to become the person we need to be to have the life we desire. What might that look like? Take a class on budget management, schedule an appointment with a counselor or life coach, or begin to change daily habits that have not yielded the results you seek (eating, exercising, spending, gossiping, etc.).

Become Comfortable with Unknowns. On the day you were born, your parents were not given a manual telling them what the future had in store for you so that they might prepare you for what lay ahead. No. You are unique; you have your own journey, but you must begin to live. Be present each day. Savor the day. Dance with it, and see your journey as a treasure hunt. Learn the lessons when they are presented to you along the way; indulge in your victories and successes, no matter how winding the path may seem. You will get there.

Technically, you are already there because you are today exactly where you need to be to get to where you want to go tomorrow, so long as you heed these seven steps. Trusting the timing of your life is not an easy thing to do, depending upon where you currently are in your life.

I am trusting life now more than I ever have. I had wanted to move to Bend more than nine years ago, but the timing in many arenas was not right (housing marketing, my teaching expertise, etc.). I tried to acquire a teaching job in 2014, and it didn't pan out. Upon reflection, that attempt fine-tuned me for my successful attempt to move to Bend in 2015. Embedded in that experience is yet another life lesson: There is no such thing as failure if you learn from it. Every life experience is offering you fuel, knowledge, and experience you can use later.

In late December during my first year in Bend, I was taking my regular weekly walk along the Deschutes River with my dogs. The afternoon sun was gradually sinking, and the sunlight danced upon the running water. As I looked out upon the river, I saw, soaring upstream, a great blue heron. Its speed was hampered by the gentle breeze, but it still proceeded upward, and as it did, a second heron came flying in from the far side of the river, heading in the same direction. The two birds' speeds became synchronized, seemingly instantaneously, as they found each other and flew off out of sight around the river's bend.

In many ways, we each are one of these herons. We must travel the direction that speaks to us, and at times we may have to soar alone, but the beauty is that we get to soar. Sometimes we will have to go against the wind, and sometimes the wind will be at our backs, but we only get further along in our journey if we soar forward. We will meet the people and the occurrences that are meant to be in our lives along this unique journey, but we must continue along it. Trust your timing.

How to Successfully Transition Your Life from One Zip Code to Another

The homes we inhabit are extensions of ourselves. They not only become the hug that greets us each evening when we return from being out in the world, with all its uncontrollable variables; they also provide a sense of security, a source of inspiration, and a place for our routines to continue, including restful sleep and meals and conversation to energize us. So relocating to another town, state, or country can be daunting and give rise to a mixed bag of emotions.

In 2015, I relocated to Bend, Oregon, after living nine years in the eastern part of the state. I never would have expected such a life transition to unfold so smoothly. I want to share with you how it happened, so that you too, whether you are simply moving from one side of town to another or to an entirely different zip code, can begin your new life on the best footing possible — rested, cognizant of what you want, knowing how to go about doing it, and giddy about your new prospects.

Before

Mail. The U.S. Post Office requires ten working days' notice to redirect your mail to your new address. Fill out the simple form at your local branch.

Subscriptions. If you change your mailing address early enough, you may be able to designate a date to have your address switched.

Financial, Insurance, Loans, Credit, Bank Accounts. Each must be updated with the new mailing address.

Driver's License. Call your state's DMV or go online to change your mailing address. A new label will be mailed to you, free, within a week to stick onto your current driver's license.

Voter Registration Card. Go to your new state's secretary of state's web page or simply type in "[state name] voter registration." As long as you have a driver's license or a Social Security number, you will be able to change your county or residence so you can vote in the next election.

Current Utilities. If you are leaving a rental, or if your house has been sold and you do not need to keep it heated, the yard watered, etc., then shut down all utilities. If your home is still for sale or the sale has not closed, keep your water, heat/AC, electricity, and gas up and running. Utilities you will want to have shut off or moved include cable, Internet, water, garbage, heat (gas and/or electric), electricity, and landlines.

Set Up New Utilities. Some utilities are simple and can be turned on at the last minute (water, electricity, etc.), but for others, a technician will need to stop by your home; for example, if you want to have television and Wi-Fi when you arrive, you will need to schedule well in advance. The utilities you might need to sign up for include cable and Internet (call three to four weeks out to schedule an appointment); water; garbage pickup (have bins dropped off before you arrive, and ask about pick-up date and times, as well as any rules or extra charges); heat (gas and/or electric); and phone (if you only have a cell phone, you generally just need to change your address).

Moving Company. While I had the wonderful help of family during earlier moves, this time I decided to hire a moving company. (Remember, the cost of the move can be written off when you file your taxes, if you itemize.) Scope out a few moving companies and schedule them to stop by to give you an estimate; ask for recommendations of customers they have worked with. Ask about purchasing insurance; movers generally offer different levels of coverage. Usually everything they pack is insured and anything you pack is not.

Plan a Moving Sale. A move is a wonderful opportunity to eliminate from your life items, furniture, clothes, and anything else you no longer use. A moving sale also makes it easy for neighbors and acquaintances to stop by, chat, and say good-bye.

Get Your Beauty Info. Gather your hair color information from your hairstylist, your tanning color from your aesthetician, and anything else that you will need as you move to a new set of professionals.

Let Your Emotions Out. Give your emotions free rein, whatever they are. Crying, dancing, cheering — just do it. It is natural. You are either grieving the loss of the life you are leaving behind or exuberantly celebrating your growth and new beginnings. Either way, feel it, move through it, and then strive forward.

Label Boxes. Make sure that all boxes are clearly labeled on the sides (not the top) with the contents of the box and the room it belongs in.

Pack a Travel Tote. Most likely you will be traveling or living out of a suitcase for a night or two. Before the movers arrive, pack your suitcase as though you were traveling, plus any pet supplies, so that you can be comfortable during the transition.

After

Set Up Mail Service. If you have a locked mailbox (such as in the block of mailboxes in many neighborhoods), stop by your local post office branch for the key. If you have to have a key made, it will cost you $40. If you have a traditional mailbox, you will typically only have to fill out a card for the mail carrier indicating the names that will accept mail at the new address.

Copy All Important Keys. Make copies of your front door and work keys right away.

Introduce Yourself to Your Immediate Neighbors. You do not need to knock on anyone's door. If you happen to see your neighbors outside, introduce yourself briefly. It is crucial to make the first meeting of neighbors a positive one. See "The Gifts of a Healthy Neighborhood," in chapter five.

Help Removing Moving Materials. Once I had unpacked all of my boxes, my garage was filled to the brim with cardboard and wrapping paper. Local moving companies will pick up (for a fee) all of your moving material.

Keep All Receipts of the Moving Process for Taxes. From the mover's receipts to the mileage on your car, keep all filed away safely for tax season; you can write off your expenses for relocating, if you itemize.

Remove or Revisit Later. If you come across boxes of things that may not work at your new home or realize you may not need them, keep them boxed up and revisit them in a year to see if you truly need them or can donate them.

Stay in the Know. Set up local newspaper delivery as a way to get to know your new community and discover events and outings to explore.

Begin Setting Up Your Home Gradually. These are the rooms that should be set up first to help you feel at home: master bedroom, kitchen, bathrooms, and living/family room. The second stage should be the laundry room, dining room, and office. Stage three is outdoor spaces, hallways, entry/foyer, extra rooms, and garage. Set a goal, one that suits your schedule, to have all of these rooms, and therefore your entire home, set up and unpacked in one week or one month. Then make steady progress.

Scope Out and Establish Regular and Necessary Haunts. From your grocer to your coffee shop, begin to explore and then eventually settle in on the shops and destinations you will be visiting regularly. As you do this, you will start to feel more and more as though your new location truly is home.

Begin Establishing a Social Circle. The beautiful opportunity of moving is a fresh start when it comes to meeting people. While our workplaces may provide a social network, it is nice and healthy as well to establish relationships outside of work. The key is to not be overeager, to have patience, to be sincerely ourselves, and to remain curious. Below are a few ways to connect with others:

- Check out Meetup.com.
- Attend events alone, as I did when I went to a Pink Martini concert. I ended up seated next to a lovely fellow fan. We struck up a conversation and exchanged numbers to meet for coffee. You never know.
- Become a regular. Once you have found a favorite coffee shop, bookstore, grocery store, etc., get to know the staff, and do not be afraid to strike up casual conversations with other regulars you see.
- Visit local parks and walking and running trails regularly.
- Attend city council meetings.

As with anything in life, if you have a plan, you will be more successful in your endeavor. As a former colleague reminded students, recalling advice from Benjamin Franklin: "If you fail to plan, you plan to fail." Moving is an enormous opportunity. Truly spread your wings, step into your new self and home, and make the most of something that does not occur that often.

Make Your Own History

Do not go where the path may lead, go instead where there is no path and leave a trail.
— Ralph Waldo Emerson

Someone recently posed the question "Why not make your own history?" and I began to turn over this idea in my head. As a history teacher and someone who has an insatiable curiosity about the past, I could not help but ask the question, How does someone consciously go about making their own history?

As young children, we are influenced and molded by the people who raise us and counsel us — for better or for worse. Unless we are able to step outside of the inner circle our family has created or have parents who allow us to see more of the world, offering us a broader perspective of all the different ways life can be lived, it is easy to be ignorant of the possibilities the world can offer.

Ultimately, whether a child has been offered the opportunity or not, there must be something within an individual that wants to create a life for themselves that is uniquely their own, tailored to their talents, passions, and abilities. And in tapping into this inner curiosity, one must be willing to face adversity. How does one go about making their own history? This is what I have learned so far:

Understand the Past

I have always been an independent person. Beginning in childhood and continuing until the present day, I refuse to be afraid to try something simply because no one wants to join me. When I began to understand the history of women and their fight for equality, votes, financial independence, and equal pay, I began to appreciate my independence much more deeply. Understanding of the past helps us determine how we want to proceed as we create our own history.

Get to Know, Respect, and Befriend Yourself

Knowing who you are when you are in your pre-teen years is far different than knowing yourself in your twenties, thirties, and beyond as so much will change (although some things will simply become clearer). The key is to continue to challenge and introduce yourself to new ideas and listen to your internal response. These moments of stillness allow you to truly understand what makes you feel comforted or unsafe, inspired or bored, curious or apathetic, so that you can continue down the path that is best suited to your authentic self.

Once you accept your quirks, strengths, and weaknesses, it is important to stop apologizing and start capitalizing on the best person you can ever be — your authentic self.

And when you begin to respect yourself, you refuse to let people speak negatively about the person standing in front of them, whom they may not understand or want to understand. You can either speak up or ignore them and move on; either way, refuse to be belittled for being the only person you can be — your best self. Everyone needs a friend who will have their back every single day. And guess what? You have always had that friend: yourself.

Create a Vision and Set Goals to Achieve It

You are capable of more than you know. Choose a goal that seems right for you and strive to be the best, however hard the path. Aim high. Behave honorably. Prepare to be alone at times, and to endure failure. Persist! The world needs all you can give.
— E. O. Wilson

Do this simple activity. If you knew you would not be judged, laughed at, or criticized, what would your dream life look like? Write it down. Now, let's step back into the real world. It is understandable why some may choose a path that is less fraught with friction, adversity, and questioning, but to not choose the life we desire in order to avoid these trials is to live someone else's history and not our own.

If you remember back to your last social studies course, history is not smooth sailing. It is littered with pain, uncertainty, and loss. But remember that, throughout history, turmoil had to occur in order for people to institute change.

Once you have your vision, break it down into small goals. So long as you are making small steps forward, the history you are creating is slowly taking shape. And before long, you will turn around and notice how that first step so very long ago was necessary to get to a milestone you may have thought was impossible to reach.

Have Resolute Belief in Yourself

Perhaps at this moment, no one understands why you would want to live the life you have envisioned. But more often than not, it is ourselves we have to convince. So long as you are being honest with yourself about what brings you joy, contentment, satisfaction, and a sense of positive contribution, you can stop being afraid of becoming your best self. And for those moments when you lose your nerve but know without question you are on the right track, make sure you have a friend or family member who is there to listen, support you, get you back on your feet, and prod you forward.

CHAPTER ELEVEN

Effortless Style: The Truth

Style is about knowing who you are and telegraphing that confidence to the world.
— Kate Betts

Our signature style is personal. It reveals to the world multiple layers of information about who we are, what we value, what we are confident about, and what we understand about ourselves physically.

During my first two years of living in Bend, my attention to my personal signature style shifted. But while I created fewer posts about it on the blog, it was not because I was not interested in the topic. At first, I was not sure what it meant. As I began dreaming about my first trip abroad since moving to Bend, planning the itinerary to the countryside of France in 2018, primarily Provence, I began to contemplate what clothing I might want to add to my wardrobe. And as I did this, I came to understand that my signature style has been evolving, and it needed time to find its bearings due in some part to how much my life had shifted. I have found this to be something to celebrate.

Part of the reason my attention shifted from my clothing (though I continue to recognize it as a valuable asset) was that I have been trying to tap into and cultivate other aspects of my life and ensure that they reflect my truest self: a daily routine I enjoy but that enables me to be productive and healthy in my new hometown; caring for my skin and hair in a far drier environment than I have ever lived in; diving headfirst into eating well and becoming more confident in the kitchen, as I now have endless food options at my fingertips; and investing in personal relationships even more deeply as I continue to strive for a balance between work and play. Most importantly, I am focusing on trusting the woman I now understand myself capable of becoming and on trusting my wardrobe decisions more instinctively, thus freeing up more energy for pursuing my passions.

During the summer of 2017, I went through my closet for the second time in two years. What occurred was a simpler purge, but it was indeed a purge. However, the decisions were far easier, made with nearly no hesitation, and in less than an hour, I had my closet reorganized with twenty to thirty fewer clothing items and two fewer pairs of shoes. And none of the items were hard for me to let go. Why? I certainly had not lost weight. In fact, the five to ten pounds I have been wanting to shed for two years now have shifted into muscle as I work out far more now, and while I eat healthily, I do not deprive myself.

Truthfully, I have begun to feel more comfortable in my own skin. No, at the moment, I am not going to fit into size 4 jeans, as I once did; however, now I find myself celebrating more substantive details throughout my days — even though I would love to do a happy dance around the house in size 4 anything. But it would be a secondary effect caused by more valuable life changes and focuses. Do I want to remain svelte? Absolutely. But I also want to enjoy my days, the people I dine with, and my time in the kitchen or in restaurants.

The truth is I love style. I love communicating with my clothing. I respect the power of a well-chosen ensemble, no matter how simple it appears. And while I do not believe we should live our lives so we can fit into our favorite clothes, I do believe that if you are living well, the clothes you wear exhibit this fact about your life.

How can you live well, making savvy sartorial decisions as you curate a signature style you love?

First, get real with yourself. Be honest. So long as you hold on to clothes you will never wear, whether they fit or not, you are keeping yourself from true growth — not only the growth of your signature style, but of the life you are living and want to live. Step into your closet and pull everything out.

As I made my list of items I needed to add or update, I found it was rather short. This was greatly satisfying but quite a change from past clean-outs, and I wondered about the reason.

Aha! Over time, I had welcomed into my closet items that were highly versatile, well-made, and classic in design, and they have taken me through many years — the simply luxurious approach. But it took time. Cultivating such a wardrobe — one that is highly versatile, interchangeable, and, most importantly, tailored to each of us individually — takes time and regular attention.

Each time I take on the task of editing of my closet, I experience a moment of reflection and introspection. The tossing has become far easier and knowing what to keep simpler, but each time I edit, I see gaps where my lifestyle no longer aligns with my wardrobe. What this realization tells me is I am ever-evolving as an individual — "Yeah! I'm growing!" — and with each passing year, I become more aware of what my true style is. Initially, frustration may set in because we want to look effortlessly stylish every day, all the time. But it takes time.

New fashions are available every season, and purchasing them is easy; it is what we do with them that is hard and that takes time — to learn what works together and to get to know ourselves and what we feel our best in. Effortless style, while not a total myth, is something that requires effort. Let's take a look at three truths about effortless style.

It Takes Time. In an interview with *Elle* magazine in 2014, former Chanel model Inès de la Fressange shared something that should be a great relief to us all: "'I just woke up like this' is a lie." When I read this interview, I relaxed. Phew! But the reality is that knowing what works well together, knowing what works well for you, and knowing where to find it takes conscious effort, patience, and time as we evolve into our most authentic selves. In the third episode of Garance Doré's podcast *Pardon My French*, she interviews two Parisiennes, who admit that acquiring effortless style took many years as they became acquainted with who they were. To make this process work, we must notice what works, be willing to try something new, invest in quality clothing and tailoring, and learn from those who know how to do it well.

It Gets Easier. The good news is that, as with most endeavors in which we invest time, maintaining a signature style does become easier. Over time, you refrain from buying items that do not complement your skin tone or body shape. You discover which outfits make you both feel the best and garner sincere compliments on a regular basis. And your style becomes more and more effortless.

It Requires Regular Editing. We are ever-evolving and continually learning as we follow our curiosities and progress as individuals, so our wardrobes must evolve as well. That does not necessarily mean that you toss everything, but wear and tear does occur, colors fade, and you can add subtle updates and updated quality to improve your wardrobe with simple changes. With each edit that I do, about twice a year, I remove fewer and fewer items, which is a good sign. I am learning and not purchasing unnecessary and unwearable clothing. When we edit, we also are reminded about what needs to be repaired, what can work well with other items, and how far we have come.

Let's Talk about Beauty

Whatever is given to you on the day you are born, you are the one who decides who you will become, every day. Beauty grows as we grow into ourselves.
— Garance Doré

The construct of beauty can serve as either a builder or a deflater. If we grow up in a family and a community that praises us for something we have no control over, as we are young, unlearned, trusting and naïve, we instinctively do more of what is praised, similar to training a pup. But if we grow up in an environment that encourages growth toward self-actualization, we are given the tools that put the ability to attain self-confidence squarely in our own hands. No approval necessary.

If we are fortunate enough to have experienced the latter childhood and young adulthood, we come to understand that beauty is more than skin deep. We see beauty as something that is found in actions, behavior, growth, and confidence. We see beauty as something that increases as we age rather than dissipates as we grow wiser and become more *bien dans sa peau* (comfortable in one's skin).

But if we only pursue superficial beauty, we will forever be insecure. Insecurity can happen for other reasons as well, but the best way to eradicate insecurity is to establish deep roots. What does that mean?

Talking about beauty means shifting the definition and the conversation. Women are not a piece of art to gawk at. If we happen to look stunning in the attire we have chosen, it is a decision based on self-expression, a decision that expresses our self-respect, a decision to engage people to further investigate and get to know the intriguing woman wearing the clothes. It is not the end of the conversation, but rather the beginning.

The difficult part is shifting the discussion we have in our own minds, perhaps unconsciously. We must not feel defeated when a crop of zits pops up out of nowhere. Swap out zits for a wrinkle or two or three. Swap it out for anything that is on the surface of who we are that we either cannot control or that is temporary. We are more than a temporary bacterial flare-up. We are more than wrinkle lines. Our words, our actions, our ease in loving the life we have created for ourselves — that is what people notice and remember. And people who are drawn to us for our words, actions, and approach to life are people we want to surround ourselves with.

Dressing well, having fun with fashion, loving your home's decor — these are passions many of you embrace, as I do. There is indeed a power that comes with creating a space that is inviting and an outfit that makes us feel our best. But these passions create the backdrop for a woman — one who has, after countless hours, months, and years of investment, cultivated deep, strong roots — to shine. Because the exterior of who we are is merely an introduction to who we are entirely.

True beauty is . . . having a solid knowledge of your worth . . . sincerity . . . kindness to all, even if occasionally we have to tactfully share a truth that hurts . . . strength found within . . . embracing a life that does not follow, but rather adheres to what is calling you . . . expressing love without expectation . . . a life filled with gratitude . . . knowing life is always offering us a chance to evolve . . . acceptance of others . . . self-respect without needing approval . . . self-confidence . . . being who you were meant to be.

Choose to grow into who you can become, not what you think you should become. Enjoy the journey of discovery. Revel in the unknown as you strive toward what is tickling your curiosities. When you are completely lost in the living of your life, when you have the wherewithal to appreciate the amazing things around you and applaud those who are engrossed in their own life's passions as well, that is when your true beauty is alive and radiating to those around you. Most importantly, when you are exuding true beauty, what the outer world thinks of you is irrelevant because your roots are deep. Here are the components of beauty:

A Healthy Body. The clothes we wear will always look their best if they are sized to fit our physique. So long as we tend to our health, eat well, and get our blood pumping on a regular basis, our size should not vary too much, which means we can wear the clothes we love for many years.

Glowing Skin. When we are born, our skin is pristine, and it is up to our parents initially and then us to refrain from bad behaviors that can have damaging, sometimes irreversible effects on our skin. Here are a few bad habits to reduce or eliminate altogether: smoking, sun-bathing, drinking alcohol, picking at your skin, eating excess sugar and salt, over-cleansing, and not getting enough sleep. But rather than focusing on what not to do, let's dive into the habits that you should include in your regular skin regimen. Just as your body needs moisture internally, it also needs to be hydrated from the outside as well. You may use more intense or lighter options with the changing of the seasons, but the key is to moisturize daily. The moment you get out of the shower or bath, moisturize everywhere. When you do this regularly, you will notice a positive difference. One simple way to add that extra subtle glow is to use primer beneath your makeup; I have been using Colorescience Pro-Line Tamer, which helps even the skin tone but also adds an extra soft touch. Another is to use a shimmer block to add a subtle sheen to your cheekbones and décolletage.

Pampered Eyes. The delicate skin around your eyes can handle rich moisture; in fact, it wants such attention. Begin this habit in your twenties.

Regular Exfoliating. Exfoliating once or twice a week will remove dead skin cells, brighten your skin, and even its tone. Choose exfoliants that are gentle; you can make your own with sugar and olive oil (great for exfoliating your entire body as well).

Weekly At-home Masques. The beauty of a masque is that you do not need to set aside any additional time. Simply apply it to your face prior to stepping into the shower, let the shower work as the humidifier, and rinse off before stepping out.

Maintenance Facials. One of the seasonal beauty routines I began incorporating into my schedule as soon as my finances made it possible was the professional spa facial. These "maintenance facials" help keep my skin on track. A facial is wonderfully pampering and luxurious, and spending time with an expert is an educational experience as well.

Knowing How to Combat Break-outs. While we can use benzoyl peroxide or salicylic acid to reduce inflammation when it occurs, there are ways to prevent break-outs from occurring. Ironically enough, often when our skin becomes excessively dry, it will produce more oil to compensate, which ultimately results in spots of acne. By choosing to regularly moisturize, we are actually being preventive. Another preventive idea is to use a masque, as it will normalize oily skin and prevent breakouts.

Hydration from Within. Drinking water throughout the day, starting the moment you wake up and ending just before you close your eyes in the evening, not only will help your skin but will also detoxify your body. Also, keep in mind that caffeine and alcohol will thwart your hydrating efforts, so drink them in moderation.

While each of these routines involves a small investment, I assure you they will make a beautiful difference. First, determine what you can invest, then shop around, meet with an aesthetician, and start asking questions. Look for my list of recommended beauty products and skin-care routines on the blog in the Beauty archives.

What Does Inner Beauty Look Like?

Personal style comes from within. It's when the woman, her individuality and spirit, comes through. She uses clothes to express who she is and how she feels.
— Donna Karan

The maxim "It's not what's on the outside that counts, but rather the inside" strikes a warm, fuzzy tone, but what the heck does it mean? Does it mean we allow ourselves to become haggard, so long as we are kind to those around us? Absolutely not. Does it mean we put others ahead of our own needs? No. Or, in a nutshell, does it prescribe an elevating of ourselves, our potential, and our unique gifts as we combine our inner and outer beauty? Yes.

If a woman wearing a beautiful outfit does not have a healthy sense of her inner beauty, it is much more difficult for her clothes to work their magic. We are much more than what we wear. Beyond first impressions, our self-confidence, thoughtfulness, creativity, and intelligence will carry us the rest of the way. I have been contemplating the elements of inner beauty, and this is what I have decided they are:

Self-Respect. Being respectful of others is most definitely an admirable quality, but more importantly, we must always respect ourselves. Once we genuinely respect who we are, the potential we can fulfill, and the dreams we dare to dream, we gain the strength to refuse to be treated disrespectfully by others who may wish to pigeonhole, stereotype, or discriminate against us.

Integrity. The first ingredient necessary for integrity is to know what we value, and what we wish to protect, encourage, and cultivate. We may not always have the support that would make it an easier journey, but knowing the direction we want to take is half the battle. Integrity involves standing up or speaking out when it is not the popular thing, but rather the right thing to do. Having integrity means staying true to your word, being honest, telling the truth, and treating others as you would prefer to be treated.

Compassion. Choose to live in such a way that you are considerate of others' feelings, and help not in order to gain something in return, but to simply offer yourself, your time, and your resources. Compassion also involves placing yourself in others' shoes, doing your best to understand how they might be feeling. Decide not to be a pleaser or a pushover simply to avoid confrontation; instead, be strong enough to reveal who you are and what you can and cannot do.

Applied Wisdom. Regardless of where we went to school, who are parents were, or where we grew up, knowledge is available for us to grab if we choose to look for it. Inner beauty suggests an inner strength to do not what may be expected, but what we wish for ourselves. When we apply that knowledge to improve our lives and the world around us, our inner beauty shines.

Perpetual Curiosity. In order to continually gain wisdom, remain forever curious. Ask questions, listen to those with more wisdom, try new things, travel, read, and be aware that the world is full of lessons to be learned and experiences to enjoy.

Seeking and Attaining Effortless Elegance

True elegance does not come from one's clothes.
— Garance Doré

The sartorial choices we make each day are merely a vehicle to a more substantive conversation we potentially can have with the world we navigate, but it is up to each of us to understand the purpose and power of the medium. As designer Oscar de la Renta, who celebrated women's clothing as a means of liberation, said, "Fashion is a trend. Style lives within a person."

Along this journey, you will explore different colors, textures, designs, and ideas, and you will discover what is best suited to you. With each lesson you learn, you will shed what is unnecessary or irrelevant and become clearer about what will become your effortless style. You will begin to walk more confidently, speak with more grace and conviction, and step into the life you have envisioned for yourself. After all, style is the exhibition of knowledge gained and consciously applied.

Habits That Result in Effortless Style

Working with women who embody a strong, yet effortless sense of style, I am continually inspired to put forth the effort, time, and attention to cultivate habits that result in an air of calm and certainty.

Reuse Classic Staples. From the white button-up shirt to a tailored navy blazer, adhere to your capsule wardrobe. Then mix and match with abandon. Discover the elements of a capsule wardrobe, see components of my capsule wardrobe, and learn how to create your own on *TSLL* blog (https://www.thesimplyluxuriouslife.com/product-category/capsulewardrobe/) as well as in chapter four of my first book.

Invest in Classic Outerwear. A camel wool trench epitomizes timeless style, but it is an expensive item. However, if you carefully save and make such a purchase, a lifetime of style can be yours. Whatever your outwear of choice — a leather jacket, a Burberry trench — invest and capture your true style.

Add a Third Piece. The basics of putting together an outfit are a top and a bottom, but as *Who What Wear* suggests, adding a third piece — a blazer, a statement accessory (hat, scarf, bold jewelry, etc.), a cardigan, a sweater over a button-up shirt, a vest — can add a special finishing touch.

Get It Tailored. Whether the inseam of your dark denim jeans needs to be shortened, your waist nipped a smidge, or a few darts added to your waist, buy a size that allows such changes to be made.

Add a Belt. Proportions are key to elongating and slimming, and just the right belt can give you a stunning silhouette.

Pressed and Primed. Buy a garment steamer, bring out your iron, take your clothes to the dry cleaner, and present a polished you.

Embrace Inspiration from Unexpected Sources. Select a handful of street style and fashion blogs to check out each week or any morning you are looking for a creative way to pull together a new outfit from what is in your closet.

Master Proportions. Understand your body, and do not divide yourself in half with your clothing. Look at yourself in the mirror. Where is the middle? If you are 5'10", where is the three-foot mark approximately? Never let your clothing (the bottom of your top, the waistline in your pants) hit that mark. Instead, strive for thirds.

Dress Up Denim. Worn with heels, polished loafers, or knee-high boots, denim will always have its place in a timeless wardrobe. The addition of a blazer or a stunning silk blouse takes denim to new heights.

Tend to Finishing Touches. Complete your look with a haircut that requires little more than a blow-out and one or two products, makeup that is minimal yet refined, and a subtle touch of your signature scent.

Save Up and Invest. While I have a capsule wardrobe of primarily investment brands, I purchased very few at full retail price. Have I been able to acquire all of the items that I have desired? No, but by knowing what I need, shopping year-round, and checking in and watching for opportunities to save, I own pieces I absolutely love.

Letting Your Signature Style Evolve

Style is something each one of us already has, we just have to find it.
— Diane von Furstenberg

Style is available to anyone. Each of us has a signature style if we will just choose to understand what it is. For each of us, this signature style will shift as we evolve as individuals.

Forget the Size. In one brand, I am a medium, and in another for the same type of item, I am a small. Especially if you are ordering online, order at least two different sizes, try the pieces on, and ship back the size that did not work.

Invest in Classic Items and Make Them Your Own. Fashion trends can sometimes lure us away from what we know works well, but classic works for a reason. I have a classic short dark denim jacket that I layer over everything in the summer. The dress, jumpsuit, or top I layer it over may change, but that jacket has been with me for four or five years, and it has never gone out of style.

Understand Which Silhouettes Are Your Friend. Knowing your shape and then dressing it well reduces the decisions you need to make when shopping at a clothing boutique in person or online.

Stock up on Spanx. Spanx and similar undergarments that smooth your shape enable you to wear what you love and feel good doing so.

Slow and Steady. Gradually add the items you need as you find what you love. Have patience, and do not feel you have to look "perfect" each time you pull an outfit together. What makes it ideal is the woman who wears it. Clothing is fun, but it is an accessory to the life we are building for ourselves. We should recognize and respect its power, because it truly is powerful if we know how to use it effectively, but choose to see building your signature style as a journey, just as life is.

Limit Bargain Hunting. The material an item is made of and the skill used to craft it are worth investing in. Stick to brands that offer quality, and do not feel you have to explore other labels to mix it up. Consignment is the perfect addition to your shopping repertoire as it often offers brands that are made to last.

Keep It Simple. Make your wardrobe a simple affair you tend to each day. Purchase the white button-up shirt, make sure your hair is coiffed as you like it, let your skin shine with just enough makeup to look effortlessly stunning, pull on denim jeans or tailored pants that create a beautiful silhouette, select shoes you love, slip on your favorite simple earrings, and sling your handbag (made by a designer who does not need to put their label everywhere) onto your arm. Voilà!

Ask yourself how your closet is working for you. How many times do you walk inside or open the door and see a multitude of items but only one or two viable options? Paradoxically, the trick is to eliminate; reduce the number of items and add just enough pieces that you are excited to wear and that can work with at least two different garments already in your closet. Then all you will need to do is maintain. Assess one or two times a year, and little by little evolve ever closer to the signature style that best aligns with who you are and wish to become.

Discover the Power of Cultivating Your Style

Fashion asks — indeed, sometimes it feels as though it demands — that we buy, spend, and spend again each season, attempting to keep up with industry trends. But if we will simply understand the difference between style and fashion, we can better appreciate and carefully select beautiful additions to our wardrobes that will enhance our style and not burden our budget. While it may be easier to pull on a ratty T-shirt and slip on loose, battered denim, choosing to craft your signature style offers a variety of benefits. This does not require a flush bank account, but it does require time, patience, and thoughtful contemplation about who you are and what truths about your identity you want to reveal to the world.

While clothing is reflective of the current culture, simply look back on your middle school and high school photographs. What did the clothes you were wearing reveal about you? Each of us will see someone different. Some of us will want the courage and confidence we exuded in high school, while others will see a clone of the peers that surround them.

Style speaks your language to the world, while fashion is a tongue in which someone else asks you to learn and be a follower. Style never follows but is rather inspired by what speaks to people, who then interpret it for themselves. Understanding this difference and embracing your own style can change your life.

Wearing the right outfit will not magically and immediately lead to winning an Oscar or improving your bank account or [insert your dream here]. But it is the vehicle with which you begin your journey in the right direction. What you wear reveals who you are. And people want to know the who they are dealing with. They want to know if they can trust you. They want to know you are worth investing in and that you are authentic. Let the world see the magnificent person you are. Find her, dress her, and let her shine without apology. Simply paying attention to the visual presentation we offer to the world each day can have profound effects on our lives — economically, socially and emotionally. Let's take a closer look:

Make a Statement, Reveal Your Identity. Style is our own unique language, a dialect of fashion that we make our own. When we first learn to speak it, we may feel intimidated and hesitate to show it to the world, especially if it is vastly different, but the more we communicate confidently, the easier it becomes to step out in our own style each and every day.

Exude Security in Yourself. An individual who takes the time to pull together a thoughtful wardrobe understands the power of clothing. An individual who dresses in a way that allows the person to shine exhibits self-awareness and self-knowledge. And when people exhibit these qualities, it becomes clear that they are secure in themselves. In order to value yourself, you must be comfortable with who you are without the external world reassuring you.

Show Your Discipline. Having style requires discipline — in how we shop; in being patient but determined; in knowing what we need in our wardrobe and taking the time to find it, sometimes tailoring it, and always caring for it properly; and in how we invest, knowing the power of quality over quantity as well as cost per wear. (If I wear a particular pair of $150 jeans 75 times, the jeans actually cost $2 per wear. It is true that my checking account is still missing $150, but the quality of the jeans allowed me to wear them 75 times, thus, saving me from buying a similar cheaper pair that would not have lasted nearly as long. If the initial cost is within your budget, in the long run you save money and time, as you look your best without having to scurry about each season to buy a replacement pair.)

Become a Person of Interest. When we dress well, we suggest that we matter. And while clothes do not determine our worth, human beings are visual. Dress well and cultivate assumptions that work in your favor.

Separate from the Crowd. The goal should never be to dress to stand out. But consistently dressing well in a manner that aligns with who you are will distinguish you from the crowd. Dressing well, whether casually or formally, depends less on the label and more on knowing how to pull together an outfit that looks good on your body, with your skin tone, hair color, etc.

Become Memorable. Maybe it is the color palette you choose, maybe it is the length and style of your skirts, or maybe it is combinations you always gravitate toward. It can be something as small as an accessory you always wear. Once you find a style that works for you, stick to it for as long as it does, as it makes you memorable.

Increase Your Salary. *Forbes* magazine has reported that dressing well and appropriately for work can increase both a man's and a woman's salary. Work ethic and results are, of course, important for whether someone receives a raise or a promotion, but human nature is still alive and well. When people see someone who dresses professionally and respectfully, they tuck this into their memory. It has never been easier to dress well, and if we choose not to, we may convey the idea that we do not take the job seriously, whether that is true or not.

Display Your Confidence. When you discover your signature style and dress to your taste, paying close attention to appropriateness and fit, you communicate that you know what you are seeking and can stand strong when others question your choices.

Improve Your Mood. Think about the last time you wore your best dress or outfit to a public event. You probably received a compliment or two on your appearance, and when we receive compliments, our mood improves as well. The medicine to spring your mood back into high gear may be that Diane von Furstenberg wrap dress that hugs your curves just enough, but not too much.

At times, pulling the proper outfit together can be confusing and even frustrating, which is why I highly recommend building a capsule wardrobe, made up of ten to fifteen items, that is tailored to your lifestyle, body, and personality. Once you create your wardrobe, you will have a variety of options for mixing and matching. Most importantly, you walk out the door confident that you look your best.

Mastering the Art of Dressing

Simple is beautiful. Working with the best materials is fundamental. Great style never goes out of style. You don't need a lot of choices to create a lot of options. Just the right ones.
— Eileen Fisher

Understanding fashion is akin to acknowledging society's rules and then breaking them in order to create the life you want. However, while being a slave to clothes and each season's trends is not a savvy pursuit, being aware of accepted mores and cultural shifts is never a bad idea.

In other words, depending upon the work or social environment, particular attire is necessary. For lawyers, yoga instructors, CEOs, and artists, certain wardrobes are acceptable, and certain styles are not. For example, most judges and courtrooms require the professionals involved in a case to wear collared shirts or suits before they can proceed as a sign of respect for the court. Knowing the requirements is crucial for success. Here are a few ways you can dress appropriately, effectively, and comfortably for the life you have chosen to live:

Ignore Fads/Trends. Chasing trends will empty your wallet and give the impression of a person whose only hobby might be how they dress. While being well dressed and well-groomed will always be a priority for me, a woman who only wears trends is a woman who does not know who she is or is afraid to reveal her authentic self. Find your signature style and revel in it. When you know what is best for your body and lifestyle, you can have fun in your own way regardless of trends.

Dress for Your Life. Depending upon your job, lifestyle, and responsibilities, you know what shoes are reasonable for your day-to-day duties and whether you can wear pants or have to wear skirts and dresses. However, often women use their lifestyle as an excuse to not dress well. Wearing a dress is often the most comfortable and easiest option in the morning for a mother or busy businesswoman, and as we know, dresses can quickly elevate one's style. The key to whatever clothing you choose is to tailor it to your body — size, length, color, and fabrics.

Beware of Black. Wearing black, while an easy option for nearly every skin tone, can be tricky if not handled properly. Worn close to the face, black can deepen the appearance of wrinkles, lines, and shadows. To mitigate this effect, choose the accessories closest to your face — necklace, scarves, and neckline details — wisely.

Spotlight the Mind, Not the Body. If you want people to respect you for your thoughts, words, and conversation, draw their attention to your face rather than your cleavage. While accentuating and tailoring clothing to fit your figure is a must, revealing too much skin or wearing clothes that are too tight is not going to leave your coworkers, boss, or date thinking about your mental and intellectual talents or charming personality. When we pay attention to beautifully designed necklines, wear hats, or adorn our shoulders and/or neck with scarves and beautiful earrings or necklaces, we spotlight where we would prefer an onlooker's attention to go.

Invest in Quality Classics. Refrain from being a slave to clothing by gradually building your closet with quality staples. When you mix and match, from year to year, with clothing that always looks good and lets your best self shine, you reduce stress and allow yourself to focus your efforts on the task at hand.

Better to Overdress. When in doubt, dress well. Even if you outshine the rest of the crowd, you will be noticed for being respectful of the moment. If you know how to dress well, you will look stunning and create moments of conversation and curiosity that reveal the gift that is you.

Why Not . . . Wear a Blazer?

Having found my dream blazer a few seasons ago, I began to see all the options it made available to me. Below I take a look at the options available when you have a blazer in your closet and how to wear it to work best with your signature style.

Work Appropriate. If you are expected to wear a suit at work, a blazer will always work. If you work in a field, such as education, that is a middle ground in terms of formal versus casual, blazers can be worn with dark denim, over sleeveless dresses, or with many other options. The coverage, collar, and layering allow you to look pulled together and professional. Roll your sleeves up to add a touch of casual, but still, you are workplace appropriate.

Casual Chic. A blazer offers an easy transition as you make your way from your workplace to a restaurant for dinner and drinks with friends. Perhaps you want to change up your accessories and even your shoes, but the blazer can remain constant and always fit in any situation.

Endless Options. The brilliance of the blazer is that you can wear it every day, as long as it is with a different top or bottom, and you will always look pulled together and in style. Choose a neutral color that works well with your capsule wardrobe — tan/wheat, charcoal, gray, black, navy or white — and it will blend in beautifully.

A Safe Option That Can Break the Rules Tastefully. One of the things I love about a blazer is that it exudes a professional touch, but you can have a bit more leeway with the bottoms. Have fun with a statement T-shirt that speaks to your sense of humor or even boyfriend jeans and a pair of flats. The juxtaposition of serious and silly or über casual can sing a very nice tune.

A Travel Go-To. Airplanes can be chilly, and wearing a scarf or coat is always a good idea, even in warmer months. However, wearing a blazer on board saves a bit of space, while offering a layer of comfort when the cabin temperature decreases.

There are many ways to wear a blazer:

As a Piece of a Suit (Skirt or Pants). A blazer is made to be paired with a bottom half — a skirt or trousers. To create a polished look that conveys you mean business, make sure it is tailored to your body, and walk confidently into that interview or into the front row during fashion week knowing you look top-notch.

With Jeans. This is my favorite, and a look that Jennifer Aniston does so well. She regularly is seen with a blazer and jeans while traveling and on the streets going about her day. Whether you choose boot-cut, skinny, straight-leg, or boyfriend, you strike a beautiful middle ground that can take you just about anywhere.

With a Scarf. Accessorizing with a scarf is simple and classic. When you have a neutral blazer, a scarf can make a statement that is immediate.

With Flats or Heels. Depending upon your preference, the event, or what looks best with your outfit, either flats or heels work well with a blazer. Especially if you are wearing a boyfriend blazer (more oversized and longer), pairing with a stunning heel is an attractive balance of masculine and feminine.

Shorts Too. If you have got the gams, wear your shorts, but do not forget the blazer for more dressed-up affairs. Whether it is a romper or a pair of tuxedo shorts, the addition of a blazer provides the finishing touch to get you into that four- or five-star restaurant without causing a stir.

Layer It Over a Dress. Perhaps you are wearing a sleeveless sheath or have a few summer dresses that would work well in the fall if only you could cover a bit more skin. Add a blazer. Even a boyfriend blazer works, as you can cinch the waist with a belt that ties it all together.

Pair with Tees. Whether you want to have some fun with statement tees or just want to run errands and pull together a quick stylish look, select a T-shirt to wear with a blazer. Always have few on hand in the neckline that is most flattering for you, and without fail, you will look effortlessly chic.

Wear with a Camisole. For a look that is a touch dressier, layer your blazer over a beautiful silk camisole. You can wear a lightweight camisole under a blazer during any season of the year; add more layers, if necessary, or just adhere to the basics.

Wear Over Stripes. Due to stripes' neutrality, you can wear a blazer of just about any color, and you will look casual, yet pulled together.

Depending upon your signature style, your profession, and your daily lifestyle, you can make a blazer shine for you in a distinctive way. The key is to choose something you can wear with many different outfits in your capsule wardrobe, adding depth to what you already have.

Why Not . . . Invest in Good Shoes?

Give a girl the right shoes, and she can conquer the world.
— Marilyn Monroe

As Mireille Guiliano reminds readers in *French Women Don't Get Facelifts*, there are particular "tells" when it comes to a woman's appearance — how she feels about herself and how she wants to be perceived by the outside world. The first tell is a woman's haircut, and the other is her shoes. Guiliano and actress Candace Bergen agree that a woman can wear expensive or inexpensive clothes, and so long as she pairs quality shoes with her outfit, she will shine. However, on the flip side, an amazingly well-styled ensemble can be decimated when you pull shabby shoes from the closet.

With an investment in well-made shoes, you can rest easy, knowing with certainty that you will present a confident and signature look, have comfortable (blister-free) feet, and enjoy years free of shoe shopping.

They Complete Any Look. A quality leather ballet flat from Lanvin paired with jeans, a classic nude pump from L. K. Bennett for work, or black over-the-knee boots from Stuart Weitzman worn over skinny jeans for evening — a classic pair of shoes should complete the outfit you have chosen, not be the look. However, perhaps your style is to wear bright, bold, unique shoes; in that case, you have even more reason to invest in quality shoes as they are the star of the show. Quality shoes not only feel good on your feet (my nude Stuart Weitzman 4" pumps look like murder, but actually mold to my feet like a glove and feel like 2" heels), but they reveal to the world someone who knows who she is and cares about her appearance, but always wants to effectively accomplish whatever she came there to do.

They Last for Years. Mireille Guiliano has two pairs of 3½" heels in her closet that she reserves for special occasions — one from Yves Saint Laurent (before they dropped the Yves) and one from Bottega Veneta. Now, no doubt, both of these heels cost more than I have ever paid for a pair of shoes, but because they are reserved for certain outfits and occasions and are created by master artisans with quality materials, Mireille should be able to wear them for decades. Shoes that hold their form, do not fall apart, and can easily be buffed up, polished, or resoled are a sound investment; find a good cobbler and you can wear your heels for the rest of your stylish days if you have them in a good rotation. Always consider the cost per wear equation to validate that beautifully made shoes are worth every penny.

They Reflect Your Signature Style. The shoes you choose — like the style and color of your hair — reveal your personality and attitude about life, and they provide a peek into how you spend your days. Love cowboy boots? Shop accordingly — look for bright, unique designs, sensational leather, or anything that speaks to your preference. Nude and black are my go-to colors for everything. I love to have fun with scarves and jewelry as well as blouses and jackets. No matter what your style, do not forget to bring your shoes into the presentation.

What shoes do you need for your lifestyle? How much will you have to save to purchase them? Now would be a good time to start; just think, by this time next season, you could have your own pair of [fill in the blank] sitting in your closet ready to be worn on a moment's notice, boosting your confidence just before you walk out the door for that interview, date, project pitch, etc.

Keeping on Top of Your Wardrobe

The closer you get to knowing yourself, what you shine in, and what works with your lifestyle, the easier decisions become. Simply keep your eyes open and update items before they need to be swapped out. When we view what we wear as a pleasure, our clothes become an extension of ourselves and help enliven our confidence, mood, and carefree attitude so we can be fully present in the moment. Clothes should not be a barrier, but rather a minor detail that with time and patience will enable you to revel in your amazing life.

Schedule a Seasonal Check-Up. Spring and fall, when the new collections appear in stores, are the best times to organize your closet and review its contents. Twice a year, I set aside a few hours to determine what I have and what I need, as well as what I should toss or donate — anything that no longer is part of my style or that no longer helps me look my best. It's quite simple and fun as well.

Carve Out Time. Choose either an entire morning or afternoon that is free so that you are not making rushed decisions and are adequately rested. You do not want to make rash decisions about the clothes, shoes, and accessories you have spent good money on.

Start from Zero. Remove everything from your closet (do one at a time if you have many), and pile everything on your bed or sofa or a clean floor.

Have a Notebook Handy. Make notes about what you need, what needs to be repaired or tailored, and any tools you can acquire to help you care for your clothes and keep them well organized (specialty hangers, dividers, jewelry organizer, etc.).

Use a Full-length Mirror. While you will not need to try on everything, you will want to refresh your memory about some items and take a hard, honest look in the mirror to recall how some garments hang on your body.

Find Two Empty, Large Boxes or Structured Bags. For each item of clothing, you will choose one of three options — keep, tailor/fix/repair, or toss/donate/consign. Make it a streamlined process by setting up two large boxes or bags for the things you will repair and the ones you will toss.

Have Your Capsule Wardrobe List Handy. As I go through my closet, I am constantly asking myself, "What will I wear this with? What does this item need to better fit my capsule wardrobe?" In order to answer these questions effectively and accurately, you must know what type of capsule wardrobe you want to create.

Proceed One by One. Go through each item and ask the following:

- Do I wear it?
- Does it fit properly?
- Does it fit in my capsule wardrobe?
- Does it need to be repaired?
- Does it need to be cleaned?
- Do I feel good wearing it?
- Can I wear it with more than one outfit?

For some items, you will get through only the first two questions; for others, you will need to go through the entire list. Once you have worked your way through these questions for each item, you have sorted your clothes.

- Clean any items that need it as soon as possible.
- For clothing you will take to a consignment shop, determine which season it is best suited for and ask the store when they accept those seasonal items. Typically, they will ask you to wash and iron items you bring in.

Hang and Store Your Things Properly. The clothes that made the cut need to be cared for, so make sure you have the right hangers, enough shelving, adequate drawer space, etc. Below is a list of hangers I use, as well as a few other items you may need.

- Non-slip hangers (for large necklines, camisoles, lightweight tops)
- Wooden skirt hangers
- Padded hangers (for high-collared garments, lingerie, dresses)
- Regular wooden hangers
- Wooden trouser/jean hangers
- Scarf hanger or designated drawer with organizer
- Belt hanger

- Hanging jewelry organizer
- Shelf dividers
- Shoe organizer. To store boots, roll up a magazine and place inside; this helps boots stand up straight and maintain their shape.

Pick up these items at an all-purpose department or specialty store such as a Container Store or Storables. Save money by looking for these items at yard sales.

Organize by Type and Color. Depending upon your preference, organize your clothing by hue or type (skirt, top, dress, etc.) — or perhaps both. Not only does this create an aesthetic that is pleasing to the eye when you open the door to your closet; it also helps you keep track of where everything is and where to hang it.

Assess What Is Missing. Now is the time to pour yourself a glass of something delicious, take out your notebook, and decide what is missing from your capsule wardrobe — items that will complement what you already have.

Plan What You Are Shopping for This Season. You probably will not be able to buy everything on your list immediately, so make savvy decisions about items to shop for now, those for which you will wait for fall and spring sales, and ones you will have to save up for.

Start Shopping. If you have access to brick-and-mortar stores, it is always a good idea to go there first; you can try things on, and often you will find items that will never be offered online — although often there are online exclusives as well. Subscribe to your favorite designers' and websites' newsletters, which will alert you to early sales or releases; be sure to act quickly for the best selection of styles and sizes. And more and more shops are offering wonderful discounts with short (two- or three-day, mid-week) sales.

Edit Regularly. As I shared previously, I usually go through my closet twice a year, typically before the spring and fall collections arrive in the stores and online boutiques. I am always fine-tuning my capsule wardrobe, and the amount of clothing I have becomes smaller and more refined, but I always check the quality and remind myself what I have to mix and match with. The purpose of diving into your closet is to reduce buyer's remorse and to help you create a capsule wardrobe that is a pleasure to wake up to every morning as you think about the outfit you will pull together.

When we feel confident about what we are wearing, that confidence rubs off on everything we do and improves the quality of our lives. So pick a day and enjoy a process that can actually be quite fun — and most certainly will be rewarding.

Thirty-Nine Essentials for a Stylish Woman in Her Thirties and Beyond

A woman, till five-and-thirty, is only looked upon as a raw girl, and can possibly make no noise in the world till about forty.
— English poet Mary Wortley Montagu

My twenties were a whirlwind of fact-finding, exploration, and dealing with insecurities. Now that I am approaching the end of my thirties, I can say with certainty that it only gets better. My nine years as a trigenarian have been far richer (primarily experientially) and more fulfilling, yet not without struggles and challenges, some more difficult than the ones I faced in my twenties. However, the gained wisdom from these lessons learned made them much easier to navigate. If Mary Wortley Montagu is correct and thirty-five is the end of being a girl, I am ready. In that spirit, here are thirty-nine things — actual physical items or intangible valuables — I have found that are beneficial for women my age and older.

- A classic shoe (flat, boot, or pump) that fits your signature style
- A quality timepiece
- A complementary lip color
- A work "uniform" that is appropriate and stylish
- A signature perfume
- A preferred flower (or one for each season)
- Jewelry that is stunning and irreplaceable
- Original art that is priceless to you
- An investment tote that can last your lifetime
- A quality, chic winter coat
- A black dress

- A hair style that reveals you are a woman who knows her unique beauty
- Regular access to knowledge and information about the world
- A growing retirement account
- The strength to say no
- The knowledge to know when to exercise that ability and when to set fears aside and say yes instead
- The courage to take a risk on her dreams
- An understanding of good health: more water, less sugar, more exercise, less body loathing, more real food, less quick, processed food
- The ability to cook a delicious meal
- Knowing that having cooking abilities does not mean she must cook simply because she is a woman
- Her own definition for a contented life
- How to fall in love without losing herself in the process
- Respect for her body — physically (a fitness regimen), objectively (remaining immune to fawning charm from those who might see a woman's body and nothing else), and mentally (eating well to nourish, not diminish, the brain's abilities)
- Signature stationery and the knowledge of how to craft a lovely thank-you
- A small handful of trusted confidants
- At least one tremendous risk that she is unapologetically proud to have taken
- A broken heart that has rebounded and stepped forward from the past
- Rejection or challenges that have made her appreciate the success that followed
- The knowledge of common grammar rules (e.g., *How are you doing? I'm doing well*)
- Nourishing, rich night and/or eye cream
- An understanding that drama should be reserved for film, the theater, and television, not one's daily behavior and conversation
- Time or financial support (large or small) for causes she is passionate about

- The habit of regularly reading books and credible, quality journalism
- An aesthetician she trusts for her beauty needs — waxing, massage, facial, nails
- A passport and evidence of the beginning of a well-traveled life
- Peace of mind knowing that the journey she travels is and will be as unique as the woman taking each step
- A sincere enjoyment of her own company
- An open mind for observing and considering new ideas, cultures, and beliefs, as she understands the world is not as simple as black and white, but rather involves many gradations of gray
- An understanding that "luck" does not happen without planning, patience, passion, and the willingness to seize upon opportunities that have no guarantees

I am eager to see what the future has in store and confident that, while I will make mistakes along the way, the positive things I learn will help make each year richer and more wonderful.

CHAPTER TWELVE

Enjoying Eating and Being Healthy

One cannot think well, love well, sleep well, if one has not dined well.
— Virginia Woolf

Since arriving at my rental cottage in Bend, I have been spoiled for food and produce options. Doing my best to capitalize on this opportunity while staying within my budget, I have been cooking and experimenting far more than I have done in the past. But my experimenting is not with grand, complicated recipes. With so many wonderful resources at my disposal, I set out to discover the skills for making delicious meals with whatever happened to be in my refrigerator and available at that time of year. It has been a delicious journey of discovery.

It is pure pleasure to step into my kitchen each day and see what I can come up with. The past and the future nearly evaporate, and I am in my bubble. The oil or butter in the pan sizzling, the water boiling, the zester buzzing, and the fresh scent of herbs in the summer and the cinnamon on the apple tart in the winter — all deepen my love and appreciation for knowing how to cook.

My new vodcast, *The Simply Luxurious Kitchen*, focuses on seasonal fare to elevate the everyday meal. Much of what is shared, and far more, is detailed for you in this chapter. Let's get started. Discover the ingredients you should always have on hand, how to shop seasonally, and how to eat and cook well on a budget —a simple approach to weekday eating.

Have a Love Affair with Food

Below are simple tips on how to eat well without the guilt, while unearthing your most beautiful and healthy physique. What's not to love?

Listen to Your Body and Retrain Your Mind

Let food be thy medicine.
— Hippocrates, ancient Greek philosopher, the father of medicine

Our body knows what it needs; we just have to figure out the language in which it is communicating. If you have not been in tune with your body for a while, you may not be feeding it what it needs. As Carol Cottrill reminds readers in *The French Twist*, we are all on a diet, no matter what we eat; however, the word *diet* has been turned into something that conjures up deprivation and restriction. But food is to be enjoyed. There is so much amazingly wonderful, delicious, and nourishing food out there; the stuff in boxes cannot hold a candle to what Mother Nature offers.

Three healthy and balanced meals plus two snacks is more than enough to get you through your day. It is a priceless gift to be able to go about our business and to see clearly, sleep calmly, speak eloquently, and laugh exuberantly without worry or fear. However, we are the chemist in a dynamic and fascinating chemistry experiment. Our body works extremely hard to function, but there are many ignorant choices we can make that hinder its optimal performance.

The term to keep in mind is *nourishment*. How are you feeding your body and brain? They crave real food, so make sure that is what you are giving them. You will see amazing changes, and it will not just be in your weight. You will be less likely to come down with a cold or flu, you will have increased energy to finish your daily to-do list, your sleep will become sounder, and your thoughts will be clearer. I cannot think of a better reason to eat well. While I, and perhaps you too, may have initially wanted to eat better to slip into a smaller size, the health benefits are far more motivating.

Knowing how to feed your body will allow you to reach your full potential. Wellness begins from within; eating unprocessed and nourishing food enables you to live a healthier, happier, and more energized life.

Essential Items for Your Grocery List. Bring home food grown or raised in nature — pulled from the ground, off a tree, or from a ranch. Focus on real food that provides a balanced diet. It is easy to make such a diet a way of life because it delivers big-time flavor and satisfies the palette. Below is a list of basic food groups that will give your body the fuel it craves so it can perform at its highest potential.

- Fruit — apples, oranges, berries, bananas, kiwi, plums, pears
- Vegetables — broccoli, carrots, beets, green beans, brussels sprouts
- Animal protein — poultry, pork, lean red meat, fish, eggs
- Vegetable protein — legumes (beans), nuts, tofu
- Whole grains — brown rice, steel-cut oatmeal
- Whole wheat flour — carbohydrates for energy
- Vegetable oils — olive, coconut, sesame, safflower, peanut, canola, grape seed, flaxseed
- Butter — salted or unsalted, with a high butterfat content (80–82 percent minimum)
- Herbs and spices — oregano, thyme, basil, tarragon, cumin, turmeric, salt, pepper

What to Reduce or Eliminate

Whether you follow a vegan, paleo, vegetarian, or any other eating regimen, simply refuse to eat anything out of a box or anything with a distant expiration date. When you purchase only food stocked on the outer edges of the supermarket, you are choosing real food. This food generally will expire in a matter of days, but you are nourishing your body with the nutrients it is craving. Food groups to limit include:

- Refined grains — good grains gone bad, as Carol Cottrill calls them
- Added sugar — in ketchup, cereal, store-bought spaghetti sauce, granola, pretzels, etc.
- High-fructose corn syrup — lots of added sugars give it extra calories
- Saturated and trans fats — saturated fats are found in animal products like meat, and whole-fat butter, milk, and yogurt, as well as some vegetable oils, like coconut oil; trans fats (man-made fats) include margarine and vegetable shortening
- Alcohol (including wine and beer) — always pair with food

Being aware of the effects any ingredient, not just sugar, has on the mind and the body is vital information to be aware of. Notice that I did not say to eliminate added sugars because we all may want a bowl of cereal or a slice of cake from time to time, but knowing what has added sugar, and the value of reducing your intake, is a helpful step in the best interest of your health.

Make Water Your Drink of Choice. Drinking water regularly flushes out toxins from your vital organs, provides nutrients to your cells, and prevents dehydration so that you continue to feel energized throughout the day. The Institute of Medicine recommends "adequate intakes" for women of 2.2. liters (about 9 cups) a day and for men 3 liters (about 13 cups).

Sit Down and Savor Your Food. Multitasking is one of the best habits to lose, especially when it comes to enjoying your meals. Choose instead to enjoy the conversation or just your own thoughts or something engaging to read, but respect the ritual of enjoying your food. Refuse to eat while driving, standing up, or walking down the street. Eating is a pleasure that deserves to be savored. Savor your food in small portions. When you savor your food, you slow down, and when you slow down the pace of your eating, you tend to decrease the number of calories you consume. It takes approximately twenty minutes for your mind to get the message that you are full, so take your time and let the message arrive. Enjoy your company and the flavors the cook took such care to incorporate.

Eat Local and Eat in Season. When you eat fresh fruits and vegetables, especially when they are in season (the times of year when they yield their harvest naturally), you will enjoy their peak flavor without adding extra ingredients and unnecessary sugars. Pick up pears and brussels sprouts in the fall, asparagus and rhubarb in the spring, berries and tomatoes in the summer, and turnips and mandarin oranges in the winter. Similarly, when you purchase your bread from a local bakery or your milk and eggs straight from the farm, you are likely reducing the hormones you will ingest. And you are supporting local farmers.

Supermarkets have made the food we love available for consumers year-round, but we all know a tomato in December here in the States tastes nothing like its summer counterpart. Instead, pick up an apple or, if you are in Hawaii or on the West Coast, a rambutan (seasonally available September through March). Satisfy your sweet tooth and eat what is readily available and full of flavor. When I am tempted to fall into the habit of eating the same vegetables, fruits, and even entire meals year-round, it is partly because it is easy, and I think it saves time. While it does ease the need to plan what to eat each night or for lunch, it isn't actually the best choice for my health.

Initially, it will take time and your full attention to learn what is in season and what to do with it when you get it back to your kitchen, but once gained, this knowledge becomes a habit. In essence, you become your own home chef, capable of cooking anything with fresh ingredients and what is in your *épicerie*. Most of us eat at home most of the time, so it does not have to be a passion, and you do not have to be a foodie to learn the basics of seasonal cooking.

Have a Plan and Keep It Simple. The primary reason I created seasonal capsule menus (details below) is to provide a foundation for how to cook seasonally. With time and practice, you will begin to incorporate your favorite ingredients and discover which recipes you like and even create your own. The best meal you will make on a regular basis can be simple, because it is the quality of the food that makes it excellent. For example, my go-to recipe for vegetables year-round is to roast them. Name the vegetable and, with few exceptions, I will roast it. In the spring, I add lemon juice and a bay leaf to asparagus; in summer and fall, I drizzle olive oil and sprinkle salt and pepper over zucchini and yellow squash; the same in fall and winter for broccoli — then roast at 400 degrees for 20–25 minutes. And I recently tried roasted cauliflower and finished it in the final two minutes with a sprinkle of Gruyère and Parmigiano Reggiano — delicious!

Learn and Incorporate a New Habit Each Week. Perhaps one week you will learn and become confident with roasting; maybe the next week you will make your own herb butter, and then the next a tasty vinaigrette. Whenever you eat out and you taste something you love, ask how it was made. A few summers ago, I had the most delicious huckleberry ricotta mousse. The restaurant staff happily shared the ingredients, and I went online and found a ricotta mousse recipe from a trusted source and adapted it to my taste. (I even learned how to make my own ricotta — so simple!)

Fall in Love with Food Again. Once you establish a healthy relationship with food and remain consistent with these simple habits, you will begin to see positive changes. While it will take time, the changes will become permanent; eating habits like these deliver such unmistakable benefits that it is simple to maintain them for life. Making the shift from eating well for your health rather than to fit into your jeans has a powerful effect on your motivation.

Outfit Your Kitchen

The more time we spend in the kitchen and the more familiar we become with the techniques, the more magnificent the outcomes can be. Do not get me wrong; there will be cringe-worthy moments, but take it from someone who has been tinkering and exploring in the kitchen since I was a young girl: The outcomes become more and more successful and enjoyable. Granted, you must know what you are doing, but enjoy the process; do not rush the chopping of the vegetables, the sautéing of the garlic and shallots, and the resting of the protein. Gather the necessary tools, come with as much knowledge as you can (while always being willing to learn more), and dive into the present.

There are certain essentials when it comes to the ingredients necessary to be successful in the kitchen. And you do not need fancy gadgets. As anyone who has traveled in Europe will attest, kitchens there are very small, even in the grandest of cities. Cooking in a small kitchen is quite possible. Do not let the size of your kitchen be a roadblock. But make sure you have the basic tools and a well-stocked *épicerie*.

Tools

These are the essential tools for an enjoyable cooking experience.

Two Cutting Boards. One for nearly everything, and the other (perhaps smaller) for the items with a strong scent (garlic, onions, etc.).

Three Good and Proper Knives. A cook will find constant use for a classic chef's knife, a small paring knife, and a serrated knife for bread. If you are going to invest in one good knife and save up for the other two, start with a chef's knife.

Four Good and Proper Pans. Start with two skillets (8" and 12") and two saucepans (small and medium). Purchase the best quality you can afford; it will improve your cooking experience. Copper is expensive but performs fantastically, so plan to slowly add copper pans and skillets to your kitchen.

French Butter Keeper. This pottery container consists of two parts: a lid that resembles a bell, in which you pack the butter; and the base, into which the lid is placed and which contains water, about 1/4"–1/2" depending on how big your butter keeper is. The lid combined with the water creates an airtight seal that keeps oxygen out, thus negating the need for refrigeration and allowing the butter to remain spreadable.

Ceramic Utensil Holder. Having all of your tools within arm's reach is a must for a seamless experience in the kitchen: spatulas (metal and rubber), wooden spoons, zester, metal tongs, spider strainer, fish spatula, and French rolling pin.

Tea Kettle. From boiling water for a cup of tea, in the morning, to enjoy with my steel-cut oats and, at the end of the day, another cup to savor with a dark chocolate peanut butter truffle, a tea kettle is a must.

Olive Oil and Balsamic Vinegar Dispensers. Choose glass, preferably opaque, or ceramic containers with a simple spout. Keep them in a cool, but convenient place on your countertop.

Pepper Mill. Fresh grinding means the peppercorns' flavor and oils will be at their freshest. A classic wooden peppermill is as stylish as it is functional, so keep it on your counter near your stovetop.

Sets of Ramekins and Graduated Bowls. They are great for organizing your ingredients before you begin.

Finally, make sure you are working in a clean environment. Organize your kitchen so that your counters are as clean and clear as possible and your stovetop is prepped and ready to use, along with all the dishes, pots, pans, and utensils you will need. Visit *TSLL* blog to discover all the kitchen tools I recommend; use this link — https://www.thesimplyluxuriouslife.com/product-category/kitchen/ — or click on *TSLL* Shop in the menu and click on "Kitchen" in the drop-down. You can also view my vodcast *The Simply Luxurious Kitchen* on the blog, YouTube, or iTunes, to see the tools in action in my kitchen as I prepare seasonal fare to elevate the everyday.

A Well-Stocked *Épicerie*

The items below are for the pantry, the counter, the freezer, and the fridge — the things you always want to have on hand. These are not the fresh ingredients you will purchase each week, but rather the staples that complete and complement dishes each time you step into the kitchen.

Fresh herbs and spices. Grow your own herbs (outdoors or inside) and keep a variety of spices handy. They will add a depth of flavor to amplify your dishes.

Two types of salt. Fleur de sol or gray sea salt for cooking, and finishing salt such as Maldon's flaky sea salt.

Pepper. Choose whole peppercorns, and grind them while preparing your meal in a pepper mill for the full peppery flavor.

Oils. Begin with extra virgin olive oil, then expand as you prefer. Some cooks keep specialty oils on hand for favorite salad dressings: sesame seed oil, grapeseed oil, olive oils flavored with basil or truffles, etc.

Vinegar. My favorite is balsamic. Others you might like for specialty dressings include white- and red-wine vinegar as well as apple cider vinegar. Also use balsamic vinegar to finish a vegetable dish such as brussels sprouts roasted with pancetta.

Garlic. A head of garlic full of fresh cloves ready to be smashed and sliced.

Lemons. I usually have on hand two lemons for a regular week of cooking.

Butter. Unsalted and salted, preferably French butter or butter with a high butterfat content (80–82 percent or higher).

Good cheese. Have on hand Parmigiano-Reggiano, as well as a soft cheese, a hard cheese, and perhaps a blue cheese.

Eggs. Farm-fresh eggs offer a brilliant yellow color and, most importantly, gorgeous flavor; they are also a way to support local farmers.

Steel-cut oats. My preferred brands are Bob's Red Mill or McCann's; choose the original rather than quick cooking.

Potatoes. Sweet potatoes or traditional spuds make a wonderful, simple side dish when roasted and seasoned with salt and pepper.

Tea/coffee. To begin the day, to wrap up the evening, or for afternoon tea, I keep a stock of teas from Palais des Thés, Fortnum and Mason, and Mariage Frères.

Lentils. They make a fantastic base for fish, mixed with vegetables and a simple vinaigrette dressing.

Pasta. The options are endless, from whole wheat to gluten-free; choose a varietal and size that best pleases your palette and works well with the sauce.

Canned tomato sauce. A classic staple to have on hand for flavoring protein or making sauce for your pasta.
Mustard. Keep three main types on hand: classic Dijon, whole-grain, and honey Dijon.

Mayonnaise. Make your own or seek out top-quality flavor, which will add a satisfying binder to your dish, dip, or dressing.

Freezer food. Seafood (shrimp is my favorite), meat (chicken, sausage, beef, etc.), extra butter, ice cream and gelato (vanilla and chocolate at a minimum).

For baking: flour, sugar (brown and white), yeast. For freshly made bread or a pastry crust perfect for quiche or a fruit tart.

Chocolate: semisweet, bittersweet, or dark (minimum 70 percent cacao). The higher the cacao content, the less sugar. Dark chocolate is better for your health and satisfies your palette more efficiently.

Sliced, toasted almonds, and other nuts. For tossing onto a salad, making a praline paste for a batch of cookies, or simply to nibble on as a snack.

Raisins. For breakfast (to top my steel-cut oats), for snacking (paired with almonds), or for dinner (include in a delicious sauce for slow-roasted salmon along with an onion, capers, olives, and a few tablespoons of rum).

Honey. Instead of adding granulated sugar to my steel-cut oats for a touch of sweetness, I add a teaspoon of honey. I also drizzle honey over my prosciutto-wrapped and goat-cheese-stuffed figs; it is the perfect subtle, sweet finishing taste.

Jam. For croissants on the weekends —*bien sûr!*

Wine. A white and a red (and a rosé in warmer months). If you like to drink it, it will taste delicious in the food you prepare.

While this list may seem long, once you have all of these items stocked, it will take some time for many of them to run out, and you will be doing weekly or bi-weekly restocking for only a handful (for me, lemons, eggs, and sometimes butter). Knowing you have everything on hand for the basics of everyday cooking and baking will make it all the more enjoyable to step into your kitchen and get lost in the moment.

Recently, Giada de Laurentiis shared in an interview that you must "create a space in your kitchen that you enjoy being in." Organize your kitchen so that it is easy to navigate, the necessary supplies are readily at hand, cupboard clutter is at a minimum, and the counters are as clear as possible. When your space is inviting, when you have beautiful and highly functional tools to use, you will want to step into the space and work your magic.

Get Comfortable with Basic Kitchen Skills

The only real stumbling block is fear of failure. In cooking you've got to have a what-the-hell attitude.
— Julia Child

Learning how to cook well is no different than learning how to strengthen the tools in your toolbox, as discussed in chapters eight and nine. Conscious effort, a desire to learn, and multiple opportunities to practice are all you need to become the cook you want to be. Have fun in the kitchen and see each meal as an opportunity to practice.

Today the Internet is at our fingertips, and we can easily find demonstrations of various cooking techniques. I learned how to properly chop an onion by watching one of the first episodes of Julia Child's *The French Chef*. No longer am I worried that I will slice my fingertips off (the secret is to curl your fingers, so the knife cannot even find your fingertips).

Chop Garlic. Trim, crush (using a broad knife held flat over the clove and smashing it with your fist), and chop.

Cut an Onion. To learn to prepare one of the most essential vegetables, watch this informative video produced by America's Test Kitchen: https://www.youtube.com/watch?v=Znv46pRiDIk.

Learn Basic Knife Skills. This BBC video is a short course in knife handling: https://www.bbcgoodfood.com/videos/techniques/knife-skills.

Cook Pasta. Al dente, al dente, al dente. If you are cooking with fresh pasta, it will take just a few minutes — not five, not four, just two or three. In all cases, read the packaging, and do not let it get mushy. Al dente, al dente, al dente.

Make a Classic Vinaigrette. My recipe is 1/4 cup balsamic vinegar (or any vinegar you prefer) with 3/4 cup extra virgin olive oil, 1/4 teaspoon Dijon mustard, a dash of salt and pepper, and voilà!

Prepare Baking Tins. For cakes, pies, and tarts (removable bottoms for tart pans). For cakes that come out of the tins, butter and then line with parchment paper along all sides and the bottom.

Tenderize Meat. Cover the meat with waxed paper and pound until about 1/8"–1/4" thick, using the flat/smooth side of a mallet.

Fry an Egg. Add 1–2 tablespoons of olive oil or butter to a properly seasoned pan that has been brought to medium heat, crack the egg gently so as not to break the yolk, and sprinkle with flaky sea salt and freshly ground pepper. For sunny side up, cook for 2–4 minutes until the white is opaque and the yolk is still mobile. For over-easy, flip quickly at this point and let cook for another 30–45 seconds. Remove with a spatula.

Make an Omelet. View my vodcast *The Simply Luxurious Kitchen*, season 1, episode 5.

Roast a Chicken. I defer to the Barefoot Contessa for the perfectly roasted chicken. Visit https://barefootcontessa.com/recipes/perfect-roast-chicken.

Steam Vegetables. Bring a large saucepan of water (about 1" deep) to boil. Once the water is boiling, place a steamer basket on top of the water. Place chopped vegetables in the steamer, cover, and reduce to medium heat. After a couple of minutes, check for tenderness. For extra flavor, toss with olive oil, fresh lemon juice, salt, or butter.

Roast Vegetables. Drizzle bite-size chopped vegetables with olive oil, salt, and pepper, toss, and put in a 400-degree oven for 20–25 minutes.

Blanche Vegetables. If you want vegetables to be cooked but still have a crunch, blanching is the best. Bring a pot of water — deep enough for all vegetables to be submerged (although they will rise to the top) — to boiling. Toss your chopped vegetables into the water. Keep the water boiling for 3–4 minutes, just until the color of the broccoli, for example, turns brilliant green. Remove with a wire strainer and immediately place in a bowl of ice water to retain the color and stop the cooking.

Make Pan Sauce. A pan sauce makes an amazing difference, and once you know the "how" of making one, you will be able to enhance every fish or beef or pork dish you make. Visit Bon Appétit's "Basically" website to get started: https://www.bonappetit.com/test-kitchen/how-to/article/perfect-pan-sauce.

To see all of these skills and more demonstrated, check out my vodcast, *The Simply Luxurious Kitchen*, on the blog, iTunes, or YouTube (channel: Shannon Ables). Each season, 8–10 new episodes will demonstrate how to elevate the everyday meal.

Capsule Menus: How to Create Yours

A full life — a life of contentment that is balanced with continual opportunities for growth and the ability to reach our goals —requires us to eat well. Most of us are balancing work and personal lives, and finding time to go to the market, pick up the necessary ingredients, and cook delicious, healthy meals can be tough. Even if from time to time we order in or go out for a meal, we derive a special pleasure from cooking meals for ourselves and those we love. Much like curating a capsule wardrobe for spring and fall, adhering to a capsule menu for regular weekly meals is a simple, but dependable way to eat well, always have on hand what you need, and fuel your body efficiently.

The concept began to bounce around in my mind after an extremely busy year balancing a new life in Bend while doing my best to produce quality work on the blog and settle into a new teaching position with AP students. Bend offers an ample supply of quality food; within a ten-mile radius of my house, I can stop into a Market of Choice, Safeway, Whole Foods, Trader Joe's, and Newport Market, plus, during the summer, a fresh produce stand and bi-weekly farmers markets. I knew I had the ingredients to eat well and give my body an excellent diet. Now it was up to me to devise a plan to make this a reality with my full schedule. Here it is.

Capsule Weekly Menu Basics

For each day, plan breakfast, lunch, and dinner. Build each meal around the following plate proportion goals:

- 1/2 low-starch veggies and/or leafy greens, anything that can be enjoyed in its raw state
- 1/4 high-starch veggies and/or whole-grain carbohydrates: Most high-starch veggies have to be cooked before you eat them; 100 percent whole-grain (not multigrain) brown rice, farro, oats, bulgur, rye, quinoa, barley, buckwheat, whole corn, or homemade popcorn
- 1/4 lean protein or legumes (lentils and beans)

One or two snacks can help balance your diet and fill in for what you missed at mealtime. They should combine protein and carbs that contain fiber, which helps regulate the body's use of sugars and helps keep hunger in check. Choose snacks that encourage you to chew. Examples of protein snacks: plain Greek yogurt, eggs, edamame, flaxseeds, peanut butter, pumpkin seeds, quinoa, milk, broccoli, tuna, white-meat poultry, pork, soy, beans, cheese, lentils, and fish. High-fiber snacks include bran, broccoli, cabbage, berries (raspberries, strawberries, blueberries), leafy greens, celery, beans, mushrooms, raisins, figs, bananas, apples with skin, pears, and nuts.

When I plan my weekly shopping list, I look for the following items:

- Two or three versatile proteins or legumes

- Three or four vegetables (2/3 low starch, 1/3 high starch)
- Two or three healthy whole grains
- Snacks (with fiber and protein)
- One or two breakfast options
- Ingredients for one or two desserts
- Ingredients for a comfort meal

My Capsule Menu Shopping List

Below I lay out my general capsule menu weekly shopping list, which I use throughout the year. For my recipes, take a look at my detailed capsule menus. Download each seasonal capsule menu for free (spring, summer, fall, winter): https://www.thesimplyluxuriouslife.com/product-category/capsulemenus/.

- Salmon fillets
- Chicken breasts or chicken tenders
- Lentils
- Eggs
- Broccoli
- Spinach
- Carrots
- Green beans
- Almonds (mixed with raisins for snacking)
- Raisins
- Strawberries (sliced for morning snacking)
- Blueberries (morning snack)
- Cheese (afternoon snack with slices of apple and almonds and a cup of tea)
- Apples
- Steel-cut oats
- An apple (for a French tart)
- Vanilla gelato
- Pasta (linguini, penne, shells, etc.)
- Shrimp
- Arugula

My Capsule Planning Menu simplifies this weekly routine: Select items that can be used in a handful of meals, items that allow for a well-balanced diet, items that offer exquisite flavor, and organize your weekly meals, knowing that each time you step into the kitchen, you have the necessary ingredients. Both a notepad version and a pdf are available, and you can practice your French too as an English and a French version are available. Use the link provided above.

Refine Your Shopping

When you have the best and tastiest ingredients, you can cook very simply and the food will be extraordinary because it tastes like what it is.
— Alice Walker

A fish market, cheese shop, local bakery, farm stand — frequenting such food outlets will make your shopping experience more pleasurable than navigating a supermarket, and the food you purchase will be fresher and most likely in season. You can establish relationships with the experts who run each business, ask them questions, and learn about what you will be eating and feeding those you love.

The weekly capsule menu works wonderfully. While I typically do a weekly shopping run to my farmers market or Trader Joe's, I stop by the local produce stand or the bakery a couple times each week to ensure I have fresh ingredients. Make this a weekly ritual that you look forward to. Choose a market or markets that have most of the food you need at prices you can afford.

Take a list with you. I use my *TSLL* "To Market, To Market" notepad list, which is pinned to the corkboard in my kitchen, and after going over my Capsule Planning Menu page, which lays out each ingredient I will need, I determine which items I must shop for and add them to my list.

Why Not . . . Buy Local Produce?

Go to the farmers market and buy food there. You'll get something that's delicious.
— Alice Waters

Slices of sun-ripened strawberries, enjoyed atop homemade granola. Carrots with a natural sweetness akin to candy, enjoyed moments after being pulled from the earth. Figs, picked up late in the market season, paired with goat cheese and wrapped in prosciutto. When we eat on Mother Nature's schedule, extra sauces and processed sweeteners are not necessary. Once you have savored tasty treats like these during the time of year when they are at their peak flavor, you will not want to revert to inferior mass-produced alternatives. And when we eat in season, meals become simpler to make, and our appetites are more quickly satisfied. We gain long-term benefits as well: healthier bodies, clearer minds, longer and more satisfying lives.

What do I look for at a farmers market? I love to bring home rhubarb and make strawberry rhubarb pies or tarts. I seek out asparagus for a simple, yet delicious roasted vegetable side dish. I keep an eye out for peonies, which are available for only a short time and make elegant bouquets. Beyond that, anything else that tempts my taste buds is likely to wind up in my basket. Having fresh food at your fingertips in the town you call home is to feel truly wealthy. Eating well, having an abundance of choices, shopping outdoors, savoring Mother Nature as you peruse the selection — the entire experience is an exercise in living well.

Get Top-Quality Flavor and More Nutrients. Produce at farmers markets is picked at its peak and often sold the same day or the next, and the farmers chose the best produce to be enjoyed on that particular day. The fewer miles the food has to travel, the more nutrients and flavor the produce retains.

Eat Fresh, Organic Food and Expand Your Repertoire. Farmers markets sell what is in season. Artichokes are available as spring wraps up, followed soon by tomatoes. Visiting farmers markets, I am encouraged to try new vegetables and fruits, and I love that. For example, I had never cooked with garlic spears, but the farmer gave me some simple ideas. He also told me they are available for only a few weeks, all the more reason to give them a try when they're available.

Support the Local Farming Community. It is wonderful getting to know the farmers and their families and workers, whose livelihoods are dependent upon the weather and other variables out of their control. Supporting those who contribute to the community like these folks do shows our appreciation for their delicious, safe, and healthy produce. When we pay farmers a good price for the quality produce they offer, we are helping them maintain a profitable farm. If we want to have healthy produce, grown on clean, rich soil, and meat from animals that are treated humanely, we need to be willing to pay an extra price. Most individuals who sell the food at the market are the ones who have cared for it as it grows, and they will be able to answer your questions.

Get Ideas for Cooking. Last summer, I picked up some fava beans. These gorgeous, ginormous green pods grabbed my attention, but I honestly did not know how to cook them. However, I had just seen *Paris Can Wait*, in which Diane Lane's character enjoys bruschetta topped with fava beans. Curious about how to make such an appetizer, I asked the farmer. He gave me some delicious ideas, as well as instructions on how to properly cook the beans (blanche in the pod for a couple of minutes, pop out the beans after submerging in cold water, peel off the hard outer shell, and voilà!). He suggested pairing fava beans with capers and a little olive oil, smashing it all together, and smearing the mixture on grilled bread. He was absolutely right.

Pick Up Fresh, Seasonal Flowers. Discover flowers that can be hard to find. When I lived in Pendleton, I would stalk the farmers market in May and June, waiting for the peonies to arrive. I knew they would be available for only a few short weeks, and I did not want to miss this once-yearly opportunity. In Bend, peonies are usually available for about a month, but their appearance is brief and evanescent, which makes it all the more something to celebrate when you welcome them into your home. Just as farmers markets can introduce you to new foods, you also discover new varietals of flowers.

Leaving behind the air-conditioned supermarket and breathing in the fresh air is a memorable experience. Don your sunnies or maybe a wide-brimmed summer hat and just take everything in: the food, the people, the music, the moment.

The Simplest Solution Can Be the Best

There's an expression, or theory, that says, "The easiest solution is the best." Which goes along with something I've learned from French cuisine: You don't need to do, or add, a whole bunch of stuff to food — just let good ingredients shine.
— David Lebovitz

Julia Child was right when she said, "With enough butter, anything is good." And you do not need an excess amount of butter, just quality — and preferably French — butter. Why? The minimum fat the law requires for French butter is 82 percent, and most has at least 85 percent, while American butter averages 80 percent fat. It may not seem like a big difference, but if you have ever had Echiré, Au Bon Beurre, Lescure, or any other quality butter from France, you know the flavor is intensely different. High-quality butter is soft to the touch even as it sits in the refrigerator (not the freezer). Many American markets carry French and other European butters, which all have a higher fat component.

Your body needs fat, and when you feed it what it actually needs, you do not need a gluttonous amount. So long as you listen to it, your body will let you know what it needs and how much.

When it comes to food, eating, and dining out, keep it simple. Simple food is good food so long as quality ingredients are involved. Once you learn simple, basic cooking skills and come to trust yourself in the kitchen, you really do not need recipes. Start with ingredients you love, understand how to add flavor (herbs, spices, aromatics), and then just have fun. When we rely too much on recipes, we often limit the potential of what is right in front of us.

So much of what I am learning in the kitchen has opened my eyes about how to live well. For example, yes, we need to give ourselves the proper foundation, the fundamental skills to be successful, much like with education, which deepens our understanding of how to effectively communicate, navigate, and excel in the world. But once we know the rules, we need to pay attention to the journey. We want the citron tart to taste exquisite and look scrumptious, but how much sweetness do you need? What are the lemons giving you? When it comes to pastry, what is the humidity where you are cooking? Do you need as much water as the recipe calls for?

In the kitchen, as in life and in love, we need to trust that we have the necessary skills to survive, but we also need to let go and try whatever speaks to us. We need to trust our instincts, which have been honed over years of experience, and then let go when we run up against combinations we have never tried.

I fondly remember a first date that took place in my kitchen. We cooked a four-course meal together, and it was a rare first date that I was ecstatic about. While I was confident I knew how to cook, I was silently trembling as the evening began. But what happened was what always happens when I step into the kitchen. I lost track of time, I became completely present, and I did what I knew and learned what I did not. We cooked in the kitchen together many more times, and rarely used a recipe unless it was for a special occasion and a dish we had never made.

Love is a risk, thriving in life is a risk, but why worry about taking risks in the kitchen? Just have fun. Even if the meal does not turn out as you had hoped, just as relationships often do not last a lifetime, you learn something along the way that you can apply to future attempts in the kitchen and to opportunities for loving relationships.

Why Not . . . Create a Mini Garden?

Almost as much as I love organizing and building my wardrobe, I love the arrival of spring, as it means I get to shop for my yard and garden. Cooking for me is very pleasurable and often therapeutic, and I try to grow what I can in my herb and vegetable garden. While my plants do not always grow as I had hoped, when they do, I do a mini happy dance in my kitchen. Whether you live in a small studio in the city or on a sprawling country estate, creating a mini garden is simple and relatively affordable.

In my previous home, during the summer months, I had a small cement herb box attached to my house near my kitchen door, which allowed me to quickly step outside in my bare feet to pick a few leaves of basil, fresh flat-leaf parsley, or a handful of lettuce. In my cottage in Bend, I keep my mini garden next to my porch, so that I again can quickly step outside and snip the herbs I am looking for. I simply love cutting a few leaves of basil and drinking in their fragrance, which to me symbolizes summer, good health, and scrumptious eating.

Whether you have a large plot of land or a windowsill, plant what you can and what you are curious about, and with each year, try something new. Try to plant something to be enjoyed in each season: rhubarb in the early spring, strawberries in late spring, fresh herbs all summer (sometimes year-round, depending upon where you keep them and where you live), squash and pumpkin in the fall — the possibilities are endless. Here are a few things you will need to know to get started:

Seek Out the Sunshine. Most herbs and vegetables need access to full sun at some point during the day. Whether you are placing small pots on a windowsill inside your home or keeping them outside on your porch, determine how much space you have to work with.

Pick Out the Containers. Perhaps you would like to use a handful of small pots or one large one, or maybe you have a creative planter in mind. Have fun picking out the size, color, and material, but make sure you choose one that allows the soil to drain properly (terra-cotta works, but so do other pots with holes in the bottom).

Choose Your Herbs and/or Vegetables. Knowing that cut basil at the store or farm stand costs at least three dollars for one meal and that I can purchase a basil plant for four dollars and grow enough to last the entire season motivates me to grow my own. Determine which herbs you enjoy with your food, as well as vegetables you want to have on hand throughout the summer, then seek them out; most farmers markets and nurseries sell seedlings. My favorites are sweet basil, Italian (Genovese) basil, Thai basil, dark opal basil (purple), sage, rosemary, dill, lemon thyme, thyme, oregano, chives, Italian flat-leaf parsley, Roma and heirloom tomatoes, and lettuces.

Soil and Water. You might have to pick up some potting soil. Just regular potting soil works fine. Be sure to water your plants regularly, especially when temperatures soar. Buy a fun watering can, indulge your green thumb, and enjoy.

Read Cookbooks for Pleasure

Yet every recipe, whether we cook it or not, offers a vision of the good life, and a way of tasting food in your brain.
— Bee Wilson, *The New Yorker*

The sizzle of aromatic ingredients, finely chopped and dropped atop olive oil or butter in a pre-heated skillet. The steady hum of bubbles in a pot ready for fresh pasta. The splash of red wine poured into a stemmed glass. Cooking after work has wrapped up and the day is winding down has always reminded me of a symphony of food and a build-up of anticipation for the meal that is being created. The simple, soothing sounds and gestures in the kitchen during the buildup to the meal are always a welcome melody. There are a hundred multiplied by infinity recipes I have yet to try, as well as numerous approaches and techniques and lessons I am curious to learn. Thus my passion for cookbooks.

I was reminded of how much I enjoy reading cookbooks for pleasure when Susan Hermann Loomis's *In a French Kitchen* was released a few years ago and I did not want it to end. In the same way a cozy mystery transfixes me with its details, settings, and characters rather than the murder plot itself, I wanted to continue to roam the community she writes about, read more about the food and the gardens, and dawdle with the secondary characters. Hermann Loomis skillfully sprinkles a few recipes at the end of each chapter that correspond with the seasons, and her stories and images of home cooks in their kitchens kept me spellbound. Likewise, Elizabeth Bard's Francophile must-have *Dinner Chez Moi: 50 French Secrets to Joyful Eating and Entertaining* is full of personal stories and anecdotes, as well as recipes; upon opening the book, I feel temporarily transported to Provence, which this New Yorker now calls home with her family.

While we may never actually make most of the recipes we read about — I came across this text in the cookbook section of my local bookshop: "Meals you intend to make, but never will" — cookbooks are a soothing respite. No tragedy, no news, no unexpected surprises (except maybe a renewed appetite). Simply deliciously curated flavors, often exquisite photography, and inspiration and motivation that I too can create something beautiful, nourishing, and brilliant in my own kitchen. I highly recommend the cookbooks described below.

The Art of Simple Food: Notes, Recipes, and Lessons from a Delicious Revolution, by Alice Waters. The author is the West Coast food expert and founder of the famed Chez Panisse who brought to our attention the value of seasonal, local, and sustainably produced foods. She encourages her readers to grow a garden, cook simply, cook together, and be mindful of the food and its origins. The first chapter alone will give you a grasp of the foundations of a kitchen that creates delicious food simply.

Mastering the Art of French Cooking, by Julia Child. I "got to know" Julia Child in *Dearie: The Remarkable Life of Julia Child*, by Bob Spitz; *As Always, Julia: The Letters of Julia Child and Avis DeVoto*; and Child's memoir *My Life in France*. I have long relied on *Mastering the Art of French Cooking* for the wealth of cooking questions she answers. If you love baking, *Baking with Julia* is a must-have resource. Next on my list to read is *Julia's Kitchen Wisdom*, in which Child offers answers to seemingly simple, but pesky questions: the proper proportions for vinaigrette, the quickest way to sauté, tips and tricks for bread making, ideas for soups, and much more.

Sauces: Classic and Contemporary Sauce Making, by James Peterson. Dive into the first chapter of this tome of a cookbook and become acquainted with the history of sauce making through the centuries; shift to the necessary and proper equipment and ingredients in chapter two; and finally, devour chapters that each focus on a particular type of sauce — brown sauces, crustacean sauces, mayonnaise-based sauces, egg yolk sauces, butter sauces, etc. If you want to become a gourmand, pick up this invaluable resource for sauce making.

Tartine All Day: Modern Recipes for the Home Cook, by Elisabeth Prueitt. The scrumptious descriptions of each recipe by this author, cofounder of San Francisco's Tartine bakery and restaurant, will leave you ready for a meal or a snack no matter how full you thought you were. Prueitt's simple recipes deliver big, surefire flavor and leave you confident you can make what she describes.

How to Cook Everything: 2,000 Simple Recipes for Great Food, by Mark Bittman. Learn the simple techniques of everyday cooking, discover the power of quality, fresh, natural ingredients, and come to understand that you do not need complicated gadgetry, just basic equipment, to be successful in the kitchen.

Barefoot in Paris: Easy French Food You Can Make at Home, by Ina Garten. Each of the Barefoot Contessa's cookbooks are a treat to read, and her latest, *Cooking for Jeffrey*, is no exception. In *Barefoot in Paris*, I especially enjoyed the photography of Ina's favorite stops in the city of light (Poilâne in St. Germaine, for example) and the commentary in each chapter about French ways of cooking, shopping for cookware, and setting the table, and her other experiences in France.

On Food and Cooking: The Science and Lore of the Kitchen, by Harold McGee. This kitchen classic, glowingly reviewed by more than 500 readers since it was published in 1984, is the go-to resource "for an understanding of where our foods come from, what exactly they are made of, and how cooking transforms them into something new and delicious." A wonderful, informative read.

My Master Recipes: 165 Recipes to Inspire Confidence in the Kitchen, by Patricia Wells. If you have ever wondered what blanching, searing, poaching, or any other cooking technique means and how to do it properly, you will love the most recent cookbook from food writer and journalist Patricia Wells, the woman behind cooking schools in Paris and Provence. Each chapter revolves around one cooking skill, detailing "how to" and then offering a variety of recipes to build your cooking expertise.

My Paris Kitchen: Recipes and Stories, by David Lebovitz. The first section alone is a reason to bring this book home as it is a wealth of a resource for determining which foods to have on hand for any recipe you may want to try. Lebovitz, who has made Paris his home for the past twenty years, adds his personal touches to classic French recipes both sweet and savory.

If you are looking for more ideas and titles, stop by my *TSLL* Shop, click on "Cookbooks" in the drop-down menu, and discover my entire list of cookbook recommendations, which is updated each week.

living Small

Own less stuff. Enjoy more freedom. It really is that simple.
— Joshua Becker, the *Becoming Minimalist* blog

ess house, more time to enjoy living. Less to clean, more time to experience and explore. More time to dream, to let your curiosities lead you where they might, and to dive deeper into the depths of what it truly takes to live a fulfilling life.

My first home as a child was in a nice, friendly neighborhood in a 2,000-person town. It had a yard, a garden, and a sandbox, and a bedroom I shared with my younger brother until I was five years old. I have fond memories of that home. It was cozy, it seemed large, it was warm, and I felt safe.

When I was five, my parents purchased property in the country to build a family home on ten acres. It took many years for us to live entirely in the house as my parents stayed within their budget and built when they could. Until it was livable, we lived in a barn on the property, a one-room living and sleeping space (bedrooms, living room, family room) with a nearby trailer for the kitchen and bathroom. We lived in this setup for about four years while we watched our large family home being built. I did not mind the small space because I had the outdoors at my fingertips and was always exploring the wilderness with my animals alongside.

It was not until I was in high school that the house was entirely finished. Now my parents live in this grand abode, complete with expansive and bucolic grounds, a large garden where my mother exercises her talented green thumb, a shop for my father's many projects, and acres of grounds for animals and other lovers of the outdoors to roam. It is stunning, but I know how much time and work it takes to maintain it. At this point, they are contemplating how much longer they can live there and tend to it properly as it is a place they truly love.

Each of us will choose something different when it comes to defining a sanctuary in which we spend our everydays. What is important is to choose something enlivening, something that will awaken your best self, something that will give you the opportunity to share your gifts and your love with the world.

Since leaving the countryside of Alder Slope in Wallowa County when I graduated from high school, I have set myself on a journey to explore the world and to pursue what piques my curiosity. I have doggedly chased down answers to my many why's about the wider world and have come to better understand how to best navigate it and how to grow and progress, instead of shrinking in fear of what I do not know. What I continue to discover is that a rich, fulfilling, contented life has everything to do with how one lives their everydays and very little with what society would purport to be necessary for a good life.

More is not better. It is truly just more. More to care for, more to clean, more to pay for. The key is to find the right balance — between square footage and contentment, between stuff to enhance versus stuff that interferes. Each of us will settle on a different equation, and I have realized that my equation is different than my parents'. It does not mean they chose too much. For thirty plus years, they have built and are living a life they love, and I loved growing up there. Having had the experiences I had as a child, I know what brings me joy: proximity to nature, the ability to rest and read for hours without interruption, quiet time to create and dream and discover, regular moments with a hot cup of something delicious, some homemade food, and conversations with loved ones. None of these requires a large home. All require time to inquire into one's being and see what brings peace and contentment, and my family's country home provided this opportunity from which I could then strive along my journey.

The first home I owned was so large I lived in only half of it. Now I live in more or less the square footage of the half I lived in previously — 1,200 square feet, with a yard on a quiet street. I have more time to write and dream and be curious, and I spend less time cleaning and tending to the yard and house. However, I do gain inspiration from a welcoming sanctuary and a yard that I care for as a home for birds, squirrels, and even deer from time to time, so I have struck a better balance here in Bend, and it began with understanding myself and the life I am living and building.

Why Not . . . Consume Less?

With the personal storage business ballooning into a $22 billion industry and advertisers incessantly vying for our attention at every turn, a life of minimalism is a never-ending exercise in saying no.

Why do we feel the urge to buy our way to happiness? Why do we need to collect, devour, and charge our way through life? I will give advertisers their due. They have studied and researched their targeted audience. They have come to understand with precision how to attract the eye of the consumer, but when we understand their goals, we can make the decision to ignore, turn off, or turn away from their pleadings so that we put ourselves back in control. Choosing to consume less puts us in the driver's seat, rather than the world of commerce that is swirling around us. It is the primary premise of living a simply luxurious life that we be selective about what we bring into our lives so as not to drown in unnecessary excess that reduces our ability to enjoy the life we want to live.

If we want to reduce stress and create a more enjoyable life, one focused on quality rather than quantity, a good starting point is to begin to consume less. Below is a list of areas in which consuming less may indeed allow us to live lives of greater fulfillment and contentment:

Clothing. I am not advocating against shopping as a whole — I love expressing myself through my style — but rather suggesting that we shop smarter. Purchasing fewer, but better-quality items reduces the amount of shopping we do and helps support better working environments in clothing factories around the world.

Fossil Fuels. While not everyone has the luxury of leaving their vehicle in the garage in favor of public transportation, it is interesting to note that fewer and fewer teenagers are seeking a driver's license than in decades past. A mobile piece of steel is no longer an essential part of the American dream, partly because of the expense and partly because of the ability to communicate via technology no matter where one lives. The reduction of face-to-face interaction is not something to applaud, but the reality is that today's teenagers can communicate quite simply without picking up their best friend to go cruising. As we consume fewer of the earth's resources, we help care for the planet.

Food. Did you know that the National Resources Defense Council found that 40 percent of food purchased by Americans eventually lands in the trash? As with fossil fuels, consuming less helps the planet and its animals, and by focusing on quality food, we satisfy our appetites without eating in excess, thereby reducing our waistlines and expanding our longevity.

Television. We can save money by canceling our cable connection in favor of viewing online for lower cost, and it is ever more possible to be selective about when and what we watch. And even if we do not cut the cord entirely, choosing to consume quality programming via a cable network is a means of communicating what is worth producing and what is not.

Social Media. As a blogger, I fully appreciate the reach social media affords me to share ideas and meet readers from around the globe, yet there is such a thing as too much. One of social media's primary goals is to connect people, but it is important to self-assess regularly to determine if we are using it to connect or keep our distance and boundaries up, which prevents us from forging deep, lasting connections.

Space. Why does the average American household (2.6 people) need 2,466 square feet to live their life? With more space, one is often more propelled to fill it up with unnecessary stuff. Which means more money spent, more stuff to tend to, increased stress, and more energy for heating and cooling the residence. Less can be surprisingly more fulfilling, refreshingly less stressful, and ultimately more in line with a life lived to be luxurious but not bulging at the seams.

Gadgets. Technology has produced amazing gadgets, helpful aids, and organizational tools with the goal of simplifying our lives, but when do the gadgets begin to deflate one's quality of life? When they reduce our ability to form quality relationships, blossom into our best selves, and truly appreciate the world around us. If we allow gadgets to become enablers, preventing us from effectively learning, growing, connecting, and being compassionate toward one another, then we need to put them down or at least pick up fewer than we are used to.

Most of the time, living well requires that we avoid living with excess. When we choose to consume less, we allow opportunities to present themselves that may not have been previously available.

Why Less Is More

The secret of happiness is not found in seeking more, but in developing the capacity to enjoy less.
— Socrates

Wearing a stunning white Chanel gown accessorized with only simple diamond studs . . . choosing a timeless color for the rooms of your home, making sure the paint is of superb quality . . . tending to a few meaningful and time-tested friendships. These scenarios all involve consciously choosing less rather than more and bringing more value and beautiful memories and moments into your life.

A few years ago, I turned on the tail end of the Golden Globe Awards to see Anne Hathaway on stage with the entire *Les Misérables* cast and crew after learning they had won Best Picture – Musical or Comedy. While her attire was only the exterior aspect of her exuberant beauty, I could not help but applaud her stylist Rachel Zoe's choice of the white Chanel two-piece gown and barely any other accessories. Chanel is more than just a tad out of my reach, but such an image teaches an invaluable lesson. When we choose to bring material items and more people into our lives, it is not about how many we can acquire; it is about building something of quality.

Before moving to Bend, I took on the task of remodeling, reorganizing, and simplifying my kitchen. It was only when everything had been painted and only the necessary items were placed in the cupboards and everything else was packed away for a future garage sale that I realized the value of what I had done — fewer dishes, but better quality; less clutter, more function; less chaos of colors and more tranquility; the ability to find not only beauty in what I am eating, but beauty in the preparation.

There are so many ways we can welcome more quality and less quantity into our lives. Here are a few:

- Focus on the quality of the friendships you have, not the number of friends you have accumulated on social media accounts.
- Choose one fabulous, quality piece of statement jewelry to accessorize your outfit.
- Pay attention to the fabric for furniture, clothing, etc., as well as the craftsmanship.

- Cook with food grown or raised locally by farmers who adhere to better standards of production.
- Maintain a small wardrobe of quality pieces, which will last much longer and is certain to look its best for more than just a season.
- Refuse to purchase something simply because it is beautiful. If you do not need it, if it does not serve a purpose, or you already have one just like it, appreciate it from afar but do not bring clutter into your life.
- Take on fewer responsibilities, so that you can give 100 percent of your attention and effort to those you hold on to.

Creating a life of quality rather than quantity takes time, but gradually your conscious decision making results in a life of substance that you are proud to say you are purposely and continually creating. Be discerning of the people, food, clothes, furniture, thoughts, and anything else you bring into your life. More is simply more, and nothing becomes special when you say yes to everything.

The Pleasures of Living in a Smaller Home

With the Great Recession, McMansions began to be less desirable to potential homeowners. As a result of the housing crisis, the average square footage of primary residences dropped to 2,300 square feet. While it has slowly crept back up, many people are finding the luxury of living in smaller homes to be very attractive. Not only is it less expensive to own a smaller home or apartment, but it also provides many unforeseen opportunities to enrich our lives.

Approximately eight years ago, while I was still living in eastern Oregon, I had an itch to move back to Portland or at least rent a studio in the city to escape to on weekends and during the summer months. At the time, I was already a homeowner who was taking care of a yard and more than 2,600 square feet of living space, and I became intrigued by the thought of living in a 500- to 600-square-foot studio in Portland. Acquiescing to my curiosities, I rented a pied-à-terre in the Rose City. Why? With less space to decorate and care for, I could simply enjoy all that the city had to offer. If Powell's Bookstore was calling my name, I could easily arrange my schedule. If a stroll through the famed Japanese Gardens tugged at my need for tranquility, I could indulge without feeling guilty that something was being left unattended to at home. If a friend wanted to drop in, I could quickly pick up the studio at the last minute and thoroughly enjoy their company. In other words, with fewer material items and space to tend to, I would have more opportunities to improve the quality of my life rather than living a life based on quantity.

I understand that such realizations may seem obvious or commonsense, but in a world that bombards us with unrelenting advertisements in magazines, on the radio and television, and online, if we do not consciously limit these intrusions, subconsciously we become persuaded, ever so slowly and subtly. Living with less can be the foundation of a more fulfilling life if indeed what we seek is a life of more memorable moments and fewer material goods. Below are a few benefits we gain when we choose to live small.

Save Money and Energy. Buying or renting a smaller home saves you money — money that can be placed in savings each month. Money that can be spent traveling to Bordeaux, France, as you have dreamed of doing. Money that can be spent any way you want, instead of having to spend it as you must. So maybe in a studio you do not have a formal dining room. Purchase a chic bistro table and dine as though you were in Paris gazing at the passersby or the stars. A home can become a sanctuary no matter what the size. When we live in a smaller house or apartment, we consume less energy on heating and air conditioning. As energy costs rise, smaller homes are becoming the choice of more buyers and are proving to be more marketable than larger homes.

Gain Free Time and Have Less Stress. This benefit has always been a selling point for me. I clean my home on Friday in order to spend the weekend in a clean house; yet, of course, after a long workweek, I would rather relax than vacuum the floors. While there will always be cleaning to do, no matter a home's size, having less to tend to shortens the time we have to spend keeping things clean and tidy. We all look for ways to reduce stress, and when we have a smaller home to care for, there is less of everything — think pipes, windows, roof, yard, etc. — to repair or replace.

Trade Quantity for Quality. While initially having less space may make us feel cramped, it is actually the amount of stuff we have that creates the illusion of spacious living rooms or itty-bitty bedrooms. Once we have less space, we must be mindful about what we bring into our homes in order to maintain open living areas. And when we no longer need lots of furniture to fill our home, what we do purchase can be of much higher quality, which will make it useful for far longer.

Less Space Can Strengthen Relationships. In his fascinating book *Going Solo*, Eric Klinenberg makes an interesting observation: People are becoming more accustomed to living alone in part because, as children, many Generation Xers had their own rooms, as their Baby Boomer parents were able to afford larger homes. While I will always want to have my own bedroom, if we take this need for more personal space even further (the McMansion craze, for example), we begin to live in homes so large we can easily avoid the ones we live with. And you have to wonder, if you are living with someone you do not particularly want to come into contact with, why are you living with them? Choosing to live in a small home creates an environment of interaction and an opportunity to work together, respect the small space we each may need from time to time, and strengthen the bonds with those we love.

If you wonder why you have less time to do the things you enjoy and smaller stashes of cash than you would like, consider living in a smaller home. Quality truly does surpass quantity when it comes to creating a life of fulfillment. Having a bigger house will not make you any happier if you do not already know how to live well. For each of us, the proper size will be unique to our needs and those of our family, but the key is to find the tipping point between enough and too much.

A Small and Simple Sanctuary = A Grand and Full Life

There is nothing like staying at home for real comfort.
— Jane Austen

Oprah Winfrey always ends her weekly *Super Soul Sunday* on OWN with a handful of questions, and one of them is "What is the soul?" While it is clear that there are just as many definitions as there are guests on her program, the idea that keeps being repeated in one form or another is that the soul is our true and most authentic self, the element within us that cannot be taken away, die, or change significantly. When we look at the definition of "soul" through such a lens, the necessity of taking care of our soul is profoundly crucial to reaching our full potential.

Since we need to tend to our soul regularly, a sanctuary must be more than just our home. We all need to have sanctuaries where we can be left alone, unbothered, to discover what is waiting to be realized within in each of us.

Some of us enjoy alone time more than others, but solitude is actually beneficial for us all. Part of the reason we each need to be comfortable just being in our own company is that we need to be able to understand the crutches in our lives. Some examples: television and the advertisements and talking heads that fill the background even when we think we are not listening; reliance on anyone who takes care of our basic needs — food, cleaning, laundry, bills, etc.; social, government, and community constructs and what they provide that we take for granted (roads, mail service, education, etc.).

Once you recognize and begin to either appreciate or edit out crutches that are detrimental to your growth as a person, you can begin to live more consciously. And when you live more consciously, you begin to tap into your true potential. Will you be able to be entirely free from nagging commercials and uncomfortable situations and people? Absolutely not. But you can begin to limit their disturbance in your life and thus become clear about who you truly are, what your heart is longing for, and perhaps see and feel authentically without being influenced as much by the world and people around you. Because when we step into our full potential, we see improvement in not only our own lives, but in the community and world around us as well.

As the 21st century unfolds and we are now a decade removed from the Great Recession, the hope would be that we will apply the lessons learned and refrain from making the same mistakes. For example, after the 2008 economic dive, many people began to seek simpler ways of living; some chose smaller homes and became more efficient with energy, partly out of need, but also out of an awareness of what is truly necessary to live well.

When I moved to Bend, I was determined to downsize for many different reasons. After visiting London and Paris, I was mesmerized by how well two, three, even four people can live in an apartment that is fewer than 1,000 square feet. Likewise, I saw how few appliances and furniture are needed to live well and be truly comfortable. Small refrigerators, no microwaves, galley kitchens, to room-enlarging high ceilings, large windows that admit ample natural light and air — the gift of living well comes not from square footage but rather from how we live in the spaces we inhabit.

Once I moved into a much smaller house, I found that since I need to spend less time on cleaning, I have more time to enjoy doing what tickles my curiosities. With less space to decorate, I have more money in the bank. With a smaller yard to maintain, I have the benefits of playing in the dirt without spending lots of time and energy on upkeep. With less square footage to heat or cool, my energy bills are lower, and my social calendar is full and more of a pleasure because I am able to live in the town I have dreamed about and have time to enjoy its offerings.

But it is not just about living in a smaller space; it is about how you live in the space you call home. No matter where you call home at any given time, even on an extended vacation, the key is to pay attention to the details. The home you reside in need not be large; it need not be new or, for that matter, historic, but it needs to be your sanctuary. Here are fifteen simple ways to make your home your sanctuary.

Respect the Architectural Design. A French chateau can no more be decorated with modern, streamlined interiors than a couture Giambattista Valli skirt can be paired with a grunge flannel button-up. While yes, the unexpected pairing would make a statement and may be trendy for a moment, it is not something you would find yourself wearing very often. When it comes to your home, decorate in a way that will stand the test of time and that you can build upon, continually add to, and finesse over the years.

Spruce Up the Exterior. An easy way to spruce up your home, no matter its architectural exterior, is to turn to Mother Nature. In the front, place a pair of matching pots with annuals or perennials that you will plant after the summer somewhere else in the yard. Add a hanging basket or two. If you have tables and pedestals, add pots and plants as well. For your door, add a wreath if the design calls for it, and keep the stoop swept and welcoming for guests. If you have a balcony or a back patio, plant a mini herb garden, find a simple, but basic patio set with table and chairs, accessorizing with outdoor pillows. You will enjoy this space in the mornings as you savor your breakfast, and your guests will as well when you have them over for a dinner party al fresco.

Keep It Clean. It takes me fewer than thirty minutes to clean my house each week. That time is so brief because of my habit of tending to daily upkeep. I recently read that one of the habits of productive people is to immediately complete any task that will take fewer than two minutes. Direct, simple, and true. Whether it is wiping kitchen counters, putting away dishes, straightening or recycling newspapers that are spread on the table, or making the bed in the morning, simple attention to small tasks throughout the day makes weekly and seasonal cleaning tasks much easier and allows our sanctuaries to be places of refuge and comfort every day of the week.

Use Space Efficiently. Living in a small space may at first appear to be problematic when it comes to designing an office space, as well as a designated foyer for shoes, keys, etc., but ingenuity is spurred into action when there is a need. More and more retailers are creating multi-use products, streamlined storage, and hideaway bins and drawers that allow for stylish and comfortable living even in the tiniest of places.

Create Rooms of Comfort. Wherever you like to spend your time in your home — a kitchen nook, a reading chair, or your office — take time to curate spaces that beckon you to sit down and just relax. One way to decorate or stock such nooks of comfort is to create shelves of comfort — for tea or coffee in your kitchen or lined walls of books and favorite reading material in your living room or office space. The goal in creating rooms of comfort is to create a luxurious space where you can look forward to enjoying your everyday routines. Don't forget your bedroom; add a lavender candle and a favorite book or two, and get rid of unnecessary clutter.

Pay Attention to Details. For the areas where you like to read, sip, and relax, select furniture that is comfortable, reupholstering if necessary to fit your decor. Pick up a simple table or pedestal that does not take up much space but provides a place to set your hot drink while you read your newspaper or book.

Keep Counters and Tables Clear. No matter how big or small your home, if counters and tabletops are cluttered, the rooms can seem smaller, almost claustrophobic. One change I made after returning from Europe some years ago was to get rid of my microwave. In my home at the time, I did not have a built-in, so the one I had was taking up counter space. I did not use one for two weeks in the apartments I vacationed in and discovered I did not really need it. I got rid of my microwave, now heat up leftovers in my oven, and have not looked back. Ask yourself whether items you leave permanently on your kitchen counters have a purpose or a need to be visible each day. If they do not, find a home for them in a cupboard or get rid of them entirely.

Let the Daylight In. If you have a choice, always choose a home with as much natural light and as many windows as possible; light opens up the space, making it appear larger than it actually is. Two walls with windows would be a dream, but even one wall with floor-to-ceiling windows will do wonders for your mood. I have never understood why people cover windows. Granted, for privacy at night, warmth in the winter, and keeping the house cool in the summer, it is best to draw the curtains, but the benefits of daylight are immense. When you have access to daylight, let it in. If you live close to your neighbors, be creative with sheers and blinds, but do what you can to let in as much light as possible. This will make the space appear larger, and the connection to nature will be good for your spirit.

Add Mirrors. When you live in a small space, it is not about vanity; it is about necessity. Mirrors are a small home dweller's best friend. Mirrors instantly create the illusion of more square footage. Arrange three or four small mirrors on a wall as decoration, or use a full-length mirror as part of a contemporary scheme. Thrift shops usually offer mirrors that will instantly enlarge your living space.

The Interplay of Color and Light. The color of your walls, whether you paint them or wallpaper them, can have a tremendous effect on your mood. For example, your bedroom — the room in which you spend at least one-third of your time — should instill in you a feeling of calm and comfort. Choosing soft neutrals for your bedroom is never a bad idea, as you can always add personality with furniture and other accessories. A monochromatic approach goes a long way to creating a sophisticated, chic look. The details can be colorful, but keep the fundamentals within the same color family. When you live in a small space, the fewer differing colors and busy prints, the more open and spacious your home will feel. My approach is always to choose colors for the walls and major furniture pieces that are solid and neutral. The smaller details, such as throw pillows and table and wall decor, can then be bright, full of prints, and playful — and easily changed according to mood and season.

The Power of Light Fixtures. Floor lamps, table lamps, sconces, pendants, chandeliers. You name it, the lighting you choose has an influence on the mood that is created in each room of your home. For example, the only place to use overhead lighting is a room where you need to pay precise attention to detail — the kitchen, bathroom, laundry room, sometimes the office. Otherwise, do your best to cast the best lighting possible with table lamps, floor lamps, and wall lighting. If you already have ceiling lighting — chandeliers or built-in can lighting — add a dimmer to control the "temperature" of the room.

Let the Sofa Sing. If you have room for a sofa, or even a love seat, invest. Buying a sofa requires patience. Why? It is one of the most powerful players in the primary common area of your home. When you get the style, the color, and the size right, everything you pair it with is elevated. Whether you plan to buy it brand-new or purchase a consignment piece and have it reupholstered, take the time to determine what you want and then be willing to wait until you find exactly what you are looking for.

Blankets, Pillows, Blankets, and More Pillows. Such simple additions to any room can sometimes be the toughest decisions. When you eventually decide on the proper print and hue for your sofa, armchairs, beds, and reading nooks, blankets and pillows finish the space and beg to be enjoyed. Sometimes the colors and prints you want can be found at local boutiques, and sometimes you might go to a fabric store, pick exactly what you want, and have someone make a pillow for you. Your patience and knowledge of what you need will pay off when it all comes together. Appreciate the power of perfect throw pillows, which can elevate neutral furniture and complete a room. Welcome variety — texture, color, print — and bring your room to life. And consider making your own. Use natural fibers. From bed linens, to slipcovers and throws to snuggle up in on the sofa, pay attention to the fabrics that will surround your body.

Vases. I am loving my ritual of having at least two fresh bouquets in my house. I can usually pick up two bunches of flowers for fewer than five dollars and have bright bouquets on my dining room table and in my living room for two weeks. (Refill with fresh water every three to five days, trim the stems, and they will last longer than you think.) As the flowers are always different, I have a variety of vases —from bud vases to square vases, clear glass, and colorful, opaque, whimsical designs. This simple decor detail can create a great signature touch.

Bed Linens. The master bedroom is the space where we let all of our defenses down each and every night. Investing in your boudoir is not an excessive expense, especially when you understand the power of a good night's sleep. Choosing natural fibers, such as 100 percent Egyptian cotton or French or Belgium linen for your bed linens, is one of the simplest, yet necessary investments to make when it comes to ensuring a sound night's sleep. For less than $50 on Overstock.com or Amazon, you can purchase luxury bed sheets and be set for a blissfully deep slumber. I recently purchased a down feather bed pillow and love it. And do not forget quality bath linens. My go-to towels from Beecrowbee are made from bamboo. When you slip into your bed between 500-thread-count Egyptian cotton sheets with just enough layers for warmth, you will thank yourself.

How to Decorate Small Spaces

Less time spent cleaning, less furniture to buy, and more money for the quality decor that you love — these are just three of the many benefits of living in a small home. Whether you are living in a studio, a one-bedroom flat, or a cozy cottage, you want items that make the space feel as welcoming as possible, yet uncluttered. Here are some ideas for creating a sanctuary that promotes tranquility.

Show Some Leg. Choose a sofa, chairs, and dining tables that have visible legs. Eliminate dust ruffles and the boxy solid look, as it weighs furniture down and makes it appear heavier and larger. Simple wooden, acrylic, or metal legs allow the eye to see through the furniture, creating an illusion of more space.

Clear = Invisible = More Space. One of the best ideas for tables in a small space is to choose items that are made of acrylic or clear glass. Being able to see through pieces of furniture opens up the space and creates less clutter, while also providing the functionality you need.

Decorate Up. Do not forget about the walls. Use floating shelves for pictures or place a tall, narrow bookshelf in a quiet corner that does not take up much floor space but draws the eye up and keeps your home organized.

Be Smart and Buy Multi-Use Pieces. Anytime you can purchase an item you love that can serve two purposes, you automatically save space. An ottoman with internal storage; a headboard that serves as a room divider in a small studio; a standing tray table that serves as a table in your entry during the week and a bar on the weekends for dinner parties — all are great ideas to look into.

Go for Bigger and Less, Rather than Smaller and More. While proportions should always be considered, placing one impressive framed print or piece of art or even a large mirror, rather than many small items, on a wall creates a grand tone that suggests the idea of living large.

Hang Closet Organizers. A large dresser is not always a possibility when you live in a small space. The best thing to do is stop into your local Storables or Container Store and pick up hanging organizers, which are available in all shapes, colors, and styles (sweaters, shoes, jeans, etc.). Use them for items you would normally fold and place in drawers, and hang them in your closet to create tidy organization and save space.

Rely on Rugs. Living in a studio or small apartment often requires that two rooms become one. Decorate with area rugs to create designated spaces — living area, kitchen, bedroom, office, etc. It is a simple matter of training the eye and the mind about where one room ends and the other begins. Large or small, expensive or Ikea, area rugs define a space. Keep it simple and allow them to be an unexpected element; you can layer one rug on top of another, even if you have carpeting.

All of these simple touches make the space you call home more beckoning at the end of each day. No matter how big or small your space, respect it and understand the power it can have in your everyday life. Harness this power to support you, inspire you, and leave you a more fulfilled individual as you start each day.

Quantity is never a substitute for quality. So long as you carefully and tastefully decorate the space you live in and create a space that becomes your sanctuary the moment you cross the threshold, it does not matter how large it is. The quality of the life we live is determined by how we spend our time, what we value, and the relationships we build. A bigger home does not necessarily ensure this, but a well-cared-for space decorated with details that enliven our everyday experience certainly does.

The sanctuary we call home is a place to relax, unwind, and recharge for tomorrow. By investing in these simple ideas up front, you are ensuring continued comfort and far less stress over the long haul as you chase your dreams and enjoy your life. Consider your sanctuary an integral piece in the foundation of your simply luxurious journey; it truly is that powerful.

Create a Grown-up's Living Space

A home should be a distillation of your interests, of who you really are. If you're happy with your life, your space will reflect that.
— Designer Rafael de Cárdenas

The destination we come home to each night after a long day's work, after an exhilarating evening out, or after stepping off a plane should be a place where we feel most ourselves, where we can be most comfortable, and where we will be rejuvenated. As a junior in high school, I became ecstatic when my mother gave me permission to redecorate my bedroom, and I have stepped into each new space I have lived in and done my best (with the funds available) to make it a sanctuary.

While the details, size, and budget will differ, no matter what your age, you can live in a home that is tailored to your needs, that reflects your unique self, and that welcomes any guests you entertain in your home. After all, we all need a blissfully cozy bed to sleep in each night; we all need a place to restore us so that we are our best selves as a new day begins, and that is what you get when you invest in a simply luxurious sanctuary. Take steps like the following to fine-tune.

Display Original Art that Speaks to You. Whether it is framed photographs that you have taken or a piece from a local artist, welcome into your home and proudly display original art that speaks to you. Each time you see it, you should be inspired by what was sparked within you when you acquired it.

Matching Dishes/Wineglasses/Silverware. When in doubt, go with basic white for your dishes (as I did in my kitchen). If you like an eclectic look, then at least stick with the same shapes. By adhering to a matching formula, you create a purposeful, thoughtful presentation that makes your food all the more inviting.

Thoughtful Organization, Clutter-Free Living. A grown-up home is a clean and clutter-free space. You do not have to live like a minimalist, with only 100 items in your entire home, to reap the benefits of living in a clutter-free environment. Studies have shown that excess in our homes increases stress, which over time is damaging to our health.

The Power of One Unexpected Element. Only you can determine what the perfect unexpected element is for your home, but when you see it, you will know. The key is to choose one item; otherwise, the attention that the original item was intended to grab will be diluted. It could be a red wall or a purple couch or perhaps a unique collection of items on a designated shelf — whatever it is, welcome it and accessorize accordingly. And when you are ready to change (as I was after a year of living with a red living room), you will know. After all, that is what another can of paint is for.

A Designated Buffet Table/Cart for Entertaining. Any piece of furniture that you can creatively use to serve appetizers, tea, or the evening aperitif is a great addition. Think a bar cart or a console table, and when it is not in use for entertaining, add a beautiful bouquet or a unique bowl or bust.

Conversation Rather than Television. If you only have a living room (without an additional family or recreational room), there will most likely be a television, whether it is front and center or tucked away in a corner. Do your best to arrange your furniture so it encourages conversation rather than watching TV.

An Office Space That Encourages Productivity. A place for your computer and file storage and an environment suited to contemplation and creation indicate that you value productivity and organization. Whether you have a separate room or simply create an area within a larger space, organize it in such a way that it helps you sit down and get busy.

Through trial and error, you will gradually come to discover what makes you feel most at home and at peace. Enjoy the journey, have patience with yourself, and trust your instincts.

Consignment Decor

Your home can become a canvas for your passions, your experiences, your dreams, and your sense of humor. One of the best ways to showcase your signature style in your home, without breaking the bank, is to shop in a consignment decor boutique. During the holidays a handful of years ago, I stepped into a boutique called DeBouche, in Walla Walla, Washington, and immediately lost all track of time as treasure after treasure caught my eye. My project at the time was giving my living and dining room a facelift, and I knew instantly that I had found a destination for the finishing touches that would complete my tabletop vignettes and add the polish and personality I was looking for.

Much like turning to consignment stores for clothing, shopping at consignment decor boutiques requires time and patience, but you will be rewarded with the discovery of unique and intriguing pieces that you will appreciate far more than a cookie-cutter design everyone and your neighbor can pick up for themselves at a moment's notice. After all, shouldn't our homes bring together reminders of the world we have seen, love, and cherish? The way to do that is to gradually and patiently meander along, looking for the perfect item.

New Fabric with a Classic Structure. Sometimes consignment shops offer classic pieces of furniture that have been completely reupholstered with new, contemporary colors, fabrics, and designs. So, yes, you are bringing home a previously used piece of furniture that offers a classic or retro shape, and you are also able to enjoy a brand-new and original item.

Unique Lighting Details. Consignment shops can be a source for chic, yet affordable lampshades you will not find at your local Home Depot.

Signature Accessories. When I shop in decor boutiques, I spend most of my time hunting for accessories and details to finish a tabletop or an empty shelf, or for stemware for a buffet that can start a conversation between strangers. In a consignment shop, the possibilities are endless.

Retro Decor. Each of us has an aesthetic we gravitate toward. Perhaps we have fond memories of our grandmother's shag rug from the seventies and nibbling on cookies while lounging on it, away from mom and dad. Or maybe a favorite film, such as *Designing Woman*, starring Lauren Bacall, grabbed our attention years ago and we want to create a similar look or feel or evoke a certain mood. Whatever your preference, stepping into a consignment shop invites you to experiment with what catches your eye. Trust it, try it, and who knows what you will unearth?

Save Money. The key to living simply luxuriously is to become a savvy shopper. More should not be the goal, but rather a focus on acquiring items that have the value and function you want. English designer William Morris once said, "Have nothing in your home that you don't know to be useful or believe to be beautiful." When you stop into a consignment decor boutique, you are exposed to plentiful opportunities to acquire beauty without having to break the bank.

Respect the Planet While Welcoming Style into Your Home. While consignment boutiques are not antiques shops, they let us discover well-cared-for items that are in need of a home. Rather than purchasing another item that countless other shoppers can easily get their hands on, choose instead to reveal your ingenuity and expertise by hunting for a perfect, unique item. In doing so, you can also feel assured that, in a small way, you have reduced your carbon footprint.

While those who can afford it might hire an interior designer, taking the time to carefully decorate our homes so that they reflect who we are, the journey we have traveled, and the person we are becoming is something that hired help cannot do. Maybe your home is not exactly as you would prefer it, but it can slowly evolve into what you want it to be. Have patience, and enjoy the treasure hunt.

Refuse to Conform and Consume, and Welcome a Life of Riches

To be nobody-but-yourself — in a world which is doing its best, night and day, to make you everybody else — means to fight the hardest battle which any human being can fight; and never stop fighting.
— E. E. Cummings

The world, with all its intriguing people, adventures, and destinations, will always offer something more, something we have not done, or something we hope to see, try, or become. However, a life well lived is one of refusal. What? Didn't I just claim that the world offers us endless options? Yes, and that is why, when we discover the path that works for our contentment, our passions, and our purpose, it becomes much easier to not be distracted by what will not fulfill us. The key is to get to know ourselves.

At first glance, a comfortable, fulfilling life may appear to require masses of money, but the more I inquire, observe, and experience, the more I realize that people who genuinely live comfortably and enjoy financially secure lives are people who say no; they are people who do not purchase everything they can but instead acquire what they need and tuck away the remaining money in a stellar investment fund or savings account. Examples include adhering to a capsule wardrobe instead of purchasing the newest trends and latest accessories every season, and taking one grand vacation every year and then enjoying day or weekend trips to nearby destinations the rest of the year.

The slogan for *TSLL* blog — *Cultivating the art of living well, for a life of quality over quantity* — is based on my personal experience and my observations of others with little or ginormous sums of money. Those who are swimming in greenbacks can feel just as strapped and stressed as someone making $40,000 a year if they continually expand their lifestyle to live in a way they think they should. Simply having more money does not mean people live a more contented life. According to a study from Princeton University's Woodrow Wilson School, while there is a minimum amount one needs to live comfortably, there is a maximum — $75,000 — after which earning more does not make you happier. Ultimately, it comes down to how we handle the money we have earned.

After all, when we know who we are, what we need, and what we can do without, we are better able to say no thank you to offers, temptations, and societal expectations that do not line up with our priorities and way of living.

Living life on our terms, terms with which we are most comfortable, is a constant battle, turning away from temptations, and keeping our hard-earned money in our pocket when we do not need to be spending it. The clearer you become about the direction you want to take your life and the goals you want to achieve, the easier it becomes to know whether you should say yes or no. When you are uncertain of your direction, even the slightest breeze can empty your pockets, slow down your progress, or alter your direction entirely. Saying no to what you do not need eventually becomes quite easy. With patience, perseverance, and diligent focus, a contented and fulfilling life is possible, no matter what your income.

CHAPTER FOURTEEN

Cultivating True Contentment

Once you have achieved a state of happiness, you must never become lax about maintaining it, you must make a mighty effort to keep swimming upward into that happiness forever, to stay afloat on top of it.
— Elizabeth Gilbert

Fully grasping what is and what is not in our control elevates our lives to their fullest potential. We cannot just wait; we have to wait and work for it as well. We have to practice enjoying the everydays, reminding ourselves that they are really all we have. If we properly tend to what we have control over, when those magnificent life moments arrive — financial success, a loving partner, a fulfilling job, a sanctuary to call home — we can absolutely celebrate them. But the gift we have given ourselves long before these wonderful events arrive is to be comfortable stepping back into our everyday lives because we have made them truly breathtaking.

The How of Happiness: Controlling and Mastering What You Can

A sign of significant prosperity is simply having the time and ability to think about what makes one happy and then cultivating a life that is even more attractive to moments of happiness. The important part is to shift how you go about experiencing happiness. Do not let the outside world, the marketing world, tell you what it takes to attain happiness. Rather, discover how to make the shift in your daily life from seeking happiness to cultivating a life of contentment.

Strengthen Key Skills

When we strengthen the skills of trust, confidence, hope, and faith, we are strengthening our happiness muscles. In other words, when we see negative events in a temporary fashion (*Oops, my lack of sleep last night kept me from doing my best on the test*) rather than with a negative response (*I'm so stupid! No wonder I failed*), we are practicing optimism. The same goes for the flip side: having a permanent positive response (*I'm resilient. I'll figure a way out of this*) rather than a negative temporary response (*I just got lucky*). When we regularly practice the skills that lead to more favorable outcomes, we form the right type of habits, and before we realize it, we have created a happy life for ourselves and those we make contact with on any given day.

Learned optimism is a vital skill in our search for happiness. For anyone who is logical and rational, and cringes at the simplistic maxims that get tossed around in the guise of positive thinking, learned optimism makes more sense. It is one thing to be positive (*I know my wisdom guides me to the right decision*), but if you do not have the wisdom to make the right decision, then how well will that serve you? Learned optimism is much like being a detective. You need concrete pieces of evidence to remind you that no, you are not stupid. The fact is, you had a bad day because you did not prepare, did not sleep well and could not focus, or did not have the information available to demonstrate your understanding. In other words, the truth matters, but sometimes we overreact, and that is not helpful.

Exercise your strengths. Strengths are qualities you possess and exercise without having to put them on your "to do" list. Strengths are what come most innately to you. No one has to poke or prod you to do them. And because you enjoy doing them, you can lose all track of time. Exercise your strengths. Happiness resides in the moments when you are engaged with your strengths and the skills you have worked to develop.

Money and Marriage Are Not the Answers

As I mentioned in chapter thirteen, a study says there is an average amount of annual income that will improve the level of happiness in one's life — $75,000 — but after that point, more money earned does not directly improve one's level of happiness. In another study, those who defined themselves as happy were more likely to value time than money. In other words, experiences, not material things, support an increase in happiness

Study after study reports that marriage is a precursor for happiness. However, there are many ways to look at the data. The National Opinion Research Center reported in 2004 that after surveying 35,000 people, 40 percent of those who were married reported being "very happy." But let's look at the data another way: 60 percent did not report being "very happy." And according to a study shared by the Council on Contemporary Families in 2013 and reported by the *New York Times*, "Almost 80 percent [of people in the study] already reported high levels of well-being before getting married, with no significant increase afterward." In other words, do not get married in hopes of finally becoming happy; instead be someone who already knows how to be happy in order to continue being so once married. One can be single and happy as well as married and happy.

Be Able to Adapt, and Limit Shortcuts

Making the assumption that more wealth, better looks, a bigger house, more clothes, etc. will equate to more happiness is a fool's pursuit. What will improve your happiness is the experiences you cultivate with your good health and your money: buying tickets to travel or see a play, or engaging in activities that deepen relationships and lead to moments of wonder and awe. Limit the shortcuts. Drugs, chocolate, loveless sex, shopping, television — these "feel good" choices are not a foundation for lasting happiness.

Don't Give the Past Power

If we assume the past is destined to repeat itself only when it has treated us poorly, we will never have the courage or curiosity to seek out a happier route. Dwelling on the past is similar to being unable to forgive and move on. We have a finite amount of energy on any given day, so choose to expend your energy for the better. The truth is we have the power in the present to shift the direction of our lives no matter what circumstances have brought us to this point.

Be able to forgive. When we forgive, we make room to feel contentment and satisfaction about our lives, but when we choose to dwell in bitterness, hatred, pride, and a desire for revenge, we leave no room for positive emotions to emerge. Allowing ourselves to forgive and move on allows the mind to forget so that it can focus on cultivating a life of positivity.

Don't Let Emotions Rule Your Actions

As teenagers and even as early twenty-year-olds, our minds are not fully developed. The understanding of what we should actually be fearful of has not fully developed; emotions adults would call irrational can feel completely legitimate to younger people. As we come to recognize and manage our emotions, not allowing them to hold sway over us, we find that within twenty-four hours most disruptive emotions dissipate, and we are usually grateful we did not act on that emotional response.

Cultivate a Balanced Social Life

In *Authentic Happiness*, Martin E. P. Seligman shares that happy people spend the least amount of time alone and most of their time socializing. When I read this, I instantly froze because such a life sounds absolutely miserable to me. I also know that about two-thirds of the population self-identifies as being extroverted, and that means 33 percent identify as introverts. Introverts covet time alone and find great satisfaction in their private pursuits. The key is yes, we need human interaction as a means of feeling happy, but the degree, frequency, and depth of intimacy is based on the individual. My advice, based on my experience and conversations with a handful of close friends who self-identify as introverts, as well as authors who have researched the subject, is to cultivate the social network that works for you. Listen to yourself, trust yourself, and then invest.

Shift Your Perspective

Understand that fear of the unknown is a good sign, and not being happy does not mean you are sad. The expectation of constant happiness gets in the way of learning how to feel and exist with other emotions that are not all the opposite of happy. We can be curious, interested, ambivalent, neutral, focused, challenged, and I am just barely scratching the surface. Our job is to properly identify what we are feeling; while sometimes we may be able to explain why, we do not actually have to always know the root of each feeling.

Simply knowing what we are feeling and letting ourselves experience that emotion is a very healthy skill. Practice handling negative situations in a productive way. Doing so builds your resilience and persistence, and thus your chances of experiencing happiness when opportunities present themselves.

Act from Confidence and Strength

Practice patience and mindfulness. Let go of the need for fast fixes. Being mindful is being present, which requires us to have the ability to be the captain of our mind. Strive to improve your self-awareness. Our natural state needs to be content rather than happy. Once we realize and practice building and living a life of contentment, we broaden the opportunity for happiness.

When you work to bolster your strengths, you begin to see how you can tie them to a grander purpose for your life's work or legacy. Most often, we do not reach enduring happiness via shortcuts. Getting there takes time, work, dedication, and clarity about our purpose and direction.

Practice Gratitude

Last but not least, express gratitude regularly — whether it is at the end of each day, writing in a journal and reminding yourself of all the small and large events and moments that went well, or simply sitting quietly in the morning, lost in thought, allowing yourself to smile as you contemplate the amazing life you are fortunate to live.

Eight Truths about Contentment That Seem Impossible . . .

. . . until we experience them. There are innumerable axioms about living a happy life: Marry your best friend . . . live like today is your last . . . life is what happens while you are busy making other plans. But wait. Didn't Diane von Furstenberg tell us to be our own best friend, so how would that work? If I live like today is my last, I will have no money in my bank account, and if I am making other plans, that is my life. There is a reason some pearls of wisdom continue to be shared; sometimes, as with the three above, it is simply because they are easy to memorize and repeat, not because they are entirely true.

Many words of wisdom are true, but when we first hear them, we think they cannot be worthwhile. Sometimes it is not until we experience these ideas for ourselves that we finally come to understand and see the truth behind them. Here are eight truths I have observed about contented people

When You Love Your Life, You Do Not Rush through It. When I was in my twenties and met someone I was interested in romantically, I could not wait until the next date . . . so much so that I would unconsciously put the rest of my life on hold. I now know that I was not in love with my life fifteen years ago. I was still in the process of building, learning, and seeking the type of life I wanted, whether I was single or coupled, and that meant I was not at peace. If we love the routines and rituals we have cultivated for ourselves, instead of depending on others for our contentment, we do not want to rush through them. We do not want to rush to the next date because we want to savor what has taken place, as well as be able to step back into our daily routines to regain our balance, knowing while we do indeed want to love, we also are thankful that it is the icing on the cake.

Taking Care of Your Body Feels Amazing. When we eat or drink too much or eat something that does not agree with us, we are reminded of the power of eating well and taking care of our bodies. The foundation of all happiness is physical and mental well-being, so that we can partake in the life we love and have built for ourselves. In a moment when you are hungry or weak, you may gravitate toward what will not truly feed your hunger, but if you can catch yourself and remember the simple gift you can give your body and mind, the decision to eat well and stay active will become easier.

Live with Hope, but Let Go of Expectations. Letting go is crucial if we are to attain happiness. Economists Rakesh Sarin and Manel Baucells revealed their equation for attaining happiness in their book *Engineering Happiness*: "Happiness equals reality minus expectations." Often we become overly committed to a vision of how things will work out, and our rigidity zaps other beautiful possibilities from maturing or even being considered. In our efforts to reach our fullest potential, all we have control over is ourselves and our own development. We cannot know how people and the world at large will respond to what we offer. But when we let go of our expectations and those of the people and organizations around us, we allow an entire world of possibilities to unfold.

Worry Is the Bandit of Contentment. Ninety percent of what we worry about does not materialize, so why do we worry? Biologically, we may be conditioned to protect ourselves, but that is a weak excuse for individuals who are intelligent, analytical, and self-sufficient. Worrying robs our days of joy. When we worry about outcomes, others' opinions, and the future, we tend to stumble and miss opportunities to connect more deeply, laugh more fully, and grow into our fullest potential.

The Power of Nature Is Profound. Regular time in nature reduces stress, puts our worries into perspective, and helps our minds to wander, discovering creative ideas we otherwise may never have grasped.

Taking Risks Opens Doors to the Unexpected. Not all the risks you take will pan out in the precisely way you had hoped (but remember, no expectations). However, even from unfilled hopes you build courage and tenacity, and you evolve into someone stronger, more confident, and resilient with the lessons you acquire. Taking risks is a must if we are going to live a life we enjoy living each day. We must figure out what we want, be able to see what is not working and why, and then have the courage to make a change.

Giving "Just Because" Brings an Abundance of Peace. Thinking of others and knowing what would help them or express our love for them is to be truly loving. Love does not ask for reciprocity; it gives simply to enliven and bring comfort.

Savoring Sweet Memories Is as Wonderful as Creating Them. When we allow ourselves to be fully present, vulnerable, and engaged as well as free of expectations, resistance, and fear of limitation, we can experience amazing moments. And while we do not know in such a moment if it will ever happen again, knowing that we let go and stepped into the opportunity allows us to reflect, in the weeks, months, and years to follow, with a smile and complete joy as we savor what occurred.

These life truths can be hard to accept until we experience them for ourselves. While there are many lessons we can learn simply through observation of others, sometimes we have to get our hands dirty and see what it feels like to leap, trusting that, no matter what happens, we will be just fine. Because we have become clearer about what we want and have begun to build a life that we enjoy living each day.

Nine Habits to Cultivate for Contentment

You'll never know everything about anything, especially something you love.
— Julia Child

An oft-cited quote has been attributed to both Aristotle and Albert Einstein. It goes something like this: "The more I learn, the more I realize how much I don't know." This quote contains an underlying understanding — that we are not in control of all aspects of our lives. For example, not all of the factors that align for financial success are under our control: economic downturns and upswings, banking regulations, tax law, the financial needs of loved ones, to name a few. That realization may initially be frightening or frustrating, but ultimately it can be liberating and lead to a life of true contentment.

If you are living a life of true contentment, you embody certain qualities, a particular mind-set, and an approach to living each day that is distinctly different from someone who is trying to control everything and everyone. To become content, develop these abilities:

Get to Know Yourself. This is a process, and it will take time. Initially, spending time with ourselves is awkward if we have never done it. Just as pushing off from the edge of the swimming pool is initially scary, if we never leave our comfort zone, we will never reap the benefits of knowing who we truly are. An important part of knowing yourself is understanding your emotions — why you feel the way you do in certain situations and determining which emotions you should respect and which you need to let go. When you know yourself, you know how to make the best decisions for yourself. And when you know you will make the best decisions for yourself today and down the road, you can be at peace about your future even if you do not know precisely how it will unfold.

Trust Your Instincts. If you have taken the time to get to know yourself, you have probably been listening to your gut. But if you are new to this activity, what your gut is telling you can feel like a foreign language, and the way you respond may lead you into odd or unwanted situations. However, even in the instances that do not pan out as you had hoped, you are gaining valuable information. If you keep listening and responding, eventually your gut will become a finely tuned

THE SIMPLY LUXURIOUS LIFE | 353

instrument you can rely on in situations that you have never been in before with people you are meeting for the first time. Your instincts, your gut, are a part of you, but you need to learn their language and practice this new second tongue.

Live Each Day in the Present. A sense of liberation will wash over you when you begin to live in the present. When you choose to be aware of the moment — the details, the people, the environment, the beauty of the world — you will have less time to worry about the past or stress about the future. Your anxiety will diminish, and your joy will soar. When you are able to live in the present, you are at peace with where you have come from and confident that you know how to forge forward successfully into your future.

Strengthen Your Emotional Intelligence. Put simply, the emotional intelligence quotient (EQ) is a person's ability to perceive, control, evaluate, and express emotions (see discussion in chapter nine). Your EQ is just as telling about your potential in life as your IQ. Even if you have a high IQ, if your EQ is low, life can be difficult for you. For example, one of the significant emotions that squashes the ability to be present is fear. When you realize what fear feels like, realize you will never eradicate it entirely, and accept that it is how you handle it that will make the difference, your EQ becomes far stronger.

Don't Seek Perfection. A person who seeks perfection lacks the belief that they are enough and what they do is enough. That person needs to stop seeking external approval and instead seek approval from within. This process can take time. First, it takes awareness to recognize "perfectionitis" in ourselves and to understand why we seek this impossible outcome. Then you need to begin to like who you are and what you have to offer, and grow a thicker skin to help shield you from those who harp on what they see as not enough. Once you are at peace with the effort you have made and with the life you have chosen, dismissing critical remarks from others becomes easier. Give yourself approval, and simply strive to do your best rather than to be perfect.

Focus on What You Can Do. The truth is that not everything is under your control, no matter how much you may want it to be. After all, the only person you can control is yourself; trying to control others is called manipulation. You will never know how your unique life will unfold, but you can put the odds in your favor with the thoughts you allow to dance in your mind on a daily basis, the way you spend your money, the words you choose to utter, the behavior you exhibit, the courage you muster, and the curiosity you allow to drive you forward into new ventures and discoveries. So, no, not everything is under your control, but so much is.

Understand the Fictitious Nature of Limits. The only limits that truly hold us back are ones we either set for ourselves — *There's no way I can run a marathon* — and the fallacious ones we let society impose upon us — *A woman's brain is inferior to a man's*. The way to break these limits, even when we do not know what is beyond them, is to allow our dreams to run wild. Be infinitely curious. Ask why not? And refuse to accept no when it comes to an intriguing idea you have seen in your mind's eye.

Realize That Growth Can Occur Only When You Let Go. In order to reach the other end of the swimming pool, you must let go of the edge and swim. You may not reach the other side when you had hoped, and you may need a floating apparatus to help you as you learn how to swim, but the only way you can make it is if you let go. Growth can happen for each of us, but you have to let go of old habits, past events, old selves, and limiting beliefs. It is the only way. It is simple, but initially difficult; however, when you have made it halfway, the desire to return to old ways will be far less desirable because you will begin to see the reality you are swimming toward. That will motivate you to keep moving forward.

Recognize That Knowledge Is Power. When you know what you do not know, you have done your homework. When you are clear on the facts, figures, and loose ends that need to be tended to, you can find people with more expertise than you to tidy them up. But until you do your homework, you are walking into a potential and absolutely unnecessary mess. Choose to build the foundation of your dreams on cement rather than sand and you will find your contentment.

Contentment is possible when we accept that we cannot control everything. As Herman Hesse reminds us, "Some of us think holding on makes us strong, but sometimes it is letting go." Strength, peace of mind, and contentment come from acceptance that even if we do not know how it will all work out, we know how we will respond. We know we have prepared as much as possible. The rest is a wondrous journey that reveals itself anew every day so long as we are open to the possibilities.

The gift of being passionate about living well is that there will always be something new around the corner that you never expected, that you never could have anticipated, and what an amazing gift that is. More specifically, when you are truly dialed in to living your authentic life, you will not have all the answers, you will not know what will unfold moving forward, but you will be loving your life, making it all but impossible not to live in the present and revel in it.

Why Not . . . Celebrate the Ordinary?

The invariable mark of wisdom is to see the miraculous in the common.
— Ralph Waldo Emerson

The entire premise of living a simply luxurious life is understanding and then putting into action ways to live an extraordinary life in the everyday ordinary moments. Such moments are the tasks and routines we tend to each day — breakfast, a job that pays the bills, time with those we love, seven or eight hours of sleep each night.

Some people know how to turn the ordinary into truly extraordinary circumstances and experiences, while others just make it through the day. It truly is a skill, a choice, a way of living, and it does not require a certain amount of money, a home with a particular amount of square footage, or a particular wardrobe. What it does require is something we each can find within ourselves if we choose to look. What is it we are looking for? The beauty and opportunity in each moment, and then choosing to make the most of it.

Why not . . .

. . . savor everyday routines such as grocery shopping, your daily walk, making breakfast, or even cleaning the house?
. . . revel in the rest you give yourself each day?
. . . create your own simple rituals, events you look forward to and lose all track of time while enjoying?
. . . simplify, but at the same time elevate your workweek style in order to look and feel your best?
. . . eradicate negativity so that you can experience and luxuriate in all the goodness that surrounds you every day?
. . . spend time in nature regularly?
. . . discover how to design a happy life that truly brings you joy, rather than trying to mimic what society says your life should look like?

. . . be inspired by cultures that fascinate you?

. . . recognize that whether you are able to get away on a vacation or not, life can still be quite grand?

. . . understand and master the basics and build a solid foundation in your everyday life so that you can springboard into the extraordinary, no matter where your curiosities take you?

What separates the ordinary from the extraordinary is how we dance with each of these details. Instead of begrudgingly making dinner, why not make it a fun affair? Why not have a theme night, or perhaps make it an experience in which the music is on, the television is off, and anyone who steps foot into the kitchen has to wear a fun apron? When it is time to relax after a long day, put on soothing tunes rather than the drone of the television, pour yourself a crisp glass of water with a squeeze of lemon, and allow yourself to close your eyes or talk about your day with a loved one. When we celebrate the ordinary moments in our lives, we can make them extraordinary, elevating not only our lives but the lives that we touch or are intertwined with.

Each of us has a choice. It is easy to be ordinary, to do what everyone else approves of and accepts, but if that does not sit well, you can elevate your life. Do that by celebrating the seemingly ordinary moments — the chirp on a spring morning of mating birds, the sweet smell of gently falling rain, a snuggle with a pup or a child as you sit in your favorite chair, the playful whisper of sweet words from your love, savoring a well-written opinion piece in the morning newspaper while sipping your coffee — and doing what you can to enliven the everyday at every turn.

How can you make the everyday of someone you love more lovely? How can you shift gears from humdrum to happy dance? Ask yourself, what pulls you down? Do you pull yourself down? Are you focusing on what frustrates you, slows you down, or seems to get in your way? Why not focus on what is working? Why not focus on your gifts — a job you love or good health that keeps your heart and mind at their optimum performance? Why not focus on the lovely sleep you had last night or the sensual perfume you wear each day? Why not focus on the greatest gift you have — the chance to live today better than you did yesterday?

The habit of celebrating the ordinary provides the foundation for an overall well-lived life. When you can find the beauty in events, things, and people that others pass by, the experience of the extraordinary is all the more powerful and life-changing. It often strikes me that if we did not have the ordinary, we might not know how to fully appreciate the unique and extraordinary when they enter our lives. When the hoped for but unexpected has entered my life, I have found I was all the more stunned, dumbstruck, and appreciative, bathing myself in each and every moment so as not to forget its magic, not sure if such events were a dream or a dream come true, but knowing I would never forget they occurred.

The gift, for those who celebrate the ordinary moments, are the moments I spoke of that take our breath away. And with the combination of ordinary and extraordinary moments making up our lives, what amazing lives we have the opportunity to live each and every day. Today and every day, why not revel in the everyday routines you have established, honed, and polished (and if necessary, toss those that are not working) so that every day can be one you look forward to?

How to Reach Your Full Potential

Do you ever take time to people watch — simply take in the world that walks past you on a daily basis? Ever wonder how one woman becomes a successful entrepreneur while another struggles to pay the bills? Or why one family has raised children who are concerned, diligent citizens, while another has a hard time keeping their children in school? The ways our lives ultimately play out come down to the decisions we make, big and small, on a daily basis. The attitudes we choose, the foresight and knowledge we bring to situations, the people we spend time with and seek advice from — all affect how our lives evolve.

Whether times are going well or are challenging, the way we handle each scenario will determine how tomorrow goes. In particular, it is the challenging times that determine our fate. While there may be people who have experienced similar setbacks and challenges, nobody has experienced exactly what you have gone through to get where you are. And the only way to conquer the challenges that come your way is to strategize an idea and then put it into action.

Challenges are put in front of us not to destroy us, but to show us what we are truly capable of. Whether it is something as simple as learning to balance your budget each month or something as grand as becoming the master of your mind so you can eliminate self-sabotage and engage in positive self-talk in the most frustrating moments — when you handle what was once a challenge, you realize your full potential. More importantly, you realize you are capable of much more than you may have realized. Instead of viewing challenges as roadblocks, view them as opportunities that let you know there is even more amazing life magic available to you than you thought.

The Missing Piece: Trust

Trust is choosing to risk making something you value vulnerable to another person's actions.
— Charles Feltman, *The Thin Book of Trust*

There is a goal I once hesitated to place on my New Year's resolutions list because I did not know how to accomplish it: to cultivate trust.

As much as we can blame the outside world for some of the frustrations and headaches in our lives, we also must take responsibility for sometimes creating frustrations and headaches for ourselves. Part of it is ignorance; another part is thinking that in no way could we be at fault; it must be something or someone else. The beautiful realization is that often what needs to be fixed, after we have changed everything on the outside that can be changed, is our cognitive response.

Each of us has endured a loss of trust in some form, in either our personal or our professional lives. But what does losing trust look like? When we say we do not trust someone or something, what are we really saying? How do we build trust? How do we begin to trust others? Most importantly, how do we trust ourselves?

In 2015, I found the courage to let go of some comfort and began again here in Bend. It was, without question, the right move for the life I want to lead, but there is still work to be done: learning to build trust and be more trustworthy, recognizing why I cannot continue certain past relationships, and recognizing that I can be in relationships as I move forward if I engage and exhibit trust.

Instead of assuming someone new will be untrustworthy based on past relationships, assess them by what they show you. We may have reasons to be guarded, but when we examine and come to understand why our cognition is working in this way, we can retrain our minds, and begin to behave and respond differently so that the results will be different as well. If you begin to act and think differently, the world will begin to respond differently. You have more power within you than you realize.

Nine Ways to Trust Your Inner Compass

Just trust yourself, then you will know how to live.
— Johann Wolfgang von Goethe

A knotted stomach. A racing pulse. A situation that is not entirely in your control. Stepping into your potential future boss's office to be interviewed, pitching your idea to a crowd of onlookers, gazing into your future, trying to decide which way to go — such scenarios can understandably provoke even the most confident of us to internally shake just a bit. What makes the difference between knocking it out of the park and simply getting through any of these situations is trusting that we have everything we need. Whether we possess the ability, brains, creativity, gumption, and tenacity to swing big depends on whether we trust ourselves.

To merely exist is to waste the opportunity to truly live. We can timidly get by, tiptoeing to ensure we avoid make glaring mistakes, but wouldn't that be the most significant mistake of all? There will always be moments of uncertainty. If we are growing, evolving, learning, and discovering, we are encountering new people and new experiences that of course involve unknowns. The only way to navigate is to trust ourselves. When you trust what you know about the person who is on the journey (that would be you), you will know how to proceed. How does one do it? How do any of us become better in sync with our inner compass?

Look for Consistencies. Take time to notice the situations in which you are most at ease. In what situations are you most inspired? At first, you may not see the commonalities, but look again, and ask yourself what specifically made you feel anxious, inspired, curious, or calm? Was it a certain time of day, certain people, lack of or a satisfying amount of respect? Keep track of your observations, as they are a map helping to direct you down the right path.

Ask Why. Upon discovering the consistencies (the positive and the negative), do a bit of analysis and ask the question "Why?" Why did you feel secure even if others did not? Did it have to do with your knowledge or experience? Why did you feel intimidated? Why did you feel a sense of tranquility? Getting to know yourself leads to trusting yourself when it comes to making decisions, even when the future that you are walking toward is uncertain. If you can trust that you can (or cannot) handle or feel comfortable in certain situations, wouldn't feel comfortable or be your best self in certain situations, then you are in tune with your inner compass.

Reflect on Successes. Even after asking "Why?" you may still have uncertainties. If so, reflect upon your previous successes. When was the

last time you exceeded what you thought you were initially capable of?
When was last time you acted despite others' caution and demonstrated
that a risk was worth it? Reflect on such moments to build your
confidence and remind yourself that you indeed already have an inner
compass that speaks to you, if only you would listen to it.

Assess Mistakes. Not everything you reflect on is going to be a roaring
success. Mistakes happen. But when they do, the key is to take the time
to assess why it did not work and move forward with the knowledge.

Take a Time Out. In order to become in tune with your inner compass,
you must become still every once in a while. Quiet yourself, converse
with yourself, and give yourself time to work through some of the
habits discussed here. If you move blindly from one mistake to the next,
you are not taking advantage of the available knowledge and almost
guaranteeing you will make similar mistakes again.

Never Stop Learning. The best way to gain self-confidence and bolster
your inner compass is to continually become better acquainted with the
world. When you come to understand how the world functions — how
it functioned in the past and how people previously lived, currently live,
and potentially can live — you put the odds in your favor that the
decisions and direction you take are based on knowledge, not simply
belief. That is the difference between standing on quicksand or cement.

Find Your Faith. Martin Luther King Jr. said, "Faith is taking the first
step even when you don't see the whole staircase." Even with all of the
knowledge you can gather, there will still be unknowns. After all, each
of us is a unique individual with unique circumstances, so in order to
move forward, trusting your inner compass, you must fill the unknowns
(the gaps, as I like to call them) with your faith. I am not necessarily
talking about religious faith, although that might be part of it for some,
but a universal faith that allows you to stride forward with confidence.

Take Action. With as much knowledge and insight as you can possess
at that moment, strike out in a fashion that is not timid; rather, be
assured that you are endeavoring in the direction that is best for you.
You have done your homework, listened to your previous experiences,
and absorbed all that they have to teach you, and you have a vision for
the life you want to live. Go forward with resolute determination.
Others may not understand, but you do.

So long as you stride forward, you can only fall forward. It is when you are timid and leaning back with uncertainty that the winds can easily push you back. Trust yourself, because even if you should trip, the experience you have will be invaluable, and you will have still gained ground despite the misstep.

How to Let Go of Cynicism

Nobody knows enough to be pessimistic.
— Daniel Goleman

The beauty of self-reflection is that it allows us to see what we were not able to understand at the time. Due to a handful of painful emotional experiences during my early and mid-thirties, I had slowly but steadily developed a tendency to assume a negative attitude as a means of protecting myself from hurt. I would not say I had become cynical, but I was aware of something I wanted to change.

It is hard to share this realization because it means that, at the time, I was not as secure in myself in certain areas of my life as I thought I was; on the flip side, it has reassured me that my instincts were correct — I needed a significant shift. I had tried a multitude of angles, approaches, and ideas, and nothing was working. I needed to uproot myself and move to a new town a couple of hundred miles away to begin to trust life again.

I am now able to see that indeed I was not where I needed to be to grow more fully into the person I want to become. I needed room to grow and space to stretch into the person I am excited to evolve into. Do I, do any of us, know who this "other" version is or could be? No, but I am, as always, enjoying the journey.

Why does one gravitate toward being a cynic or immediately default to a defensive stance rather than assuming a positive response or outcome? Psychologists say that it often results from prior negative experiences. We want to protect ourselves and eliminate the possibility for more pain.

After all, when we refrain from cynicism and instead select hope or put our faith in the process, people, or anything that is out of our control, we make ourselves vulnerable. It takes an extremely secure person to do this, to be secure in what we can offer, knowing that whether the outcome is positive or negative, it may have nothing to do with us but rather depends on the other person or the situation. Insecure people often assume it has something to do with them, and as a protection, they label all "men/women," "Democrats/Republicans," or [category or label of your choice] as something to be wary of.

Over three months, the change I had made was giving me the opportunity to take down my walls. It has been a refreshing realization. In many ways, I feel I can breathe again, truly be myself, and know that if I am disappointed in someone or something, I will be fine because at least I am not standing behind a false version of who I am.

Our overall contentment in life has everything to do with how we approach each day — our attitudes, our expectations, our responses to events and people we will never have control over. But what must we do to eliminate the cynicism?

Establish a Secure Sense of Self. Get to know yourself. Stand in your truth. When you do these things, you will set yourself free.

Stop Assuming the Worst. We can only see what we look for, and if we are focused on looking for the worst, we will miss the good that surrounds us.

Put Forth More Goodwill into the World. Do so with your words, your actions, what you support, how you spend your time, without expectation of anything in return. You will be amazed at the environment of opportunities you are cultivating.

Practice Meditation. As shared in chapter nine, regular meditation offers a myriad of benefits to enhance the quality of our lives: reduced anxiety and stress, a stronger memory, appreciation of the present and thus stronger relationships, as well as a sound understanding of our emotions and their often-ephemeral nature.

Try Something New. Refrain from returning to the source of your pain and expecting a different outcome. Whether it is an individual, a job, a town, or an activity, if you have tried to present the new you and still the outcome is hurtful, negative, and destructive, move on.

Be Creative. Follow Yoko Ono's advice: "Experiencing sadness and anger can make you feel more creative, and by being creative, you can get beyond your pain or negativity."

One of the hardest parts of letting go of cynicism is helping those around you to see either why you are moving on or why you are choosing to change. Often those with whom we find ourselves in a web of negativity are not ready or willing to see what life could be if they chose to let go of the defense of cynicism. Sometimes we will not know either, but at least we know we want something better. And based on the people, experiences, and places I have had the opportunity to enjoy firsthand, it is indeed worth it — far beyond anything I could have imagined — to look for the good and stop assuming the worst. My job now is to keep cultivating, keep growing, and squash any negative tendencies. I can honestly say fewer and fewer are arising, and that, in itself, is an amazing victory.

Why Not . . . Have Self-Compassion?

Self-compassion provides an island of calm, a refuge from the stormy seas of endless positive and negative self-judgment, so that we can finally stop asking, "Am I as good as they are? Am I good enough?"
— Dr. Kristin Neff, *Self-Compassion*

Is there a voice in your head that is always contemplating the negative or worst-case scenario, an inner critic who berates you for your mistakes, no matter how minor, and refuses to congratulate you if a flaw or wrinkle is apparent? The irony is that while we think being tough on ourselves and holding our feet to the fire is beneficial on the road toward success and ultimately happiness, the opposite is actually true. In *Self-Compassion: The Proven Power of Being Kind to Yourself*, Dr. Kristin Neff explains that self-compassion is the key to the successful and content life we seek.

How do we develop the voice in our head that does us no favors, even if we initially think it does? According to Dr. Neff, the way we were raised, how we were taught, and the community around us bolster the belief that tough love is the best love for getting something done. You may be wondering, shouldn't we be disciplined and be given guidelines to follow in order to be safe and successful? Absolutely. But the extreme scenarios, ones that are used to scare, do us a disservice.

When we seek the truth and acquire knowledge, providing ourselves with options and scenarios, we realize that mistakes are inevitable, and that beating ourselves up for making them only prevents us from moving forward.

I have been very hard on myself, starting at a young age, but I have become aware that being overly self-critical is not beneficial. It attacks my self-esteem, it weakens my self-confidence, and the only person I have to blame is myself. I used to think I was helping myself out by being tough on myself. And I did not feel it was right to be caught "bragging" about my accomplishments. In reality, it is not bragging if it is the truth; someone asks and you respond with decorum. Confidence and success are contagious, and people innately want to be around these qualities. Let's talk about the benefits Dr. Neff shares.

You Will Have Fewer Negative Thoughts and Emotions. Whether it is fear, irritability, anxiety, or anger, negative feelings become fewer and fewer for those who embrace the habit of being self-compassionate. How? It has to do with mindfulness — the ability to be aware of your thoughts without accepting them as being entirely true (or even true at all). The key is to acknowledge how you are feeling, and to have the wherewithal to note that these are feelings and they will pass and you need not accept them entirely.

You Will Deal with Negative Emotions and Move On. As much as we might want all negative emotions to be erased from our lives, in reality, this can never happen. But when we refuse to deal with what we are feeling, refuse to find out why we are feeling that way, we cause ourselves unnecessary suffering. When we practice self-compassion, we trust ourselves to be able to deal with our emotions, the good and the bad — to face them, deal with them, and allow ourselves to move forward.

You Will Understand That Perfection Is Not Possible. When we truly accept that we are imperfect beings, we liberate ourselves. We know that we are doing our best, and that sometimes our best will not be enough. During the times when things do not work out, we must not beat ourselves up, but rather turn to the habit of self-compassion to nurture ourselves back to feeling good about ourselves.

You Will Increase Your Emotional Intelligence (EQ). According to Daniel Goleman's book *Emotional Intelligence*, those with more self-compassion have a higher EQ. Self-compassion helps us recover from tough emotional experiences rather than be weighed down by them. Emotionally intelligent people have a better perspective on their problems; they understand they are not the only ones who have experienced what is causing them pain at the moment, and they understand it will pass.

You Will Have More Success in Attaining Goals. Individuals who practice self-compassion experience more success because they get out of their own way. When the going gets tough, they realize the only way to respond is to move through it, not be held back by it. Using the approaches to negative emotions and difficulties discussed in this chapter, they are not held down by imaginary obstacles.

You Will Enjoy Healthier Relationships. When you have self-compassion, you rely less on others to fulfill you, and instead look to yourself, with the confidence that you can take care of your own emotional needs. And when you are secure in your ability to care for yourself, the relationships you seek and build are healthier, and you are capable of giving more fully and without expectations.

You Will Change the Overall Quality of Your Life. Self-compassion is a vital tool in cultivating a life that is full of contentment no matter what is going on. How? It is a mind shift. The quality of our lives is due in part to how we think we are doing. When an obstacle or challenge arises, all we can do is respond to the best of our ability. When we are self-compassionate, we do not expect more, and we applaud ourselves for all that we have done and are doing. While most of us do not want to brag or come across as narcissistic, we do need to pat ourselves on the back regularly, whether in a daily journal, a mindful meditation, or a walk in which we revel in the ability to savor the everyday moments we are given and have created for ourselves.

When we embrace the idea of being self-compassionate, we embrace the reality that, whether or not anyone else tells us so, we are okay just as we are. It all begins with believing it ourselves. And when we do that, we do not need to seek outside approval.

The more you practice self-compassion, the easier it becomes to confront and more quickly move through negative thoughts, emotions, and experiences. When you open your heart to yourself, you will be better able to open it to the world and trust that no matter what the world does, you will be just fine as you have built a foundation of comfort within yourself.

The Difference Between Pleasure and Joy

Pleasure is always derived from something outside you, whereas joy arises from within.
— Eckhart Tolle

One of the most empowering realizations is to understand that much of what we seek in order to create a fulfilling life already exists within us and is within our control, rather than outside of us and beyond our control. When I came to understand this life lesson, a huge sense of relief washed over me. While it was something I knew subconsciously as a young woman, as I became curious about the world and began exploring after leaving my parents' home, I seemed to have forgotten such a vital concept, which is necessary for the dream I sought — fulfillment.

Throughout my late teenage years and twenties, I far too often sought the acceptance of others and the consumer goods of retailers in hopes that they would lead me to the contentment I desired. Thankfully, a handful of lessons (many small, yet quite powerful) showed me that life is about going within to discover the contentment we seek rather than gobbling up more from the outside world.

The jockeying back and forth between our inner world and the outer world is what brings me to the difference between joy and pleasure. Pleasure, fleeting and often elusive, is sought by humans for a reason — it makes us feel euphoric and perhaps somewhat removed from the present moment. However, because it is something that we seek outside of ourselves, we do not have complete control over it, if any at all.

Joy, on the other hand is a pursuit that requires that we dive deep within ourselves. It is something that cannot be taken away and that builds like interest once we become better in tune with ourselves and learn to discover it within our thoughts, being, and overall existence.

While pleasure may cost money, it is rather easy to attain, and it does not add to the quality of our lives but does add exclamation points along the way. Joy, on the other hand, requires more time, attention, and thoughtfulness from us, but the rewards are enormous because of their durability and substance.

Of course, we should not eliminate pleasure from our lives. A decadent meal, a beautifully tailored outfit, an intimate experience with our partner — these pleasures add to the richness of our lives. But when we are not clear about the difference between joy and pleasure, we can seek one all the while thinking it is the other. The key to creating a fulfilling life is to build your foundation on joy and adorn it occasionally with pleasure. So long as we do not rely on pleasure to provide us with contentment, we can appreciate it for what it is — a temporary moment to appreciate fully but not become attached to.

Welcome More Joy into Your Life

Here's how:

- Take time to meditate or pray, and be still.
- Look inward — become at peace with who you are, and celebrate your uniqueness.
- Allow external inspiration (art, nature, music, conversation) to stir your creativity, and act upon those moments of inspiration to dream and create.
- Figure out your purpose/passion, and then pursue it.
- Be thankful for what you already have, rather than what you lack.
- Give when you have the resources, time, and energy to do so.
- Pursue dreams that are meaningful and align with your values.
- Plan activities that cultivate more moments of joy — simple meals, gatherings, events you are curious about.

Knowledge is truly power. And when we understand the difference between joy and pleasure, we become not a feather in the wind, randomly blown from one pleasurable moment to the next, but an oak tree that bends with the gusts yet is always rooted in what provides security and certainty.

CHAPTER FIFTEEN

Savor the Life You Have Created

Just imagine — you wake up with excitement, go through your day with clarity, and unwind in the evening with peace of mind and a dose of pleasure and extraordinary comfort. In a very succinct way, this is what living a simply luxurious life is about. What do we need to do now to enjoy this state of being each and every day?

What does a simply luxurious life mean? The answer will be different and unique for each person, just as we are different and unique individuals in this vast and amazing world, learning what is joyful, pleasurable, and lovely in our everyday routines. Below are my thoughts on what a simply luxurious life entails and how it will feel as you are living it. A simply luxurious life involves:

Knowing Yourself. You know what you need and what you want. You give to yourself with self-respect and self-compassion, and find the inner strength to successfully attain your goals.

Being Clear about What You Value. Eliminating responsibilities, activities, and relationships that do not support your primary values requires regular reassessment.

Letting Yourself Feel What You Are Feeling. Do not numb yourself when difficulties arise. When you allow your feelings to emerge, you allow yourself to move forward with clarity, compassion, and awareness.

Finding a Purpose That Aligns with Your Passions. Once you discover what enlivens you, sparks your curiosity, and fits with your talents, the world will feel brand-new in beautiful ways; you have found your direction, and that will make all other decisions far easier moving forward.

Always Learning and Remaining Curious. The universe always offers something new. Once you answer one question, two more will appear based on what you now know. Curiosity propels you toward a purpose that speaks authentically to you.

Establishing Routines That Enable Spontaneity. It sounds incongruous, but when we establish routines, we set our minds free to dance with ideas, entertain possibilities, and discover creative ways to enjoy today and tomorrow.

Traveling Regularly. Visiting other places and cultures is a must as we grow and evolve. Make your trips luxurious, with proper attention to advance planning and details for a simple and enjoyable itinerary to be savored.

Striking a Balance between Your Work and Your Personal Life. We need to determine the amounts of time we spend with work and in our private life as we explore what is most rewarding for not only ourselves but those we want to strengthen bonds with both professionally and personally.

Investing in a Healthy Social Circle. Put the focus on quality, not quantity.

Being Compassionate but Having Firm Boundaries. Knowing how much we can give to others is showing respect not only to ourselves, but to those who ask for more than we can give. Establishing boundaries communicates self-respect.

Being Open to Love. Take your time, learning from past mistakes and knowing what you can and cannot compromise on.
Maintaining a Sturdy Three-legged Stool of Health. A diet of moderation built around real food; daily, simple, enjoyable aerobic

exercise, combined with strength training and stretching; and mastery of your mind — conscious decision making, positive self-talk, meditation, and a regular good night's sleep.

Living within Your Means. Be sure that your spending includes investing in yourself. The key is to have your financial security in your complete control. Continue to educate yourself so you can take risks but also remain financially savvy.

Creating a Sanctuary, a comfortable home to wake up in each morning and fall asleep in every night. Keep it decluttered, organized, and stocked with the simple pleasures for your daily, weekly, and monthly rituals so that it is simple to maintain and a pleasure to live in.

Looking Great in a Chic, Stylish Wardrobe. This is something you can do while adhering to your budget and not letting trends and the media master you.

Allowing Room for Luxuries. Luxury can be both extraordinary and routine — think flowers, massages, facials, pedicures and manicures, entertainment, dining out, etc. Regularly plan special moments — no matter how small, and at least one each day — to celebrate or appreciate something that is going well.

What You Will Feel as You Live a Simply Luxurious Life

These are some of the emotions, mental states, spiritual conditions, and attitudes you are likely to feel when you have discovered the keys to living in simple luxury:

Contentment . . . uncertainty, which tells you to seek answers and knowledge but also to trust yourself . . . peace . . . initial doubt, followed by confidence . . . gratitude . . . excitement . . . security . . . determination . . . freedom . . . curiosity . . . a sense of being engrossed . . . reassurance . . . calm . . . relaxation . . . delight . . . joy.

You will have the confidence to face any uncertainty. You will have the ability to appreciate where you are, what you have, and how far you have come. You will be in touch with yourself so that you understand your emotions, and that is why the negative emotions do not often rise to the surface. You may initially feel frustration or anger due to another's actions or the outcome of a scenario that did not go your way, but you will know how to respond effectively; you will know what to let go of and will not burden yourself with unnecessary angst.

My work on my blog and on now two books is part of my attempt to understand myself and the world as a 21st-century woman who values her independence, intelligence, and femininity. I try to reach my full potential, while at the same time savoring each and every day. How fortunate I am to have the opportunity to share as I go, revealing the *aha* moments I experience with each challenge I overcome. This simply luxurious life continues to become extraordinary beyond my wildest expectations, and I want you to experience this as well because you absolutely can.

To the casual observer, your life may not be extraordinary or magnificent. But you know the transformation you have undergone. You will feel all the feelings noted above, and you will wake up with excitement, go through your day with clarity, and unwind in the evening with peace of mind and a dose of pleasure and extraordinary comfort every single day. The simply luxurious life is worth living, and you hold all the power to make it so.

How to Turn Fairy Tales into Reality

Do not lose hope — what you seek will be found.
— Neil Gaiman

In our modern world, the mere mention of fairy tales brings to mind Disney, Prince Charming, and glass slippers. The real history of fairy tales is a ghastly one. The Brothers Grimm, along with many other authors, included in their stories considerable violence and extensive gruesome details that have been washed away in versions sanitized for children to enjoy. Did you know that one of the evil stepsisters in Cinderella cut parts of her feet off in order to fit into the glass slippers? Or that in the original French version of Little Red Riding Hood by Charles Perrault, the young girl is actually eaten by the wolf, not saved?

I share these examples not to dissuade you from fairy tales, but to help us all recognize that each of these stories that we most likely adored during childhood were extended metaphors devised to teach us life lessons — never, for example, try to be someone you are not, and do not give your trust to people who have yet to earn it. Yet such tales are not to be taken literally, which makes me wonder, what was the story of Prince Charming's tale trying to teach us?

If "happily ever after" means finding a metaphorical Prince Charming, perhaps what it means is not that we should all aspire to find that one person to complete our lives. Instead, perhaps it is telling us to dare to dream grand, amazing dreams that surpass even our own expectations. A life rich with travel and endless new experiences — it can happen. A life lived as a well-paid writer, graphic designer, chef — it can happen. A life that involves owning your own boutique selling beautiful garments and accessories from independent designers — it can happen. A life of public service that leads to the Oval Office — it can happen.

Fairy tales never exclude the obstacles. There will always be evil stepmothers, a ticking clock at midnight, a queen who wants her competition destroyed. But fairy tales remind us that if we choose wisely, we can overcome.

Each of us will have our own fairy tale; in fact, you are living yours right now. It is simply a matter of redefining "fairy tale." The way we move forward, what we work toward, who we spend our lives with, the challenges we take on and refuse to be defeated by — all come together to form our own unique fairy tale. The way you look at your life, as drudgery or a fantastic experiment, is up to you.

The gift of living a fairy tale is that so long as we define it by what we find to be worth pursuing — what brings us bliss, contentment, and fulfillment — we allow our lives to be richer. Your Prince Charming may be living life on your own terms, and if that is the case for you, as it is for me, you are already living a fairy tale.

Create Your Own Happy Ending

A bird sitting on a tree is never afraid of the branch breaking because its trust is not on the branch but on its own wings.
— Anonymous

It is easy, and quite healthy, to forget mind-sets and limiting beliefs we had as young adults and in our earlier adult years about the trajectory one's life should follow in order to attain contentment. It is always amazing to me how quickly we can become inured to our current situation and forget the hard work, progress, and difficult decisions it took to arrive at our destination. However, with each year and life hurdle, my appreciation for the journey increases.

I am thankful that I broadened my perspective, stepped out of my comfort zone several years ago, and began to live life using my own compass and with the help of endless firsthand lessons learned from my mistakes. I by no means am mistake-free now, but thankfully, my current mistakes are different ones that continually allow me to grow and improve.

What our lives are supposed to look like is something we must all reassess. We must first understand where the conception of "happy endings" comes from. Happiness is something only each one of us can do for ourselves. To live someone else's definition of happiness is to throw away the gift that resides in each of us that the world is waiting to be introduced to.

One popular maxim is that lessons repeat themselves until they are learned. While I have heard this before, I have always felt there was a negative aspect to the reappearance of a life lesson. It is as though we are saying, You failed, so let's try it again. And when we look at any life situation through such a negative lens, it can be difficult to have confidence that we will be successful. But remember: Our lives are full of spirals, events, situations, and recurring lessons so that we can apply knowledge we did not have the first time around. We can only do our best at the time a lesson presents itself. When we have experienced a lesson once, we have gained new information that will enable us to do better when a similar situation arises.

I see lessons repeating themselves in a positive light. I view them as opportunities to reap the benefits we were not initially able to garner on the first go-round. Rather than viewing the second or third attempt as a punishment, why not view it as an opportunity to earn the rewards we did not receive the first time? In order to live in this dynamic fashion, we must cultivate certain habits that stimulate a continual progress that allows us to grow. Read on to consider habits that, once ingrained in your way of living, allow you to regularly grow, learn and, most importantly, flourish.

Be a Friend to Yourself. The only way to build healthy friendships is to be a friend to yourself. When you realize what you need to be healthy, safe, and content, then you can recognize how to be a better friend to someone else. Another benefit: You can more readily recognize someone who is not friend material.

Respect Yourself. Choosing to respect yourself — to discover and realize that you are worthy of being respected — is a fundamental step to creating boundaries. When we respect ourselves, we teach others how to treat us, and we create opportunities to develop stronger, healthier relationships built on mutual respect.

Create a Solid Financial Foundation. Regardless of the relationships you are stepping into — marriage, co-habitation, business venture, etc. — if you know you have your financial house in order, you will be able to stand on your own two feet should things go south. However, on the flip side, if you rely on someone else for financial support, you are giving them a certain amount of control over your life's path. We all need freedom in order to create, to venture, and to eventually soar into our true potential. This is why it is so important to build your own financial stability.

Recognize the Lesson That Keeps Returning. Growth requires recognition. We must be able to recognize when patterns occur in our lives. When lines of communication keep breaking down or we feel we are butting our heads against a wall at work, we must take responsibility and realize the lesson that has again appeared in our lives, begging to be learned. Once we recognize it, we can fix it.

Reflect and Be Honest with Yourself. Now that we have recognized a lesson, we need to find time to self-assess. Why do I choose unavailable people? Why do I procrastinate at work? Sitting down with ourselves and being honest can initially be uncomfortable, but it lets us experience amazing *aha* moments.

Don't Take It Personally. As humans, our psychology is designed to protect us, to prevent anything from causing pain. In other words, we are preconditioned to take things personally. When we fail to keep this innate reflex in check, we are letting fear run our lives. And when we let fear rule, we are giving up control. How do we not take hurtful comments or behavior personally? First, recognize that the behavior of others is a reflection of who they are, not you. Second, when certain reactions or comments cause us to bristle, often it is because we have wounds that have not yet healed. When we can understand ourselves more fully and heal ourselves, we will be far better at not taking others' words and actions personally and better able to deal with them in a healthy and effective manner.

While on the surface, these habits may appear simple, they will take targeted, conscious focus to become habituated into your daily routine. Once they do, your spontaneous response will be positive and healthy, and will open up amazing opportunities you did not experience the first time around.

Maintaining a Simply Luxurious Life

A simple life is not seeing how little we can get by with — that's poverty — but how efficiently we can put first things first. . . . When you're clear about your purpose and your priorities, you can painlessly discard whatever does not support these, whether it's clutter in your cabinets or commitments on your calendar.
— Victoria Moran

Just as one must work out regularly, eat in moderation, and visit the dentist for regular cleanings in order to maintain a healthy life, we must also put in place routine practices to ensure we are living simply luxuriously. In other words, we must dedicate ourselves to maintaining the life we have created for ourselves.

If you have already taken steps to restructure your life — creating a more simplistic approach, editing out the unnecessary, and delineating your priorities — the maintenance will be easier. However, it is only by creating a maintenance plan that we can ensure that our simply luxurious way of life will remain intact, as our lives are always changing and evolving.

Over the past two years, I have had to make conscious choices about what I can and cannot do in order to live my own simply luxurious life. While it may be frustrating to hear that choosing to live well is not a one-and-done process, the good news is if the path you have paved for yourself is in line with your values, all you need to do is check in regularly and perform a tune-up when the need arises.

I have devised a list of routines that can help keep the unnecessary to a minimum and allow you to continue to live a life of quality and contentment. I have broken down these routines into four categories: everyday living, health, wardrobe, and relationships.

Everyday Living

Organize Your E-mail Inbox. It is vital to set up your e-mail account so it does not overwhelm you and gobble up unnecessary time when you finally get around to making your way through your inbox. Put in place the appropriate blocks, create mailboxes/folders for e-mails you want to save, subscribe only to newsletters and alerts that assist you in living a more simple and luxurious life, and delete anything you no longer need.

Be Smart about Snail Mail. Removing your address from catalog mailing lists will greatly reduce the mail delivered to your door each day. Set up a system for dealing with your mail; put it somewhere you cannot ignore, then review it regularly, and throw out what you do not need.

Set up a House-Cleaning Schedule. Keep it simple. There is no need to deep-clean your oven every week, but with regular tidying up, you can keep stress at a minimum, and you can enjoy walking across your threshold each night.

Outsource as Necessary. Consider your time as a valuable commodity. If you do not have time to mow your lawn and could use a few extra hours on the weekend to enjoy time with your family and friends or to relax, hire a service to care for your lawn. Or hire someone to regularly clean your house, if your budget allows. Do not feel guilty for protecting your time and energy.

Monthly Budget. Financial wealth is crucial for peace of mind and future success. Choose a date each month when you sit down and reconcile your income and expenses. Knowing where your money is going will help you make good decisions.

Health

Weekly Grocery Shopping. Choose a time each week or so to pick up the essentials for your upcoming meals. For example, each week I stop by my local bakery and pick up a fresh loaf of bread or a baguette, followed by a visit to a local farm stand for a dozen fresh eggs. I also pick up at my local market the fruit and vegetables, protein, and other regular items I need for breakfasts, lunches, and dinners. (A reader once asked me how I keep a baguette fresh all week when it is just me that I am cooking for. While the initial crunch and inner chewy goodness won't be as ideal after the first day, you can easily make it last for another two to four days. Slice in half, or small enough to fit, and place in a plastic storage bag. Usually, I enjoy the baguette as is on the first day and then toast it for bruschetta the rest of the week or make sandwiches.) The key is to have a default grocery list that you follow each week and edit or add to as necessary so that you can quickly take care of this task without spending unnecessarily.

Weekly Food Prep. Nell Stephenson, the original paleoista, shared this simple trick. On Sunday or the day before your workweek begins, slice and dice all of the veggies and fruit you will be enjoying throughout the week. Place them in containers in your refrigerator. As you need the food for lunches or snacks, pull them out and you are ready to go. You have saved time and are eating healthy, as you had planned.

Fitness Routine. Respect your workout routine just as you would a meeting at work. Keep it simple, but follow it consistently. And while you can certainly mix it up, during busy weeks, when you have no time to think about what you are doing, you will be thankful for the fitness habit you have created.

Water, Water, Water. A simple trick is to go to bed with a bottle of water. Drink a healthy glassful so your body will not be dehydrated when it wakes up. When you get up, immediately drink the remaining water, as your body needs hydration after its overnight hibernation. You are giving the body what it needs and kick-starting the cleansing process.

Stock Your Pantry and Refrigerator Responsibly. One thing that used to confuse my niece and nephew was the lack of snacks in my house. I just do not have them — packaged snacks, that is. They ended up snacking on fruit instead, which they love. Keep your shelves stocked with food you should eat, not snacks that lack solid nutritional value. During moments of weakness, you may become frustrated that you do not have "cheat food" at the ready, but eventually you will eat in a balanced way, and such weak moments occur less frequently because your body is receiving the nutrients it needs.

Wardrobe

Cost per Wear. While initially it may be hard to pay a significant amount of your monthly budget for a quality pair of shoes or any essential item, in the long run you are saving yourself time and money, as you won't have to run to the store for yet another pair of flats anytime soon. Additionally, you will reduce your stress because you can confidently walk into a meeting or interview knowing you look great.

Repair as Necessary. Whether there is a ripped seam on your favorite skirt or coat or the soles of your shoes are becoming worn, tend to your clothing keep it looking its best. By repairing rather than immediately replacing (quality clothing will continue to look great), you are saving yourself money and time.

Save and Wait. As someone who keeps my eye on favorite items as they are released in fall and spring, I also do not or cannot pay full price. So rather than visiting a site multiple times a week to see if an item goes on sale, I set a Shoptagr alert, which e-mails me immediately when a flash sale is on or the item goes on the sale list. You would be amazed at how much of my DVF wardrobe has been discovered with this alert. Money saved, style intact.

Bi-Annual Closet Analysis. A simple way to keep your closet updated and at the ready for any occasion is to perform a bi-annual closet analysis. See my detailed advice in chapter eleven.

Relationships

Weekly/Monthly Dates. For friends with busy lives, one of the easiest ways to stay caught up and enjoy each other's company is to create a regular date. Whether it is a phone conversation, a coffee date, or a group brunch, make your relationships a priority and nurture them regularly.

Keep Stationery at the Ready. Always have stationery ready to use for any number of occasions. The best stationery is blank so that you can insert any message. A thoughtful note from a friend or neighbor shows forethought and consideration. It is a simple gesture that speaks volumes.

Quality, Quality, Quality. When it comes to any number of relationships — romantic, friendships, work — we need to be aware of our time and resources, but also of the effect any of these connections has on our energy, well-being, and sense of self-worth. So long as we nurture relationships that are healthy, our quest for a contented life is on the right track.

With simple routines set in place, we become better adept at knowing what to avoid and what to welcome into our lives. The habits we create and stick to on a daily basis help us to not waste time or energy on unnecessary stressors or triggers that take us off track.

Whenever you have a significant life change (job, move, relationship, etc.), or even at the beginning of a new season or school year, it may be a good idea to assess how each of your systems are working and adjust accordingly for even better performance. I usually sit down in August before the school year and consider which routines worked well the previous year and which did not. If they did not work well, I try to determine why and then edit as necessary. Take time regularly to check in with your life. Most likely you are doing great, so keep up the good work.

How to Live a Courageous Life

Fear is powerful. The point during our lives when we are exposed to fearful situations will determine the effect such exposure has. It is very important to raise a child in a safe home environment, but whether or not we were protected from dangers early in life, we can unlearn an irrational fear response. In other words, all of us have the capacity to be courageous. But how?

Widen Your Perspective and look at Your Fears Objectively

Often our fears are a result of old innate survival responses. Our job is to determine which fears are rational and which are not. Rational fear would keep you from reaching for your phone while driving. But being fearful about doing something new because you do not know how it will turn out is irrational. It comes back to doing your homework, realizing that everything has to have a beginning and we all have to try something for the first time, and, regardless of the outcome, chalking up the experience to growth and lessons learned.

I have noticed that I am a fantastic storyteller, and by story, I mean an account of the doom and gloom of what will happen to my life if my risk-taking does not work out. I have to admit, however, that those stories I feared would unfold never have. I am not saying we should not consider everything that could happen and be reasonable in our approach, but we must also refuse to underestimate ourselves.

Brain science has revealed that neurologically we remain hard-wired to seek out security and survival. When we do something that may threaten our survival (our financial earnings, the roof over our heads, etc.), our minds go into alert mode and, well, panic. It is our job to understand this about ourselves, and then do the necessary homework to prepare for the change we are about to make. Will the timing ever be perfect to leap? No, there will never be a perfect time. Do your due diligence, have patience, and then attempt what you dare. What's the worst-case scenario? What happens if you do not get exactly what you want? Allow perspective, taking yourself out of the spotlight, to help motivate you to at least try. You will be glad you did when it is all said and done.

Exercise the Fearlessness Muscle

Stepping into our fears becomes easier with practice. Each attempt becomes less fraught as we gradually build up to more significant new experiences. One example is traveling by ourselves. For many of us, it is second nature, but for others, this may be a terrifying thing to do. What if I miss my flight? What if I don't hear the announcement? Part of our fear is rooted in the unknown. Anyone can travel by themselves, but it is experience that teaches us how. You just have to practice. If you have never traveled alone, first make a short trip to build up to traveling across the country or internationally. Practice fine-tunes our skills and calms our fears.

Choose Your True Potential and Understand Your Capabilities

Settling is always an option. When we know that things could be much worse than they are, we may choose to settle rather than striving forward toward something that has been aching inside of us. But as Arianna Huffington said, "A fear-driven life is a life not fully lived," and I wholeheartedly agree.

While we live in a modern society with technological advancements, we still have hard-wiring in our minds that can be described as animalistic. Our instinctive urges to obtain sex, food, and security are natural responses. However, often they are responses we should not heed each time they arise if we are going to flourish in our civilized society. When we look our fears in the face and step forward toward them anyway, it is natural to be feel trepidation. Face them, and go forward knowing why you feel the way you do. That alone will give you the power to accept and successfully maneuver beyond the challenge.

Talk It Out

Our closest confidantes most likely do not hold a degree in psychology, but we share our woes and worries with them anyway, hoping they will know why something happened and what we should do. And while they can give their best advice based on their experience, really what we are accessing in such conversations is the opportunity to share, vent, and work through what is running through our minds.

Talking often proves to be the elixir to many of my fears. Our friends and family tend to have ways to help us eradicate irrational worry, allowing us to hear how absurd our worries are. When we hear ourselves saying some of our fears out loud, we often can laugh at ourselves and move forward with reassurance.

Pat Yourself on the Back

No matter how small your achievement, allow yourself a celebration. Treat yourself to a massage, a new pair of shoes, or a nice bottle of champagne. Sometimes we have to be our own cheerleaders, and if we have friends who want to join us, we should celebrate with them as well.

In many ways, the fears that pop up in our lives are a road map, a guide for where we should take our lives or at least a reminder of what we value highly. Those who take risks assure those who are timidly waiting and not acting that their fears tell them what they care most passionately about. Heed these signs, do the homework, then strive boldly in the direction that continually pops up in your mind.

None of us will ever eradicate fear from our lives, but we can learn to master it, use it to our advantage, and allow it to propel us on the road to reaching our full potential.

Face the Unknowns and Manage Stress Wisely

Often we are fearful because we do not know enough about what we are considering or what has been presented to us. What can we do? Educate ourselves. Do the homework. When we do not have to rely on ignorant, baseless platitudes and instead can rely confidently on facts, truths, and the knowledge of what we are capable of, we are in a good position to take back the power over our lives.

Our fears can increase our stress, which then turns into an ugly cycle, because our fears make us less able to be rational, and they increase tenfold. A better approach is to be preventive. Make regular exercise and meditation part of your daily or weekly routine. Will this eliminate all stress from our lives? No, but it will mitigate it, lessen it, and help us to think more clearly when events seem to have spun out of control. The key is to know when our anxiety is ratcheting up. When we can recognize this, we can avoid making rash decisions or succumbing to our fears.

Choose Courage Over Security

I can only speak for myself, but I have a feeling I am not in the minority. Part of the reason change, such as taking a leap we have never tried before, facing down a fear, or taking a risk, is daunting is because we suppose that our security — our job, our relationship, our safety, the comforts we have grown accustomed to — will evaporate if we make the courageous decision we are contemplating.

While we must respect this valid feeling, we must not choose "comfort" in a bad job, a miserable marriage, or any other unhealthy situation over the opportunity to improve our life circumstances. While we may have to stretch and ride out an uncertain and bumpy transition, it is temporary and will subside. Once it does, life will reward us for stepping into our fears rather than being ruled by them.

How to Savor Your Simply Luxurious Life

To know the mind is to know oneself. To know oneself is to discover a place of quiet confidence. To know this confidence is to be able to fearlessly express our potential.
— Andy Puddicombe

From the infancy of *TSLL* blog back in 2009, the premise of living simply luxuriously has always been about appreciating the powerful joy in everyday moments, cultivating a life of quality, and then expressing and sharing what we discover with the world and those around us in a way that is authentic to each of us.

Each year, my world becomes more streamlined and edited with regards to letting go of what is no longer necessary and freeing myself from what is no longer working. As I go through this process, simple, unassumingly powerful moments have much more of an effect on my appreciation each and every day.

When excesses in our life cloud our ability to focus, to live fully, and to be able to be in the moment with absolute appreciation for the life we have been cultivating for ourselves, we must wash them away. And when we do, the clear, crystalized view we are granted says that it is worth letting go of what no longer serves the life we wish to build.

Here is a list of things I do that help me savor my life and that I recommend to one and all:

Awake to gentle classical music melodies.
Challenge the mind with a daily crossword puzzle.
Cook a simple, delicious breakfast to jump-start the day.
Eagerly walk across the threshold of my home after a productive day at work.
Receive love, smiles, and kisses from loved ones.
Bask in the sunshine.
Watch the rain.
Enjoy time with Mother Nature.
Marvel at fresh flowers.
Celebrate moments of serendipity.
Have patience and see it pay off.
Drink a glass of fresh, cool water.
Listen to birds chirping in the morning.
Look forward to a day that is wide open, with no plans.
Receive unexpected thank-yous.
Send unexpected thank-yous.
Find exactly what I have been looking for.
Lose track of time doing what I love.
Detect savory deliciousness wafting from the kitchen.
Cultivate savory deliciousness by cooking with the offerings of the season.
Pour a glass of wine and have the time to enjoy it with a simple, scrumptious meal.
Unwind in a beckoning bubble bath.
Become engrossed in a newspaper or magazine article.
Sip a cup of a favorite tea or freshly ground coffee.
Allow time at the end of the day to read.
Open the page of a new book.
Close the cover of a book that broadened my mind.
Sleep deeply.
Wake to enjoy another day.

A simple everyday life such as the one outlined above offers an abundance of luxury — a realization of how magnificent our lives are regardless of superficial definitions and exterior demonstrations and "proofs" of wealth.

The fundamental purpose of living simply luxuriously is to discover what we uniquely can offer the world if only we would have the courage to shed the layers of expectation that do not align with our authentic selves. In so doing, we discover the amazing person we have the potential to become through the revelation of our strengths and the development of the skills to enhance who we innately are.

It is then that we find the quiet confidence that enables us to savor our carefully curated everydays, elevating them to the extraordinary experiences that they have the ability to be and luxuriating in them. Finally, when we are calm and centered, we free our mind and our potential to discover the ideas, dreams, and curiosities that only we can bring to fruition through our unique talents, capabilities, and passions.

Acknowledgments

To readers, listeners, and viewers around the globe, thank you for being curious about curating a simply luxurious life. Thank you for being courageous in choosing to design your best life, a life that we are all capable of unearthing. Many readers have e-mailed and shared comments about their journey toward a life that is in authentic alignment with their innate passions and curiosities, even when those around them might not understand. Thank you for being tenacious and determined, strong and genuine.

For every time I was rejected, denied, or had what seemed to have been an embarrassing failure, and for the initially regrettable moments when I was reminded that I should have followed my instincts, I offer my sincerest gratitude to the universe, although it is hindsight that allows me to be appreciative. It has been my mission to learn the lessons presented at each of these moments, to share what I have learned, and to keep striving forward.

To my editor, Patricia Fogarty, my simple thanks will never be enough for helping me do what I have dreamed about doing since I was a young girl: to write and to do it so well so that I can share my discoveries with readers.

While blogging is a delightful career choice for an introvert, as I have the opportunity to work alone with my two spaniels napping nearby, I would not be able to deliver the experience readers of the blog discover each day without the talent, kindness, and hard work of my web designers and book cover design team at Dash Creative, Mike Trobiano and J. Aller. Thank you for bringing my ideas to the screen.

To Inslee Farris, the artist behind the illustrations that enhance the front and back covers of the book, as well as *TSLL*, thank you for continuing to work with me. Our journey began in 2011, and you have taken every idea I have shared and have masterfully brought it to life.

To my friends and family members, thank you for honoring the time and space I needed to write, explore, and create. Thank you for being my cheerleaders (Mom and Dad and the Fowlers), for discovering that my journey may be unlike yours, but that, like yours, it is a choice and one I feel fortunate to live. Thank you to my mentor, Marthe, for being exactly who you are, which demonstrated to me at the age of twenty-one that the best way to live is to love the way you live your life, not someone else's.

ABOUT THE AUTHOR

Shannon Ables has been living in Bend, Oregon, since 2015 with her two spaniels, Oscar and Norman. She founded her lifestyle blog, *The Simply Luxurious Life*, in 2009 and a complementary weekly podcast, *The Simple Sophisticate*, in 2014. Her new vodcast, *The Simply Luxurious Kitchen*, provides the inspiration for elevating everyday meals using seasonal fare. Shannon is also a regular contributing guest on Portland, Oregon's KATU *Afternoon Live* and appears on *AM Northwest* as their resident lifestyle expert. Find and follow *TSLL* on Instagram @thesimplyluxuriouslife.